The History and Politics of Exhumation

Michael L. Nash

The History and Politics of Exhumation

Royal Bodies and Lesser Mortals

palgrave
macmillan

Michael L. Nash
Norwich Business School
University of East Anglia
Norwich, UK

ISBN 978-3-030-24046-2 ISBN 978-3-030-24047-9 (eBook)
https://doi.org/10.1007/978-3-030-24047-9

This Palgrave Macmillan imprint is published by the registered company Springer Nature Switzerland AG.
The registered company address is: Gewerbestrasse 11, 6330 Cham, Switzerland

P.M.S.N.

To my wife Ann, my muse and my inspiration

Foreword

Death is serious business. The tradition of the careful disposal of bodies and the rites connected with that disposal is evident across time and cultures. Whilst some may believe in an afterlife, there is an important sense that death extinguishes the worldly personality that the remaining cadaver is merely the external residue and reminder of the individual who has ceased, in a very real sense, to exist. Yet, this does not mean that this residue is unimportant. There have been those who believe that the integrity of corporeal remains is essential for a proper physical Resurrection, explaining why amputated limbs might be preserved for later burial with the rest of the corpse which had survived their loss, or why riots broke out to rescue the cadavers of hanged felons before they could be handed over to surgeon to be anatomised in eighteenth-century England. But even those who held no such eschatological beliefs were not immune from the desire, perhaps at some deep level the need, to accord respect to the treatment of the dead body in most cases. And the disposal of that body was and is, for the most part, regarded as a final one. "Rest in peace", people still intone ritually, where the rest is not only to be understood as respite from the cares of the world, but figuratively as the last, undisturbed sleep in the "final resting place".

Yet, not all resting places are final, nor all sleeps undisturbed. Exhumation has been practised for centuries for a variety of reasons. Some are pragmatic, such as the use of ossuaries to save space in burial grounds, some are spiritual, such as the "translation" of the bones of a saint to confer sanctity on an institution, some financial, as the attraction of relics could draw pilgrims and their resources to the site of that institution.

Some are evidential, of crime or of identity, some accidental, as were an earlier grave is uncovered in the course of other operations. Some are political too, the corpse being considered to have been deposited in a place too humble or too grand for the symbolic importance it is thought that the individual merited. These are not the only reasons for exhumation, nor indeed are they mutually exclusive, but they indicate that exhumation is often a deliberate willed act which breaks an otherwise anticipated and ritualised continuity. As such the practice, its motivations, and its consequences deserve both attention and scholarly study.

The "turn towards the body" has been an interesting development in recent historical writing. Yet the body most closely interrogated in that writing has been the living one, its gestures, postures, and decoration, rather than the lifeless matter which remains when these ephemeral matters lack the agency which animated them. However, as the following pages will demonstrate that history (all history) is controversial. Historical claims for the identity or significance of a corpse will often be disputed, depending on the beliefs, experience, and temporal position of those making those claims, and no historian, of course, is immune from the impact of those factors on his or her interpretation of the actions or mentalities of those in earlier times. The past is indeed a foreign country and its language and customs may look very strange indeed.

If the historian faces problems, what of the lawyer? The traditional major concerns of the law, the protection of life and property, run up against the problem of the corpse, which lacks the former and is, in some particular way, not compatible with the general conception (at least to a common lawyer) of the latter. Much of the law's history has been concerned with death. The descent of land, in those fortunate enough to hold it, or of personal property (once the preserve of the church, indicative of the fact that the disposition of goods should benefit the soul, rather than the vessel it had departed) have been, and are still, major items of the lawyers' business. The law has claimed, still claims in some jurisdictions, the right to kill, and in many now faces questions as to whether it should recognise a right to die. Yet, though death might still require the services of a lawyer, the dead themselves, as physical entities, are usually less present in the offices of the typical solicitor. The use of the gibbet to display the corpse of criminals as a deterrent to the population, or the "auto-icon" of the legal reformer Jeremy Bentham intended to act as a positive encouragement to medical research, are well known to law students. But the dead themselves normally occupy other specialists nowadays, namely doctors and undertakers. There are, it is true, individuals who fulfil the functions *post-mortem* of one of the most ancient offices of English law, that of coroner, and church courts retain rights to determine matters concerning the dead as vestigial survivors of an extensive jurisdiction which they once held over all. However, many lawyers, like many others, will never have to deal with a dead body.

Yet, as I have said, the exhumation of dead bodies is a matter which should interest both lawyers and historians. On first reading the accounts of these procedures there is a tendency to concentrate on the macabre details of the practice; the effects of decay, the acts of pilferage. But many very deep issues merit the reader's attention. How far, and to what extent, can personality, or ideology, or power be attributed to dry bones? What explains the change of social or individual responses towards the product of a process which is universal and in itself unchanging? How can we in an increasingly secular and scientific age explain the observations and beliefs of individuals in earlier times confronting the manifestations of death? If our confrontations with the dead in this volume confirm one thing, then it is a sense of our own eventual fate: "Quod sum, eris: Quod es, olim fui" the figure of Death says to happy individuals in mediaeval wall painting, "What I am, you will be: what you are, once I was". Yet, as this book's attention to the fate of the bodies of royalty, saints, and politicians discloses, such democratic sentiment does not necessarily hold so true with regard to exhumation. In this respect, at least, we may question the idea that death is "The Great Leveller".

Lecturer Emeritus, Aberystwyth University, Aberystwyth, Wales, UK

Richard W. Ireland

Acknowledgements

The Dean and Chapter of Westminster Abbey for access to the diaries of Lawrence Tanner (Archivist, Keeper of the Muniments, and member of the Society of Antiquaries);

Dr. Tony Trowles, Librarian of Westminster Abbey, for his great assistance and thanks to Miss Christine Reynolds, Deputy Librarian;

Dr. Stefan Fogelberg Rota, of the Universities of Umea and Uppsala, Sweden, for his great assistance in obtaining copies of the works of Carl-Hermann Hjortso;

Jan Mispelaere, Archivist and Historian at the Riksarkivet, Stockholm, for his assistance with records of Erick XIV and Gustav Vasa;

Richard Ireland, Lecturer Emeritus of the University of Aberystwyth, for valuable advice concerning the Foreword of this book;

Ricardo Javier Mateos Sainz de Medrano, for his invaluable assistance with research works into the story of Ines de Castro;

Maria Pilar Queralt de Hierro, for much appreciated information from her seminal work on Ines de Castro, *La Leyenda de la muyer que reine despues la muerta*;

Fr. David Middleton, of Clare Priory, Suffolk, for his great assistance in putting books at my disposal in Clare Priory library, on the life and exhumations of Lionel, Duke of Clarence, and for a tour of the ancient Priory;

Fr. Gregory Corcoran, of Quarr Abbey, Isle of Wight, for giving me his memories of the exhumation of Mother Ahelheid, the former soi disant Queen of Portugal;

Carys Lewis, of the National Portrait Gallery Archives, for her much appreciated assistance with the notebooks of Sir George Scharf;

Alison Dyer, Kate Squire, Zoe White, and staff of the Library of the University of East Anglia, who were immensely helpful and instrumental in obtaining rare books and monographs;

Daniel Clarke, Heritage Officer, St. Edmundsbury Borough Council Heritage Service of Moyse's Hall Museum, Bury St. Edmunds, Suffolk, for valuable information and photos concerning Mary Tudor and Thomas Beaufort;

Hugo Vickers for his much appreciated assistance and information concerning Princess Alice of Greece and Princess Elizabeth of Hesse (the Grand Duchess Serge);

Katrina Warne, Assistant Editor of *Eurohistory*, for access to her articles and photos concerning Princess Alice and Princess Elizabeth of Hesse;

My son Joseph for bringing my attention to news items I would otherwise have missed concerning the Five Archbishops of Canterbury and a relic of Pope Clement;

All my family, friends, and colleagues, who have been so very helpful and supportive of me, especially my long-suffering wife Ann, my four sons, and my daughter;

Anyone I have missed, please forgive the omission.

Contents

List of Figures

CHAPTER 1

Introduction

When I had written my previous book, on Royal Wills, in 2017, I thought I would write another one: but on what subject? I narrowed it down to two topics which had always interested me: the Sumptuary Laws and the History of Exhumation. It had to be another niche area. These two topics had always interested me from the standpoint of legal history. On checking, I found that several books and articles had been written on the Sumptuary Laws since 1996, so my search went to Exhumation. Here, nothing major had been written since c. 1934, when Richard Haestier wrote his somewhat remarkable book entitled *Dead Men Tell Tales*, in the wake of the exhumation of the Princes in the Tower in 1933. Apart from that, there were some books with popular appeal, of which the most notable is *Rest in Pieces*, a study of the dismemberment of famous bodies, by Bess Lovejoy. Both of these books gave me much information to work from.

Many years ago, when I first considered writing on this topic, I borrowed a book from Southampton Public Library on this arcane subject, written by an American with an extraordinary name (not unusual among Americans), but this book I cannot now trace. I had intended to write an article for a journal to which I often contributed, and even discussed it with the editor, but in the end, nothing came of it. So, it had been more than eighty years since there had been something more major on exhumation, and this is how I came to write it.

There have been many important exhumations since 1934. The most important of them, The Romanovs and Richard III, who together with

M. L. Nash, *The History and Politics of Exhumation*,
https://doi.org/10.1007/978-3-030-24047-9_1

Tut-an-khamoun and the Princes in the Tower, form the four which most caught the public imagination, I felt at once that I would not trespass on the work of those who had gone before and covered them so well. I had to make an exception for the Princes in the Tower because I had access to the diaries of Laurence Tanner, the archivist of Westminster Abbey, and the light he throws on their exhumation, where he was a leading investigator, is refreshing and different, being a man of much learning and not a little wit and humour.

The idea of writing about exhumation was often there, in the back of my mind: after all, it was an extraordinary thing to do, digging up bodies, opening coffins, examining bones, why would anyone do it, and indeed, should they do it?

It proved to be one of those subjects of the most enduring fascination, for all kinds of reasons. When I was a boy, my Father, who had been a chauffeur-Tour guide for my grandfather's business, proved himself to be a mine of information, about things historical, geographical, architectural, social, and cultural, gleaned from this occupation and his own inherent interest. He told me many tales and repeated many myths, inscriptions, and epitaphs from Winchester, Canterbury, Cambridge, Oxford, Greenwich, and beyond. One of these tales stuck in my mind, and it is still there today: how the coffin of William Rufus was opened and inside was the king's body or skeleton, still with its red hair, and a dead rat curled up inside his skull. This in a way said it all: identification, confirmation, surprise, and shock. William Rufus anyway had always intrigued me and still does. Why, of all his brothers, was he the only one with red hair? So red, apparently, that together with his ruddy complexion, was called Will le Rous, Rufus, a nickname which has come down the centuries. He was an enigmatic and elusive character, the only adult sovereign of these Isles not ever to marry. He was killed hunting in the New Forest as the eleventh century turned into the twelfth; killed by a stray arrow which glanced off an oak tree and killed him instantly. His companion, Sir Walter Tyrrell, fled to France, fearing he would be blamed and unlikely to get a fair trial. The mystery of the king's death remained. His body was found by a charcoal burner, Purkiss, who took it on his cart to Winchester Cathedral, where it was hastily buried. A trail of the king's blood on the forest floor had followed the cart. Within three days, his brother Henry had seized the Treasury and begun his thirty-five-year reign. When I was a young man, I had worked with a girl named Wendy Purkiss, who proudly claimed descent from Purkiss, the charcoal burner, his name etched into local history. I had been several times to see the Rufus Stone, originally erected by John, Lord Delaware, in 1745, as he had seen the very oak tree, now no longer there. A century later, the stone had become so worn it was enclosed in metal, with the original inscription, by William Sturgess Bourne, one of the Forest Wardens, in 1841. There it still is, at Canterton, near Cadnam. I was born in the New Forest, at Ashurst, not far away. I rode in the Forest for many years with my brother. Perhaps, this is why I feel a resonance with Rufus, perhaps even sympathy for a king pursued by demons. My Father had taken my brother and myself to see the Rufus Stone. It may have been on one of these occasions that he told us about the exhumation of the Red King.

Henry I was Henry Beauclerk, Henry the educated; so different from the bad boy Rufus, who never listened to anyone, not even the saintly Anselm, unless he was ill. Yet, it is Rufus who fascinates. Cardinal Basil Hume, long the Headmaster of Ampleforth College, said once that he liked the bad boys, and this reminded me of the invocation: May God make all the bad people good, and all the good people interesting!

This is a book which attempts to fill in the background of those who have been exhumed, and why they have been the subjects or victims of this practice, which, initially, would seem to go against all human instinct and sensibility. The coverage is full of surprises and shocks: empty tombs, tombs, or coffins with the wrong bodies in them; more than one body; parts of bodies mixed up with other remains; bodies remarkably well preserved; bodies embalmed; fragrant bodies; bodies with evil odours; relics stolen, taken, surreptitiously secreted. There are bodies of saints, criminals, royal persons of all degrees, those who, like Potemkin, were "parvenus, but in some sense royal", as Simon Sebag Montefiore has memorably put it. Where does "royalty" begin, anyway? Was Napoleon royal?

It is in this spirit of inquiry and investigation, of seeking to sift evidence over eleven centuries, that this present work is offered. It could not have been written without the help and encouragement of many people, in Europe and beyond, of which my wife is always in the forefront.

CHAPTER 2

Royal Bodies and Lesser Mortals

The exhumation of the bones of Richard III in 2012 from underneath a car park in Leicester was described by *The Guardian* as "a blockbuster exhumation"[1] which not only had extraordinary consequences but was the catalyst for a new interest in knowledge of the past through a certain medium. It was from this that the present writer took his cue for this work. Questions of identity and scientific investigation and analysis, combined with the glamour and romance of a Shakespearian icon, all combined to rivet the public imagination. Even current questions of how disabilities are treated and viewed came into the interested public view; after all, the discovery confirmed that Richard had a crooked spine. The hype of the twenty-first century suddenly met an age which was 500 years earlier. The statue of Richard and the ground in front of Leicester Cathedral was covered with white roses, the symbol of the Yorkist dynasty. Richard was the last Yorkist and the last Plantagenet. The box had been opened, and many interesting issues and problems emerged from it.

The discovery immediately set off searches for other lost sovereigns and lesser royal persons; perhaps more importantly, it brought into focus the reasons why exhumations take place at all. It is not just historical fascination with questions of identity. The reasons turn out to be many indeed. They may be the result of genuine and perhaps accidental discoveries during archaeological excavations. These discoveries are sometimes fortuitous and sometimes disconcerting. Falling into this category are the discoveries purporting to be Thomas Becket, the murdered Archbishop of Canterbury.

M. L. Nash, *The History and Politics of Exhumation*,
https://doi.org/10.1007/978-3-030-24047-9_2

A skeleton found in Canterbury Cathedral in 1888 set off a chain of investigations which continue to the present day. Was the skeleton his or not?[2] Then there is the discovery by workmen (and it is often workmen) of the coffin of the infant Duchess of York, Anne Mowbray, in 1965.[3] In 2017, an astonishing discovery was made in the grounds of Lambeth Palace, namely the bodies of past Archbishops of Canterbury. In the words of the old Music hall song, "Nobody knew there were there".[4]

The current fascination with all things Tudor, and just before and just after, means that there is an enduring interest in the rediscovery of the *Mary Rose*, the favourite ship of Henry VIII. It was named after his favourite sister, Mary Tudor the elder, Queen of France and then Duchess of Suffolk. Among the thousands of artefacts salvaged from the ship (actually half a ship) in 1982 (and before and after) were many skeletons. One of them is now buried in Portsmouth Cathedral, as the grave of the Unknown Sailor. The huge importance and interest generated by the sight of the ship arising from the sea (it had not been seen above water since 1545) was, according to the historian David Starkey, "almost like the opening of the tomb of Tut-an-kamoun". A programme featured by the BBC on Channel 4 on March 18, 2019[5] raised the fascinating question: how English was the crew of the *Mary Rose*? The last words heard by the much stressed captain of the ship, Sir George Carew, who shouted to a passing ship, were "I have the kind of knaves I cannot rule!" In other words, for reasons probably of language and understanding, and sheer pressure of numbers (there were 500 on board, far too many), he has lost control of both the ship and the men. It was no wonder it sank. Now DNA techniques and isotope analysis reveal that the ship "may actually have been a melting pot of nationalities and races". To this, some historians would immediately reply "Well, of course it was", because of the regular employment by kings of mercenaries from many parts. This had been a feature of nearly all conflicts since Roman times and before. But now, with modern techniques, we have fresh proof. For decades now, the skeletons and bones have been in an ossuary in Portsmouth awaiting their analysis. Using digital analysis, it is now suggested that one skeleton belonged to a man who may have been black. Rather like the DNA required for the identification of the bones of Richard III, descendants, actual or collateral, are required. But the analysis required here lesser mortals rather than royal bodies, immediately making things rather more testing. However, the descendants of the only two crew members whose names are known can be traced. Even more interesting is the little-known story of a West African diver, Jacques

Francis, who, two years after the ship went down, somehow managed to salvage several treasures, including a cannon in 1547 that was quite a feat.[6]

To show again how current and continuing exhumation is, a team of biological anthropologists from the University of Bristol had examined 1300 bones in Winchester cathedral, and in particular the mortuary chests, which, it can now be established, contain the bones of no less than twenty-three individuals. This is not very surprising because when the bones were disturbed during the Civil War in 1642, the chests were then repacked by local people, with no precise knowledge of the bones. Among these are Queen Emma, which was previously known, and two teenage boys, whose existence was not. The contents of the mortuary chests have been analysed and radiocarbon-dated.[7]

Sometimes the exhumations are ordered and official. Falling into this category are those of the American Presidents Polk, Lincoln, and Kennedy[8]; the rock singer Elvis Presley[9]; the Nazi deputy leader Rudolph Hess[10]; the Polish president; and ninety-five other important Polish dignitaries, killed in an air crash returning from Russia in 2010. Because of the controversy concerning the last, the remains of the President and his wife were exhumed from their place in Wawel cathedral in Krakow in 2016, with very surprising results.[11] Only very recently, it was reported in *The Times* on June 30, 2018 that one of the Mandela clan in South Africa, Mandla, had had the remains of three members of his family exhumed and moved to another village where he is the tribal chief. His aunt, Pumla, and fourteen other members of the clan then took him to court to have the bodies returned to Mandela's home town. Legal consequences and wrangles often initiate exhumations and often follow them.[12]

Though official, the reasons for these exhumations may be rather different. For Polk, Lincoln, and Kennedy, it was so that their bodies could be situated in more appropriate places. In the case of Rudolph Hess, it was the opposite reason. There was a fear that Hess's burial place might become a Nazi shrine, and so the exhumation was followed by cremation and scattering of the ashes in the sea.

The desire to honour the dead is another valid reason for exhumation. Thus, Napoleon was moved from St. Helena back to Paris in 1840. It was also the occasion for a rapprochement between the traditional enemies, France and England.

The world famous Marie Curie and her husband Pierre were exhumed from a family grave in Sceaux, in France, and re-interred in the national mausoleum, the Pantheon, in honour of themselves and their pioneering work.

Becket himself, whose shrine was perhaps the greatest pilgrimage destination in Europe, became something of a cause celebre for Henry VIII, who saw in his story a mirror image of what had happened between him and Thomas More. Because of this, he had the whole shrine and every reference to Becket erased and removed, as if he had never existed. But he was not successful. Henry himself in his heart of hearts, which remained obstinately Catholic, was ambivalent about it all and hesitated. However, the Achilles' heel of this basically unhappy monarch was women, and it was the perhaps unexpected appearance of one particular woman, and her reactions to the shrine, which tipped the balance against Becket and for destruction and iconoclasm. Attempts to obliterate the past, its cultures and practice, are all too familiar today.

Then there is a category where exhumation is for revenge or retribution, again to try and atone for the past. The exhumations of the sixteenth-century reformers Martin Bucer and Paul Phagius in Oxford during the reign of Mary Tudor and of Peter Martyr's innocent wife in Cambridge shortly after illustrate this,[13] as do the exhumations of Cromwell, Ireton, and Bradshaw in the middle of the seventeenth century.[14] It simply meant that the opposite party was now in power and meant to show it by every means, symbolic and otherwise. England has done this at various times in its long history: reformers and Catholics, Cavaliers and Roundheads, factory and mine owners and workers, and even now with the nation divided between Brexiteers and Remainers. Who is right but repulsive and who is wrong but romantic? The exhumations of these persons were certainly not romantic nor did everyone think it right, but it did happen, and it did have consequences.

If one goes back to the ninth century, it becomes apparent that this revengeful exhumation, visiting wrath even on the dead and unfeeling, is nothing new. Pope Formosus, who was a controversial character and divided a beleaguered church in Rome into his followers and his opponents, suffered the same indignity. After his death, his successor, one of his bitterest opponents, full of ire and frustration, had his body exhumed in what became known as the Cadaver or Corpse Synod, dressed it in papal robes, and put it on trial.[15] This ghastly parody was repeated in the case of Thomas Becket,[16] while in twelfth-century Portugal, the King, anguished that his mistress had been killed with his father's connivance, not only sought her murderers but had her own corpse exhumed and clad in royal robes and crown to sit beside him, thus reigning after death. The tale of Ines de Castro has not only entered literature and drama but given rise to an expression still known in Portugal, to wit, "It is too late; Ines is dead", rather akin to the English expression "Queen Anne's dead" when one hears stale news. For the King, his posthumous attempt to rehabilitate the great love of his death was both anguished and in vain.[17]

Yet again, exhumation may concern what the Catholic Church calls the "Odour of Sanctity".[18] Both actual and metaphorical: an extraordinary reason and phenomenon. The actuality of this has been dissected with some persuasion by writers in very recent times.

The cult of relics, or relics resulting in a cult, gives validation sometimes to the dismemberment of saintly bodies, and their distribution among various shrines and locations associated with the person, and sometimes these relics end up with individuals. A bone purporting to belong to St. Clement, an early Pope, and the patron of those travelling by water, recently turned up in England and was claimed by Hungary and Ukraine, although ending up in Westminster Cathedral.[19]

Occasionally, the exhumation of bodies, or the attempt to do so, is frustrated. The exhumation of John Henry Cardinal Newman in 2010 is a case in point. The Cardinal had foreseen that this might happen and so had directed that substances be put into his grave which would dissolve his body. Followers must be content with second and third class relics of the great man.[20]

At the other end of the spectrum, exhumation sometimes confirms that the body of the deceased is incorrupt. How has this happened? It might perhaps be the result of very successful embalming or other preservation, but could it be a mark of the saintliness of the deceased? Most of these incorrupt bodies are those of women, but occasionally it happens with men. One of these was the Emperor Karl of Austria, who had died in Madeira in exile in 1922. Was this a mark of his holiness? Pope John Paul II thought so and declared him blessed. His body was not removed from its resting place in Madeira, to rest with his many Habsburg ancestors and relatives in Vienna, but remained as the centre of a shrine to his memory.[21] Pilgrimage and tourism, with all its material benefits, so often contrive to go together, as every reader of Chaucer will know. The sacred and the secular nudge each other down the centuries and millennia.

Then there is a darker side to exhumation: the darkest of all it gets is perhaps the Resurrection Men in the 1820s and before, when corpses as fresh as possible were exhumed, as there was a ready market by medical men and students for dissection.[22] Such trade had been going on at least since the Renaissance. Sometimes the Church connived at it, as in the case of Leonardo da Vinci and Michelangelo. Their amazing works often would not have been possible without it.

However, before the Resurrection Men, an alarming cult had grown up between around 1720 and 1820 to exhume bodies for the thrill and the terror of it: a truly Gothic cull, fuelled by the novels of Horace Walpole and Mrs Radcliffe. Every famous, or even royal, body was at risk. During this period, many kings, queens, and lesser mortals were exhumed. The chief horror was the lack of sensibility or respect for the bodies. The eighteenth century, so cultured and enlightened and sophisticated in many ways, did not scruple to cut off the hair of these bodies, and even pieces of flesh; some of the bones were made into knife handles and cruet pots.

Later ages attempted to rectify these enormities. But they were not just committed by men. Sometimes it was a group of women, fired by what they had read or discussed, determined to search for and exhume a famous dead body. When they did find it, it might, like the body of Mary Tudor, who had been a Queen and a Duchess, and the sister of Henry VIII, have ended on a dung heap. Thankfully, more civilised individuals often rescued the remains and gave them decent burial again.[23]

Enduring fascination with mysterious deaths and disappearances are of course covered here and account for the exhumation of many famous individuals. How did these unfortunates meet their end? Is it now possible to find out? Can new techniques prove identification? Most prominent in English history are the Princes in the Tower, whose purported bones rest in an urn in Westminster Abbey. But are the bones really of the princes? Exhumation and examination in 1933 thought they were. The diaries of the archivist shed some interesting light on it all. Unfortunately, modern applications to re-examine them have been declined by both Chapter and royal patron because the craze to do it might result in another free for all, for all royal bodies, in the twenty-first century, reminding us of the eighteenth century. It is true that the archivist involved in the Westminster Abbey examination became so fired by it all that he almost immediately began looking for the bones of Thomas More.[24]

The desire to carry out genuine investigations for scientific and medical reasons stretches from that of the body of Queen Christina of Sweden, who had died in Rome, and whose remains were examined in 1965,[25] to that of Sir Mark Wright in England, who had died during the Spanish flu epidemic of 1918. It was thought in the latter case that because he had been buried in a lead-lined coffin, the original virus might have survived, and so, an examination might help sufferers now.[26]

Lastly, there are the examinations which have been carried out to restore the bodies to a family or dynastic vault. The agenda behind this is often of a serious political nature. In this category come the Russian, Serbian, and Portuguese royal families, it being the purpose and the policy of the present governments of these states to either consider restoring their former royal families or at least rehabilitate them in their respective national histories. Thus, bringing as many bodies of their former rulers and their consorts home to their dynastic vaults gives a new impetus to exhumation. The restoration gives another part to the fractured mosaic of an otherwise convoluted history. In Russia and Serbia, the Orthodox Church gave full support, even in Russia to the canonisation of some members of the former Imperial family.[27] In Portugal, it began as a deliberate and overt attempt to restore the Portuguese monarchy, which had been abolished in 1910, the dictator Salazar following the example of Franco in Spain. The attempt was frustrated by certain personalities involved, but the exhumations served a purpose at restoring Portuguese pride and dignity in their past. The retrieval of scattered royal bodies somehow lends a reality to the purpose.[28]

Extraordinarily, it is not only the bodies of human beings which may be exhumed but those of animals, particularly famous horses. A recent author, Christopher McGrath, has recorded in his memorable volume on racing that the exhumations of both humans and animals involved in the dizzying world of top-class racing. Sidney Herbert, the half-brother of the Earl of Pembroke, had entered the House of Commons in the 1820s, handsome, intelligent, and refined, and one of the outstanding prospects of his generation. He also inherited the Wilton stud, among whom was the famous thoroughbred, Sir Hercules. Unfortunately for the stud, Herbert's devout new wife was having none of it and also introduced the hapless Sidney to Florence Nightingale. Between them they sent him off on a new direction altogether, and within four years nothing remained of the Wilton stud. The famous Sir Hercules was sold to one Escricke Phillips, a farmer near Wolverhampton, "for a few sovereigns". The first foal sired by Sir Hercules after this was bought by a doctor from Rugely, William Palmer. But Palmer was deeply in debt to London moneylenders, and the new owner was shortly afterwards charged with the murder of a friend, John Cook. Despite the professional ministrations of Palmer, Cook had died of "wild-eyed convulsions", after celebrating with Palmer, when he, Cook, had won a large bet. During the post-mortem, Palmer jolted the surgeon just as he took a sample from Cook's stomach. At the inquest, a toxicologist heard a chambermaid describe Cook's reactions to Palmer's pills and declared it consistent by poisoning with strychnine. None had been found in Cook's system, but judicious dosing might leave no trace but death. The bodies of Palmer's wife and brother were now exhumed for analysis, both having died prematurely, and his horses put up for sale. Palmer denied his guilt throughout, albeit with what McGrath calls "provoking ambiguity". "I am innocent of poisoning Cook by strychnine" he specified, walking jauntily onto the scaffold at Stafford, before a crowd of 50,000 in 1856.[29]

The actual identity, or indeed, the age, of horses is of course vital in determining if the right horse should be awarded a race and declared the winner. The five "Classic" races can only be run by three-year-olds, but certainly in the early days of racing, four-year-olds were sometimes substituted. Given also that racing is heavily dependent on correct breeding and genealogies, the parentage of horses is likewise often vital. A case in which this was all important was that of Bend Or, a colt which had belonged to the Duke of Westminster and his Eaton stud. Bend Or was ridden by the most famous jockey of all time, Fred Archer, and the horse which stood perhaps the best chance to win the 1880 Derby, Robert the Devil, was ridden by a last-minute substitute, Rossiter. Both horses crossed the line together, but a Stewards' Inquiry was inevitable, as it was alleged that Bend Or was in fact another horse, Tadcaster. The two horses were both sired by the famous Doncaster, but with different dams. It was decided that the colt was indeed Bend Or, but the challenge was embarrassing to all concerned, as the stud books at Eaton had been negligently kept.

This case and its lessons persisted in the racing world until, in 2012, scientists took a sample from the mandible of Bend Or, whose skeleton is preserved at the Natural History Museum. Using mitochondrial DNA analysis, they established that his genes were characteristic of the maternal family of Clemence, not of Rose Rouge; so after the protesting groom, Arnull, was probably right, and it had been Tadcaster who had won, and not Bend Or at all. Nevertheless, they were both sons of the great Doncaster.[30]

This is the stuff of history. Every exhumation adds to knowledge, historical and scientific and political, and most of all knowledge of human behaviour and outlook.

The law of course takes a hand in this, as it does in everything; sometimes restrictive, sometimes wise and enlightened. Even here there is much to learn, where applications to exhume in England at least are shared by the secular and spiritual authorities. Perhaps this is well, as the subject matter involves not only the physical bodies, or what remains of them, but the spirit and personality which animated them.

Every historian wishes to arrive at the truth of the matter. Absolute or detailed truth is often simply not possible. The most one can do is to sift evidence and consider the opinions of others, particularly contemporaries, as to the matter in hand. Is it possible to become completely detached from the evidence before you so that your own take on the matter is as neutral as possible? Would this make it colourless to the reader? The present writer of course has his own opinions but throughout this study is seeking to present evidence in such a way that the reader can consider his or her own judgment. A comparison of two writers on one subject, namely the reign of the Pope John XII, in the tenth century, may serve the point here. John XII reigned just after the time of the first case in the study, Pope Formosus, and his reign is generally considered to be the nadir of the Papacy, both in fortune and reputation.

Here is the take of the respected Catholic historian, J.D.N. Kelly:

> On his deathbed, Alberic, Prince and all-powerful ruler of Rome, obliged the leading Romans to swear that, when the reigning Pope, Agapitus II, died, they would elect Octavian, (who was the bastard son of Alberic, and hardly eighteen years old. Octavian was to succeed him as Prince, and Pope as well. Although this undertaking violated the decree of Pope Symmachus (1st March, 499) forbidding agreements during a Pope's lifetime about the choice of his successor, it was carried out, Octavian changing his name (only the second Pope to do so) to John. Already in orders, he was hardly eighteen, contemporary reports agree about his disinterest in spiritual things, addiction to boorish pleasures, and uninhibitedly debauched life. Gossipy tongues accused him of turning the Lateran palace into a brothel.
>
> However scandalous his conduct, John maintained a show of administrative activity, seizing every to assert the Papal authority. His standing in the church at large was not apparently affected....

And this is what another respected historian, Chris Wickham, writes of the same man and period:

> if ever there was a moment when Rome might have shifted from an episcopal to a dynastic model of government, if was then. But it was Alberic him-

> self who reversed this trend, when, on his deathbed, he made the nobles of Rome swear not only to accept the young Octavian as princeps, but to elect him as Pope at the next vacancy, which they duly did, just over a year later, in 956. This may seem like the culmination of Theophylact power (the dynasty of Alberic and Octavian) with one person henceforth holding both supreme positions, lay and ecclesiastical alike.... And, indeed Octavian, as John XII, not only found time to have an imaginative private life, like his father and possibly his grandmother, but also kept his power and his popularity in Rome intact...John XII was also the most ambitious of the Theophylacts in his foreign policy...John XII deserves consideration as, at least, no worse than a fairly typical tenth-century ruler. But Alberic's choice to make him Pope, instead of simply princeps, was a step back. Rather than moving Rome more surely to a dynastic tradition, this was a recognition that lasting legitimacy in Rome was, even after half a century of the Theophylacts, still episcopal.

The point of emphasis of the first is on Canon Law and the inappropriateness of Octavian's behaviour, while acknowledging his wider administrative and political competence. The emphasis of the second is on which type of government would endure in Rome. Octavian's behaviour, pitchforked by his father into a double role which he found irksome, becomes secondary. Both these accounts are valid, but the writers see the situation through a different prism.

The net result of exhumations has informed and often illumined the history of those involved and continues to do so. It is in this spirit that the present study is now offered; but the story is of course a continuing one and not over yet.

Notes

1. *The Guardian*, 23 May 2015.
2. A skeleton found in Canterbury cathedral in 1888: See Chap. 3: *Retribution and Reparation*.
3. The discovery of the coffin of the infant Duchess of York, 1965. See Watson, Bruce, *Society of Antiquaries Address*, February 2019 & Chap. 2.
4. Remains of five "lost" Archbishops of Canterbury found, *BBC News Daily*, 16 April 2017.
5. *Secret History*, Channel 4, 18 March 2019.
6. Joe Clay, in his commentary on the programme, 18 March 2019. The present writer was himself a presenter for the *Mary Rose Trust* for many years until 2002, giving over one hundred lectures.

7. "Queen's bones found in Winchester Cathedral royal chests": *BBC Regional News* (Hampshire and the Isle of Wight), May 16, 2019.
8. American Presidents Polk, Lincoln and Taylor: See Chap. 10: *Reasons Many and Various.* Elvis Presley's remains were moved from his original grave in Memphis to the grounds of his Graceland mansion, following an attempt to steal his body.
9. Rudolph Hess, Nazi deputy leader: See Chap. 10: *Reasons Many and Various.*
10. Polish President killed in air crash, 2010: See Chap. 10: *Reasons Many and Various.*
11. *The Times*, June 30, 2018, Bell Machell, *Living with Mandela (Ndaba Mandela).*
12. Martin Bucer, Paul Phagius, and Catherine Danmartin: See Chap. 3: *Retribution and Reparation.*
13. Cromwell, Ireton and Bradshaw: See Chap. 3: *Retribution and Reparation.*
14. The Cadaver or Corpse synod (Pope Formosus): See Chap. 3: *Retribution and Reparation.*
15. Ines de Castro: See Chap. 2: *Retribution and Reparation.*
16. The Odour of Sanctity: See Chap. 7.
17. A bone purporting to be that of Pope Clement, St.: See Chap. 7: *The Odour of Sanctity.*
18. John Henry Cardinal Newman, 2010: See Chap. 7: *The Odour of Sanctity.*
19. Emperor Karl of Austria, 1922, 2008: See Chap. 7: *The Odour of Sanctity.*
20. The Resurrection Men: See Chap. 6: *A Gothic Cult.*
21. A Gothic Cult, c.1720–c. 1820: Chap. 6.
22. The exhumation of the bones of the Princes in the Tower, 1933: See Chap. 3: *Retribution and Reparation.*
23. Queen Christina of Sweden, 1965: See Chap. 8: *Royal Requiem.*
24. Sir Mark Sykes, 1918: See Chap. 10: *Reasons Many and Various.*
25. Russia, and Serbia: royal repatriation of bodies: See Chap. 8: *Royal Requiem.*
26. Portugal, Salazar and the Isle of Wight, 1966: See Chap. 8: *Royal Requiem.*
27. Kelly, J.D.N., *History of the Popes*, Oxford, pp. 126–7.
28. Wickham, Chris., op. cit., pp. 160–1.
29. McGrath, Christopher, *Mr. Darley's Arabian*, John Murray (2016), pp. 144–6.
30. Ibid., pp. 199–200.

CHAPTER 3

Retribution and Reparation

Exhumation seems often to be the result of having a controversial figure, who polarised the people of their day, and afterwards, and created two distinct camps, pro and anti. Nowhere was this more obvious and more divisive than in the case of a Pope of the ninth century, namely, Formosus. He reigned from 891 to 896, but both during his life and for a long time afterwards, he was the central figure of the Church. He was obviously someone one loved or hated; there seemed to be no middle ground. Why was this?

The Catholic Church, indeed the Christian Church as a whole, was coming to the end of its first millennium, just as the present world has just come to the end of its second millennium. Interestingly, like the world today, the old world order was not only being seriously questioned. It was actually disintegrating. It was a very unstable period both politically and religiously. The Church was not yet divided into two, between the Catholic and the Orthodox: that would wait another two centuries. But the political order was seriously shifting. The two worlds, political and religious, were of course not only interconnected, but difficult to disentangle. At the beginning of the ninth century the European world had been dominated by the figure of Charlemagne, Carolus Magnus, who in the year 800 was crowned by the Pope in Rome as a new type of Roman Emperor, the Roman empire in the West having finally disappeared in 476. Into this world Formosus was born, in 815, one year after the death of Charlemagne. The European world of Formosus was now divided between the three

M. L. Nash, *The History and Politics of Exhumation*,
https://doi.org/10.1007/978-3-030-24047-9_3

sons of Charlemagne, confirmed by the Treaty of Verdun in 843, into very roughly the divisions which we now name France, Germany, and Italy, but then up to 1945, the actual borders were in constant dispute. What was a Pope to do? His first role would be to protect the Church and his own authority. He had after all succeeded to one of the titles of the defunct Roman Emperor of the West, namely, that of Pontifex Maximus, the highest priest, a legend which still appears on Papal coinage.

Formosus had been born probably in Rome He was gifted and well-educated. Not only that, but he was by all accounts good-looking as well. His name is indicative. Formosus means beautiful in Latin, but in the sense of being comely, shapely, and graceful. A later Pope, vain as Formosus might have been, tried to adopt this name, but was dissuaded. The reason was that Formosus was to be the subject, not only in his life, of controversy, but after his death, the subject of a ghastly trial and tribunal, known as the Corpse Tribunal or the Cadaver Tribunal. The rise of Formosus in his chosen career was predictable. Despite the fact that transport remained the same for a thousand years, travel around Europe and the Mediterranean was astonishing. Formosus became a brilliant missionary to Bulgaria, so good in fact that the King of Bulgaria, Boris I., petitioned not one, but two popes, Nicholas I. and Hadrian II, to appoint Formosus as Metropolitan of that country. This meteoric rise would certainly have one consequence: bitter envy and rivalry from some of his fellow priests. Both Popes refused the request on the grounds of Canon Law, namely, that it was forbidden at that time to translate bishops from one see to another. This excessive legalism was to prove a key point in the story of Formosus, Formosus alive, and Formosus dead.

But his career continued. He became Papal legate in both France and Germany. Pope John VIII, playing the game of Imperial politics, entrusted Formosus with the task of offering the Imperial crown to Charles II (Charles the Bald) in 875. The developing duality of Pope and Emperor, papal and imperial power and influence, inchoate at this time, would reach a turning point in the next century, in 962, when the "new" Roman Emperor would adopt the extraordinary title of Holy Roman Emperor, a title which would last until 1806. It was a title extraordinary in both name and pretensions.

Formosus seems to have polarised everyone who knew him or met him. They either loved him or hated him. For someone so far back in history, we cannot now be sure quite why this was. The combination of physical beauty and religious authority was both magnetic and deeply disturbing, as perhaps it has always been. Someone who seemed to have so many gifts was bound to incur resentment in those of smaller minds. Jealousy, suspicion, and hostility were certainly present. Unfortunately, at this point Pope John VIII fell out with Formosus, and, in a dramatic turn of events, excommunicated him in 876, deposed him on charges of treason, and deprived him of his See (he was at this time Bishop of Porto). Formosus fled from Rome, but by 878 the vacillating Pope had modified his stance, and admitted Formosus to lay communion, after he had apparently abjectly avowed his guilt (quite what were the charges precisely it is difficult to know, but they must have involved ambition, which Formosus certainly had). Formosus took an oath to remain permanently in exile, and never to try and regain his See, an unwise move perhaps, as he had so many supporters. From such a degradation the only way could be up. From such a situation there was bound to be a reaction. When Pope John became the first Pope to be assassinated (probably by one of his own entourage) the next pope, Marinus I, recalled Formosus from exile in France, rehabilitated him, and restored him as Bishop of Porto. He also released him from the vows he had made under Pope John, as they had been made under duress.

Succeeding popes however now made the life of Formosus very difficult, as some supported him, and some were violently opposed to him. Opposing political policies were carried out with deadly intent, and Formosus became a symbol of this discord. His chequered existence was to continue for twenty-five years, both during his lifetime, and, in a most macabre way, after his death. The Papacy had seriously begun to lose its way and was to stray very far indeed from its original mission. The long night was just beginning.

Eventually, on the death of Pope Stephen V (VI) the moment came: Formosus himself was elected Pope in October 891. If he had indeed been born in 815, this would make him seventy-six years old. Already therefore of advanced years, he was caught up in the struggles of rival dynasties. The family of Charlemagne, by the third generation, was disintegrating further. Like previous Popes, for his own safety and that of his authority, Formosus had to choose. Arnulf, the King of the East Franks (who was actually a bastard son), now came to his rescue from the clutches of the Spoletan dynasty, and Formosus then crowned him as Emperor, and his son as co-Emperor. Fate intervened, and Arnulf was struck down by paralysis (probably a stroke), had to abandon Rome, and returned to Germany. On April 4, 896, the same year, Formosus died, at the age of eighty-one.

Worse was now to follow. The hatred within the Church against him by his enemies was married to the political alignments he had chosen. His choice of Arnulf was unforgiven.

It is possible that what happened after the death of Formosus had not only a religious vendetta element to it but also a political one. Every pope at this period had to choose between a series of candidates for the Imperial title, and most of them wavered from one to another; Formosus was no exception. The rival to Arnulf had been Lambert, whom Formosus had crowned as co-ruler of what was to become the Holy Roman Empire, in 892. Lambert's own father, Guy III of Spoleto, had been crowned before by Pope John VIII. But by 893 Formosus had been seriously concerned by the aggressive attitudes of the Spoletan dynasty, which aimed to make the popes their puppets, and that was when he had turned to Arnulf. Guy himself also had died. After Formosus's death, one pope, Boniface VI, reigned very briefly for two weeks, and then Lambert, and his dominatrix mother the Empress Angiltrude, entered Rome about the same time that Stephen VI, Formosus's great enemy, was elected Pope. It was this Pope who convened the notorious Cadaver synod, early in 897. Modern research and interpretation, at least since 1932, has taken the view that it was not the empress and her son, but the disaffected Guy IV, Lambert's cousin, who had entered Rome with them, who was the moving power behind the synod. History, we are told, is written by the victors, but whoever writes history is usually motivated by prejudice and propaganda to some extent. Rival writers during this period were either pro or anti-Formosus. Liutprand, the Bishop of Cremona, was anti-Formosus, and Auxilius was pro-Formosus. Balancing the accounts of these two may give us some true idea of the events that followed.

The new pope, Stephen VI, ordered that the body of Formosus be exhumed, removed from his tomb and brought to the papal court for judgment, a posthumous revenge of the most macabre kind. With the corpse propped up on the throne, dressed in full papal robes, a deacon was appointed to answer for the deceased pontiff.

Formosus was accused of transmigrating sees in contravention of canon law, of perjury, and of serving as a bishop while actually a layman. Eventually, the corpse was found guilty. Liutprand and other sources then say that the corpse being stripped of its vestments (divestment, a degradation which was common in both ecclesiastical and military law), Stephen then himself cut off the three fingers of the right hand which had been used for blessing, then formally invalidating all of Formosus's acts and ordinations (which included the ordination of Stephen himself as bishop of Anagni), and finally the body was re-interred in a graveyard for foreigners, only to be exhumed once again, tied to weights, and cast into the Tiber. According to Liutprand's version, Stephen addressed the corpse during the "trial" by asking it "When you were bishop of Porto, did you usurp the universal Roman see in such a spirit of ambition?"

But such things work their own reaction. The Roman populace turned against Stephen. By some chance the body of Formosus was washed up in a turning of the river, and some authorities day it was retrieved by a hermit, others by fishermen. Inevitably, reports of miracles performed by the body began to circulate. Formosus was re-buried in the old St. Peter's, which he had completed during his reign, and his name restored to the list of the popes buried there. As for Stephen, he was deposed during a public uprising against him, imprisoned, and eight months after the synod, he was strangled.

In December 897, Pope Theodore II convened another synod which annulled the Cadaver synod and rehabilitated Formosus. The next year, Pope John IX also annulled the Cadaver synod, and ordered the acta of the Cadaver synod to be destroyed, excommunicated seven cardinals who had taken part in it, and prohibited any future trial of a dead person.

However, Pope Sergius III, who reigned from 904 to 911, who as bishop had taken part in the Cadaver synod as a co-judge, overturned the rulings of Theodore II and John IX, confirming the conviction of Formosus, and had a laudatory epitaph inscribed on the tomb of Stephen VI.

In the words of the modern historian Chris Wickham, "Each faction was unprepared to give legitimacy to the other, while at the same time being unable to eradicate the other".[1]

The inability to separate the secular and spiritual powers was soon to be demonstrated in the nadir of the papacy under the later popes of the tenth century. The scene now moves to Iberia in the twelfth and thirteenth centuries, and another story which has been, like that of Formosus, the subject of drama, literature and poetry, to such an extent that the true facts are difficult to extract from the fiction.

Portugal and Castile were often locked in deadly combat, especially as Portugal was trying desperately to assert its own independence from its powerful rival. The King of Portugal, Alfonso (Affonso) contracted his heir, Prince Pedro, to marry an Aragonese princess, Constanza Manuel. Eventually she was able to cross Castile to marry him. She brought in her train, however, a very beautiful Galician lady of high birth, Ines Pires de Castro. Predictably, the marriage to Constanza being an arranged and political one, Pedro became hopelessly infatuated with the lady-in-waiting. The words are not an understatement. Even across the centuries, the accounts of this passionate affair seem to sear the pages. Constanza died after five years, giving birth to a prince, Fernando, who would eventually became the heir. King Affonso wished his son to marry again and suggested a number of suitable candidates, but Pedro was not in the least interested. To spare Ines being the subject of gossip at the court, he installed her in a palace near Coimbra, where she bore him several children, of whom the three boys survived. The trouble was that Ines herself had brothers, and they had aligned themselves with the Castilian cause, which meant the absorption of Portugal into Castile. To the king and his advisers it appeared that there were snakes in the grass. This threat would be removed or mitigated if Ines herself was removed. The king, in the last stages of his reign, weak and prone to anxiety that Ines's brothers would direct the affairs of Portugal, let himself be persuaded that the hapless Ines must be the victim. On January 7, 1355, whilst Pedro was absent, the king and three of his advisers visited Ines. This is the point where it is difficult to separate fact from fiction, so powerful have the dramas and operas concerning Ines become. The king rode from Montemor to the estate of Ines, accompanied by the Chief Justice, Alvaro Goncalves, Pedro Coelho, and Diego Lopes Pacheco. Affonso IV had an interview with Ines and then left. His counsellors returned however, pursued Ines as she fled through the gardens, and then beheaded her. The place where she died is known to this day as the *Quinta des Lagrimas*, the garden of tears.

As this whole story is such a gift to dramatists and poets, they have Ines pleading with the old king, and the king leaving with his grandsons, Joao and Dinis, while Ines flees into the garden. What is certain is the anguish and rage of Pedro when he was told, and his life being hell-bent on revenge and retribution. When he was told the story, which dies hard, is that they said "It is too late; Ines is dead". This expression has entered the Portuguese language, and is akin to the English "Queen Anne's dead" meaning it is stale news. In the case of Pedro and Ines, the implication was that now you can do nothing, but there they were wrong.

It must be noted that, despite his anguish and his continuing infatuation with the memory of Ines, this did not prevent Pedro from taking another mistress, Theresa Lourenco, who bore him the son Joao, who was to be the first of the famed Braganca dynasty, the kings and queens who were to rule until 1910.

Pedro declared war on his father, and civil war was only averted by the intercession of the Queen, but father and son never saw each other again. The predicted fear of Ines's brothers was also real, because they now invaded Portugal from Galicia, their homeland. The fighting continued during the summer of 1355, but a truce was called on August 15. The old king pardoned his son and awarded him the administration of justice in return for a promise that the three murderers should be spared. Pedro was simply waiting his time. When Affonso died in May 1357, the three culprits immediately fled to Castile, where Pedro sought their extradition. Diego Pacheco fled further to England and escaped, but the other two were caught by Pedro in 1360, and were executed at Santarem. The method, or a part of it, of their execution, was particularly repellent, and Pedro, who seems to have been something of a student of methods of execution, may have learnt of it from the Norsemen and the Vikings. This is because it bore a close resemblance to what the Vikings called the "Bloody eagle", that is, the lungs were pulled out of the back of the victim, and spread-eagled on the shoulder blades. Pedro adapted this by having the heart of one pulled through the front and the other through the back. There was no doubt of his revengefulness.

Pedro then proclaimed that he had been married to Ines, presumably after the death of Dona Constanza. They may have gone through a secret ceremony in Braga cathedral before the Archbishop of Braga. Some said that they had been married at the mountaintop town of Genarda before the bishop of that place.

Whatever be the truth, Pedro did go through four wild years at the beginning of his reign, alternating between deep depression and unrestrained licence. It is quite possible that he was partly deranged during this period, something which reminds one of the subsequent stories of Ivan the Terrible and Peter the Great of Russia, both of whom killed their own sons and heirs in fits of rage, and then fell into black depression, remorse, and guilt.

Then, early in 1361, on 24 April, Pedro took the final step in this grisly drama. He had the body of Ines exhumed, clothed in royal robes and crowned, and placed the body on a throne besides him in the sanctuary of Santa Clara, where she had been buried. The horrified courtiers were then made to line up before it, and, at his terrible cry of "The Queen of Portugal!", file past and kiss its hand.

There followed a funeral procession of immense pomp, by night, from Coimbra to the Cistercian Abbey of Alcobaca, a distance of nearly eighty miles, lined by thousands of men with flaming torches. Pedro had a splendid tomb erected for her; when he himself died he was buried foot to foot with her, so that at the day of Judgement their first sight, when they arose from their tombs, should be each other.

On January 18, 1367, Pedro died; now his bearded effigy, crowned, hands clasped on sword, lies foot to foot with Ines, whose seraphic beauty is matched by the weeping cherubim who cluster round her tomb.

But, similar to the Cadaver synod, such acts of macabre revenge and even more macabre retribution were to usher in a period of lust, violence, and murder into the early history of Portugal. Meanwhile, in neighbouring Castile, the story of Ines and Pedro was to be replicated in the story of Pedro the Cruel and Maria de Padilla, and their romances would be inevitably conflated.

The story of Pedro has become well known through certain chroniclers, and the stories about him have grown with the re-telling, something in common with most of the subjects in this study. The use by Pedro Lopez de Ayala of anti-Petrine ballads canonised propaganda into history, a memorable and repeatable phrase.[2] Ayala's literary skill cannot clear him here of the charge of "political journalism". Ballads and "prophecies" together with skilful innuendo, give us the king whom Ayala presented as Pedro the Cruel. Even a chronicle written for a descendant of one of Pedro's loyal followers sees him as ruined by a Jewish adviser and by his mistress, the famous Maria de Padilla. Pedro's government was, a Muslim contemporary said "hard and tyrannical"; in this he was not exceptional for his age. "…Pedro's use of Jewish advisers and Muslim troops was part of the traditional policy of convivencia. Because he was not understood beyond the Pyrenees it does not prove that he was irreligious. Pedro was also unfortunate in being uninterested in the cult of chivalry embodied in the Black Prince, and admired by Ayala".[3]

Tall (1.83 m), blond, blue-eyed, and muscular, Pedro had been obliged to marry a French princess, Blanche of Bourbon, by his chief adviser Albuquerque, when he was nineteen years old, and she was fourteen. Three days later he abandoned her and imprisoned her in the castle of Jerez. The hapless princess was then moved to Medina Sidonia, further south, to lessen the possibility of rescue by her French relatives. Again, the authorities must be seen through the prism of their prejudices and agenda. Was Blanche murdered? Her marriage was annulled, at the insistence of Pedro, by the bishops of Avila and Salamanca. Pero Lopez de Ayala says that Pedro contrived her death in 1361, when she was twenty-two. Zuniga amended Ayala' chronicle and says that Pedro's partisans said the death was natural. That she was poisoned by herbs is repeated by Juan de Mariana, while the French historians stated that Pedro paid two Jews to murder her. It seems clear that the governor of the prison in Jerez refused to countenance her death, so Pedro contrived to induce a crossbowman to execute her. The tragic Blanche may actually have died of plague.

Even the attitude of the Pope at the time, Innocent VI, was motivated by the fact that he had found it hard to collect papal revenues from Castile, and so joined forces with the controlling adviser Albuquerque and Pedro's bastard brothers to force the king to return to Blanche. Pedro might have been already married to Maria at this time. One of the stories was that Fadrique Alfonso, one of the bastard brothers, had had an affair with Blanche as she was en route across Spain.

Pedro's reputation was not improved by his marriage to a widow, Juana de Castro, as, after two nights he deserted her, leaving her pregnant. Some people do not help their own situations.

Pedro had probably met Maria, a Castilian noblewoman who might have herself been of converso Jewish descent, through her maternal uncle, who was Pedro's favoured adviser. She was described as "Very beautiful, intelligent and small of body", and she and Pedro had a lasting affair, which produced at least four children, and reflected the passion of Pedro of Portugal and Ines de Castro. Fortunately it did not have the same end. Maria died, probably of plague, and was buried first in the royal monastery of Santa Clara in Astudillo, which she had founded in 1353. However, on the orders of Pedro, a short time afterwards her remains were exhumed and taken to be buried in the royal vaults in Seville cathedral, with other royal persons. Not only this, but the Castilian Cortes twice legitimated the children of Maria de Padilla, and as she had been de facto Queen during her lifetime, by a special Act of the Cortes she was declared de jure Queen after it.

Religious and political upheavals have contributed to most of the subjects in this study. Nowhere was this more so than in the exhumation of the bones or remains of Thomas Becket, Archbishop of Canterbury, and pre-eminent martyr of England, whose shrine had become perhaps the most famous and the most visited in the whole of Europe. The symbolism of the destruction of the shrine in 1538, on the orders of Henry VIII and his servant Thomas Cromwell and his minions, cannot be underestimated.

The story of Becket should perhaps be retold at least in outline. Beginning as the boon companion of King Henry II, and enjoying all the pursuits of a life-loving and pleasure-loving king, Becket seemed, at least to the king, to change personality when he was appointed Archbishop of Canterbury. He became very serious about his office and his duties, and, most trying of all, he became extremely defensive and protective of the rights of the Church when these clashed with those of the king himself. Henry Plantagenet was not a patient man at the best of times, and, driven to exasperation, uttered the fateful words: "Who will rid me of this turbulent priest?" Four knights crossed the sea from France and promptly murdered the Archbishop in his own cathedral, while he was saying Mass, on December 29, 1170. The outrage across Europe echoes across the centuries, as it was to do when Henry VIII repeated this in the case of Thomas Becket in 1538. The only difference was that Thomas Becket was dead for four centuries, and the outrage was upon his remains and his shrine. Why Henry Plantagenet uttered his fateful words is clear, but why Henry VIII visited this strange posthumous revenge on a much revered saint needs further analysis.

Interestingly, Becket, like many revered Archbishops, had already been exhumed twice, in order to further honour him by moving his body to another shrine. The first burial had been understandably quick by his own shattered monastic community. Even at the beginning, it is possible that his head, which had certainly suffered considerable damage during his killing, had been separated from his body and kept in another part of the cathedral. But on July 20, 1220, fifty years after his death, his remains were translated, or transferred, from his relatively humble grave to a new and magnificent shrine in the Trinity chapel above. Attended by the young king, Henry III, who was thirteen, Archbishop Stephen Langton provided barrels of wine for the populace at each gate leading into the city. It was a time of celebration and festival, something not lost on those of a more commercial instinct. Polistorie, a Canterbury chronicle in French, described the scene:

> They lifted him and put him in a seemly wooden chest, adorned for the purpose, the which was well strengthened with iron, and they fastened it also carefully with iron nail, and then carried him to a seemly and secret place, until they should celebrate solemnly on the morrow, the day of the translation.

But a somewhat different account is given in the Quadrilogues, a thirteenth-century conflation of five different biographies of Becket.

According to this, the body had already been removed on June 27. The body was first taken by the monks and given to the Archbishop, who himself placed it in a "feretrum", or iron container, having first reserved a few small bones for distribution to great men and famous churches. The feretrum was then fastened with iron nail, and carried by the monks to a bier, in an honourable place, where it rested until the ceremony of the translation on the July 7.

The removal of the bones by Langton is of particular interest. Down through the ages, it seems that this temptation to take small parts of a holy body which has been exhumed (and not just holy bodies) is too much even for those in the highest office. Thus bodies become diminished, as will be seen when later discoveries take place, especially the archaeological discoveries of 1888, which will be covered in another chapter.

However, according to the Icelandic Saga of Thomas, an early fourteenth biography of Becket based on Robert of Cricklade's Life of the Saint, the body of the saint crumbled to dust when it was removed from the coffin (which would have been expected if it had not been embalmed) and what was placed in the feretrum was not a body, but a collection of bones. The Saga corroborates the evidence that a small number of bones were kept aside for later distribution.

The shrine itself was to become famous throughout Christendom because of the many, many gifts and donations which were made to it. It had been constructed by two clerical craftsmen, Walter of Colchester and Elyas of Dereham. It was raised up on steps and comprised three parts: a stone plinth, with an open arcaded base, the richly gilded and decorated wooden casket in which the feretrum containing the relics was laid, and a painted wooden canopy, suspended from the roof by a series of pulleys, that enabled it to be raised or lowered to reveal or cover the casket itself. The casket was covered with gold plate and decorated with fine golden trellis work. Affixed to the gold plate were innumerable jewels which had been donated or sent by the high and mighty. The most famous was La Regale of France, an enormous ruby which had been donated by King Louis VII of France, when he visited the shrine in 1179, eight years after the murder, and when Henry II was still reigning. But among the many others there were pearls, sapphires, diamonds, and emeralds, together with rings and cameos of sculptured agate, cornelian, and onyx. Those who sought the "holy, blissful martyr" would also be dazzled by his shrine.

But what the pilgrims did not see were the actual remains of Becket. These were safely contained within the feretrum, in which they had been placed by Stephen Langton and the monks during the ceremony in the crypt in 1220. There appears to be no exact record of what relics were placed in the feretrum, or how they were arranged, and this then compounds the difficulty in ascertaining their fate in 1538.

There was an inscription, however, and the late-sixteenth century Annals of John Stowe, and the Cottonian drawing, reads thus:

> "This chest of iron contained (note past tense) the bones of Thomas Becket, skill and all, with the wound of his death and the pece (sic) cast out of his skull laid in the same wounde". To which can be added: "Something purporting to be part of Becket's skull was shown to the pilgrims".

When the great scholars, Erasmus and John Colet, visited the shrine in 1512, they were offended by certain aspects of it, and certainly the superstitions it seemed to foster, and the reprehensible commercial aspects, exhibited even by certain of the monks.

But the core of all this is not superstition and not the commercial aspects, it was the fact that Becket was not a saint like other saints. His particular and despicable crime, in the eyes of Henry VIII, who, it must be remembered, was also a master of self-deception and persuasion, had been the challenge of Becket to the royal authority. His was a special cult, and now, when his remains and shrine were under threat, he required perhaps special treatment.

In September 1538, the Royal Commissioners for the Destruction of Shrines, headed by Dr. Richard Layton, Archdeacon of Buckingham, arrived in Canterbury to do their business. The bones of Becket were to be removed from the feretrum, where they had been for 318 years.

However, there is another, and important, factor here. This is what remains of the king's religious scruples. Henry VIII always believed he was a Catholic, but one shorn of the Papal authority. He was a second son, destined, according to some authorities, by his father for the Church. He had been greatly influenced by his over pious grandmother, Lady Margaret Beaufort, who had acted as regent during the first two months of his reign, and had chosen his first ministers, while disposing of two unpopular ones. Something deep in his psyche was telling him to pause before he did this thing.

The French have a telling expression: Cherchez la femme. At this very point, a lady entered the king's life who was to tip the balance. Henry VIII at this time was forty-seven years old. He was, for the first and only time, a widower. News came to him that a distinguished French lady of noble connections, whose family occupied a very high place at the French court, was travelling through England from Scotland on her way back to France. During 1538 Henry was looking for a French bride. At the end of August, he indulged his temporary Francophile passion by giving a lavish welcome in London to Madame de Montreuil, a former senior attendant of the recently deceased Queen Madeleine of Scotland… Henry decided to mix business with pleasure by making a rendez-vous with her after he had inspected the defences at Dover; she was accompanied south by the French ambassador. Her English escort was Sir William Penison, who noted her reactions and observations.[4]

Anne de Boissy, Madame de Montreuil, had been the governess and then principal lady-in-waiting of the Princess Madeleine of France, who had married James V of Scotland and become known to the Scots as the Midsummer Queen. She had died in 1537 at the age of seventeen. Having welcomed the new Queen, Marie de Guise, Madame de Montreuil felt she had done her duty in Scotland and wished to return to France. She had neither enjoyed the climate nor the cuisine. Would His Majesty of England give her safe passage? Henry liked the company of women and he invited her to come, not only to his court in London, but to accompany him on his visit to Canterbury, on her way to Dover. This visit proved the turning point.

Madame de Montreuil requested a visit both to the cathedral and the shrine. It was a prestigious visit under the royal auspices. The monks were aware of this. At the end of August 1538, she arrived in Canterbury, and on September 1, Sir William Pennison wrote to Thomas Cromwell about "a visit that was paid to the shrine upon Friday last at 6, by Mme de Montreuil". The letter describes in some detail the French lady's tour of the Cathedral, culminating in a visit to the shrine itself.[5]

> Thus over looking and viewing more than an owre, as well the shrine, as Saint Thomas hed, being at both sett coushions to knyle, and the Pryour, opening Saint Thomas hed, saying to her 3 tymes, 'This is Saint Thomas hed,' and offering her to kisse it; but she nother knyled, not would kissue it, but still viewing the riches thereof, she deparated and went to her lodgings to dynner.

Thus we have the report that, despite being given every comfort and encouragement to honour the relics, the lady declined to do so, but nevertheless, still looked, in an inscrutable manner, at all the riches of the shrine. There is of course a subtext to tall this. We cannot know now if Henry VIII knew of what kind of bent she was concerning the Reformation. He might have done. But it is hard to escape the conclusion that she was a kind of test, an acid test, before the shrine. She was a great lady who knew two royal courts intimately. What would she do? If she had knelt devoutly and kissed the relic, perhaps he might have held his hand. She did not do so.

Diarmaid MacCulloch, in his biography of Thomas Cranmer (1996), makes a pertinent comment on the visit of Mme de Montreuil. "Prior Goldwell never again had a chance to show off the holy skull, and one wonders whether Madame's visit clinched a plan of actions already in Henry's mind".[6]

But what of the leanings of this redoubtable lady? Buchanan, who was the most distinguished Scottish neo-Latinist of his day and was briefly a member of the court of James V, has been described as a "vanguard humanist susceptible to evangelical currents" says MacFarlane, his biographer. He seems to have come under the influence of Erasmus, and, returning to Scotland in 1535, became tutor to one of the king's illegitimate sons, Lord James Stewart, between 1536 and 1539, precisely the period when Madame de Montreuil was in Scotland. He was later to become classical tutor to Mary Queen of Scots and then to her son James VI.

When Queen Madeleine died in July 1537 a number of epitaphs were written for the dead queen. One of these was by Jean Demoutiers, a learned gentleman in the household of King Francis I of France, Madeleine's father; he had already written a History of Scotland for her coming queenship. The other three epitaphs were by Etienne Dolet, Jean Visagier, and Nicolas Defrenes. These names are significant, for they seem to indicate that there was substance to Buchanan's view that Queen Madeleine herself (reminiscent perhaps of both Edward VI and Lady Jane Grey in their adolescent precocity) was inclined to evangelism, since Dolet's advanced opinions brought him under suspicion of heresy in the late 1530s, and he was eventually burnt at the stake in 1546. Defrenes, a Louvain theologian, was also in the evangelical camp, and Visagier was to produce two other neo-Latin poems to commemorate Madeleine's death, which were published in Paris in 1538. Buchanan himself became the object of a heresy enquiry.

That the doctrinal disputes of the Renaissance humanists had already impinged on the court of James V even before the advent of Buchanan cannot be in question. Queen Madeleine herself and the little court she took to Scotland seemed to have become a focus of evangelism there, even though a closet or covert one. The attitude of Madame at the shrine of Becket seems to leave no doubt at all of her opinions. Madeleine may well have learnt from her. Whatever the details, the outcome was what Henry VIII had been looking for. He was, after all, always looking for someone else to blame for what he did.

Something akin to what happened all those centuries before to Pope Formosus, now happened to the remains of Thomas Becket. He was cited by Proclamation to appear before the king, to answer charges of rebellion and treason; he not appearing counsel pleaded for him, without any avail; the saint was stripped of his title, became plain Bishop Becket, and the court made order that "his pictures and images throughout the whole realm should be put down and avoided out of all churches, chapels and other places, and that from henceforth the days used to be festival in his name should not be observed, nor the service, antiphons and prayers in his name read, but razed and put out of all books, because he died like a traitor and a rebel to his Prince".

His bones accordingly were burnt, "so that there shall no more mention be made of him never".[7]

But did this happen? Were the bones burnt, as was reported, or were there other possibilities? Modern research has suggested that there may be grounds for thinking that they may have been buried, either by the monks, knowing what was likely to happen, or even with the collusion of the Commissioners. What makes this less likely is that Cardinal Pole, when he came to Canterbury as Archbishop in 1556 did not seek them or re-instate the shrine; indeed Mary Tudor only reinstated one famous saint, St. Edward the Confessor, in Westminster Abbey. The truth is that both Mary and Pole had had a humanist education, and what they sought to re-establish was a rather different edition of Catholicism than that of 1538. (See Butler, J. The Quest for Becket's bones Yale, 1995, and ...) The story that the bones of Becket had been burnt appears to have originated on the mainland of Europe, where Catholic opinion was outraged at the king's action. At a Consistory in Rome on October 25, 1538, the Pope "announced the new cruelty and impiety of the King of England, who had commanded the body of St. Thomas of Canterbury to be burnt, and the ashes scattered to the wind". A few weeks later, on December 6, 1538, Castelnau, Bishop of Tarbes, noted in a letter that

> "the Pope's nuncio presses for vengeance for the relics of St. Edward (the Confessor) and St. Thomas of Canterbury; and later the same month, December 17th, Pope Paul III promulgated a bull of excommunication against Henry VIII, that had first been prepared, but never executed, in 1535, (after the executions of Bishop Fisher and Thomas More). In it the Pope specifically accused the king of having ordered the burning of St. Thomas's bones, following a mock trial..." "To be summoned to a trial... and declared a traitor, he has commanded those bones *to be exhumed and burned*, and the ashes scattered to the wind".

One commentator has said: "the curious use of the word *exhumed* may be noted. It may means nothing more than that the bones were taken out of the shrine before being burned; but the word *exhumed* and the original Latin word *exhumari*, usually suggests the removal of a body or bones from the earth." The hint in the Bull that the bones of Becket may have been buried somewhere else before being burned, is of interest in the light of the hypotheses that they were either buried by the monks elsewhere or possibly mixed with the bones of others, deliberately, so that one could not be told from the other.

Curiously, Henry VIII was so sure of his own orthodox Catholicism that the Six Articles of 1539 reflect his own views to the dismay of many of the reformers. In the same year, when the Empress Isabella died, Henry had a full requiem said for her, with every traditional ceremony. But Henry had equated heresy in his own eyes with treason, and that view was to haunt every Tudor to the end of their dynasty. A particular irony, as MacCulloch points out, is that the very Archbishop whom Henry appointed to do his bidding, Thomas Cranmer, died defying his sovereign in the name of conscience.

The scene now moves indeed to the latter part of the reign of Queen Mary Tudor and the instructions or directions of Cardinal Pole, regarding certain bodies to be exhumed. These were the bodies of Martin Bucer, Paul Fagius (or Phagius), and the wife of Peter Martyr. All three of these men had been (and, in the case of Martyr, still was) famous icons of the Reformation. Martin Bucer or Butzer had been born in 1491 in Alsace; Paul Phagius had been born at Rheinzabern in 1504 and had studied at Heidelberg. Both had been invited by Thomas Cranmer to come to Cambridge in 1551, during the very radical government of the boy king Edward VI.

Peter Martyr, whose original name was Vermigli, had been born in Florence in 1499 and educated at the University of Padua. All three of these men had been Catholic priests, and, in the case of Martyr, had been both Prior and Abbot. Interestingly, Martyr had certainly made the acquaintance of Cardinal Pole, together with Pietro Bembo, Marcantonio Flaminio, and other illuminati, at Padua, for all were interested in the Spirituali movement, which sought to introduce the spirit of Humanism into Christianity. Martyr had changed his name, adopting that of a Dominican saint, Peter of Verona. When he became abbot of the monastery of San Pietro ad Aram, at Naples, he then became acquainted with Juan de Valdes, who was one of the leaders of the Spirituali movement. In 1541, when he was elected to the important post of Prior of the Basilica of San Frediano in Lucca, he set up a college there based on the humanist principles of St. John's College, Cambridge, and Corpus Christi College, Oxford. This seemingly unstoppable rise was indeed stopped by the reconstitution of the Roman Inquisition in 1542, and Martyr fled, first to Pisa, and then via Ferrara and Verona, to Zurich. By 1544 he had already been elected Canon of St. Thomas's Church in Strasbourg: Peter Martyr was indeed a big fish for the Reformers to catch. Then Martyr did something which put him further outside the Catholic pale and would be the reason for one of the exhumations. He married. Not only that, but his wife, as seems to be so often the case, was a former nun, Catherine Danmartin, from Metz. It is of interest that Martyr, at least to begin with, spoke no German, and Catherine no Italian. It is assumed that they spoke Latin!

Once Henry VIII was dead, Cranmer invited both Martyr and Bernardino Ochino to England, and in November1547, they sailed into another life. As ever, his rise was predictable. He replaced Richard Smyth in 1548 as second Regius Professor of Divinity at Oxford. This was the most influential post at a University which had been slow to accept reform. To many it was a deliberate provocation.

For Martyr it proved to be a baptism of fire. He left after some riots, and then returned and became first Canon of Christ Church in January 1551. He was the first married priest at Oxford, at a time when celibacy and the academic and clerical life were strongly linked together, which indeed was provided for in the University statutes. It was bound to provoke controversy, and it did. When Martyr brought his wife into his rooms overlooking Fish Street at the great Quadrangle, there was consternation. It was akin to bringing a woman on board a ship; evil consequences would be bound to follow. After his windows were smashed several times, which would have continued, he moved to a location in the cloisters, where he had a fortified stone study. It gives a good idea of how polarised and riven society had become by the new doctrines and practices. Peter Martyr then assisted in the re-drafting of the Canon Law of England in October 1551. This by draft was published by John Foxe (he of the Book of Martyrs fame) in 1552. The Canon Law of England had of course been an integral part of English law, but now, with the establishment of the Anglican church, this Canon Law, being the rules of a theocracy based in Rome, had to be replaced by a national and reformed edition. Since then there have been two sets of Canon law in England: one for Anglicans and one for Catholics, although in many essentials they remained the same, or at least similar.

When Mary Tudor became Queen in July 1553 Peter Martyr re-thought his options. His fellow reformers, Martin Bucer and Paul Fagius, had both died in England: Bucer had died in Cambridge on February 28, 1551, perhaps of tuberculosis, and Fagius had already died of the plague on November 13, 1549. Bucer was buried in St. Mary's, the main church of Cambridge, and Fagius in the church of St. Michael.

Mary's reign opened with great good will and optimism. It is true that all foreign preachers were required to leave the country in September 1553, but the statutes against heresy of 1401 (originally to deal with the Lollards) were not to be revived until February 1555. Why there could not have been a new statute, rather than reviving one a century and a half old, is a good question. The answer may be that the government of Mary Tudor wished the suppression of heresy to be seen as a continuance rather than something new.

Peter Martyr lost no time in removing himself, and by October was in Strasbourg. His much-loved wife Catherine Danmartin, who, though childless herself, had endeared herself to the ordinary people of Oxford, by caring for expectant mothers and the poor generally, had died however in February 1553, and been buried in Christ Church, near to the Holy Virgin St. Frideswiede, the patroness saint of the University. Peter Martyr married again in 1559 and died himself in Zurich in 1562, leaving his second wife pregnant. The posthumous daughter survived.

It is of considerable interest that Martin Bucer himself had predicted the Marian persecution before he died in 1551. He had written to Calvin in 1550, informing him that the English Church (i.e., the Church of England) was in a perilous state; only the godliness of a few individuals stood between the corruption of power and the divine wrath. Not only would persecution be a deserved chastisement, for their failure and short-comings, it would also be *a purging fire*, and a means of confirming to men of passionate sincerity the validity of their elation. Be careful what you wish for.

Of course, what Bucer did not factor in, in all this, and probably simply did not understand, was the coolness of the English towards any form of extremism, something which has become indelible in the English psyche, and continues to this day. It is not for nothing that the historian David Starkey has compared the fateful referendum of 2016 and the ensuing division between Remainers and Brexiteers as the Reformation movement of our own day.

What Bucer also did not anticipate was what was to happen to his own body, that of Fagius and that of the poor hapless Catherine Danmartin. The pursuers of heresy might not be able to get hold of the living reformers and they could not extradite Peter Martyr, but they could exert revenge on the dead bodies. Accordingly, all three bodies were exhumed, and their cases examined for heresy. The prime mover behind this was the legal adviser and datary of Cardinal Pole, one Nicolo Ormanetto. He had been Vicar-General under the famous Carlo Borromeo in Milan, implementing the decrees of the Council of Trent, the forum and apparatus of the Counter Reformation within the Catholic Church, which was still in the midst of its deliberations in 1557, and would not close its doors until 1563.

Reform there might be, but the Counter Reformation also included the rooting out of what was not orthodox, that is, heresy. What was, and what was not, heresy, tended to be a shifting target, almost like quicksilver, changing as the years advanced, and the players came and went. Pole himself, so nearly elected Pope in 1549, was himself to be accused of heresy by the firebrand Paul IV, known as the Inquisitor Pope. Such movements as the Spirituali, to which Pole was certainly attached, were considered by the unbalanced Neapolitan pope to be not humanist reform but heresy. Pole was also disturbed by the burning of heretics, and was enough of an Englishman to remember that, as a Plantagenet he was hesitant about the efficacy of such extremism. "It was noticed that he preferred to order that the dead carcasses of Bucer and Phagius should be dug up and burned, than that living heretics should go to the stake; this perhaps, as Foxe himself suggests, he was 'loth to be so cruel to the other'".[8] Let us not forget, however, that the Spanish theologian, polymath and humanist Michael Servetus had been burnt at the stake in Geneva in October 1553, on the orders of the magistrates of that city. Servetus was the great rival of Calvin, who did not have the power in Geneva at that time he was to have later, and the execution was approved by all the Swiss Protestant cantons. There was a strong political element therefore in the burning, although Servetus had sailed very close to the wind, and had already been condemned to death by the Catholic church. What is clear here is the ambivalence and hesitation over the burning of heretics by many rulers.[9]

But by the time Pole became Archbishop of Canterbury in 1556, the business of persecution was well-advanced, and trials for heresy commonplace. The inquisitors who now descended upon Oxford and Cambridge were commissioners with almost unlimited powers. On January 9, 1557, they arrived in Cambridge to purge the University of heresy. The next day, the 10th, the two churches, St. Mary's and St. Michaels's, where Bucer and Fagius were buried, were put under an interdict. On the 12th, the inquisition began, and while the colleges were searched for condemned books, the commissioners debated on the fate of men already dead. Trials of dead men for heresy were not infrequent in the annals of the Catholic Church, but they were rare in England. Far from being ebullitions of sheer malice they had their origins in the law which said that the entire property of the heretic would be forfeit to the Church, condemning the dependents and descendants of the heretic to complete and utter destitution.[10] Such a harsh interpretation may be compared with how the church and the state generally treated suicide until the reforms of the 1960s in England.[11]

The whole process, and thinking behind it, also contains the idea of contamination, that it, even the dead body can contaminate other, and more holy bodies, when they are buried together; and this thinking has continued into the legal cases being brought in the twenty-first century.

On the January 26, 1557, the sentence of condemnation for proven heresy was read out in St. Mary's. The bodies of the heretics were to be disinterred, exhumed, degraded from Holy Orders, delivered over to the secular arm, and burnt. (It may be noted here that the actual carrying out of the execution or burning was transferred to a power outside, perhaps also to obviate the risk of contamination, and certainly to transfer blame.) The sentence was carried out on February 6. On that day the coffins were taken to the market place, set on end, and fastened to a great stake, faggots were piled against them, and, as the fire consumed the dead bodies, condemned books, bibles, and prayer books, were cast into the flames. The University would show its gratitude for being so ridded so finally of two redoubtable heretics, by conferring the degree of Doctor on Cole and Ormanetto. They then both proceeded to Oxford, to deal with the dead body of Peter Martyr's wife, Catherine.

Catherine Danmartin had been buried near St. Friedeswide. It is an interesting fact that the most trusted companion and servant of the Queen, Mary Tudor, had been named after this saint, Friedeswide Strelly. She had the dubious, though appreciated, honour of telling the queen she was not pregnant when she continued to persuade herself she was.

But here Ormanetto could discover nothing in the lady's life to her detriment, for what she believed she had not taught. She could not, therefore, be burnt, alive, or dead, for proven heresy. Ormanetto thereupon wrote to Pole for advice. Pole appeared to think that the proximity in death of the married nun to the virgin saint was an insult to holy bones, and he advised that Catherine's body should be disinterred, exhumed, and cast out. Marshal, the Dean of Christ Church, complied, and the wife of Peter Martyr was exhumed and re-buried in a dunghill. Catherine had been described as "an honest, grave and sober matron, while she lived, and of poor people a great helper". As for St. Friedeswide, when Henry VIII refounded what had been Wolsey's great project, Cardinal College, as Christ Church, in 1532, her shrine was left undisturbed. But it was despoiled by the commissioners in 1538. It was restored, however, by Queen Mary, one of only two she restored, and it is not entirely fanciful to suggest that she was encouraged, or perhaps implored to do this, by the faithful Friedeswide Strelly.

In 1558, however, presumably after the death of Mary Tudor (which occurred on November 17) a new outrage occurred. The shrine was further desecrated, in the eyes of some at least, by the bones of St. Friedeswide being mixed with those of Catherine Danmartin. This was achieved by James Calfhill, a Calvinist divine, intent on the suppression of St. Friedeswide's cult. Foxe accepted this act of unnecessary vandalism, not unsurprisingly, as a fait accompli, writing: "(Queen)Elizabeth willed to take her (Catherine) out of that unclean and dishonest place (the dunghill) where she lay, and, in the face of the whole town, (sic) to bury her again in a more decent and honest monument" and so "she was restored and translated to her proper place, and withal coupled with Friedeswide's bones, that in case any cardinal will be so mad hereafter to remove this woman's bones again, it shall be hard for them to discern the bones".[12]

A modern addendum to this might be that sophisticated modern techniques could indeed distinguish the bones from one another, and probably could have done it at the time, for some of the bones were from the eighth century and some from the sixteenth! Ironically, like many saints, St. Friedeswide's body had already been exhumed and moved twice, in

1180 and 1289. Her cult had certainly been strengthened by being adopted as patroness of the University of Oxford in the fifteenth century. St. Friedeswide had been of royal blood, an abbess, and contemporary of the Venerable Bede, and so was worthy of the honour.

As for Bucer and Fagius, they too were rehabilitated by Queen Elizabeth on July 22, 1560. A brass plaque in St. Mary's Church marks the spot of the original grave of Bucer, and Fagius too had a memorial set up to him also in 1560.

As for James Calfhill, he who had mixed the bones, he was elected Bishop of Worcester, but mercifully or otherwise for the inhabitants of that city, died before consecration; while Queen Elizabeth's Archbishop of Canterbury, the Norwich-born Matthew Parker, who had been Bucer's executor in Cambridge, inherited much of Bucer's incoming, and outgoing correspondence.

The polarisation and division of opinions are behind the grisly story of the next exhumations, the most famous or infamous in British history, on January 30, 1661. This was the anniversary of the execution of King Charles I in 1649. Those who had been vanquished at that time, the Royalists and their sympathisers, were now back in power, after eleven years of Republican rule. Those who had signed the death warrant of Charles I., the Regicides, were now being hunted down. All those who had fled abroad were attainted, and the same penalty was posthumously extended to the prominent offenders who had escaped punishment by death.

The three chief regicides, Cromwell, his son-in-law Ireton, and Bradshaw, were thus exhumed, hanged at Tyburn and buried beneath the gallows. "Thus," as Richard Lodge wrote in his volume of *The Political History of England Vol. VIII 1660–1702*, "the dust of one of the most redoubtable of English rulers was committed to an unhonoured and untraceable grave. It may have been a grim consolation to the defeated republicans that the intended re-interment of the 'royal martyr' at Westminster was rendered impossible because none of the witnesses of the hurried funeral at Windsor could identify the precise place of burial."[13]

This is of course simply touching the surface of a very complex story, both before and after the exhumations. The biographical details of the three men involved need some elucidation. John Bradshaw, the least likeable of some very dour companions, had been the President of the Court which condemned the king. On that occasion, his manners were as short as his speeches were lengthy. Permanent president of the Council of State, and Chancellor of the Duchy of Lancaster (it is interesting that republicans kept a duchy), his "stiff republicanism" estranged him from Cromwell. Not surprisingly, he opposed Cromwell's gradual assumption of arbitrary power, a temptation for all rulers, both before and after Lord Acton's famous aphorism. He had been buried in Westminster Abbey after his death in 1659.

Henry Ireton, Cromwell's son-in-law (he had married Bridget Cromwell) from 1646, had in 1647 proposed a constitutional monarchy (the so-called *Heads of the Proposals*) and even suggested Charles's deposition in favour of one of his three sons, but, despite this, later signed the death warrant of the king. Cromwell made him Lieutenant Governor of Ireland, and he died there, much regretted by many, probably of the plague, in 1651.

Of Cromwell himself (who died in September 1658) more will be said shortly. Firstly, the details of the exhumations after the Bill of Attainder. The three corpses were exhumed from the Abbey by a mason named John Lewis, who was paid 17 shillings for his task. Cromwell and Ireton had been embalmed, and their corpses were in a reasonable state, but that of Bradshaw was in a most unpleasant condition. The corpses were taken to the Red Lion Inn at Holborn to await their fate, and the following day were dragged to Tyburn on hurdles, as had happened to living persons, and hung on a triple tree. Bradshaw was hung in the middle; he was obviously considered to be the greatest traitor. Here they remained until the following day. In the late afternoon, they were taken down and their heads hacked off. It took eight blows to separate Cromwell's head from his body, considerably more than was usual if the body had been living. It took a further six blows to remove the head of Ireton. Nor was that the only incision now performed upon those inanimate unprotesting objects, as Antonia Fraser terms them.[14] It seems that fingers and toes were hacked off at the same time, and it may have been while this was being done that Cromwell lost an ear from the skull. The fascinating parallel with what happened to Pope Formosus should not be lost here. Clearly, it the case of the papal fingers, they had been used for blessing; but Cromwell's fingers and toes? The headless corpses were then put into a large pit, below the gallows at Tyburn. The heads were taken to Westminster Hall (where the trial of Charles I. had taken place) and there stuck on poles tipped with iron, then placed high on display. Here they were to remain until 1684, for almost all the reign of Charles II. A wind blew down the pole which had held Cromwell's head, and a guard. It was reported, took it as a souvenir.

The whole of this narrative now needs to be dissected and analysed: was it all true? Was any of it true? Obviously the public had seen three bodies treated in this way, but what had actually happened? There are several accounts suggesting that Cromwell himself, foreseeing what might *happen, actually took steps to see that no revenge was taken on him after death. One account says* that his body was taken to the field of the Battle of Naseby, and there buried in the field; another that he was taken by boat, and his body tipped into the Thames; still others that he arranged for his body to be substituted for that of Charles I at Windsor, although it is known this was false, as they could not even find the king's body (although they did later). Taking a balanced view, historians think it seems most unlikely that Cromwell would think of taking such evasive action. There remains, however, a more realistic possibility that the soldiers who had taken Cromwell's body to the Red Lion could have been bribed to substitute another body during the night he lay there. Cromwell's daughter Mary Fauconberg might have managed this. There is an account of her burying a body at Newburgh Priory, where there is a tomb. This story cannot be substantiated, because the owners of the Priory have never allowed the tomb to be inspected (a common frustration in these cases) even when King Edward VII, no less, took an interest. It is more reasonable to assume that the headless body lies in the ground at Tyburn, near to the present-day Marble Arch.

The fate of Cromwell's head is another matter. It remained, as has been seen, on a spike at Westminster Hall, until it was blown down early in the reign of James II (1684–1685). (It should be remembered that James began to reign legally in 1684, because the legal new year did not begin until March 25, and Charles II had died on February 6.) One of the sentinels saw what had happened, recognised the head for what it was, and, taking it under his cloak, took it home. His daughter eventually sold it to a Cambridge family, from whom it passed to a drunken actor, Samuel Russell. It is true that the stories about exhumations and their aftermaths are sometimes hard to improve on. In about 1781 the head was "picked up as a bargain for £118" by a James Cox, the proprietor of a private museum. Here it is pertinent to intersperse that 1780 puts this story right in the middle of what was, in the eighteenth and early nineteenth centuries, a Gothic cult, which would indeed have collected such relics, and will be dealt with at length in a subsequent chapter. Anyway, James Cox recognised its display value and acquired it for this purpose. He then sold it for £230, a large sum for those days, to three speculators, a syndicate, who again exhibited it, and charged the public two shillings and sixpence a time to see it.[15] How are the mighty fallen: from the splendours of state to three dubious characters out to make profit. All three speculators died violent deaths, but this might simply have been the risks they ran in the sort of circles they came from, for no other superstition attaches to this relic. From here, it was passed to a Josiah Wilkinson, and so eventually to someone, at least by calling, of a higher order, Canon Wilkinson, who left it in his will to Sidney Sussex College in Cambridge, where it still is. This was Cromwell's own college. At this time, again, as so often happens, there were two heads, and the owners were both claiming that his was the authentic one. One was in the possession of Wilkinson and the other was at Oxford. Wilkinson was sure that his head was the genuine one; and in pursuit of this, there was a newspaper article in December 1933, which stated that the Canon's great-grandfather had acquired the skull at the end of the eighteenth century. In order to satisfy himself that the skill he had was really that of Cromwell, the Canon had it photographed and measured by experts, who compared it with the measurements with a death mask of Cromwell which is now in the British Museum. The measurements corresponded exactly. Furthermore, the skull in the Canon's possession has a hole in the lower portion of it. This, it was claimed, was made by the spike at the top of the pole on which it was impaled. The spike entered underneath the lower jaw, and went through the top of the skull. The head was exhibited in 1911, before the Royal Archaeological Institute, and in the same year Asquith, the Prime Minister, was asked to facilitate an official enquiry into the provenance and authenticity of the head, but refused to intervene.

The 1930s, as will be seen, following the sensational discovery of Tut-an-khamoun in Egypt in 1922, proved a fertile ground for exhumations and re-examinations of famous bodies and bones. Thus the head was examined by Dr. Mornat and Mr. Pearson. They noted that the head was of a man of about sixty years. (Cromwell was fifty-nine years old when he died.) The head had a hole in it, which would have been used for trepanning after death, as was necessary for embalming, and it had been severed from the body after death by a number of strokes. They published their complete findings in *Biometrika*, and there seemed to be no doubt that the head was, to them, authentic. Sidney Sussex College decided to give the head a proper burial. Accordingly, a plaque has been placed near the chapel entrance which reads: "Near to this place was buried, on March 25th, 1960 the head of Oliver Cromwell, Lord Protector of the Commonwealth of England, Scotland and Ireland, Fellow Commoner of this College 1616–17." The exact whereabouts of the head is a secret guarded like the recipe for Chartreuse.

However, some doubt persists. Cromwell's body underwent a post-mortem examination by Dr. Bate, after Cromwell had died in 1658. Part of this examination is worth repeating. "…the middle of the spleen was liquefied, which is not characteristic of malaria, although the spleen is otherwise affected by the disease. The embalmers filled the body cavities with aromatics, removed the brain, and then enclosed the body in a wooden coffin. This was placed in a second lead coffin. In spite of this, 'yet the filth broke through them all', and the stench became overbearing, as is typical with death from uraemia. It was found to be necessary to bury the body with all haste, and this was done while preparations were made for the official burial ceremony."

A vast lying-in-state was arranged to take place at Somerset House. Four rooms were prepared and arranged for the public to pass through, the first being filled with the objects of State. In the fourth room was the great wax image of the Protector. In the first few days this lay like a huge doll, clothed in imperial robes, with a large crown above, and holding in one hand the orb, and the other the sceptre. The whole was illuminated by four huge candlesticks. Whether this exaggerated usurpation of the trappings of monarchy proved too much for some or perhaps it was something else, but after a few more days the lying-in-state was altered, with the wax image now standing upright, and crown placed on his head with the eyes opened. Thus Cromwell, like Ines de Castro, was crowned after death; there is no doubt that this symbolism was deliberate.

Arrangements were now made for the funeral itself. It should be noted here that the making of wax effigies was a traditional way of honouring and marking the funeral of a dead sovereign or royal person, and the outrage felt by royalists when Cromwell's followers hijacked this meant that the practice of having the wax effigy on the coffin at the funeral was discontinued, although some wax effigies were still made; and perhaps, even more interestingly, they began to be made for great figures of state, comparable to Cromwell, for example, Nelson.

The funeral itself, which took place on November 23, 1658, started with a huge procession from Somerset House to Westminster Hall, with the effigy in a great hearse. Unfortunately the dark November day had brought a gloom to the Abbey, which was freezing cold. No arrangements had been made for lighting or heating, so that the elaborate hearse was simply left there, in the chapel, without any orations, sermons, or other rites. The hearse and the effigy remained in this position *for several months*, with the public paying to obtain admission. This commercial element often raises its head in these stories of royal bodies and lesser mortals.

Cromwell's favourite daughter, Betty Claypole, had died just before her father, on August 6, 1658, and been buried in the Abbey. She was the only member of her family not to be disturbed at the Restoration, and the reason was the same as in the quest for the body of Charles I. Nobody knew its whereabouts, which seems extraordinary, as the time lapse was only two years and five months. Obviously someone knew, but no-one was telling; and so it was not until 1725, when workmen came upon her tomb by accident, that she was found, and she remains in the Abbey to this day.[16]

As Olivia Bland says, "Cromwell's obsequies were performed in all respects like those of a king, and played a major part in the development of the tradition of royal funerals as we know them today."

But what of Cromwell's actual body? It was said that it had been buried in the Abbey before all these elaborate ceremonies began, due to a bungled embalming. The hasty burial may also have been that it was feared that someone might steal the body. As has been noted, when the bodies of Cromwell, Ireton and Bradshaw were exhumed, the first two were apparently in a good state of preservation.

Sergeant Norfolk may have taken the gold gorget from Cromwell's body, but if he did he must have been disappointed, for it proved to be copper gilt. The taking of items and "souvenirs" from graves at exhumations proved to be a regular feature.

The ordering of the funeral was undertaken by the Heralds' Office. How interesting that these trappings of a monarchical state were retained by the Republicans. The cost has been estimated at £100, 000 in contemporary terms, a great sum, and more than double what the funeral of James I had cost in 1625, on which it was modelled. Thirty-thousand yards of black cloth were issued for mourning, and the New Model Army lined the streets in force, in their buff uniforms with black mourning facings, their buttons blacked and colours draped with cypress, the forerunner of crape. From this grew a tradition which remains to this day: monarchists took from republicans, and republicans took from monarchists.

A slab in the floor of the central eastern chapel of the Abbey marks the original burial place of Oliver Cromwell, various members of his family, and some of the leaders of the great Parliamentary party. These were all exhumed at the time of the Restoration; those of Cromwell, Ireton, and Bradshaw suffered the fate which has been described, but the other bodies (with the exception of Elizabeth (Betty) Claypole) were re-interred in the "north green" outside the Abbey. Again here the idea of "contamination" is present. They had to be removed. The resting place of Betty Claypole, when it was rediscovered in 1725, was on the north side of the tomb of Henry VII. In fact the contemporary writer Dart wrote: "This melancholy wretch is said to have ended his course in the blackest desperation; but that a Church roof was the rest of such an Unclean bird I have not heard… is it is not improbable that is some of his fits he might retire to a place very well suited to such a temper." Such partisan vitriol has of course to be properly balanced, but it is as well also to record that Churchill, in his *History of the English Speaking Peoples*, did not write favourably of Cromwell. He spoke of his "smoky soul".

The Royalist John Evelyn, describing the funeral of Cromwell with some mischief, wrote: "it was the joyfullest funeral that ever I saw, for there were none that cried, but dogs, which the soldiers hooted away with as barbarous noise, drinking and taking tobacco in the streets as they went." These scenes, however, record the feelings of royalists and seem to foreshadow the coming re-action in men's minds. A more impartial observer would probably have gathered a rather different impression, from the solemn ceremonial, a nation's tribute to one of its greatest sons. Thus thought Troutbeck in 1900.[17] However, when Cromwell's body was removed, there was now an empty tomb, a vacant vault. This was used as the burial place of James Butler, Duke of Ormonde, who died in 1688, and all his family after him, several English noblemen, and more ironic of all, several of the illegitimate descendants of Charles II. Not only that, but the favourite of William III, William Bentinck, Earl of Portland, was buried here in 1709, and the great Duke of Marlborough, Churchill's ancestor, was buried here on August 9, 1722. However his body was exhumed and re-buried in the chapel at Blenheim in 1746. Was there a fear of contamination, one wonders?

The body of Henry Ireton had been conveyed to the Abbey a full ten years before the exhumations, he having died in Ireland in November 1651, and on this occurrence hangs so many tales and legends that it is difficult, perhaps impossible now, to disentangle them, and to do the more creditable ones justice. A decade previously things were very different. The nation had felt raw at all the changes, deep, ineradicable changes.

Ireton was the eminence grise of Cromwell, a very remarkable young man who would probably have succeeded him if he had lived. The questions involve such issues as, what did he die of? Who was present? What was done with his body? Was it really his body or an empty coffin which was taken across the Irish sea to Bristol and then all the way to London? The answers must be largely unresolved ones.

Firstly, what did Ireton die of? McMains, in an important work published in 2000,[18] thinks he did not die of plague or even of typhus, as has often been thought. These diseases would have precluded his embalming of his body, or even the removal of it to London. The fear of infection was too great. Was he then buried in Ireland? Lucy Hutchinson, the wife of Colonel Hutchinson, and intimate of Ireton's, noted in her biography of her husband that "Cromwell…order'd all things" concerning Ireton's funeral. Bulstrode, that redoubtable ambassador of Cromwell's (we shall come across him in discussing the exhumation of Queen Christina of Sweden: Bulstrode was ambassador there) wrote letters from Ireland to the Council of State: his final letter stated that a decision had been made in Ireland and that "his body was to be carried over into England". The decision had been taken by someone in Ireland, in Limerick, where Ireton had died. This person was none other than Henry Cromwell, then aged 23, the son of Oliver. However, was this a smokescreen? The letter contained information not then reported regarding shipment *of a coffin* to the west of England for cartage to London. The council of England with the Irish and Scottish committees "to consider what is fit to be done in receiving *the corpse* of the late Lord Deputy of Ireland, which is to come to Bristol, and also *for its interment*". Parliament itself directed the Council to arrange Ireton's interment at State expense, making the funeral public business. How to interpret these letters?

It is possible to think that a coffin simply meant a ceremonial coffin, and that Ireton's body had been already buried in Ireland. It was decided that the body should rest in Somerset House, as was to be done in 1658, for Cromwell himself. The chief mourner was to be John Ireton, Henry's brother. The interment in Westminster Abbey, however, raised some controversy, but Cromwell overruled this in mid-December 1651. (Ireton had died on November 26.)

On the journey of the cortege from Bristol to London every possible respect was paid to the coffin, whether or not the body was in it. When the ship arrived in Bristol it was taken by a longboat draped in a black cloth, and then placed under a canopy, and brought up the Avon to a landing at

Beck. Covered with velvet, it was then conveyed to the Castle, accompanied by every known City dignitary, and, whether from curiosity or genuine respect a "multitude of inhabitants". Salvos were fired from the castle and Fort cannon. The coffin lay at the Castle until Christmas eve. There was no public viewing at this time. A chariot and six horses then conveyed the coffin to London. At the beginning of its journey all the dignitaries and many inhabitants followed it, together with 800 local militiamen and 500 soldiers. The procession wound its way round the City until Lawford's Gate, when a salute of three vollies of shots were fired. Even then some senior dignitaries accompanied the coffin for the rest of the first day. It took six days to reach London. They were six days of spectacle. The late Lord Deputy's Regiment accompanied the chariot all the way. As they approached London many people joined the cortege. On the evening of December 29, 1651, the coffin reached Somerset House accompanied by a greatly inflated procession of military guards and others.

Funeral arrangements were not completed until the end of January 1652. One of the escutcheons over the gate at Somerset House read: "Dulce est pro patria mori" (It is sweet to die for one's country) which, as Antonia Fraser relates, "naughty Cavaliers" misinterpreted as "It is good for the country that he is dead."

In the London ceremonies that now followed lay no indication that Ireton's remains were present. McMains makes the pertinent comment that "Puritan theology did not require glorification and preservation of the body; it emphasised salvation." Contemporary accounts do not refer to his body, but only to the coffin and the effigy. The ceremonies at Westminster and at Somerset House, like Cromwell's later, were all conducted with an effigy. Lucy Hutchinson was within the Commonwealth elite, and she wrote "But God cut him short by death, and whether his body *or an empty hearse* was brought into England, something in his name came to London and was to be by Cromwell's procurement magnificently buried among the kings at Westminster."

But if there was no body, then what did the mason John Lewis exhume in 1661? It can only be concluded that there really was a body, which had been embalmed, or that another body was substituted to satisfy the need for retribution visited upon the regicides.

The Memoirs of General Edmund Ludlow, who became an exile in Geneva for the rest of his life after a hairbreadth's escape at the Restoration, may shed some light here. Though not in Limerick when Ireton died, there survives a fragment from the Memoirs which has not been heavily docked and annotated. This, fortunately, is the part covering 1660–1662. It was first published c.1980. From it, Ludlow's deep religious faith, political cynicism and access to sources are all fully apparent. Referring to the 1661 exhumations of Cromwell's and Ireton's bodies, this original mss makes passing reference to Ireton's burial, confirming Lucy Hutchinson's suspicions, "the wise providence of God so ordered it that his body being interred in Ireland..."[19]

It is worth reflecting on Ireton's actual funeral. The Venetian ambassador reported, on February 6, 1652: "they gave a sumptuous funeral for Lord Ireton". But the underlying strains within the elite soon showed themselves. Cromwell apparently did not invite Colonel Hutchinson, who was Ireton's cousin, to join the official mourners; whereupon Hutchinson appeared in the chief mourner's room wearing a scarlet cloak, "publickly to reproach their neglects".

After the very magnificent funeral, Cromwell ordered William Wright, "graver in stone to the Protector", to prepare a monument. How easily, and how soon, the republicans assumed even things such as patronage and appointment in the regal style. Under the supervision of Hugh Peters, Cromwell's chaplain, the marble tomb was apparently in place by Spring 1654.

General Ludlow had reflected that Puritan belief (was) that embalming and preservation were unnecessary... republicans and radicals thought that the spirit of AntiChrist had appeared in "the vain pomp at the funeral of Lord Ireton (which) was very offensive to many." Thus they "solemnized the funeral of the late Lord Deputy" and "magnificently buried among the kings "the purported mortain remains". There was, of course, said McMains, no interment.[20]

The weight of evidence indicates, writes McMains, that two of the three bodies at Tyburn were bogus. There was an irreconcilable disparity between Cromwell's corrupted corpse buried in Westminster Abbey and the fresh one hanged at Tyburn. This does not answer, however, the question of the head, which later appeared authentic, when measured and compared with the death mask. Only the body of Bradshaw, says McMains, was genuine.

Had Cromwell's body actually been buried secretly somewhere else? In late July 1790, workmen found a coffin beneath the pavement where the common councilmen's pew stood, in St. Giles, Cripplegate. The gravedigger Elizabeth Grant charged the curious sixpence to look, with a candle, into the excavation. On August 4 and 5, 1790, the coffin was publicly displayed and caused public controversy, as to whether the corpse was that of the poet John Milton. It is not surprising that a fellow poet, William Cowper, showing more sensitivity that most Georgians, thought that disturbing the corpse for any reason was an indecency.

This discovery may have been deliberate, for it followed the publication of Sir John Prestwich's *The Secret in 1787* referring to Cromwell's burial. His authority for what he alleged was probably his Cromwellian forebear, the Reverend John Prestwich. In 1799 another publication, *Anecdotes and biography London*, by Leman Thomas Redes, said quite explicitly that "the Protector's friends" had obtained his body and buried it "in a meadow to the north of Holborn", He wrote that "it was known" at the time that Cromwell's remains had been secretly buried after the exhumation.

This points up what was perhaps an urban myth which will not go away, namely that Cromwell was buried in Red Lion Square (presumably during the night his body lay at the Inn, and by his supporters) and that "the obelisk is thought by many to be a memorial erected to his manes by an apothecary who was attached to Cromwell's principles, and had so much influence in the building of the square, as to manage the marking of the ground". Thus wrote Leman Rede when he published his book in 1799, and the apothecary was identified as one Ebenezer Heathcote.

Enter one Nicholas Barton, who was to anticipate the decade of the notorious "Resurrection Men" of the 1820s. He arranged with the Resurrection men of 1661 for corpses to represent Ireton and Cromwell. Nicholas was the son of Praisegod Barbon (really Barebones), a Cromwellian follower, and Nicholas was soon to obtain his medical degree from Utrecht, and later to become an honorary fellow of the College of Physicians. Barbon later bought Red Lion fields, so the story in some particulars fits together; enough to raise doubts of the official presentation anyway.

There was to have been a fourth man exhumed: this was Colonel Thomas Pride, but, as he had been buried in Surrey, in the end his corpse eluded its grisly fate, due to the slackness of the Sheriff of Middlesex, which may of course have been deliberate.

Napoleon Bonaparte has some resonances with Oliver Cromwell, and what happened to them when they died. Both were extraordinary generals and leaders. Bonaparte, despite the dark reputation he had built up among those who opposed him, was spared the post-mortem humiliations which visited the bodies of Cromwell and his confederates.

It is common knowledge that after his defeat at Waterloo, Napoleon was taken to the Island of St. Helena in the South Atlantic, aboard a British warship, to become "an eagle chained to a rock". Less well known, perhaps, are the three stages which followed his death in 1821, six years later. Napoleon died at Longwood House, where he had lived out his exile, on May 5, 1821. Like so many other leaders or deposed kings, who die in prison or incarceration, there were suspicions that his death was not natural. An autopsy took place. Sir Hudson Lowe, the Governor of St. Helena, had little love for his illustrious captive, and when Napoleon complained of a mysterious stomach ailment in the last months of his life, Lowe dismissed this as "a slight anaemia". Napoleon knew different. Knowing he was dying, he made out a detailed will, stating that he wished for his body to be buried on the banks of the Seine, "in the midst of the French people I have loved so well". It is sometimes forgotten that Napoleon was a Corsican of Italian descent, and all his life spoke French with a marked accent.

Lowe had no intention of letting this happen. When Napoleon did die, at 6 pm on that Spring evening, his valet said that his life went "out, as the light of a lamp goes out". During the autopsy which followed, parts of Napoleon started disappearing, much as has been seen in the exhumations following the deaths of kings and saints: in other words, people were intending to take relics. When Napoleon's doctor, an Italian named Francesco Antommarchi, cut into his stomach, he found an ulcer big enough to stick a small finger inside.[21] The rest of the organ looked as if it might have been riddled with cancer, although experts are now divided as to whether it was complications from the ulcer or cancer which killed him. During the autopsy, however, Antommarchi cut out both Napoleon's heart and his stomach, placing them in separate silver vases filled with spirits. Readers of the twenty-first century may find this nauseous, but it must be remembered that for centuries it had been normal practice to do this with royal bodies and other celebrated mortals. The heart was supposed to go to Napoleon's second wife, the Empress Marie Louise, now the ruler of an Italian state for her lifetime, but the destination of the stomach was not made clear. The tales that Antommarchi also cut off Napoleon's penis, perhaps as an act of petty revenge because he felt he had not been treated properly (he had been frequently abused by the dying emperor) can probably be discounted as sensationalism. It does seem that the first owner of the object was Napoleon's priest, Fr. Ange Paul Vignali, who took it, along with a number of Napoleon's personal effects to his

Corsican village, including a copy of his will, his waistcoat, some hair, and a pair of his breeches. These objects went on to form the Vignali collection. Although an object which was claimed to be such (and identified indeed as a penis by an American urologist, John K. Lattimer, who purchased it in a Paris auction in 1977) there is no proof that it belonged to Napoleon, and, indeed, the French government has always refused to acknowledge it as belonging to him.

Napoleon's body was now sewn together again, he was dressed in his battle uniform, and placed within four nested coffins. On the orders of the British, the vases of viscera were placed in the innermost coffin, along with some of Napoleon's good silverware. Then each coffin was soldered tight. The funeral cortege then wound its way across the island to a peaceful willow grove, where the body was laid to rest. But someone as restless as Napoleon was in life could not expect much rest in death. Although Madame Mere, Napoleon's mother, who long outlived most members of her very extraordinary family, requested his body to be returned to her, in 1821, this did not happen. Betrand had also asked for his body to be returned at this time, but was told by the British government that this was a matter for the French government. Certainly the restored Bourbons, "who had learnt nothing and forgotten nothing" did not want the physical presence of Napoleon's body in France, a threat even when deceased.

In 1840, nineteen years later, King Louis-Philippe, the Citizen King (who had signed the death warrant of his cousin Louis XVI) and who stands curiously poised between the Bourbon ascendancy and the Revolution, asked the British government for the return of Napoleon's body. Fortunately for him, the Tories were out of office, and the beneficent Melbourne was Prime Minister for the young, and very untried, Queen Victoria. He gave a sympathetic audience to the envoy of the French king. Thus Napoleon was exhumed in September 1840. It seems possible that the good citizens of St. Helena, who had profited by the presence of Napoleon's body, knew nothing of what was going to happen.

September 15, 1840, was 25 years to the day since Napoleon had arrived at St. Helena. It was raining heavily. Two tents were set up. One was giving protection to the men who were excavating the tomb. The other was set up as a chapel. In this a number of local officials were gathered, as well as a party of Frenchmen, most of whom had shared the Emperor's exile, and had come to take his body home. The work was taking longer than anticipated the thick cement protecting the tomb was hard to penetrate and the excavators had to work through the night. At

8.00 am on September 16 they finally broke through and at 9.30 am they caught sight of the coffin: soon they were able to enter into the tomb and inspect it.

Then the coffin was lifted out and moved into the chapel. As John Tyrrell has commented: “Nothing between England and France is ever quite straightforward, and this occasion was no exception.”

The French had wanted to exhume the body themselves, and the leader of the French party, the king’s son the Prince of Joinville, expressed his displeasure at not being allowed to do so by remaining on board the *Belle Poule*. Now, with the coffin in the chapel objections were made and recorded by a local judge, concerning the correct procedure that should be gone through when a coffin is unsealed.

At last the coffin was opened. For two minutes Napoleon’s remains were exposed to those present. But this was not long enough for the daguerreotype that someone had brought with them to record the occasion. The witnesses were able to verify that it did indeed contain the body of the Emperor, and not the quicklime that persistent rumour had suggested. It is impossible to imagine what must have gone through the minds of those who had shared the Emperor’s exile as the coffin was opened. As the body was revealed they were amazed to find it so well preserved; whilst they had grown older, he to some at least seemed younger than when he had died nineteen years earlier.

The following account, in response to a comment that the Emperor’s body was well preserved, was given to a visiting seaman by someone who said he had been present:

> *Yes; externally it was perfect. The least touch, however, made an indenture. His nose was the only part which did not retain its original fullness. It hung upon the bone, and greatly disfigured his countenance. I saw him by torchlight, and a more ghastly object I never looked upon. The night was dark, and, when the lid of the coffin was raised, the glare of light shed upon his pale features gave them an additional ghastliness. His eyes were much sunken, and his lips slightly parted. There was nothing of sternness in the expression of his countenance. It was rather that of pain. He looked as if he had fallen into an uneasy sleep after a long fit of illness. His liver and heart, which were embalmed, and placed upon his breast, were uninjured.*[22]

The coffin was then re-sealed, now with six layers instead of four, and weighing 1200 kilos. It was carried up the track by forty-three soldiers and placed on a carriage that had been reinforced to bear its heavy weight. At this point a British officer from a famous military family, Major-General Churchill, Chief of Staff of the Indian Army, came running to pay his respects, and he and his two aides-de-camp joined the procession into Jamestown.

In Jamestown flags were at half-mast and shops closed. All the windows were crowded with onlookers. The ladies of St. Helena had woven a large tricolour flag for the occasion.

The sick Governor (it may have been a diplomatic sickness) General Middlemore who had walked the six kilometres into Jamestown behind the procession, then formally handed over the coffin to the French. The Prince de Joinville then thanked him for the sympathy and respect with which the ceremony had been conducted.

As soon as the coffin reached the French ship, flags were unfurled, drums beaten, and salvoes fired. Gilbert Martineau described it as "*the end of the most horrible misunderstanding in history*".[23]

One John Henry Lefroy, then a young lieutenant, had been sent to St. Helena to study magnetic phenomena, and was permitted to witness the exhumation, but was not among the select few allowed into the tent to see the opening of the coffin. He chose also not to join the funeral procession to see the embarkation of the coffin aboard the *Belle Poule*, the ship sent by Louis-Philippe. But Lefroy's reports are very well worth reading. In his recollection, he says that General Middlemore, a veteran of the Peninsular War, not surprisingly hated the whole thing. He even shut himself up in Plantation House, although he claimed to be ill, and left all the negotiations to Colonel Hamelin Trelawney.

Lefroy was not himself sympathetic to the operation. Napoleon had, after all, been the arch enemy for over twenty years. He was however impressed by the young prince whom Louis-Philippe had also sent, his own son the Prince de Joinville, one of four sons. He described him as "a fine young man, about six feet three inches in height…He declined society, and went about in his loose white trousers, old coat and tarpaulin hat", but then he was the son of the Citizen king.

Lefroy asked him if he might show him around the house (Longwood, presumably) to which the Prince who Lefroy says was proficient in English and Spanish, bizzarely replied: "Thank you, Sare, I never drink wine". Perhaps the lack of proficiency was on the part of Lefroy.

Leroy was amused that the French party wanted relics, not of course of Napoleon himself, but of his place of exile: handfuls of earth, water from

Napoleon's spring, leaves, flowers, bulbs… there was definitely something quasi-religious about it all.

In a letter to his sister, dated October 17, 1840, which reflects his feelings at the time, he described somewhat disrespectfully, but maybe not atypically, *the removal of Boney's remains.* In a neat turn of phrase he noted that *corruption and the worm had spared him who had given them so many a banquet.* His description of the scene of the exhumation is evocative:

> *…the midnight formed as picturesque a scene as I have ever witnessed. The sentries posted on the hill, the black labourers, the soldiers of the guard and working party, mixed up with the muffled figures of the authorities attending, in the imperfect light of the lanterns, by which they worked, would have formed a scene for Rembrandt.*

He also expressed his disapproval of the way the Governor had in his view ceded to the demands of the French party:

> *Minute guns were fired all the way, and a royal salute from the battery, but not from the English man-of-war. However, with this latter exception, everything was done as if he were the emperor, a thing never acknowledged before, which makes the amends to France, and directly inculpates all preceding governments. I would have stuck to the "General Bonaparte" as long as there was "a shot in the locker.*

Finally, he refers to the ongoing diplomatic dispute between England and France over Syria (something which was indeed worrying Melbourne at the time, despite his unruffled exterior). *A declaration of war was daily expected.* Apparently to the great amusement of Thackeray, this was also to cause much concern aboard the *Belle Poule*, on its journey back to France with its precious cargo. The *Belle Poule* was not the only ship to panic over the imminent declaration of war between England and France. An English merchant vessel arrived at St. Helena just as the French were firing salutes, and the crew clearly thought that they were attacking the island, and the ship *fled for her life*. Likewise, as the *Belle Poule* left St. Helena, "*Littlehales, in HMS Dolphin, followed her at a safe distance, determined if he got a chance, to pitch a shell or two into 'old Boney's coffin'*".

The letter concludes somewhat abruptly, and in view of the foregoing somewhat strangely, "*The French behaved handsomely*". Perhaps Leroy was won over by the prepossessing prince.

War was not declared, to the relief of both sides. Good relations between the old enemies of eight centuries duration were finally under way from now on.[24]

Interestingly, these accounts make it clear that at last the British Government would refer to Bonaparte as "The Emperor", something not done before. But the government was still concerned not to do anything which could be criticised by the Tory Opposition. It was made clear therefore that the Governor should not say anything which in any way appeared to criticise the decision of 1815 (to send Napoleon to St. Helena). The French Government, for its part, indicated that the former captives now returning (the Emperor's small entourage) would be told to be silent and unemotional.

Honour was observed.

Then the third part of the saga was enacted as the *Belle Poule* arrived in Paris. This part is known in French as "Le Retour des Cendres".[25]

Even now, there were conspiracy stories that it was not really the body of Napoleon, but that of his butler, Jean-Baptiste Cipriani, who apparently bore him a close resemblance. It was reported on August 17, 2002 that Bruno Roy-Henn, a legal expert and amateur historian, had asked for a DNA test to be carried out on the body, but in was declined.[26]

The return of Napoleon's body had been engineered by King Louis-Philippe and the Prime Minister of France, Adolphe Thiers; but before the ceremonies were complete, Thiers had fallen from power. What was their agenda in bringing the body back? Certainly part of it was to fill in one of the mosaic pieces of French identity, especially *La Gloire*, that feeling of triumph that Henri Quatre, Louis XIV and Napoleon had given to France. The title of Louis-Philippe, who called himself King of the French instead of King of France, was akin to, and following Napoleon's title of "Emperor of the French", meaning all French people everywhere in the world. This concept has descended to the present day, with MPs being returned to the Parliament in Paris from all over the world.

There was also a French physician sent by Louis-Philippe to St. Helena, Dr. Guillard. It seems unlikely that it was not the body of Napoleon.

The ceremonious return brought out huge crowds in Paris, a glimpse of the nationalist feeling among the urban population of France, again perhaps a questionable component of perceived French identity. As Robert Tombs opines: "War…was another obsessive theme, and it too greatly shaped French identity…The cult of Napoleon was a major consequence, and it provided one of the century's great moments of national communion."

Napoleon's remains were taken slowly up the Seine to the crypt in Les Invalides. "Before the days of mass politics, mass literacy and mass media, hundreds of thousands of people waited fervently in the freezing cold to welcome *L'Empereur*...the people, the genuine people, cried "*Vive L'Empereur!,*"wanted to unharness the horses and pull the funeral car. A suburban (National Guard) company went down on its knees, men and women kissed the drapes of the catafalque. It was perhaps the century's biggest, and largely spontaneous, expression of national identity and it showed how much a sense of being French owed to the Napoleonic epic"[27] It also showed how almost mediaeval was the demonstration, as if the remains were holy, relics, the bones of a venerated saint. It never seems to quite disappear from human emotional demonstrations en masse. One only has to think of how the Russian peasantry dodged about in crowds to stand in the shadow cast by the passing Tsar (and this the last Tsar, Nicholas II, in 1913) or the almost embarrassing lamentations and keening during the funeral of Princess Diana in 1997, and the throwing of thousands of carnations at her coffin, hoping that the one thrown by you would land on it, and stay there.

Thiers's idea to bring back Napoleon's remains from St. Helena was one of the great patriotic gestures of the century, the grandiose culmination of the Napoleonic gestures that the July monarchy, on Thiers's prompting, had been making for years. The completion of the Arc de Triomphe, replacing Napoleon's statue on the Vendome column, and so on, had shown this.

But, as Tombs goes on, "Nationalism was a dangerous tool; by the time Napoleon's remains returned in pomp to Paris in December, 1840, Thiers was out of office, amid foreign and domestic crises, that were fuelled by nationalist excitement." It was almost as if the gestures had turned against their maker.

There was a postscript to this. In 1855, on her second State visit to Paris (the first had been to Louis-Philippe) Queen Victoria and Prince Albert took their two eldest children, Vicky, the Princess Royal, and Bertie, the Prince of Wales, who were then fourteen and thirteen, respectively. They visited the tomb by torchlight and recorded that the experience was "strange and marvellous"; but then the French were always adept at timing and theatricality, perhaps lost on the visitors. But, most extraordinary of all, Queen Victoria made the Prince of Wales kneel by the tomb. In turn, this was a gesture of huge proportions not lost on the French, and, for the Prince, it would be the beginning of a life-long love affair with France, and especially Paris, and a half century later in the *Entente Cordiale*; indeed, the starstruck Prince, also entranced by the demi-monde court of Napoleon III and the Empress Eugenie, wanted to remain in Paris, and, when reminded of his duties retorted "But there are eight of us!"

In 2012, the bones of King Richard III were found beneath a municipal car park in Leicester, appropriately under the space allotted to the letter "R". The discovery was a major one in the history of archaeology and of exhumations and caused a national sensation. Richard III had been one of the most vilified persons in history; it was only his desperate physical courage, especially on the day he was cut down on Bosworth Field, that was looked upon as his redeeming grace and virtue. The reason primarily for his vilification was his connection with the disappearance of his two nephews, known to history as "The Princes in the Tower". Their own particular discovery, if that is what it was, is dealt with in another chapter, but Richard himself certainly falls into the category of Retribution and Reparation. The treatment of his corpse after the battle, on August 22, 1485, was reprehensible to a degree. Richard was certainly the victim of propaganda canonised into history, one of the leitmotifs of this study. Unfortunately most of this was taken up by Shakespeare, who, like Camoes in Portugal, turned history into drama, which was then accepted as the received version. Of course the truth, what one is able to extract, is rather different. It is impossible not to sympathise with the Princes in the Tower and their fate: the elder had been accepted for two months as the King of England. They were boys of twelve and ten years old. So why has Richard been so vilified as one of the demons of history? Because in the received version he authorised the murder of his nephews, so that he could become king himself; and then, by extension of his evil reputation, he must also have been responsible for the death of the old, deluded King Henry VI, of his son the Prince of Wales, and of Richard's own brother, George, Duke of Clarence, who, it must be admitted, died a colourful, unusual and memorable death. If he was so bad, then he could be blamed for all of these. But Richard, when he died, was a mere thirty-three years old. It is true he had had a very full life, but he was very much a younger brother to the tall, athletic, glamorous, and charismatic Edward IV, to whom his loyalty never wavered. What then, changed all that? Most of the answer must lie in his sister-in-law, the commoner Elizabeth Woodville, a widow with two sons when Edward married her. It was not so much Elizabeth herself, but her relatives which so angered and alienated Richard, and there were so many of them. From the beginning, the Queen set about tirelessly promoting them. Richard watched, glowering, from the side-lines, and kept his peace; but he plotted. As their joint histories unfolded, time favoured first one and then the other: the Woodville clan, or Prince Richard, Duke of Gloucester, and his supporters. During his lifetime, Edward IV on the whole allowed his wife and her family to have their heads, and that is why Richard waited, and saw his chance when Edward died, at the age of 41. If only Edward Prince of Wales had been twenty and not twelve, things might have been very different. One cannot discount that Richard was perhaps ambitious for the throne and saw his nephews inevitably well disposed towards the Woodvilles, because they had grown up with them and they were his mother's people. The Princes became both pawns and victims. Their story will be told in a later chapter.

Richard's great Lancastrian rival was of course Henry Tudor, who, through his grandmother Katherine of Valois (who will also feature in this study) was closely related also to the French royal family. The Battle of Bosworth Field in 1485 was decisive, because Richard III was killed, fighting to the very last moment. The retribution wreaked on his body needs to be told. He had been, whatever the truth of the matter, a crowned and anointed King of England; as he fell his helmet was lost, it was said, in a thorn bush, probably hawthorn. A private soldier found it. This was Sir Reginald Bray, who handed it to Stanley, the Earl of Derby, the husband of Lady Margaret Beaufort and the stepfather of Henry Tudor. He promptly crowned his stepson with it, on the battlefield.

The body of Richard, bearing terrible injuries which had caused his death, was now subjected to additional posthumous humiliations. The *Croyland Chronicle*, written by someone well placed within the Yorkist government at the time, records that Richard's body was offered "many other insults" and treated with "insufficient humanity". He was stripped naked, as Holinshed records, "not so much as a clout to cover his private members" and carried "trussed...like a hog or calf, his head and arms hanging on one side of the horse, and his legs on the other side, and all besprinkled with mire and blood". His white boar badge was "violently razed and plucked down from every sign" because those rejoicing at his death "wished the memorie of him to be buried with his carren corpse".

More followed. His body was put on display. The politics of this was of course to show to the public that he really was dead. Holinshed continues that Richard "there laie like a miserable spectacle" but, as Amy Licence relates in her illuminating short study, "a spectacle was exactly what he was intended to be".[28] Richard's own inability to display the bodies of his nephews, was, as she rightly writes, the root of many immediate problems and the foundation of centuries of speculation.

Three days later Richard was buried in the Church of Greyfriars, the church of the convent of the Friars Minor. Polydore Vergil, who was the court historian of Henry Tudor (VII), described how he was buried "without any pompe or solemn funeral, at th' abbaye of monks Franciscane at Leycester". Several authorities confirm that his hands were still tied together, crossed right over left over the pelvis, and that he had not been provided with any shroud or coffin. Moreover, the space into which he was placed was too small, with the result that his head and shoulders were thrust forwards. His body was twisted and his jaw hung open.[29]

It was in this position, minus his feet, which had probably been cut off by Victorian workmen, during extensions to property, that the redoubtable Philippa Langley and her co-workers found him in 2012. It is no wonder that she was filled with unwilling disbelief that it was really him. "No, I can't take it in. Are they saying this is Richard? I look again at the acute 'S' shape of the spine. If this is Richard, how can he have worn armour with hump on his back? ...but it doesn't add up. How could he fight with his head tilted downwards? How could he see?"[30]

This study does, and will not, in any way, trespass on grounds which have been covered so well and in so much detail, and with such commitment, by Langley and Jones in their ground-breaking cause which met with such supreme success. But Richard must be included here, as he was indeed someone who met with retribution at his death, and then, at his exhumation, received perhaps the reparation that was owing to him. Not exactly rehabilitation, but recognition of him as being as good, or as bad as most Yorkist, Lancastrian and Tudor kings. This has resulted in his final resting place being in a white marble tomb in Leicester cathedral, having been identified as the lost king of legend and drama, now restored by the extraordinary and sophisticated techniques off the twenty-first century, 527 years after his death.

In 1819, a rather different sort of exhumation took place in New York State. This concerned the famous (and indeed, infamous) patriot and writer, Thomas Paine. It is difficult to underestimate the effect the writings and speeches of Paine had on the emerging American revolution of 1776, especially in his book *Common Sense*, which most literate Americans had read. Paine had been born in Thetford, Norfolk, England, in 1737, but he quickly became both a firebrand and a participator in what was happening in France and in the American colonies. He even became a member of the French National Convention and narrowly escaped the guillotine. As his impressive statue in Thetford reads: He was a British citizen by birth, a French citizen by decree, and an American citizen by adoption, a truly International figure. But, like so many incendiary writers and speakers, he went too far for his many, many disciples. In 1794, he began writing a series of pamphlets entitled *The Age of Reason*, which attacked organised religion, whether "Jewish, Christian or Turkish (Moslem)". This was a fatal error, in a land where so many of the immigrants were there simply to practice their form of religious worship without hindrance.

Paine was ostracised, denied a pension, and denied the vote. However, in his last years, he was befriended again by two figures from his French past, M. & Mme Bonneville. It was a friendship of mutuality, because M. de Bonneville had published *The Rights of Man, and The Age of Reason* in France. Marguerite de Bonneville had arrived in 2003, with their three sons, Benjamin, Louis, and Thomas, the last named for Paine himself. The Bonnevilles lived with Paine, and he began to write for Bonneville's newspaper, *Le Bien Informe*. He died in Greenwich Village in New York on June 8, 1809. Paine had wished to be buried in a Quaker cemetery, but even this was denied him, and there were just six mourners at his funeral, including a rebellious Quaker who took the funeral, and two negro slaves. His monument simply identified him as the author of *Common Sense*, but even this did not last. Retribution set in over his dead body, almost in the same way as Cromwell and his confederates, and Richard III. People walking by pelted it with stones, and even when an innkeeper incorporated what was left of the monument in the wall of the tavern, even this was chipped away in flakes by local drunks as souvenirs.[31]

There was another side to it. Mme de Bonneville remembered in his final moments he had said: "I am very sorry that I returned to this country". After he had been refused a plot in New York's Quaker cemetery, Mme de Bonneville confirmed with him personally that he wanted to be buried at New Rochelle, and he replied, "I have no objection to that. The farm will be sold, and they will dig up my bones before they be half rotten". Mme be Bonneville insisted that this would never happen. "I have confidence in my friends, I assure you, that the place where you will be buried shall never be sold". When her sons' share of one-half of the property was sold in 1818 at a price of $3,625, she paid $50 to keep her word, with the forty-five-foot square gravesite withheld from the transaction.

One year later, Mr. William Cobbett, his son James, aged nineteen, and his hired hand appeared with their bags and shovels.[32]

The body had actually however been buried under a walnut tree on Paine's own farm of two hundred and seventy seven acres in New Rochelle, which had been awarded to him by New York State in 1784. At least that had not been taken from him.

It is at this point that the date is important in the context of the Gothic cult of the eighteenth and early nineteenth centuries. Respect for the dead body was simply not what is has been at other times and when, in the September of 1819 one William Cobbett arrived from England and dug up what remained of Paine, no-one seemed to bat an eyelid. "I found him", wrote Cobbett, "lying in the corner of a rugged, barren field!"

Cobbett, himself the celebrated author of *Rural Rides*, and a notable political figure in his own right, had been diametrically opposed to Paine at one point, and they exchanged discourtesies, in a manner only known to politicians. However, after Paine died, Cobbett re-read his works, decided a grave injustice had been done to him on his death, and resolved to make amends. Thus it was that he arrived at Liverpool docks in November 1819, with a large trunk containing the remains of Thomas Paine. Obviously and fortunately Customs officers were not then what they were to become later.

Cobbett wanted to give his former enemy a proper funeral, through streets lined with flowers, and to have a magnificent mausoleum dedicated to him and his remains. But the plan backfired. He had not reckoned with the virulent cartoonists of Regency times, such as Gillray and Cruikshank. He found himself depicted in one cartoon as a "bone-grubber", and a tramp, with a sack of Paine's bones slung over his back. The age of the Resurrection Men was anyway upon England. The side was beginning to turn against this treatment of corpses. Cobbett found himself in his own words, denounced by three hundred newspapers, and speaking in the House of Lords, Lord Grosvenor opined: "Was there ever subject treated with more laughter, contempt and derision than the introduction of these miserable bones?" This last statement is a loaded one, for of course Paine had had no time or place for the aristocracy and to honour his bones was the last thing they wanted.

The coup de grace was delivered on January 29, 1820 (which, according to some calculations, had been Paine's birthday, using the Old Style reckoning) when the King, George III, the same king excoriated by the

American revolutionaries, died. This was the very day when Cobbett had planned a huge fund-raising dinner for his cause.

Cobbett became discouraged and lost interest. The bones remained in the trunk in the attic of his house in Ash, Normandy, Surrey. Cobbett died there in 1835, it being only a few miles from where he had been born in Farnham. Unlike Paine, who died worth $1 million in today's money, William Cobbett died in debt, so all his goods were auctioned off, with one exception: the trunk. The auctioneer refused to deal in human remains, although, interestingly, a moulding had been made from the already decomposing body in 1822, three years after its return to England. J.P. Cobbett, the eldest son, who had actually helped extricate the bones from the soil of La Rochelle, authenticated them, by marking them with inscriptions and indexing them in a journal. The trunk therefore (for whatever reason) went first to a Hampshire day labourer, or they fell into the receivership of Cobbett's neighbour, a farmer named George West, along with the rest of Cobbett's unsold estate. This was when the unfortunate J.P. was himself incarcerated for debt. West himself had no idea what to do with the bones, and so around 1844 he sold them it to Cobbett's former secretary, Ben Tilley, who had become a London furniture salesman. Of Number 13, Bedford Square East. The remains were certainly collecting provenance by this stage. There was also a story that in 1835 Cobbett's son had buried the remains in the family plot. But to return to the secretary. Tilley was by then working as a tailor in London and was in dire straits. He had no means to bury the body. The trunk was used as a stool in the tailor's shop. But, like his former employer, Tilley eventually had to sell all his goods at auction. This time the auctioneer was less reluctant to deal with human remains. He sold the trunk to a radical publisher named James Watson. It is at this stage that the records are not so certain. One source says that it was Tilley who sold at least part of the skeleton to the Reverend Robert Ainslie, who insisted in 1854 that he owned the skill and the right hand, but refused to let anyone see them. When Ainslie's daughter was questioned about this later she said the bones had been lost, but in fact they had been taken by her brother Oliver, to be examined by the Royal College of Surgeons' anatomist John Marshall, who determined that "the head was…small for a man, and of the Celtic type, I should say, and somewhat conical in shape, and with more cerebellum than frontal development". Others have claimed that they have buttons carved from Paine's bones, and there were constant rumours of a rib cage surfacing in France. (When James Watson died in 1874 a Unitarian minister named Alexander Gordon said that he had got hold of the trunk and buried its contents, but he wouldn't give any further details. That might have been the end of the trunk, but of course it was not the end of the story.)

In 1864, according to Bess Lovejoy, that is, ten years earlier, an American abolitionist named Moncure Conway had moved to England to advocate the cause of the North, during the American Civil War. He was an admirer of Paine, and like Cobbett, made it his mission to track down his bones. During a lecture he gave in 1876, that is, two years after the death of Watson, Conway received a letter from a London bookseller saying he remembered a customer boasting that he had the skull and the right hand of Thomas Paine. Conway wrote to this customer, whom the bookseller had recognised as the Reverend Robert Ainslie, a very conservative minister. By ill luck it arrived just after Ainslie had died; and the story then was that Ainslie's son had thrown out these articles into the rubbish.

Does the story rest there? These stories never rest. It transpired that in 1833, when Tilly was still working as Cobbett's secretary, and during a move, decided himself to take a souvenir out of the trunk. This is of course in time-honoured tradition that, no matter who you are, you take or reserve to yourself a bone, or a body part. Tilly took a hard, blackish lump—all that was left of Thomas Paine's brain. Tilly wrapped it in a cloth, and neatly labelled it, attaching a note as to its provenance. If only all takers of such relics would do this! After Tilly died, both brain and note were found in his rooms. The intrepid Mercure Conway tracked them down, and purchased them for £5 in 1900, a sum then worth five weeks' wages to a working man. By then the brain had shrunk to the size of a fist, and was "quite hard".

Conway took the brain back to America with him, and the Thomas Paine National Historical Association, which Conway helped to found, buried it in a secret location on the same farm in New Rochelle which had belonged to Paine. The New York Times, however, pinpointed another location. In a report published on October 19, 1905, it said that part of the patriot's brain was to rest under the shaft of the monument in the same grounds, apparently in a hollow portion below the bust. His hair (detached from the brain?) is said to be in the museum in New Rochelle: hair particularly is of course a good source of DNA, but again a comparator is needed, and probably Paine left no descendants, or, if he did, they had to be from an illegitimate child.

Rumours as to the rest of the contents of the trunk have continued to circulate. In the 1930s, a woman in Brighton claimed to have his jawbone. This story is recounted in Craig Nelson's book. "My granmother's first husband, Mr. Wilkinson, was a Customs Officer in Liverpool at the time William Cobbett brought over Thomas Paine's bones for burial in England. Mr. Cobbett gave Mr. Wilkinson Mr. Paine's 'jawbone'. My grandmother thought so much of it that she took it with her to her new home when she became the wife of Richard Beverley, a schoolmaster of Eglwysbach, North Wales. My mother used to play with it as a child, but after her marriage and when on a visit to her old home, she thought that it should have a decent burial. Her father gave his consent, and she placed it in an open grave in the village churchyard. It must therefore have had a Christian burial."[33]

Provenance is always important in these stories. There is a note in Cobbett's archive, which reads: "On Tuesday, January 27, 1833, I went to Bolt Court, Fleet Street, and there in company with Mr. Antsell and Mr. Dean, I saw at the house of Mr. Cobbett the remains of Mr. Thomas Paine, when I procured some of his hair, and from his skull I took a portion of his brain, which has become hard, and is almost black—B Tilly." When Benjamin Tilly himself became a bankrupt, this relic ended up in the hands of his landlords, the Ginn family. Baptist minister George Reynolds visited the Ginns and asked to see the Tilly Paine items; Mr. Ginn said he did not know their whereabouts, his wife was away, and when the wife returned, she explained that the keepsakes had been tossed out with the other rubbish left behind by Tilly when he died. Over time, Reynolds was able to unearth the hair and brain, which he eventually sold to the herbalist Louis Breeze, who in turn sold them to Paine biographer Conway, who gave them to Dr. Edward Bliss Foote, who interred them in the obelisk marking the Thomas Paine National Historical Association in New Rochelle in 1905.

No Catholic saint ever had his or her relics more subject to fate and fortune. As Craig Nelson says: "One of the Church's harshest critics has had his bones treated in the fashion of the reliquaries of the most pious of saints….one of the greatest proponents of Diogenes' 'citizen of the world' has his remains scattered across a global network of attics and basements."

But other proponents of the Enlightenment were similarly treated in further examples of retribution. After the Bourbons returned to power in 1814, "having learnt nothing and forgotten nothing", royalist fanatics stormed the Pantheon, tore open the lead coffins, gathered the corpses of

Voltaire and Rousseau into cloth bags, and rode out to the Barriere de la Gare, where a pit of quicklime had been prepared. Into this pit the bones of the philosophes were cast, and dissolved.[34]

In 1987 an Australian businessman claimed to have bought his skull in London. He then sold it to a fellow Australian, John Burgess, who claimed to be the descendant of an illegitimate child of Paine. It is true that Paine had no children from either of his two marriages.

But, after almost a century, reparation had been made to Thomas Paine's remains.

Notes

1. Wickham, Chris, The Romans according to their malign custom: Rome and Italy in the late ninth and tenth centuries, p. 152. Also, pp. 114–20; *Gregorovius, Ferdinand, History of the City of Rome in the Middle Ages*, transl. from the 4th edition German by Annie Hamilton (and a very elegant translation it is), Vol. III, London, George Bell, 1895; Llewellyn, Peter, Rome in the Dark Ages, Faber & Faber, London (1971); and Early Mediaeval Rome & the Christian West, (Essays in honour of Donald A. Bullough) ed. Julia M.H. Smith, Brill, Leiden, Boston, Koln (2000).
2. Hilgarth, J.N., *The Spanish Kingdoms*, Oxford (1976), p. 373.
3. Russell, P.E., *The English Intervention in Spain & Portugal*, Oxford (1955), pp. 16–22.
4. MacCulloch, Diarmaid, Thomas Cranmer (1996), pp. 226–9.
5. L & P XIII, pt. II, 257; Hamilton, W.D. (ed.) *A Chronicle of England during the Reign of the Tudors (1485–1559)*; Charles Wriothesley, Windsor Herald, London, Camden Society (1875), p. 86, and p. 87 n.
6. MacCulloch, op. cit., pp. 226, 228.
7. Simpson, Helen DeGuerry, Henry VIII, Peter Davies (1934), pp. 130–1.
8. Quoted in Prescott, H.M., Spanish Tudor (1940), p. 387.
9. See the *New Focus* article, 28 December 2005.
10. White, Beatrice, Mary Tudor (1936), p. 390.
11. See Williams, Glanville, *The Sanctity of Life and the Criminal Law*.
12. Foxe, Vol. VIII, p. 269.
13. See also Clarendon, Life, ii. 30, Oxford (1759).
14. Fraser, Antonia, *Cromwell: Our Chief of Men*, pp. 692–3.
15. Haestier, Richard, *Dead Men Tell Tales*, John Long, London (1934), pp. 49–52.
16. Brewer, Clifford, *The Death of Kings: A Medical History of the Kings & Queens of England*, Abson Books (2000), 5th impression (2005), pp. 168–74. It is interesting to note that Cromwell is included in this treatment of

kings and queens, something which Olivia Bland also does in *The Royal Way of Death*, Constable (1986), pp. 57–8.

17. Troutbeck, G.E., *Westminster Abbey*, Methuen (1900), pp. 126–8.
18. McMains, *The Death of Oliver Cromwell*, University Press of Kentucky.
19. Worden, A.B., Introduction to Ludlow, Voyce from the Watchtower, 1–5, p. 272. Ludlow had first-hand knowledge for this statement, but not for the remainder of the sentences that allege the burial of Charles Stuart's friend in his place. See also *Oliver Cromwell and the Rule of the Puritans in England* (1901), Reprint London (1938).
20. McMains, op. cit., pp. 53–9.
21. Lovejoy, Bess, *Rest in Pieces: The Curious Fate of Famous Corpses*, Simon & Schuster (2013), paperback (2016), pp. 206–7, et seq.
22. Ross Browne, J., *Etchings of a Whaling Cruise*, quoted by John Tyrrell, in his blog, 8 March 2008.
23. Martineau, Gilbert, *Napoleon's Last Journey*.
24. I am indebted for the above to Thiessen, A.D., The Removal of Napoleon's Remains from St. Helena to France, October 1840, *Journal of the Royal Astronomical Society of Canada*, Vol. 36, p. 66; to Thackeray, William Makepeace, *The Second Funeral of Napoleon*, and to the blog of John Tyrrell, 17 January 2010, and 8 March 2008.
25. Tombs, Robert, Napoleon, Longmans (1996).
26. Report in *Daily Telegraph* by Philip Delves Broughton in Paris.
27. Tombs, op. cit., p. 364, n. 29.
28. Licence, Amy, *Richard III: The Road to Leicester*, Amberley (2014), p. 63.
29. Ibid., pp. 64–5.
30. Langley, Philippa, and Jones, Michael, *The Search for Richard III: The King's Grave*, John Murray (2013), p. 137.
31. Lovejoy, Bess, pp. 187–91.
32. Nelson, Craig, Thomas Paine, Profile Books (2006), pp. 324–5.
33. Nelson, Craig, op.cit., p. 328.
34. Nelson, op. cit., p. 329.

CHAPTER 4

Identity & Investigation: I

Exhumation sometimes takes place to establish the correct or ascertainable identity of someone buried or whose remains have been placed in a tomb or urn. This type of or reason for, exhumation, may then result in analysis and investigation of the remains, whether for legal, political, medical, or scientific reasons. The discovery of remains found by archaeology obviously also fall into this section.

The discovery of the Egyptian pharaoh, Tut-an-khamoun, in 1922, caused a sensation worldwide and of course resulted in analysis and investigation, which has continued ever since. In the realm of enduring public fascination, it ranks with the volcanic eruptions which destroyed Pompeii and Herculaneum, the loss of *The Titanic*, and the discovery of the Princes in the Tower.

The discovery of the body of the boy Pharaoh Tut-an-khamoun in 1922, cannot be in any way underestimated. It had been exactly a century since Jean-François Champollion the younger, opened the great book of Ancient Egypt, sealed for two thousand years but now decipherable. On November 25th, 1922, the first stone was moved at the entrance to the Pharoah's tomb and Lord Caernarvon, his daughter Lady Evelyn Herbert, and Howard Carter caught a glimpse of the most incredible burial treasure in existence still today.[1]

But Lord Caernarvon and his fellow seekers had broken a powerful law, which forbade the disturbance of the kingdom of the dead, which every

M. L. Nash, *The History and Politics of Exhumation*,
https://doi.org/10.1007/978-3-030-24047-9_4

exhumation, great and small, is bound to do. "The living, who come to violate the dead", was an ancient prohibition.

In the March following that November 1922, Lord Caernarvon was bitten by a mosquito; the bite turned septic, and the infection rapidly spread. The infection yielded to treatment in Cairo, where Lord Caernarvon had retreated, but towards the end of March he contracted pneumonia. His son, Lord Porchester, who was serving in the Army in India, was summoned at once, and made the voyage across the Indian Ocean with many Moslem pilgrims, who prayed for the recovery of the noble lord. He died, however, at five minutes to two in the morning of April 5th, 1923, without ever having recognised his son. At that precise moment, two incidents occurred, which still send a shiver down the spine almost one hundred years later. In Cairo, all the lights went out in the hotel and remained out for some time. But it was not until the new earl went to call on the High Commissioner, Field Marshal Lord Allenby, that he learned that it was not only the hotel, but the whole of Cairo: every single light had gone out. Lord Allenby asked the English engineer in charge of the electricity the cause of this strange power failure, but received no satisfactory technical explanation. The other incident concerns the dog which Lord Portchester had left in his father's care when he sailed for India, and which had grown so fond of its new master that it had pined in his absence. At the exact moment of Lord Caernarvon's death in Egypt, the animal left in England howled inconsolably and died. As Christian Desroches-Noblecourt says, this was the "flotsam of a superstition as lively as ever in the twentieth century".

To add to the general fascination of a public mesmerised by these reports, two other members of the excavation team also died swiftly, one after the other: George Benedite, the Head of the Department of Egyptian Antiquities at the Louvre in Paris, who died of a stroke brought on by the stifling heat of the Valley of the Kings; and Arthur Mace, the Assistant Keeper of the Department of Egyptian Antiquities at the Metropolitan Museum of Art in New York also died.

But then the "curse", if that is what it was, seemed to stop. Howard Carter himself was unaffected, and died in 1939. Why had the other three met such swift retribution?

On the more positive side, it may be that Caernarvon had in some way at last released the spirit of the young king. Following Tut-an-khamoun's death, a new pharaoh, from a new dynasty, was determined on the cultural obliteration of his predecessor, who was considered a heretic. Thus,

Tut-an-khamoun was deprived of the rites and the prayers, which should have followed his death. He was deserted in his tomb. His name was wiped out, surviving only in a corner of a monument in Karnak, carved by a faithful follower. This remained hidden and was spared. Caernarvon had proved that the curse of the vengeful Horemheb could be rendered powerless: at last perhaps the seekers had exorcised it. As Christiane Desroches-Noblecourt memorably put it: "His (Caernarvon's) partner in glory had been waiting in the shadows for more than three thousand years".[2]

The Princes in the Tower are an enduring mystery, which unless some document or letter hitherto unfound turns up, possibly in France or what was Flanders, will never be satisfactory solved or explained. Perhaps an historian or archaeologist should never say never. Certainly, they should never say "Nobody knows", because somebody always knows or knew. The quest is then initially to find this person, or persons.

In 1674, during the reign of the restored King Charles II, a discovery was made by some workmen in the Tower of London, which was where the two princes had been in prison, and from which they disappeared from the radar, as is said now, in 1483. The last sighting of them seems to have been in August of that year. The elder of the two, who had been proclaimed King Edward V on the premature death of his father, Edward IV, in April, had indeed had a legal reign from his proclamation on April 11, 1483, until June 26, when he was deposed by his uncle (supposed to be his Protector) who then had himself crowned King in early July. The young king had reigned for seventy-six days. Edward had certainly been recognised as king, and had, for example, been entertained to dinner at Hornsey, by the Mayor and Corporation of the City of London. It was the only time he had been toasted as "King Edward V". At the time of the last sighting, Richard III, as he now was, was not in London.

Agnes Strickland, in her *Lives of the Bachelor Kings of England, published in 1861*, makes some pertinent comments concerning the discovery in 1674. The Tower of London had been, besides a feared fortress and the depository of the national treasures, a palatial residence. Sovereigns had been accustomed to reside there before their coronations, and then ride forth through the City of London to be crowned in the City of Westminster, in the Abbey. But during the Commonwealth "the few rags of old hangings had been torn to tatters, and the remains of furniture abstracted… nothing remained in the lonely suite of Anglo-Norman chambers excepting the old oaken council table. Charles II wanted a dry roof to cover great heaps of the national records; his Master of Ordinance, Sir Thomas Chichely wanted the same for his stores of artillery".

This was duly done. The vaults served for the military stores, and the beautiful and desecrated "chapel within the Tower", where former sovereigns had prayed in the manner of chivalrous knights before their anointing, together with the State Chamber suite were destined to receive the papers. Outside was an open stone staircase, which led up to the chapel in the White Tower. At this time, in 1674, it was "ruinous and inaccessible". The staircase was ordered to be repaired, and enclosed within the outer walls. It was during this work that the momentous discovery was made. When the workmen were digging at the foot of the stairs, they found buried in the earth a great chest. On opening it, the mouldering remains of two boys were discovered. Had Sir Thomas Chicheley's excavations brought to light the "long sought sepulchre of Edward V and his little brother, the Duke of York?"

It is now necessary to go back to 1483, and to examine the contemporary evidence. Mancini, who was an Italian observer at the time, wrote one record; Jean Molinet, a French writer, was another, whose *Chroniques* were published in 1504, during the reign of Henry VII. Molinet is particularly interesting as he records the personalities and natures of the two boys. They were very different. As is so often the way, the elder was simple and serious, to the point of introspection and melancholy, even though he was not yet thirteen years old; the younger, says Molinet, was "was a lively little boy, joyous and witty, nimble and ever ready for dances and games", which makes his fate all the more heart-wrenching and poignant. The description could, ironically, also belong to the ten-year-old future Henry VIII, also Duke of York, and a grandson of Edward IV. Shakespeare himself picked up the tradition of their differing personalities. One thing they did have in common was their winning and engaging appearance, what was described at the time as "their loveliness". There were eugenic reasons for this. Mancini says of Prince Edward "he had such dignity in his whole person and in his face such charm that the beholders were never tired of looking at him".

"No-one gains the complete confidence of a clever child without in some way deserving it", wrote Elizabeth Jenkins, "Edward had an unquestioning trust in his uncle Lord Rivers". Not, sadly, let it be noted, in his uncle Richard, the Duke of Gloucester.

The boys had inherited the undoubted beauty of both of their parents. Edward IV has a good claim to being the best-looking man, who ever occupied the English throne. He was six feet three and a half inches tall, brown haired, broad chested, well-built, always fashionably and extravagantly dressed, and in the opinion of all observers, extraordinarily good-looking. He was also something of an exhibitionist, loving to show off his fine physique to onlookers.[3] It is no wonder that similar onlookers never tired of looking at his sons. Indeed, all his offspring had their share of beauty.

What the elder boy did not apparently inherit was his father's robust health. This will be a crucial part of the examination of the bones of the boys in both 1674 and in 1933. Mediaeval children were, understandably, well behind most modern children in development, despite the fact that royal and aristocratic children would have had a better diet and a healthier lifestyle, together with far more attention, than children of lesser rank. Nevertheless, as has always been the case, some royal and aristocratic children turned out to be far less robust than their commoner contemporaries. But Edward and his siblings would on the whole have had the best food to eat, encouraging growth, and many boys were into puberty by twelve or thirteen. This would also be a question during the exhumations. Edward had the unenviable distinction of being born in prison (actually the Sanctuary of Westminster Abbey) and dying in prison. His short life was often a stressful one.

Dominic Mancini described the events leading up to July, 1483, when Edward had been deposed and lodged with his brother in the Tower. He gives as his source Dr. John Argentine, who was the physician to Edward, who could speak to Mancini in his native Italian. The book Mancini wrote was entitled *The Occupation of the throne of England by Richard III, (De Occupatione Regni Angliae per Ricardum Tertium)*. This book was completed in Beaugency, on December 1, 1483, Mancini having left England the week after Richard III's coronation, which had taken place on July 6, 1483. Obviously, being part of the retinue of the young king, he was not taking any chances.

Mancini says that Dr. John Argentine, who was a Strasbourg doctor, was the last of the attendants the young king enjoyed, reporting that Edward, like a victim prepared for sacrifice, sought remission of his sins by daily confession and penance, because he believed that death was facing him. After Dr. Argentine had last seen him, he was so sunk in misery and fear that he was unable to perform even basic tasks, such as dressing himself properly.[4] The original was "doing up his points", which was of course a reference to his long pointed shoes with their points which might attach to the leg.

Thomas More, in his *History of Richard III*, makes some pertinent comments, and More, although employed by the new Tudor dynasty, was always a man of scholarship and integrity. His sources have proved this in a number of ways. "The Prince, as soon as the Protector left that name, and took himself as King, had it showed unto him that he should not reign, but his uncle should have the crown. At which words, the Prince sore abashed began to sigh and said, 'Alas, I would my uncle would let me have my life yet, though I lose my kingdom'. Then he that told the tale, used him with good words, and put in the best comfort he could. But forthwith the Prince and his brother were both shut up and all others removed from them; only one called Black Will, or William Slaughter, was to serve them and see them sure. After which the Prince never tied his points, nor in any way cared for himself, but with that young babe his brother lingered in thought and heaviness".

Anthony Cheetham, in his *Life and Times of Richard III (1972)* drawing on Dominic Mancini's *Usurpation of Richard III*[5] expands this point by saying that the boy, whose attributes had been praised by Mancini, who on a very frightening occasion, had spoken up for his mother and her family, would prove more formidable as he grew older; and P.B. Pugh says that no doubt Gloucester genuinely feared that unless he took control of the government, he would before long be destroyed himself by the Woodvilles and the Greys. In Cheetham's words: "To survive, he must rule; and to rule, he must be King" (even though the last will of Edward IV had appointed him Protector). In the next century these very thoughts must have occurred to both the Seymour brothers and to John Dudley, when they fought to secure the person and control of the next boy king, Edward VI.

Elizabeth Jenkins, in her *Princes in the Tower (1978)* states chillingly concerning the disappearance of the princes, and Richard III's failure to produce them, living or dead, that "the absolute silence that covered a concealed execution created a state of waking nightmare". It was known that the princes were in the Tower; it was known that they were not in the royal apartments; Mancini, writing of the period before he left London, had said that they had been "withdrawn into the inner apartments of the Tower proper"; and in describing the charm and intelligence of the young Edward V he had added: "I have seen many men burst forth into tears and lamentations when mention was made of him after his removal from men's sight, and already there was a suspicion that he had been done away with". The immediacy of Mancini's report gives the reader, thought Jenkins, "a start of surprise". Mancini goes on: "whether, however, he has been done away with, and by what manner of death, so far I have not at all discovered".

The actual dates of the murder of the princes can be confined to a certain window. If a number of writers and authorities are taken together, and considering the report on the bones discovered in 1674 and exhumed in 1933, then a reasonable surmise may be made. *The Croyland Continuator* said that the children remained in the Tower when Richard departed on his progress after his coronation. This was on July 20, 1483. Rows, in his *Historia Regum Angliae* said that the deaths occurred three months after Richard took charge of Edward V, which would imply a date in the first week of August. Molinet says that they were murdered five weeks after they had entered the Tower. The Duke of York was taken there on June 16, five weeks before July 21. (He had been taken from Sanctuary with his mother in Westminster Abbey). James Ramsay, in his *Lancaster and York (1892)* concluded that the most likely time for the murders to have been committed was the end of July or the beginning of August. Thomas More had heard that the mandate for their deaths had been despatched from Warwick after the King & Buckingham had parted at Gloucester.

There are two other salient points. One is that Sir Robert Brackenbury was the Constable of the Tower, and he was both a friend and a supporter of Richard III. He would not have acted or instructed unless there was received unmistakable authority from the King. The second point is that Richard created his own son Prince of Wales early in August, and the investiture ceremony took place at York on September 8th. It is very unlikely he would have done this if the previous Prince of Wales was still living; indeed, it would have had no legal viability, and Richard had relied on legal documents (or what were claimed to be such) to declare his own nephews bastards, due to a pre-contract of their father with Lady Eleanor Butler. When the exhumation of Anne, Duchess of York, is considered, there will be an addendum to this.

There is a tradition that Richard III had given orders to an old priest at the Tower that the boys were to be buried "in hallowed ground". Agnes Strickland believed that if this story is true, the priest had obeyed the instructions to the very letter, as the grave…was in hallowed ground, for the entrance to the Tower chapel had certainly shared in the consecration of that place of worship. But an old priest near death himself could not have done it. His helpers would certainly have spread to others descriptions of their doings, which found their way into a chronicle; for there is described explicitly "the interment under the stair's foot, under a heap of stones, metely deep in the earth". That the bodies were put into a chest is confirmed by at least two authorities (Harrison and Toone), and arms chests were readily to hand in the arsenal of the Tower. Moreover, these chests were air tight and water tight, and they kept their secrets well. Nor, as Strickland notes, was it to be the only time, for the headless body of Anne Boleyn was enclosed in a chest kept for arrows.

But here we are on the edge of rumour and care must always be taken to consider the most reliable sources. However, it is more than interesting to note that the inscription on the Urn which later contained the bones read:

> Here lies relics of Edward V. King of England, and Richard, Duke of York, who, being confined in the Tower, and there stifled with pillows, were privately and meanly buried, by order of their perfidious uncle Richard, the usurper. Their bones, long inquired after and wished for, after lying 201 years in the rubbish of the stairs, (those lately leading to the White Tower), were, on 7th July, 1674, by undoubted proofs, discovered lying deep in that place. Charles II, pitying their unhappy fate, ordered these unfortunate princes to be laid amongst the relics of their predecessors, in the year 1678, and the 20th of his reign.

This inscription in some ways says it all. It combines history, events that certainly happened, rumour and tradition, and most of all, prejudice. The proofs were not undoubted. Even the last line is propaganda, for Charles II had only begun to reign on May 29, 1660, but of course, he dated his reign from the execution of his father, Charles I, on January 30, 1649 (1648 Old Style).

It is now to object of the writer to unpick, piece together, and give some sort of balance to these stories and allegations.

When the bones were discovered on July 17, 1674, an anonymous eyewitness wrote:

> This day I, standing by the opening, saw working men dig out of a stairway in the White Tower the bones of those two princes who were foully murdered by Richard III. They were small bones of lads in their teens, and there were pieces of rag and velvet about them.

It is significant to note that Shakespeare here, and Sir Thomas More to some extent, had done a very good job at "canonizing propaganda into history". The observer had already persuaded himself them this was the work of the wicked king who had preceded the triumphant Tudors.

Inside the chest were indeed the skeletons of two children: the taller one lay on its back, the smaller one face down on top of it. Alison Weir, in her *Princes in the Tower (1992)* certainly thought that this discovery provided the most compelling evidence of Sir Thomas More's account of the princes 'first burial: the bones had been found exactly where described: 'at the stair foot, metely deep under the ground, under a great heap of stones'.[6]

However, Audrey Williamson in her book *The Mystery of the Princes (1978, 2010)* puts quite another slant on the discovery:

> These bones have a curious history, and indeed, the Urn, when opened (here she is referring to the 1933 opening) in addition to the very incomplete bones of two children, contained three rusty nails and a good deal of fine dust. In spite of legend, the fate and burial place of the two boys had remained an entire mystery until that day in July 1674, almost two hundred years after the alleged deaths. When workmen rebuilding the stairs to the royal chapel in the White Tower, they came across a wooden chest, containing bones to which they (apparently) attached no importance, buried ten feet deep, so it is said, within or below the stairs. They threw the bones into the yard with other debris, but were soon made to recover them when their story and the possible nature of their discovery became known. (What was the time lapse here, one wonders?) Obviously some of the bones may have disappeared at this point, *or even been disposed of as relics*: certain finger bones were rumoured by one of the heralds at the time, Francis Sandford[7] to have reached the Ashmolean Museum in Oxford, but Professor Wright, one of the examiners of the bones in 1933, declared that no trace of them could be found, or any record of them confirmed, when he called the Museum to check.

He obviously did not try hard enough, so the same eyewitness account quoted by Alison Weir goes on: "on that day (the bones) were put aside in a stone coffin or coffer". It is thought that they had been damaged to some extent by the tools used by the workmen during the exhumation. (Does this mean when they were taken out of the chest?) Then it seems that they were left alongside a pile of builders' rubbish on the site at the time, whilst news of their discovery was being relayed to King Charles II. It also appears that *several people removed some of the bones as souvenirs at this time, and replaced them with animal bones from the rubbish heap.*

Francis Sandford was right to record the rumours and this one was apparently correct. Bones were sent to the Ashmolean Museum and were recorded in a seventeenth century catalogue of the Museum's treasures. But in 1728, when the celebrated antiquarian Thomas Hearne went there and asked to see the bones, the Keeper, Mr. Whiteside, could not find them! All he could say was that he had seen them, and remembered them as "very small, particularly the finger bones". This tells us of course that it was not only finger bones which had been sent to Oxford, but other bones as well. It is true that in 1933 a search was made in the Museum for the bones, but to no avail. It is no wonder that the skeletons in the Urn are incomplete.

The first *written account* (as opposed to eye-witness reports) of the discovery in 1674 was made by John Knight, the principal surgeon to King Charles II. He recorded it as follows:

> Anno 1674. In digging down a pair of stone staires leading from the King's lodgings to the chapel in the White Tower ther were found the bones of two striplings in (as it seemed) a wooden chest which upon the presumption that they were the bones of this Kin(g) and his brother Rich: D. of York, were by the command of King Charles II put into a marble Urn and deposited amongst the R. Family in H:7th;s Chappel in Westminster at my importunity: Jo:Knight.

This does not tell us a great deal, but at least it uses the word "presumption" and does not repeat the received popular story.

The second account, published in 1677, three years after the discovery, gives Knight as an authority, but presumably had listened to or read other sources, as it is a little fuller:

> ...in order to the rebuilding of the several offices in the Tower, and to clear the White Tower from all contiguous buildings, digging down the stairs which led from the King's Lodgings to the chapel in the said tower, about ten foot in the ground were found the bones of two striplings (as it seems) (in a) wooden chest, which upon the survey were found proportionable to ages of those two Brothers, viz. about thirteen and eleven years. The skul of the one being entire, the other broken, as indeed were many of the other bones, also the Chest, by the violence of the labourers, who.....cast the rubbish and threw them away together. Wherefore they were caused to sift the

rubbish, and by that means preserved all the bones, with.........Sir Thomas Chiceley, Master of the Ordinance, by whose industry the new Buildings were then in carrying on, and by Whom this matter was reported to the King.[8]

There are three more contemporary accounts. The next one is anonymous, possibly also by John Knight, which adds that "there were pieces of rag and velvet about them...Being fully recognized to be the bones of those two princes, they were carefully put aside in a stone coffin or coffer". One might add, after the initial mayhem.

The presence of velvet is very interesting. Velvet had been invented in Renaissance Italy in the fifteenth century and was not made in England until the sixteenth century. In the 1480s, the wearing of imported velvets was restricted to persons of the highest rank, not only because it was so expensive, but because of the social conventions then prevailing, that is the Sumptuary Laws, which were indeed augmented by Edward IV, the father of the princes. It was a way of monitoring and controlling the social classes. Even in the seventeenth century is was still a costly material available only to the well-to-do. The children whose bones were found in 1674 and who had been wearing velvet when they died were very high-born children, and must have died in the fifteenth century. On his accession, on April 11, 1483, Edward V had worn a blue velvet riding gown, and for the coronation which never took place, his clothes were already made or in the making, including a short gown, and a long gown of crimson cloth of gold (and), long gowns of blue velvet and purple velvet.

No other pair of well-born children had disappeared within the Tower during the previous two hundred years (and) it is a fair presumption that—forensic evidence aside—that these were indeed the bones of the princes.

The next account, by John Gibbon, Bluemantle Herald, is dated 1674:

July 17 Anno 1674 in digging some foundacons in ye Tower, were discovered ye bodies of Edw. 5 and his brother murdered 1483. I myselfe handled ye Bones especially ye Kings Skull. Ye other wch was lesser was broken in ye digging. Johan Gybbon, Blewmantle.[9]

But the most interesting contemporary account, however, is that of Sir Christopher Wren, as he would have a further involvement in the story. He was then Surveyor General to King Charles II, and gives a report, which is undated. He confirmed that the bones were found '...about 10 feet deep in the ground...as the workmen were taking away the stairs, which led from the royal lodgings into the chapel of the White Tower'.[10]

There is a time lapse between the discovery in 1674 and the interment of the bones in the Urn designed by Christopher Wren in 1678. Although the examination of the bones, at the King's orders, apparently, by the royal surgeon and a panel of experienced antiquaries, and the time taken by Wren to design and deliver the Urn, nevertheless four years seems a rather long time. Where were the bones during this time? Camden's *Britannica (1695 edition)* states that the bones remained in the Tower for four years, *except for some few that were retained as curiosities by Elias Ashmole and sent to the Ashmolean Museum in Oxford.* There seems to be no doubt about this. It was not until 1678 that Charles II asked Sir Christopher Wren "to provide a white marble coffin for the *supposed* bones of the two Princes". The use of the word "supposed" might be noted. Was Camden sceptical? The bones were translated from the Tower to Westminster Abbey and decently interred, according again to Camden, "under a curious altar of black and white marble", which may still be seen today.

The bones are unlikely to have been guarded at the Tower by Sir Thomas Chicheley, for he ceased to be Master of the Ordinance in 1674, and this rather mysterious time period of 1674 to 1678 has exercised more than one historian. However, to mark the spot where the bones were discovered, Sir Thomas Chicheley, or perhaps on the order of Charles II himself, had a mulberry tree planted. It grew for about a century and a half, according to the habits of that long lasting fruit tree, and was cut down only circa 1824, the topographer at the Tower recording that its dry trunk could still be seen standing in a corner at the entrance to the stairs leading to the upper apartments and chapel, then the Record Office, a melancholy reminder of past sad events.[11] John Morgan, an Australian professor, has written a lengthy paper now in the possession of the Richard III Society, entitled *Have the Princes' Bones been found in the Tower? An annotated summary of contemporary accounts of bones discovered in the Tower of London and alleged to be those of Edward IV's sons.* It is based on a correspondence in Notes & Queries (1889–1890) and an article by L.E. Tanner, *Recent Investigations regarding the fate of the Princes in the Tower (1934).* The material has been re-arranged and augmented from other sources to present a comparative survey of the reported discoveries". John Morgan had given a lecture (which must have been long!) to the Australian branch of the Richard III Society.

And so to 1933. The central figure in the exhumation which so riveted England in that year was the Archivist of Westminster Abbey, Lawrence Tanner. He was a remarkable man in his own right, both before, during and after the exhumation of the bones of the princes, as they were thought to be. From 1678 to 1933 they had not been touched, but it was said that King George V bowed to "public pressure". If this was the case, and this particular king was both thoughtful and shrewd, it was also because the King himself and the Dean of Westminster Abbey agreed to the exhumation. Westminster Abbey is not a church like other churches: it is not part of a diocese and therefore not subject to the jurisdiction of a bishop. It is a *royal peculiar*, which means that only the King of Queen, together with the Dean and Chapter, can give permission for such things to happen.

George V had lately taken an interest in Abbey ceremonies, prompted by his cousins, the Princesses Helena Victoria and Marie Louise. They persuaded him to take part in the Maundy ceremonies in 1932, thus reviving a royal participation which had lapsed in the eighteenth century. Since then, the event has certainly become high profile as the *Royal* Maundy, enthusiastically continued during the long, long reign of Elizabeth II.

King George had got to know some of the movers at the Abbey. So it was that on July 7, 1933, a group assembled for the momentous exhumation. They comprised the Dean, Sir Edward Knapp Fisher, myself (these notes are from Lawrence's Tanner's Diary) Lord Moynihan, Professor William Knight, Mr. Aymer Valence, The Dean's Verger (Mr. Drake) The Clerk of the Works (G. Bishop) Walter Wright, Dr Impe (a photographer), and three of the Abbey workmen (obviously too humble to be named). The very list is a snapshot of the social world of the 1930s, which still delineated a strict class division.

> The Urn was seen to be full of bones. Professor Wright took these bones carefully out and placed them on a tray held by myself. The first removed was a skull which he handed to me and which I placed carefully on the table. The bones were transferred from the tray to the table until most of the table was covered with them. It at once became apparent that these bones were those of two children of about the right age for the Princes. Parts of two skulls, two jawbones, and thighbones were seen to be there and the thighbones, when placed side by side, showed that one was slightly longer than the other. As the bones were placed on the table Lord Moynihan arranged them in groups.

What next?

Lord Moynihan was of opinion that this opportunity would never occur again and that not only should the most careful and expert report be made on the bones by Professor Wright but that every bone, or at least the most important ones, should be photographed. Sir Edward thought that the bones ought not to be removed from the Abbey, even to the Muniment Room, and eventually it was decided to close the chapel for a day or two so that Professor Wright could work there undisturbed. A chair and table were provided and a temporary lock placed on the door with five keys only/the Dean, Professor Wright, The Clerk of the Works, Drake, and myself (having them). (It is interesting to note here the security measures taken in 1933 with what might be in place today if such an event were to take place again!)

The Urn was found to have a central bar down the centre from the lid to the base. A hole had been cut in the lid, and molten lead had been poured in to fix it. Lumps of clay had been attached below to catch the lead and prevent it from dripping but this had not proved wholly successful.

There were two holes on the top of the lid evidently for the palms shown in Sandford's engraving (of the Urn). (Again, this is interesting as palms are the symbol, in Christian iconography, of martyrdom, implying that the murdered boys were considered martyrs, rather like Edward the Martyr, the murdered Saxon prince, and Charles I was to be). A large number of animal bones, probably rat and rabbit, were found mixed with the human bones. Also two or three nails. (These tallied with former accounts, and give credence to the possibility that souvenir seekers did take bones and replaced them with animal bones).

Here Lawrence Tanner makes a note that Dr. George Northcroft, OBE, assisted in examining the remains of the Princes...and his expert dental knowledge did much to establish the age at which the Princes died.[12]

Lawrence Tanner goes on: "July 7. Professor Wright tells me that he has been able definitely to assign several of the bones to Edward V or the Duke. Mr Northcroft examined the two jawbones and was immediately struck by the fact that there was a marked abnormality in both the jaws—another fact pointing to a family peculiarity, like the curious and similar formation of the two skulls which Professor Wright had already pointed out to me. The actual abnormality is somewhat technical but quite obvious to an expert who could deduce from it that the King had evidently been in trouble with his teeth.

Both Mr. Northcroft and Professor Wrightt expressed a strong desire to have the jaws x-rayed. To this I agreed on condition that I was present throughout. Mr. Northcroft and myself therefore took the jawbones to his home (115 Harley Street) where photographs were taken and they were then carefully wrapped up and taken back by us. Several other photographs of certain of the bones were also taken today by an expert photographer, Mr. George, from the College of Surgeons. These photos were taken in the chapel.

(On July 10th all these proceedings were interrupted by a visit from Princess Juliana, the heiress to the throne of the Netherlands. Lawrence Tanner's comments on this visit must be reserved for another forum).

July 11th. Today Professor Wright concluded his detailed examination of the bones of the Princes, and the final photographs were taken. The examination has shown conclusively that:

1. The bones are those of two boys probably of the ages of 13 and 9, and this appears to have been the ages of the Princes
2. The bones are those of two members of the same family—from certain peculiarities of the skull and jaws, and they were almost certainly brothers
3. There are bloodstains on the upper jaw of the Duke as would have been likely to have resulted from his having been smothered, and that the right side of the King's skull is also blood-stained, as though he had been lain on that side after death
4. The King's tear-duct is abnormally enlarged—a small and tragic point
5. There are no features inconsistent with their actually being the bones of the King and the Duke

> At four o'clock then assembled in this chapel the Dean, Sir Edward, Professor Wright and myself. The bones of the King and the Duke were placed separately on the table, and wrapped in the finest lawn—the skull, and the jawbones of the King were wrapped up separately. Some few human bones which could not be definitely assigned, were divided between the King and the Duke. On the remains were placed strips of parchment on which I had written:
>
> 1. King Edward V, July 11th, 1933
> 2. The skull of King Edward V, July 11th, 1933
> 3. Richard, Duke of York, July 11th, 1933

On a larger strip of parchment, I had written: "This tomb was opened on July 6th, 1933, with the consent of His Majesty King George V. The contents were carefully examined and on July 11th, the bones were reverently replaced, and the tomb re-sealed in the presence of (there followed their signatures):

W. Foxley Norris, Dean
Edward F. Knapp Fisher, Custodian
Laurence E. Tanner, Keeper of the Muniments
William Wright, Professor of the Anatomical Society of Great Britain and Ireland

A slight delay occurred while part of the iron bar supporting the lid of the Urn was sawn off but at length all being ready Mr Dean (in his black gown) mounted this raised platform and I handed them to him himself (who) placed the bones of Richard Duke of York, then the bones and skull of King Edward V. and finally the parchment statements within the Urn. Then, with Sir Edward, Professor Wright and myself standing just below the platform and Bishop (the Clerk of the Works) Walter Wright and two of the Abbey workmen just behind. Mr. Dean turned to us and said:

> Let us never forget that we have just placed within this Urn all that remains that was mortal of a King of England and a Prince of the Royal Blood.

With beautiful simplicity and touching appropriateness, he continued in the words of the Burial Service (perhaps the first time it had been read over the children).

The Urn was then closed down and sealed, the Dean and myself remaining until the whole was completed. As we came away, Mr. Dean said to me: "I have taken many thousands of services-of all kinds-the Thanksgiving for the King's Recovery—but I do not think that I have ever been so profoundly moved- I could hardly speak". I think we all felt the same".

The scene now moves on to December 1, 1933, and the following week. Laurence Tanner continues in his Diary:

> Last night Professor Wright and myself read our Paper on the Princes to what the *Daily Mail* called "an astounded audience of experts". It did indeed create a sensation and for the next week my life was not worth living. I was interviewed and rung up by every paper in London. The Paper itself

was reported at length, in every London and Provincial paper. I even had to give a five minute broadcast on the subject.

One cannot help feeling, and this is borne out by subsequent events, that the antiquarian Laurence Tanner rather enjoyed all this. Anyway, in 1940 he wrote: "I am now the only living person who actually handled the bones of the little Princes. (No, I had forgotten Northcroft).

There is a small feeling here that, knowing what had happened to Lord Caernarvon and some of the others who had exhumed Tut-an-khamoun in 1922, that a similar fate awaited those who had disturbed the Princes in the Tower. Laurence Tanner however lived on until 1979.

But he did learn that this story will not go away, and on January 14, 1936, he wrote: "This morning for the second time in one month I have been mentioned by name in a leading article in *The Times!* On January 9th, the second leader dealt with the Princes and this morning the fourth leader on the Abbey effigies".

Tanner then quotes from these leaders: "*The Times*: 'All who are interested (and who is not?) in the fate of the Princes...'" "....bones of fish, birds and animals were found...indeed, as some had predicted' but they were not all. It was clear that the elder child had died a violent death, almost certainly by suffocation. The 'fascinating controversy' as it has been called, is perhaps too fascinating ever to cease being debated, and Mr. Tanner and Professor Wright will not convince everyone".

But shortly afterwards, indeed only a week, the world's spotlight moved to Sandringham House, in Norfolk, where King George V died on January 20, 1936. For the moment, the "fascinating controversy" was stilled. On April 9, the new King, Edward VIII, attended the Royal Maundy in Westminster Abbey and made the distributions in person, forty-two coins for each of his years. During the distribution he became quite chatty, noted the irrepressible Tanner, and confounded the Archbishop by such questions as "Where does the money come from?" and "Is it anything to do with Queen Anne's Bounty?" The Sub-Almoner came to the rescue by piping up: "No, Sir, it comes out of your own pocket!" But Tanner's Diary had revealed another side of Edward VIII, a side later all too eagerly suppressed by the Establishment which he had seemed to challenge.

But the exhumation of the Princes had had an enduring effect on Tanner. Later that same year, on October 6, 1936, a search began for the remains of Sir Thomas More, proclaimed a saint by Pope Pius XI the year before, 1935. The remains of Sir (now Saint) Thomas More had apparently been removed to the crypt of St. Luke's Church in 1872, from the Old Church. Laurence Tanner was one of the members of the Committee charged with searching for the remains. The records seemed to show that in 1872, one coffin which was moved was shorter than the others, and (the remains) appeared to be headless. (Rather like Cromwell's head, the head of Thomas More had been taken from Tower Bridge by his daughter Margaret Roper, and so had remained separated from his body). The records of 1872 recorded that no head could be found, which is not surprising. Some late coffin plates had already been taken out in 1936. No short coffin could however be discovered and it was not possible to determine the identity of the bones. Tanner recorded the "profound disappointment".

Needless to say, the "fascinating controversy" has resounded to the present day. To conclude this perhaps most famous of all domestic exhumations, until that of Richard III himself, it is necessary to give the opinions of one or two distinguished persons, who were not present at the exhumation in 1933, but who nevertheless have weighed in and given extra dimensions to a seemingly endless debate.

In 1987, there was a lively debate between the *Times* archaeology correspondent Norman Hammond, Dr. Theya Molleson and a Mr. William White in the correspondence columns of *The Times* on the subject of the bones in the Urn.

Dr. Molleson compared her findings with tests carried out on mediaeval skeletons found in Winchester in which the incidence of hypodontia was the same as it is today (number and type of permanent teeth missing). She concluded that there was every likelihood of a blood relationship with Anne Mowbray, the child wife of Richard (the younger prince) and a third cousin of the Princes, whose bones had been subject to forensic analysis in 1965 (as will be seen), and whose permanent teeth were also incomplete.

Dr. Molleson was the only expert to pronounce on the sex of the children (which had been questioned) it being agreed by the rest that it was extremely hard to ascertain the gender of pre-pubertal skeletons. She compared the dental and skeletal maturity of Anne Mowbray's bones with those in the Urn, and concluded that the latter were probably both prepubescent boys.

In 1926, that is, seven years before the bones in the Urn were examined, Professor Wingate had written about diet in the Middle Ages and the lack of the vitamins A & D, which accelerate bone growth. This knowledge must have been used in 1933, but it emphasises the interesting question that if the boys' skeletal growth was retarded, then the bones might *appear* to be those of boys of nine and twelve, but actually they could have been eleven and fourteen, which would place their deaths later, say in 1485.

Professor John Morgan also, on recent advances in forensic study, dismisses the assumption of "evidence of consanguinity" made by Professor Wright in 1933, regarding the teeth, and like other modern experts, totally rejects the "extensive stain" on the facial bones as having anything whatever to do with death by suffocation, as the original examiners claimed. With regard to the "chronic disease affecting the lower jaw and teeth" in the elder child, he is inclined to accept that this is "possibly valid", but adds "apparent evidence of disease might on the other hand be a result of decomposition". Most authorities agree that this disease, if it existed, could have resulted in death from natural causes.

It might be added here that the poor health apparently suffered by the boy king has some echo in the physical makeup of his eldest sister, Elizabeth of York, who became the wife and queen of Henry Tudor. Her *Privy Purse Expenses, edited by the antiquarian Nichols*, show that she had a somewhat delicate constitution and make it surprising that she survived seven births before succumbing after the birth of the seventh, on her thirty-seventh birthday; and that she suffered from health described as "crazy" and "crazed", which can only be translated now as ill-health. Moreover, her grand-daughters Mary and Elizabeth Tudor always suffered with their teeth, well annotated in Mary Tudor's *Privy Purse Expenses from 1536 to 1544*.

If the modern hypotheses are taken together, certain statements can be made, always bearing in mind that anyone after 1933 did not see or handle the bones, or subject them to any kind of analysis or examination. What then are the facts? The bones were found in the Tower in 1674 in the vicinity of what were once the royal apartments. Analysis of them however gives absolutely no indication, on modern systems of examination, as to when these children died, what they died of, or what their ages were within a margin of several years. It cannot, therefore, be ascertained, whether they died in the reigns of Richard III or Henry VII, given the assumption that they died between 1483 and 1485, and this assumption on the evidence cannot be made in any case within a period of at least one hundred years in either direction. Presumably, this last statement means unless they are examined again and subjected to DNA and other modern techniques.

Although, to a lawyer, the circumstantial evidence seems very strong, the matter of the bones must remain open: nothing can be produced at the moment as “proof”. Unfortunately, or fortunately, requests to examine the bones again since the discovery of the bones of Richard III in 2012 have met with a negative response from both the Queen and the Dean of Westminster, probably for the reason that Pandora’s box has been opened, and it may result in every royal body in the kingdom being in line for exhumation!

The same archaeology correspondent of *The Times*, Norman Hammond, who had been one of the participants in the debate in 1987, contributed an important article in the same paper on November 25, 2017. This concerned the reconstruction of the face of Lady Anne Mowbray, the infant heiress who had married Richard Duke of York in 1478. Her face was reconstructed from her skeleton, while her hair and bones have yielded data on her stature and health, at the time of her death, just before her ninth birthday, in 1481. Norman Hammond makes the important statement here that “the remains of Lady Anne Mowbray also have the potential to illuminate one of English history’s greatest mysteries, the fate of the Princes in the Tower”.

This report can be interspersed with the diary of Laurence Tanner, the celebrated antiquarian and Keeper of the Muniments of Westminster Abbey:

> One day in 1964 I was rung up by the Director of the London Museum who told me that during excavations on the site of the former church of the Minoresses of St. Clare, in Clare Street in the City, a small lead coffin had been found. On it was a Latin inscription, which, when translated, read:
>
> > Here lies Anne, Duchess of York, daughter and heir of John, formerly Duke of Norfolk, Earl Marshal, Earl of Nottingham, Earl of Warenne, Marshal of England, and Lord of Mowbray, Segrave and Gower; the late wife of Richard, Duke of York, the second most illustrious Prince of Edward IV, King of England, France and Lord of Ireland; who died at Greenwich on the 19th day of November in the Year of Our Lord 1481 and in the 21st year of the reign of the said Lord King.

She had died aged eight or nine, three years after her marriage. Here was a puzzle. There was not the slightest doubt that originally she had been buried in the Old Lady Chapel of Westminster Abbey. When that chapel was pulled down in 1502, to make way for Henry VII’s Chapel, it was always believed and indeed definitely stated, that like others who had been buried in the Lady Chapel, she had been re-buried within the Abbey. Yet she was now found on the site of a City church, and the inscription on her coffin made her identification certain. It could only be assumed that the Abbey tradition was incorrect, and that either in 1502 or a few years later, the body must have been transferred to the Church of the Minoresses, in which church, as subsequent research was to show, her mother, the Duchess of Norfolk, and other members of her mother's family were buried.

I saw the body a few days after the coffin had been opened, and a very distressing sight it was; "her hair was wonderfully preserved, and despite the eyeless sockets, the fallen nose, and the upper teeth projecting over the space where the lower jaw had dropped away, the forehead of the skull, from which the hair had been swept back, still gave the idea of a little girl"[13] and again, after it had been beautifully cleaned and laid out as a skeleton in its lead coffin. She had masses of brown hair. After consultation with the authorities, the Dean, Dr E. Abbott, decided that she should be re-buried within the Abbey. I suggested that a grave should be made in one of the small chapels at the east end of Henry VII's chapel, very near the probable site of her original burial place, and within a few feet of the tomb of her sister-in-law, Elizabeth of York.

There, on a summer evening, after having laid in state covered by the Abbey Pall in the Jerusalem Chamber, the body of the child Royal Duchess was laid to rest. It was a deeply moving and impressive little service conducted by the Dean in the presence of a representative of the Queen, Lord and Lady Mowbray, Segrave and Stourton (representing Anne Mowbray's family), the Home Secretary, the Director of the London Museum and one or two others.

If, for a moment, we may assume that the bones in the north aisle of Henry VII's Chapel are really those of Anne's husband, the Duke of York, it is a curious fact that I should have been present at the re-burial of both these children 500 years after their deaths".

One might add that, unlike his apparent belief that the bones really were those of the Princes, in 1933 (as the Dean certainly seems to have done), thirty years later the good Keeper of the Muniments seems to have become a little more sceptical.

Edward IV had to obtain papal leave to have Anne Mowbray married to his younger son, the Pope being Innocent VIII?). The children were married the day before Parliament was due to convene, on January 15,

1478. It was a splendid State occasion, with almost the whole of the royal family attending. The practical facts was that Edward IV had come to an accommodation with the other heirs to the Mowbray inheritance, but there was no avoiding the fact that what he (Edward IV) had done (i.e. in making sure the young Richard had all Anne's titles and inheritance) was against all legal precedents governing the laws of inheritance, and there were many who blamed the Queen and her influence for this. Most unfortunately, she was blamed for a good deal, but she did nothing to lessen this suspicion. To appease Lord Berkeley, one of the rightful co-heirs, Edward IV excused him payment of a large debt owed to the Crown, and provided that the Mowbray inheritance should revert to Lords Berkeley and Howard, if York (the infant Richard) died without male issue (which he did). Howard, however, received nothing, not even money owed him for supplying plate for the Queen's coronation in 1465. Many lords were angered by the King's treatment of Lord Howard, and concerned that Edward's failure to respect the ancient laws of inheritance upon which their power was built, though there is no evidence that Howard himself expressed any grievance. Moreover, it should be remembered that the King of Queen is the "Fount of Honour", and what they do or undo concerning Peerage Law is certainly within their powers. If the Inheritance laws had been the subject of Parliamentary legislation then that might be a different matter. But the whole question of royal intervention to secure the Mowbray inheritance, involving two little children as pawns in the game, was to have considerable repercussions. John Mowbray VII was the last of the Mowbray Dukes of Norfolk. When he died in 1476, leaving only a daughter who could not inherit the title, Edward IV then granted it to his son Richard in 1477. When the little prince mysteriously disappeared in 1483, Richard III granted the title to John Howard, who became the first of a long line of Howard Dukes of Norfolk. This, however, is further circumstantial evidence that the princes were already dead, just as the granting of the title Prince of Wales to Richard's own son, was. John Howard was a relative of the deceased Mowbray Dukes on the distaff side, and both Mowbrays and Howards were of royal descent. John Howard had indeed already been ennobled by Edward IV in the 1460s as Lord Howard. John's mother was Lady Margaret Mowbray, and when she died at Framlingham castle, Lord Howard became the senior co-heir of the Mowbray estates. Following on the point above, concerning the involvement of Parliament, Edward IV made sure of his son's inheritance by a Statute giving the Prince the

Mowbray estates for life, even if his wife predeceased him (which she did). A further Act of Parliament followed in 1483. Richard was also created Earl of Nottingham.

Howard therefore found his inheritance blocked for immediate future by the Prince, and this in itself was enough reason for Howard to give his support to Richard, Duke of Gloucester. They both had much to gain from the bastardisation of the princes. This dark side of proceedings was to continue when, on June 28, 1483, that is two days after Edward V had been deposed, Richard created Howard Duke of Norfolk, Marshal and Earl Marshal of England, thereby reinforcing his support. He also granted him a share of the Mowbray estates. But more was to come. On 25 July (when the little princes may well have been dead), Howard was created Lord Admiral of England, Ireland and Aquitaine, and a member of the Privy Council. He had become for all to see the right-hand man of the new king. It must also be remembered that when Richard did this, the Acts of Parliament which had confirmed the titles and inheritance of the little prince had not yet been repealed, as the first Parliament of Richard's reign had yet to meet. No legislation had been passed depriving the little prince of his honours and his legitimate status. (Interestingly, Henry VIII was to learn this lesson well, and used Parliament to his advantage, both legal and personal). Yet the murky waters of Plantagenet politics would become even cloudier during the final battle of the Wars of the Roses in 1485, and are immortalised in the couplet:

> Jockey of Norfolk be not too bold
> For Dickon thy master is bought and sold.

On November 26, 1481, the *Cely Letters* recorded: "My young lady of York is dead" Anne Mowbray had died on November 19 at Greenwich Palace, just before her ninth birthday. She was buried in the chapel of St. Erasmus, the foundation of the Queen, Elizabeth Woodville, in Westminster Abbey.[14]

Thus, to pick up the modern story, workmen, while clearing bomb damage, and, unbeknownst, excavating the site of her second burial in Stepney in 1964 found her coffin, buried eleven feet deep. This discovery became the subject of a Home Office investigation. (Thus, as has been seen, Laurence Tanner recorded that the Home Secretary had been present at her re-burial in the Abbey, the third time she had been buried. This presence in itself was somewhat unusual). The coffin was removed from the site on December 11th, 1964, but the inquiry was whether permission from the Home Office should have been obtained before the coffin was moved, as is normal when a body is found. Police took the coffin from the site and it was later claimed by the London Museum, which traced Anne's history.[15]

Dr. Francis Celoria of the London Museum (now the Museum of London) realised from the finely engraved plate on the lead coffin who was inside it, and set up a multidisciplinary scientific investigation to study her remains. Most unfortunately, at this point, bureaucracy intervened, and there was "a fuss in Parliament and the Press" because a burial licence had not been obtained, and what would have been a ground-breaking study had to be curtailed. The results of the study have never been fully published. They do, however, show that the little duchess was 4 ft 4 in tall, small for a modern child nearly nine years old (but the same has been found in the case of the princes), but, concludes Norman Hammond, "the norm until the late 19th century, due to deficiencies of diet". This statement might be questioned concerning the privileged classes, however, who nearly always had access to a much wider and better choice of food and drink.

Her hair, went on the study, had high levels of arsenic and antimony, perhaps from her medicines, and she seems to have suffered from ill-health. When her body was being prepared for burial, her shroud appears to have been treated with beeswax, and decorated with gold leaf or thread, and a separate cloth covered her face. "Individuals like Anne, who are precisely dated are vital, so her remains are of international importance. A recent survey of more than 4,600 juvenile burials from 95 British medieaval and early post-medieaval burial sites included no named individuals", so their precise dates of birth and death could not be ascertained, Mr. Watson noted.

Of more general interest was a congenital dental anomaly—missing upper and lower permanent second molars on the left side—that Lady Anne shared with the two juvenile skeletons found in the Tower of London in 1674, assumed to be the missing princes. Most interestingly, although a new examination of these latter bones has been declined, a re-analysis of the photographs taken in 1933 has suggested that the two juveniles were 13 and a half to 14 and a half and 11 and a half to 12 and a half years old when they died. Thus, they could have died in 1484...a slightly later date in the reign of Henry VII is also possible.

But as is known already, "the debate over the identity of these undated juveniles will continue until their remains are re-examined. They could be radiocarbon dated, Mr. Watson opines, and DNA extracted to confirm if they are related to each other, and to Richard III (whose skeleton was found in 2012). Richard's DNA is available since the extensive and intensive investigation into his remains before his re-burial in 2015.

Norman Watson concludes: "Anne Mowbray's burial was that of an aristocrat with royal links and undoubtedly of value to our understanding of death and burial during the late 15th century". The new reconstruction of her face shows us how her princely bridegroom may have seen her.

In 1871, there were concerns that some of the royal burial vaults beneath Westminster Abbey were deteriorating. With permission of Queen Victoria (the Abbey being a royal peculiar) several of the vaults were opened and examined. The vault containing the remains of the boy king Edward VI, who had died before his sixteenth birthday, was discovered quite by accident. As there was only one lead-lined coffin in the chamber, it was deemed worthy of examination. The coffin was in poor condition through age and moisture damage. The lead lining appeared to be the only adhesive holding the container together. Without disturbing the actual contents, it was noted that the skeletal remains were visible, as were the remnants of a skull cap. The coffin lid had an inscribed plate in Latin which stated that the mortal remains within were those of Edward VI.

Interestingly, it may have been the above which led to the notable exhumation of Richard II and the proposed one of Henry III in 1871, or it may simply have been coincidence. The moving light behind this was the first Director of the National Portrait Gallery, Sir George Scharf, himself also a prolific sketcher, something which could only be of great benefit to himself and others, when carrying out his investigations: indeed, he managed to fill 230 notebooks with them, many of them still surviving. Some of these sketches include depictions of anatomical studies he made while attending the exhumations of royal bodies. Like many others, Sir George, despite his elevated position, did indeed collect some artefacts from the grave of Richard II during the exhumation, and these were eventually found in a cigarette box in the archives of the National Portrait Gallery. He had anticipated the exhumation of Richard II in 1871 by making sketches of the royal graves in Westminster Abbey in 1869. He was to go on to sketch the severed head found in Trinity Church in London, in 1877, and supposed to be the head of Henry Grey, the Duke of Suffolk, and father of the hapless Lady Jane, both executed in 1554. He also sketched the remains of that much handled lady, Queen Katherine of Valois, in December 1877 and January 1878, when they had deteriorated further from the time, they had been seen by Samuel Pepys in 1669, not surprisingly.

However, it was the Dean of Westminster Abbey, the Very Reverend Arthur Penrhyn Stanley, who was a Fellow of the Society of Antiquaries, who wrote and read the paper on the exhumation of Richard II. This took place on June 26, 1873, two years after the event.

The Dean thought the tomb had a triple interest: for Westminster Abbey itself, for English history generally; and for the Society of Antiquaries. There must always be a reason for an exhumation, which is sustainable in the face of criticism or opposition.

The story of Richard II in known to many people, both for accuracies and inaccuracies. The good Dean tried to concentrate on facts, while acknowledging the power and mystique of myth. He noted that the coronation of Richard was notable for the introduction of two elements, the appearance of the Champion (hereditary in the Dymoke family, whose task was to answer any challenge to the royal title) and the appearance of the Knights of the Bath for the first time, an important order of chivalry. Richard II had also been married in the Abbey, a distinction only shared by Henry III and Henry VII (at the time the Dean was writing) but much more common in the twentieth century. Richard's colossal badge of the White Hart hung in the Triforium, as did his portrait in the Abbey. The Dean praises the "marvellous restoration" of the said portrait by Mr. Stanley, something now certainly very questionable in the light of modern techniques.

Richard II also desired very much to be buried in the Abbey, as near to Saint Edward the Confessor, and to his own queen, Anne of Bohemia, as possible. Richard also, perhaps unconsciously, began the tradition of burying great literary and poetic figures in the Abbey.

Because of the circumstances of his deposition and forced abdication in 1399, and his subsequent death and the rumours surrounding it in February 1400, Richard was not immediately buried in the Abbey, but at King's Langley, and here is seen quite clearly the fear, all too apparent in other tombs, of it becoming a place "of pilgrimage or demonstrations by his numerous adherents". Amends were made in 1413 by the youth Richard himself had knighted, the new king, Henry V.

The Dean says, in somewhat dramatic terms "No other royal death or burial is enveloped in so fearful a mystery as that occasioned by the threefold account of his death. The doubt was entertained in his own time whether the body brought from Pontefract, through London to King's Langley, was not that of his chaplain Maudelyn...the tragedy of his life is centred in his grave".

The Dean now refers, somewhat obliquely, to the previous "very irregular investigation" which the antiquaries of the last (eighteenth) century made by thrusting their hands through the holes in the side of the tomb, and pulling about the royal bones. The Dean of that day, Dean Thomas, very properly closed the holes, and from that time no further exploration has been possible. However, the damage had been done. Not only were bones and other items taken out of the tomb at that time, but rubbish and other detritus was pushed in. Human nature does not basically change from one era to the next. When the exhumation took place, on August 3, 1871, "It was found that the contents had been subjected to much interference, and it was evident that they had been reached through the five holes formerly existing in the lower panelling of the south side, thus confirming the accounts given by historians of the abbey, which state that the five holes, caused by the displacement of so many metal shields, were used by visitors to pass in their hands, and thus the contents were felt and disturbed, and many portions abstracted, and other objects introduced, as was soon proved. Thus the first things to be noted as missing were portions of the skeletons, and both the lower jaws; and the crowns of copper said to have been seen through the holes on the south side were also not found. Dart writes. In his vol.ii, p. 45, 'From the side next the area, the arms are stolen, in the holes of which putting my hands, I could turn the boards of the coffin'". A telling extract from a letter, which had then been recently sent to the Dean, was also included by him. It was from Wouldham Rectory in Rochester, and dated June 30, 1873:

> It may be interesting to you to know that my grandfather Gerrard Andrews, afterwards Dean of Canterbury, saw a Westminster scholar poke his hand into the tomb of Richard II, in the year,1766, and fish out the lower jaw-bone of the king. My grandfather received the jaw-bone from the boy, and it is now in my possession. I have often shown it to medical men, who say it is the jaw-bone of a man in the prime of life. There are two teeth remaining in the jaw. On a card attached to the bone is written, (the handwriting is my grandfather's, Gerrard Andrews) "the jaw-bone of King Richard the Second, taken out of his coffin by a Westminster scholar in 1766". My grandfather was himself a Westminster scholar at that time, sixteen years of age, having been born in 1750. (Signed) Charles Gerrard Andrews.

In fact, the Dean of Westminster, John Thomas, had only been able to put a stop to these practices when he took office in 1768. It had been going on for quite some time before that. Interestingly, and somewhat ironically, in the light of the letter quoted above, Dean Thomas, who continued in his office until his death in 1793, a period of twenty-five years, did, by his will, endow two scholarships for boys at Westminster School, despite their occasional misdemeanours.

The exhumation also included Richard's first wife and queen, Anne of Bohemia, who had died of the plague in 1394. Richard was never the same after her death, and his decline, both psychologically and politically, began from that time". An examination of the masonry also showed that the structure had originally been made as far as possible airtight when the Queen was interred, for all the joints of the marble work were filled in with a resinous cement, technically called "grain", made of resin, wax, and stone dust; and this, having been thrust, whilst hot, into the open joints after the parts were fixed, had rendered all the junctions impervious. This precaution cannot have been repeated when the tomb was opened and again closed, after the deposition of the king's body, as the evident use of mortar in the pointing would preclude the more careful treatment which had been adopted in the first interment". The interment of Anne had been in 1394; that of Richard not until 1413, so the interval was nearly twenty years.

The exhumation began on August 3, 1871, and was carried on by the Dean, Canon Jennings, Sir Gilbert Scott, Mr. Doyne Bell, Mr. Richmond, Mr. George Scharf, Mr. Chance, Mr. C. Knight Watson, Mr. Sangster, Mr. John Scott and Mr. C.S. Perceval. Significant among these are of course Sir Gilbert Scott, but also the ubiquitous Mr. Doyne Bell and Mr. George (later Sir George) Scharf.

> ...on looking in, there were seen on the floor the broken and rotten boards of coffins, apparently in great disorder, especially two skulls which lay towards the foot of the grave. The Dean was at once summoned, and he directed and superintended a closer examination.. the rotten elm boards of the coffins were first lifted out, and then the remains of the King and the Queen were more visible; those of the King were lying chiefly on the north side, whilst those of the Queen remained on the south side as she had been placed by the King himself. These bones and the other contents of the grave were then all carefully handed out and examined by those present.

Certain parts were missing and the reason for this has already been noted above. The examination was nothing if not thorough. It was decided to sift the dust at the bottom, and indeed the entire contents of the grave, so as to bring to light any minute objects which might otherwise escape observation. This was accordingly done, and the result was the production of several other objects. An entire list was made of them, and the observant Doyne Bell as always made notes of all these proceedings. Several objects came into the category of objects thrown into the grave through the holes, but the most interesting piece was a large pair of plumber's shears, a remarkable find indeed. "This was lying by the King's leg-bones, and out of reach of the hands and fingers searching from the five holes. They were of great age, as shown by the amount of corrosion, and also by the trade stamp of a Plantagenet fleur-de-lys; this was of elegant form, and stamped on the flat surface near the swivel. It is very likely that they were forgotten and left in the grave the the plumber who assisted at the interment in 1413. The leaden covering in which the body with the exception of the face was enveloped must have been removed, as only a very small piece of sheet lead was found in the grave". Interestingly, Doyne Bell suggested that the leaden envelope might have been removed in order to enable the remains of the King either to be placed in the same wooden coffin or in immediate contiguity to the Queen (Eleanor of Provence); in accordance with the same sentiment which had prompted George II to order the sides of his coffin and that of Queen Caroline to be removed, that their dust might intermingle.

The examination of the King's skull drew some interesting conclusions. First, it agrees with his well-known character, and with the general appearance of his portrait in the Abbey. This, however, the examiners concluded proved nothing, as his chaplain Maudelyn was apparently exceedingly like him. Secondly, if these were indeed the King's remains, then the story of his murder by Sir Piers Exton is, as had long been suspected, a mere legend. There was no mark of the battle-axe on the skull.

The iron cramps were all removed, and cramps of copper substituted for them, and photographs taken of the skulls and other bones, and so on, something which of course could not have been done in most earlier exhumations". Arrangements were then made for closing the tomb, and this was done on September 18, 1871, in the presence of the Dean, the Canons in residence, Mr. Doyne Bell and Mr. George Scharf, the other gentlemen having melted away. The bones of the King and Queen being arranged as nearly as possible in their proper positions, were enclosed in a chest with a division to separate them. On the lid of the chest the following words were inscribed: "The remains of Richard II and his Queen". The objects which were believed to have accompanied the original interments were placed in another chest, and marked "Accompaniments of the interment of King Richard II and his Queen". The articles which had evidently been intruded at a later period were likewise enclosed in a chest, and inscribed "Later insertions into the tomb of King Richard the Second".

Upon these three chests was laid a wooden tablet face downwards, in order that the inscription should remain clear as long as possible, inscribed as follows: "This tomb was opened during the repairs undertaken by the Office of Works in July 1871, and the contents of the tomb were arranged by order of Arthur Penrhyn Stanley, D.D., Dean of Westminster".

On the top boarding of the ceiling above the tombs were observed very considerable droppings of wax, from the wax lights which had formerly been placed above the tombs, and several of the boards were found to be much charred, as if they had been on fire.

The paintings on the three panels were observed to be "of the best art of the period. In the centre is a representation of the Coronation of the Virgin, with two graceful figures. The panels to the east have two angels on each of them, supporting shields of arms of the King and Queen…the background of these paintings is on gesso and gilt, and most of this remains; the colouring on the mouldings and the gilt ornamentation was also in a fair state of preservation".

Mr. G. Richmond, RA, now undertook the restoration of these paintings, as indeed he had done of the large portrait of Richard II in the Abbey. Modern art historians have questioned this restoration. The original artist of the portrait may have been the Englishman Gilbert Prince or the Frenchman Andre Beauneveu. Given that Richard was much influenced by everything French, from table etiquette to clothes and pictures, the leaning must be towards the latter.

The intrepid team now turned their investigations to the tomb of King Henry III. An effigy of the king lay on the tomb, and, by means of a powerful hoisting apparatus and strong scaffold work it was lifted up to the Triforium. On Monday, November 6, 1871, a strong light was thrown into an aperture which had been observed in the marble bed which lay below the effigy. Some of the black dust on the coffin, which could be seen, being blown away, a tissue of cloth of gold was discovered in a condition of high preservation, and underneath it was perceived a sound and hard surface of wood, so compact that the touch and sound might easily have been mistaken for lead.

Animation was suspended until the return of the Dean, and with him, his authority to proceed. On Tuesday, 14 November, the Dean having returned to London, directed the two small stones in question to be removed in his presence; Mr. Doyne Bell was also on the spot! The two short stones were lifted onto the long one on the north side, so that the whole chamber or grave, with its coffin, became exposed….it could now be seen that the coffin was covered all over, top, sides, and ends, with cloth of gold, the warp of gold thread similar to that used (in 1871) by arras weavers; the weft only being of silk. It was woven into patterns of great beauty, consisting of striped stars and eight foils. Woodcuts were made of these patterns. It could be seen that this was one continuous cloth, the corners not cut away, but folded. On exposure to the air, however, the cloth, which had seemed in such good state, soon lost the strength of its woof of silk and of the silken core within the gold twist, and the air from a small pair of bellows was sufficient to blow away both dust and silk…the colour of the silken fibre was far gone, but some portions of it retained a crimson hue. (Be it remembered that even in 1871 it had been laid on the coffin in 1272).

It was noted too that "there was no evaporation arising from below, owing to the impervious nature of the marble slab forming the floor of the chamber". There was a small hole in the coffin lid, and, by inserting fingers, it could be lifted slightly, but thus proving that it was only kept in place by its own weight.

At the conclusion of this investigation, the Dean directed that the marble covering to be replaced, and the tomb to be re-opened on the following Thursday at four o'clock, requesting Mr. Doyne Bell to communicate with Mr. C. Knight Watson and Mr. Scharf, and directing Mr. Poole to inform Mr. Douglas Galton, of the Board of Works, so as to secure their attendance on the occasion. Everything must be done correctly.

On November 16, 1871, therefore, there assembled, in the guttering twilight, all the above, plus the Right Hon. A.S. Ayrton, First Commissioner of Works, plus Mr. C.S. Perceval, Mr. Buckler and Mr. Robertson. The two marble slabs were again removed, and accurate observations made of the structure, the cloth of gold and the coffin; the dimensions of the various parts were recorded, and several notes and sketches made by Mr. G. Scharf. The separation of the cloth of gold at the head of the coffin–lid, caused, perhaps, partly by the warping there, enabled the cloth to be turned over at that point, so that the surface of the wood beneath could be examined. It was then seen to be a beautiful slab of hard oak, smoothly wrought to almost a polish, thus showing that the apparent decay under the rectangular hole in the slab of marble was of but very limited extent.

> After a most minute inspection of every part that could be thus seen, it was determined to reassemble on Monday, 28th November, that the coffin-lid might be removed and the contents seen and carefully investigated; preparations were made for new copper cramps to be substituted for those of iron, and it was arranged that the final closing should take place after the examination. The two slabs were then again replaced and the company dispersed.

And then a strange thing happened, as it will sometimes. When the company reassembled and the slabs were again removed, "a feeling was found to prevail that there did not seem, upon historical grounds, to be sufficient motive to warrant the opening of the coffin. The project was therefore abandoned, the whole of the tomb finally closed in, and the effigy and bed replaced in their position over it".

Had it all ended in bathos, in anti-climax? Perhaps the Dean and others had simply had enough of the exhumations. They had no stomach now to continue. Enough was enough. Perhaps the Dean was correctly conscious that no Christian burial should be disturbed without sufficient reason, and there was none, beyond a natural curiosity. Henry III had not suffered the indignities of Richard II and his Queen, for nothing had been found inserted or intruded into their tombs.

An exhumation of more than usual interest also took place in 1876, when it was found that the pavement of the chapel of St. Peter ad Vincula in the Tower of London had sunk in two places, and needed to be replaced. When the pavement was lifted, the bones of a female were found at a depth of about two feet, not lying in their original order, but heaped together in a smaller space. These bones were then examined by a surgeon, Dr. Frederic Mouat, who confirmed in a memorandum that they belonged to "a female of between twenty-five and thirty years of age", of a delicate frame of body, and who had been of slender and perfect proportions; the forehead and lower jaw were small and especially well-formed. The vertebrae were particularly small, especially one joint, the atlas, which was next to the skull, and they bore witness (perhaps) to the neck of Anne Boleyn, who by her own admission, had "a lyttel neck". He noted that the skeleton was about 5 ft to 5ft 3in in height. A careful examination of the finger bones did not show any evidence of a sixth finger or any type of malformation. (Anne Boleyn was said to have had a sixth finger, a mark of a witch). He went on to say that the remains were consistent with descriptions of Anne and the sitter of the famous Holbein portrait of the queen.[16]

Although the bones were mixed up, no other remains were found at that spot. The bones of George Boleyn, the queen's brother, who was executed at the same time, but separately, were not found, but it was thought that the bones had been disturbed in the late eighteenth century, and his remains moved then, or that he was buried in an area not touched by the restoration work.[17]

Notes

1. Desroches-Noblecourt, Christiane, Tut-an-khamoun, published by The Connosieur &Michael Joseph (1963) by Penguin (1965) in association with George Rainbird.
2. Desroches-Noblecourt, op. cit., pp. 11, 16, 212; Carter, Howard, and Mace, Arthur, The Tomb of Tut-ank-Amen, Vol. I (1923); Carter, Howard (alone) Vol. II (1927), Vol. III (1933).
3. Weir, Alison, *The Princes in the Tower* (1992), pp. 18–19.
4. Weir, Alison, quotes, *The Princes in the Tower*, op. cit.
5. Cheetham, Anthony, *Life & Times of Richard III* (1972), drawing on Mancini, Dominic, *The Usurpation of Richard III*, edited by C. A. J. Armstrong (1936).
6. Weir, quoted, p. 249.
7. Francis Sandford (1630–1689), Royal Dragon Pursuivant, College of Arms (1661), Lancaster Herald (1676–1689). Chief work The Genealogical History of the Kings of England (1677).
8. Sir Thomas Chicely (1618–1699), Master of the Ordinance (1670–1674), MP for Cambridge.
9. John Gibson (1629–1718), Heraldry writer, Bluemantle (1671).
10. Quoted from Wren's Parentalia, p. 333, and also given by Tanner, p. 8, n. 4; but Morgan suggests that Wren's account may be secondhand.
11. Knight's London, Vol. II, *The Tower*, by Sanders, J., quoted in Strickland, *Lives of the Bachelor Kings of England* (1861), pp. 187–9.
12. Dr. Northcroft (1869–1943) died on November 17, 1943, in London. He was thus 63 years old when he examined the bones.
13. Jenkins, Elizabeth, *Princes in the Tower.*
14. Malden, H.G., *The Cely Papers* (1900).
15. Watson, Bruce, *Transactions of the London & Middlesex Archaeological Society.*

16. Mouat, Dr. Frederic J. (1816–1897) a British surgeon, chemist, and prison reformer. He had returned from India, where he had spent 30 years, and started a new career, as an inspector for the Local Government Board.
17. Bell, D.C., *Notices of Historic Persons Buried in the Tower* (1877), p. 21; Hammond, Peter, *Tower of London* (1987), Department of the Environment, pp. 34–5.

CHAPTER 5

Identity & Investigation: II

The year 1888 opened with a momentous discovery and exhumation, a discovery commenced on January 23. At the very end of the same year, the Prince of Wales restored the relics which had been taken during the exhumation of Charles I in 1813, an act of reparation.

But it had been at the beginning of this year that workmen carrying out operations in Canterbury cathedral had unearthed a large, and seemingly, complete skeleton. The result of this rather sensational discovery was that the Canon of the Cathedral, Charles F. Routledge, together with Dr. J. Brigstock Sheppard and Canon W.A. Scott Robinson, formed a three-man committee to report on it. This is now termed the First Report. During the subsequent Second Report, a medical examination of the bones was made by Mr. W. Pugin, a local surgeon. The sensation of the discovery was that the skeleton had been found where the body of Thomas Becket had been buried for the first time during the years 1170 and 1220. The archbishop had been murdered in the Cathedral on December 29, 1170, and 50 years later, his body had been translated to its famous shrine in the cathedral proper from where it had lain in the crypt.

The bones were laid around the head "in a sort of square", reported Mr. Pugin. They made up, when properly sorted, an almost complete human skeleton of an adult male of full stature and at least middle aged. Could this skeleton possibly be that of the murdered Becket?

Before the bones were re-interred once more, on February 10, 1888, a good many people had seen them. The bones were almost directly below

M. L. Nash, *The History and Politics of Exhumation*,
https://doi.org/10.1007/978-3-030-24047-9_5

the spot where the shrine of Becket had stood from 1220 until 1538, a period of 318 years. It has already been seen what happened in late August 1538, and that it was the visit of a French lady en route from the Scottish court to the French one, whose attitude to the shrine had probably tipped the balance in favour of its dismantling and destruction.

The feeling was that this would be an unusual location for the bones of anyone else but Becket, and the excitement was intense. The same question would inevitably be asked as in the case of the bones of the supposed Princes in Westminster Abbey. If they were not the bones of the Princes, then whose were they?

This now has a direct link with the story of 1538. Once the shrine had been destroyed, and Becket's name erased from everything to hand, the whole of the eastern crypt had been walled off in 1546. The crypt had been given for use as a private cellar to the Bishop of Dover, Richard Thornden, suggesting that the coffin had probably been interred at some time during the eight years following the final destruction in 1538, after which any interment would have been unlikely in what was then a private building. It was to remain a private place for precisely 300 years, until 1838, and closed to the public.

There were a few bones missing from the skeleton exhumed from the crypt. This was strikingly parallel to the account of a few of Becket's bones being reserved by Archbishop Stephen Langton prior to the translation of the shrine in 1220. Over the centuries, no-one, high or low, seems immune from the temptation of taking "souvenirs", for whatever reason.

The skull was another matter, for, like the skulls of Cromwell and Charles I later on, it acquired a special status of its own. It was especially venerated (as we have seen the last Prior, Goldwell, trying to persuade Madame de Montreuil to do it obeisance, quite unsuccessfully, in 1538). This was because there had been, at the time of the murder in 1170, a sacrilegious assault on the tonsure, or a particular haircut, of the priest. This tonsure indicated his dedicated status. The skull, therefore, was placed in a special position in the feretrum.

The skeleton had five remaining teeth, which were examined by a dental surgeon. The actual skeleton was possibly that of a man 6 ft 2 in in height and aged between forty-five and fifty-five years (Becket was actually 52 at the time of his death). At this point, it should be noted that there was obviously a latent wish in all these examinations that the skeleton was really that of Becket, just as the examiners in 1933 had the same wish that the bones were really those of the murdered Princes; this in itself is very hard to distance oneself from, but it also colours the reports.

The perceived injuries to the skull were also considered crucial. Contemporary accounts in the twelfth century seemed to agree that it had been seriously damaged by each of the four knights responsible for the murder. The 1888 skull was less damaged that might have been expected.

Interestingly, the head and base of a bishop or archbishop's effigy, sculpted in high relief in Purbeck marble, had also been found in the ground with the skeleton, "possibly indicative of the ecclesiastical office of the deceased man".

So what did the participants of 1888 think? Mr. H.G. Austin, the Cathedral surveyor, who had been in charge of the excavations in the crypt, was a prominent believer.[1] So was Canon Routledge. A third believer was Mr. Pugin Thornton.

However, there were sceptics and non-believers. The Committee itself concluded, rather rationally, that "There is no distinctive evidence to show to whom the bones belong". Perhaps the most prominent local sceptic was Dr. Joseph Brigstock Sheppard. He was supported by the Very Reverend Edmund Venables, the Precentor of Lincoln Cathedral and a member of the Royal Archaeological Institute. Fr. John Morris was also a sceptic. He had viewed the bones.

Thus, the reburial of the skeleton simply launched the debate, which has gone on until the present day.

In 1891, the Director of the Society of Antiquaries, Mr. Henry Salusbury Milman, became involved with the project. He made valuable contributions to the debate and went back to examine the contemporary reports concerning the destruction of the shrine in 1538, and the question of whether the bones of Becket had then been burnt, and reburied, something which has never been satisfactorily resolved.

The news (which may not have been true at all) that Becket's bones had been burnt outraged and shocked Catholic Europe, and particularly the Vatican. The Pope finally put into operation the bull of excommunication against Henry VIII, which had been prepared some time previously. The Popes had been reluctant to excommunicate Henry and had given him as much rope as they dared. He was, they did not forget, the king who had come out strongly against Luther in 1517, and, with the assistance of Thomas More, had written a book *In Defence of the Seven Sacraments*, which so pleased the Pope that Henry had been granted the title *Defender of the Faith, in 1521*, a title not only jealously guarded by Henry himself but also looked upon jealously by other Christian kings, including his own nephew, James V. of Scots, who tried to claim it as his own when Henry defected. Perhaps Henry was taken aback by the excommunication. Anyway, he had felt obliged to issue a public explanation of his policy towards shrines and relics in 1539. It was written in the hand of Thomas Derby, the Clerk of the Privy Council, and the critical passage is this:

> As for the shrine of Thomas Becket, sometime Archbishop of Canterbury… it was arrested that his shrynes and bones should be taken away, and bestowed *in such place as the same should cause no superstition afterwards, as it is indeed among others of that sorte conveyred and buried in a noble toure (Tower).*

The essential veracity of the 1539 statement was subsequently confirmed in 1552 in a narrative entitled *Il Pellegrino Inglese* attributed to William Thomas, "lately in the suite of the king's ambassador at Venice". The important passage in this read:

> …butte this is true, that his bones are spread amongst the bones of so many dead men, that without some greate miracle, they will not be found agayne.[2]

By way of further corroboration, Milman noted that the Cardinal Reginald Pole, Archbishop of Canterbury under Mary Tudor, from 1556 to 1558, was also buried in the Corona, above the Trinity Chapel in Canterbury cathedral, which is generally considered to be "The Tower", referred to in the statement of 1539. This was following instructions in his will that his body should be placed "in my church of Canterbury, in that chapel in which the head of the most blessed martyr Thomas, formerly Archbishop of the said church, was kept".

Why, Milman asked, did Pole choose the place where the supposed *head* of Becket had been kept, in preference to the crypt, where his entire body had originally been buried? Could it not be, he wondered, that Pole "may have known the secret of the second burial, and…thus provided, without revealing the secret, that his own bones should rest near those of his holy predecessor"?

It was noted that there was damage to the left side of the skull, where the greatest wounds were said to have been inflicted, according to contemporary reports.

Sixteen years later, in 1907, Mr. M. Beazeley, Fellow of the Royal Geographical Society (FRGS) honorary librarian to the Dean and Chapter of Canterbury, read a paper on the bones to the Society of Antiquaries. He thought there were three issues:

1. Is there evidence to show the remains found in 1888 were actually those of Becket?
2. Were Becket's bones really buried at the time of the destruction of the shrine in 1538?
3. (This one was novel) Supposing it to be ascertained that the remains in questions were not Becket's, what evidence is there to show whose they were?

   Supplementary questions included: Were the remains tall enough to be Becket's? Were there enough teeth for a man of vigorous health and diet? Some had questioned the size of the skull, but the circumference of 22.75 inches was not so unusual.

In March 1908, new evidence concerning the question of whether the bones had indeed been burnt and not buried was produced by the Jesuit priest, Fr. Pollen. He also raised the question as to whether both the King and the Lord Privy Seal (Thomas Cromwell) had been present when the shrine was opened in 1538.

A candidate other than Becket as the original of the bones was also put forward, which seemed viable, for the Abbot of the Benedictine monastery of Evesham in Worcestershire had been buried in the crypt in 1159. However, this was eleven years before Becket was murdered, and before the crypt had any special significance.

In 1912, a new librarian to the Dean and Chapter, the Reverend C. Eveleigh Woodruff, together with Canon William Danke, the Canon residentiary, wrote an exhaustive account of the history of the Cathedral. They made what was almost a passing reference to the exhumation of 1888, thus:

> a rude stone sarcophagus under the pavement of the crypt, containing the bones of a tall man with a cleft skull, and it has been argued that...the remains of Becket there hidden and removed by the monks, who substituted another to undergo the sacrilegious violence of the King[3]
>
> They concluded, distancing themselves from any commitment or belief in this direction, "Until this conjecture is supported by further evidence (that a substitute body had been burned) we prefer to accept the statement that the saint's bones were burnt OR obscurely buried".

John Butler[4] makes some pertinent comments on this. He quotes the examples of Dante's tomb which was opened on June 7, 1865, and found to be empty. What had happened to the body? Like the body of Becket, Dante's body was under physical threat when he had died in 1321. Like Becket, Dante, great as he was, had had enemies. The opening of the tomb was in response to the finding of a body in a wooden chest, which had been bricked up in an outlying chapel of the Fratri Minori in Ravenna, on the May 27, 1865. What had happened was that, fearing that something would happen to the body, his followers had taken it away and secreted it elsewhere. Could it be that this was what had happened to the body or remains of Becket in 1538? Interestingly, in Dante's case, there were a few bones missing from the wooden chest, and these were actually all that was in the tomb.

Butler now turned to the case of St. Cuthbert in Durham, faced with the same fate as that of Becket. Cuthbert had died as long ago as 687. (It is worth emphasising that Henry VIII reserved as special venom for Becket, considering him a traitor. This was not the case with Cuthbert and other major saints and shrines. Henry himself had walked barefoot as a young king from Barston (?) Manor to Walsingham). By Benedictine tradition, the monks moved the body of Cuthbert and buried it in another part of the Cathedral in Durham, while the coffin itself was re-buried behind the high altar in 1542. Henry VIII was still reigning, but he was now occupied by other matters, and the prime mover of the dissolution of the monasteries, Thomas Cromwell, had been executed in 1540. The bones from another monk, the tradition states, were substituted. Thus, by deduction, was the 1888 skeleton a substitute for the real bones of Becket?[5] After all, the monks had had three clear months' notice of what might befall their community in 1538, although the visit of Mme. De Montreuil in the August of that year does seem to indicate that Prior Goldwell and his community were still exhibiting the authentic remains.

Woodruff, writing in 1932, thought that it was inconceivable that if the bones had been those of Becket, and someone knew where they were, that they would not have been moved to a more honourable place during the reign of Mary Tudor. But what might be discounted here is that Mary Tudor had in mind the restoration of a somewhat different type of Catholicism than that which had been swept away by her father and the councillors of her adolescent brother. Indeed, as Butler says, it would be a version of Catholicism "which had absorbed the positive features of the Reformation", and in this sense it anticipated the coming influence of the Counter-Reformation. Mary had had a very humanist education, and there is much evidence to suggest that she had little time for relics or shrines. Certainly, she mentioned neither of them in her will, as the astute Agnes Strickland picked up. Indeed, she only restored two shrines: one was that of Edward the Confessor, in Westminster Abbey, and the other St. Friedeswide at Oxford; and the second one she may have been encouraged to do by her influential woman attendant who had been named after the saint, Friedeswide Strelly.

In any case, who knew where the bones were even in 1553, when Mary came to the throne, if that indeed is what happened. It is quite possible that the monks who knew in 1538 were either dead or displaced somewhere since then.

The example of St. Cuthbert also has an afterlife. In 1827, the coffin was opened. The body was in it; a thighbone reportedly damaged by the King's Commissioners in 1537 was missing. But a number of religious artefacts which were known to have been in the coffin when it was examined in 1104 were still hidden within the coverings in which the body was wrapped.

Once a coffin is opened, or a body exhumed, it seems some seal has been broken, and there is always the temptation to have a look at it again and again. Thus, in 1899, the coffin was opened yet again, and further tests were carried out, although exactly what these were is not clear. However, these tests showed such a measure of agreement between the contents and condition of the coffin that there could be no further room for doubt that the remains were indeed those of St. Cuthbert. Presumably, it means, therefore, that the body, which had been spirited away and buried in another part of the Cathedral in 1537, had already been restored to the coffin in 1542. Durham was further enough away for a distracted king, but Canterbury was not.

The constant opening of a coffin cannot but remind one of the stories of the Castilian Queen, Juana, called La Loca (The Mad) who kept the body of her dead husband with her and every night had it opened so that she could gaze on its face. This story may indeed only relate to the stages of the coffin as it was moved across Spain to its final resting place in 1506. At the time Juana was the ruling sovereign of Castile in succession to her mother, the famed Isabella, who had died in 1504, it was only sometime later that she was incarcerated in the castle of Tordesillas.

There is a further example in England of what happened during the years 1537 and 1538. The patron saint of Lichfield is St. Chad, and, knowing what might happen, the saint's bones were hurriedly removed from his shrine by one of the prebendaries c. 1537, when under threat of a visitation from the King's Commissioners.[6]

One of the problems concerning the damage to the 1888 skeleton was that an examination of the contemporary authorities resulted in the conclusion that there was no single or agreed version of the slaying of Becket. Butler sums it up thus: "after reading these strangely conflicting narratives, one is almost tempted to adopt the cynical dictum of Lord Palmerston that there is nothing more deceptive than figures, except facts". This means of course statements that are accepted as facts when they might not be, and the best which can be hoped for, as in the case of the Princes in the Tower, is strong circumstantial evidence, *unless of course* modern techniques, such as radiocarbon dating and DNA, can be applied.

The next step in the story was the intervention of Randall Thomas Davidson, the Archbishop of Canterbury (1851–1928), who commissioned Canon Arthur James Mason to assemble the documentary evidence about the 1888 skeleton, which had become known as "the skeleton in the crypt". In 1920, a publication appeared from Cambridge University Press, entitled *What became of the bones of St. Thomas?*

Butler rightly comments, of the bones: "the passing years had done nothing to dull their extraordinary magnetism", in common with those of Tut-an-khamoun and the Princes in the Tower, something which was to receive a further boost with the discovery of the bones of Richard III.

This commission, in turn, led to the decision, on Monday, July 18, 1949, to reopen the coffin, a decision taken by the Dean & Chapter of Canterbury. Thus, at 8.15 pm, a small group assembled to witness the reopening of the coffin, the same kind of cloak and dagger operation which had surrounded the reopening of the coffin of Charles I in 1888. Nothing seemed to change in these operations. The only difference here is that it was July, not December, and there was still much daylight. A report on this reopening was made by Professor Cave, during the years 1940 to 1951, but was never published. Why not?

Interestingly, the humble and essential workmen are named this time, as they had not been in 1933 when the Urn containing the Princes' bones had been opened. "Mr. Shilling and Mr. Baldock carried out the operations. Present were Canon John Shirley, the Archdeacon of Canterbury and Maidstone, Professor A.J.E. Cave, of the Anatomy Department of St. Bart's Hospital, Dr. Jack Trevor of the Faculty of Archaeology at Cambridge, a Mr. Tophill, a Mr. Anderson (who are they?) and Dr. William Urry, then the Cathedral librarian.

The lid of the coffin had sunk and split and the bones could be glimpsed for the first time (since 1888). "An unpleasant smell oozed upwards from the hole."

There are some interesting sidelights on those present, or not present. The actual Dean of Canterbury was Dr. Hewlett Johnson, who had already become known as the "Red Dean" for his political sympathies and was becoming increasingly estranged from his colleagues. He was not present. Thus, it was Jack Shirley, who had become Headmaster of the King's School in Canterbury and Canon Residentiary of the Cathedral, who was instrumental in the reopening of the coffin. Dr. Hewlett Johnson added to his sins, in the eyes of his enemies, by his longevity.

The morning after the re-exhumation, July 19, 1949, the bones were taken by Professor Cave to the Anatomy Department of St. Bart's, where they remained under examination for two years, an extraordinarily long time, compared with other exhumations. In 1951, a report was submitted by Professor Cave to the Dean and Chapter, a copy of which was placed in the Cathedral library. The Chapter expressed the hope that a full report would be published in due course, but no such general publication ever ensued. Moreover, the copy in the library disappeared!

In 1993, John Butler, the sleuthing author of *The Quest for Becket's Bones*, found by great good chance that Professor Cave was still living and had retained a copy of the Report among his papers. Signed by him, and dated May 21, 1951, it was a mere thirty-one pages, although he had retained the bones for examination for two years.

The reason for the disappearance of the report from the Cathedral library and the non-publication of the full report now became clear. Professor Cave had had to decisively refute any claim that the bones were those of Becket. But the Professor quite properly, although the result was a personal disappointment to him, had to add that the issue had had to be resolved solely on the evidence afforded by the skeleton itself.[7]

How had Professor Cave arrived at this decision? Firstly, he drew attention to the poor condition of the bones. Interestingly, the plaster mould on which Thornton had mounted the remains of the skull in 1888 and which had been buried with the bones had remained wet and plastic, but this had had unfortunate effects. By introducing moisture into the sealed coffin, the decaying process of the bones had been accelerated. Many of them had been attacked by a fungal organism. Mould growths had occurred in whitish patches on many of the bones, and some, especially the nasal bones and much of the pelvis, had disintegrated even upon the gentlest handling. The mould growth was removed, the bones were cleaned and slowly dried, and the long exacting business of identifying all the bone fragments began, many of which were no more than chips and splinters. Large parts of the skeleton were missing, including all the base of the skull, most of the face, and parts of the pelvis and spine. (Facial reconstruction, as with Richard III, might not have been possible, even now, with all these parts missing.)

As to the skull, it was this that provided the clearest evidence (though the *only* evidence) that the skeleton could not have been Becket's. Turning to the celebrated "corona", Cave first rehearsed the argument of its importance. The blow that killed Becket, he asserted, had detached the crown of the skull, the earlier blows having wounded the soft tissues only. Therefore, he maintained, "the authentic relic must show unmistakable evidence of instrumental breakage and detachment of the uppermost portion of the cranial vault". (It will be recalled that the knights who killed Becket were intent on this blow because of the great symbolic importance of the tonsure of the monk, the consecrated priest.)

Now, among the numerous pieces of bone from the cranium, Cave did indeed find a large upper calvarial fragment of irregular and angulated pentagonal outline. It was this, he thought, which in 1888 had been interpreted as the "corona" of Becket's skull. It had certainly been so mounted on the plaster block by Thornton, as to appear isolated from the rest of the vault.

Cave was absolutely sure, however, that Thornton's reconstruction of the skull had been fundamentally flawed: in fact, this piece of bone fitted naturally in its place in the rest of the skull and was nothing more than a large piece of the skull as a result of damage occurring after the death. The edges of the bone were angulated, jagged, and irregular, and they showed no evidence of contact with a cutting instrument. Rather, they displayed the ordinary natural fracture surface characteristic of buried skulls, of all periods, and tally exactly with archaeological material of Romano-British, Anglo-Saxon and XVIII century date, with which they have been compared.

Had the fractures been caused by a cutting instrument, before death, then a certain amount of bony tissue would have been missing from the surface edges, but this was not the case. They were obviously post-mortem fractures, caused by the disintegration of the entire cranium as the result of natural decay and the pressure of impacted earth. "It is quite certain", Cave concluded, "that (this piece of bone) was *not* detached instrumentally from the living head. It cannot therefore be the 'corona' of St.

Thomas, and hence the skeleton cannot be identified with the martyr's remains". (But it took no account of the views of Mason and others, based on the work of the monk Gervase (who had described the wounds most closely) that the "corona" was not a segment of bone, but the consecrated tonsure, and that the real skull need not have been damaged in that particular way.[8]

But Cave also stated that no ante-mortem wounds had been made with a cutting instrument, *anywhere* about the skull: "all the cracks, breaks, fractures, and erosions are most emphatically of a post-mortem nature". He also conceded that some damage may have been done during the removal of the skeleton in 1888.

There was, however, one arresting observation that, in addition to the bones of the skeleton, the coffin had also been found to contain an assortment of other bones, mostly animal ones (pig, sheep, or goat, small ox, a small bird, and some unidentified mammal). There was also an incomplete upper vertebra from another, smaller skeleton.

Professor Cave also highlighted the significance of this by adding: "the skeleton had originally been buried elsewhere, in a recognised burial place, and had been exhumed, along with some of the surrounding soil, containing the bone fragments of other people, and animals buried nearby, before being deposited in a coffin in the crypt, where it was found in 1888".[9]

> ...moreover, the skeleton had been directly buried in the earth, not in a coffin or other container...the earlier burial had been of a complete human corpse, not of a collection of bones...Many of the bones had been damaged by spade cuts...prior to its being placed in the coffin in the crypt, it had been exhumed in great haste, or with little care, or both..."with gross and destructive carelessness". The indications were of an incidental, rather than a deliberate exhumation.

One cannot, therefore, escape the notion that this tallies with the stories that Becket's bones were deliberately mixed up with others, to avoid detection and further degradation, or/and that a substitute body was hurriedly put in its place.

The bones were returned to the Cathedral in 1951. They were placed in a leaden coffin, the lid being sealed in the presence of Canon Shirley. They were buried, for at least the third time in their existence, by Shirley on the evening of Friday, June 15, 1951. The grave was sealed with a plain, unmarked slab.[10]

Now, not surprisingly, not all of the bones were replaced in the coffin. One tooth remained on the surface—probably the right upper canine tooth—and it now resides in the Cathedral archives—in a registered envelope marked "Cambridge, January 2nd, 1951". The envelope, presumably containing the tooth, was sent originally to Dr. Jack Trevor, a member of the scientific group that examined the skeleton, to Dr. Gosta Gustavson, in Malmo, Sweden. Accompanying the envelope in the archives is an anonymous handwritten note, undated and unaddressed, but bearing the initials "NS" It reads: "This is one of four teeth which the skeleton in the East Crypt was found to have on the occasion of our opening of the tomb. You might like it in the relics and treasures of the library. I have guarded it all the time, and, after all, it might be a saint's tooth".

Dr. Gustavson was an acknowledged international expert on dating the age of death from teeth, and Dr. Trevor was presumably given the task of sending him one of the teeth for this very purpose. Gustavson returned it to Cambridge, where it came to the care of "NS". This is probably the Very Reverend Norman Sykes, a close acquaintance of Canon Shirley. Sykes had a very distinguished academic career, as an ecclesiastical historian, in the Universities both of London and Cambridge. He must have kept possession of the tooth before handing it over to the Cathedral Archives before his death on March 1961.

If we return to the position of the shrine in Tudor times, it is striking how different was the situation between 1535 and 1538. In 1535, before the first dissolution of the monasteries and priories, Richard Layton, the Archdeacon of Buckingham and later Dean of York, who became one of the Royal Commissioners in 1538, had visited the shrine three years earlier, when it was threatened with fire. At that time, bandogs (which were a cross between a pit bull terrier and a Rottweiler!) were set to guard the shrine, and the sexton was put in the vestry to guard the jewels.

Very different was the position three years later, and it may be instructive to put it into the personal context of the life of the king, Henry VIII. In 1535, he was still married to Anne Boleyn but faced with the dilemma of close friends and respected bishops who would not accept his decision to declare himself Head of the Church in England. So More and Fisher were to go to the block. In 1536, Anne Boleyn herself fell, taking many with her, and Henry then swiftly married Jane Seymour, who gave him the son he so earnestly wished for in 1537, dying herself shortly after. There is evidence to show that she might have restrained him in his plundering of the monasteries and shrines, but she was now not there. So by 1538, he had no queen, and although three other queens were to follow, it was a period when he was lonely, introspective and generally on edge. This goes some way to explain his behaviour towards the shrines, and Becket's was singled out for special treatment.

This is backed up in the case of the shrine of St. William at York, for example, where Henry visited in 1541. His bones were actually rediscovered in 1732, although their authenticity has been questioned. At a meeting of the Privy Council at Hull in October, 1541, when Henry was on the same progress to the North, he issued a letter to all the bishops through Archbishop Cranmer, expressing his displeasure that the shrines and monuments of such things "yet remain in sundry places", and, indeed, the further north, the less the shrines were tampered with.

The special treatment meted out to Becket can be traced to the document dated April 24, 1538.[11] This document claims to be a sentence passed on Becket, following a mock trial conducted at his shrine at which, unsurprisingly, the defendant failed to appear. He was thus sentenced

> never to be named martyr in future, and his bones to be taken up and publickly burnt, and the treasures of his shrine confiscated to the King…this sentence pronounced, the King commanded it to be put into execution on 11th August. The gold and silver filled 26 wagons. On the 19th August (St. Bernard's day) the sacrilege was completed, and the relics publickly burnt and the ashes scattered.

But clearly, this has to be questioned as being a genuine document, as the dates do not tally with the facts, which were that the shrine was intact still in the last days of August, when Madame de Montreuil visited it. The main question, therefore, remains whether the bones were actually burnt or not, and, if not, could they have been buried? At the time of the finding of the skeleton in 1888, Fr. John Morris was a sceptic, and mainly because he knew that the contemporary writer, Nicholas Harpsfield, who had written a life of Thomas More, published in 1554, had been misquoted on "burnt", when what he had actually written was "buried". Fr. John had actually viewed the bones and was still a sceptic.

Moreover, the Vatican document, which actually excommunicated Henry VIII on December 17, 1538, actually uses the word "exhumed". It is also possible that the pilgrims were given a faked skull, in a silver reliquary, to kiss. There is no intimation of any burning in the Statement of Vindication (against Becket) drawn up by Thomas Derby, Clerk of the Privy Council, in 1538 or 1539. Could it, therefore, be that it was the fake head that was burned?

At this distance, the evidence is at best circumstantial, and much of the analysis conjecture. But again, the question remains still, if the skeleton is not that of Becket, then whose is it? Could it be that of St. Alphege, Archbishop of Canterbury killed by the Vikings in 1011? The historical records of the Cathedral tell us that the building of the eastern crypt was between 1179 and 1186 (during Becket's first burial) when part of the ancient graveyard at that end of the Cathedral precincts was disturbed, and some bones re-buried in a trench beneath the crypt, and the Priory infirmary.

In the 1860s, some superfluous canonical houses and their gardens were demolished, and human remains were said to have been brought into the crypt for re-burial.[12]

Another interesting possibility is that in 1571, a visiting French cardinal, Odet de Coligny, the Cardinal Chatillon, had died in England and been buried in an elaborate tomb in Canterbury Cathedral. It was intended that his body should be exhumed and repatriated to France, but this never happened. The Cathedral rule was that only saints should be buried in the chapel, but this rule had been suspended in the cases of King Henry IV, his queen, Joanna of Navarre, Nicholas Wootton, the first Dean after the breach with Rome, in 1542; William Courtenay, who was Archbishop, in 1396; and Edward, called later the Black Prince, at whose funeral Courtenay had officiated, in 1376. It was, therefore, a rule more honoured in the breach than in the observance.

Yet, something of Becket may still remain. In April 1992, a reliquary was opened in Rome in the basilica of St. Maria Maggiore. A linen tunic, sprinkled with blood, purporting to belong to Becket, was examined by two German scientists from the University of Munich, and the Professors Ursula Nilgen and Leonie von Wilckens concluded that "its authenticity can be considered a great certainty".

This was an artefact from the distant past that had probably been in intimate contact with Becket himself. In more modern times the politician and aristocrat Richard Needham had said perceptively, on wearing the cufflinks of the celebrated Prince Frank of Teck, "You cannot do this, without thinking of the shirt!"[13] It is contact which makes relics, even if there are of different classes of relics.

Finally, there are two other possibilities for the burial of the bones of Becket, after the destruction of the shrine in 1538. The first is after 1546, when Richard Thornden, the first Prebendary of the Cathedral, who remained sympathetic to the Catholic cause, may have wished the bones to be re-buried in the church, rather than in the cellar.

The second is during the Civil War and the Puritan purge of the Cathedral in 1643, when many tombs in the nave were opened, and their contents removed; something which happened during many significant revolutions and revolutionary movements, such as the French Revolution, and the Spanish Civil War of 1536–1539.

The writer of the Quest for the Bones of Becket came to two conclusions, viz.

1. The truth cannot be determined on the strict basis of the documentation which has come down to us
2. The correct identity of the 1888 skeleton cannot be discerned. That it was not Thomas Becket is indisputable.

In 1966 an academic Professor of Anatomy, Carl-Herman Hjortso, of the University of Lund in Sweden, obtained permission to exhume the body of Queen Christina of Sweden. She had died in Rome in 1689 and been buried among the tombs of the Popes, one of only three women to be given this honour; the others being Queen Charlotte of Cyprus and Maria Clementina Sobieska, the wife of the Old Pretender, James Edward Stuart.

Christina was the only child of King Gustavus Adolphus of Sweden, one of the heroes of the terrible Thirty Years War, which ravaged Germany and adjacent states from 1618 to 1648. Gustavus Adolphus died during the war, in 1632, leaving his daughter, Christina, then aged six, as an infant sovereign. The circumstances of her birth would affect her whole life, and there was hope, during the exhumation, and the report published afterwards, that the mystery and conundrum might be at least clarified, if not solved.

Queen Maria Eleanora, the mother of Christina, had, like Catherine of Aragon, an unfortunate gynaecological history. It was made more unfortunate by the fact that at this time Sweden was a world power, and it was important to continue a series of strong rulers. At that time strong meant male, primarily because of the military leadership aspect of kingship. Gustavus Adolphus had led an army into battle at the age of sixteen. However, there was in his personality a very pragmatic gene, and rather than divorcing the queen and marrying again, he simply accepted the situation and had Christina educated as if she had been a boy.

Maria Eleanora had had a stillborn daughter, then a daughter who did not live until her first birthday, and then a stillborn son. The birth of this next child proved difficult, but just before 11 pm on December 8, 1626, after a long labour, the child was born. It had a birth caul from head to knee, concealing the crucial evidence of its sex. The midwives were working by candlelight in the dark Swedish winter. The caul was removed at once, and the Queen's attendants declared it to be a boy; however, in the guttering dawn, they had another look, and they then decided it was a girl. The King, true to form, declared: "She will be clever, for she has deceived us all". It must have been apparent to all, however, as it might have been in the case of Princess Elizabeth of England in 1533, that there was room for doubt as to its sex.

Curiously, like Elizabeth of England, Christina was born on one of the feast days of the Virgin Mary. Elizabeth had been born on the eve of the Virgin's birthday and died on the eve of the Annunciation. December 8 was the Immaculate Conception of the Virgin. Doubtless Catholics at the time, even in this Lutheran state, remembered this. They and others did not know how significant it would prove.

The child was baptised Kristina Augusta.

But, as the biographer Veronica Buckley, among many others, has questioned, was the girl really a boy? Was she a hermaphrodite or a pseudohermaphrodite? Diagnosis of this kind, at a distance of centuries, must always be conjectural. It is possible that Christina was born with some kind of genital malformation, and she might even have been what is now called intersexual or transgendered. Our own statistically minded age records that about one in every hundred babies is born with malformed genitals of varying degrees of ambiguity (quite a worryingly high percentage), making it often difficult and sometimes impossible to determine the baby's sex. There are various disorders which can cause such malformations; in the case of a baby girl, the most common of them would produce a perfectly healthy infant with normal internal sex organs, but often with an enlarged clitoris and partially fused labia, easily confused at first glance with the small infant penis of a longed-for male child.[14] One might sympathise with the Swedish midwives of 1626.

Whatever the case, Christina's sex, like her sexuality, was to remain ambiguous to others and ambivalent to herself throughout her life.[15]

The case of Wallis Simpson, the celebrated Duchess of Windsor, who, despite three husbands, had no children, might also have been a similar case. But in the twentieth century, corrective surgery could be attempted.

There is evidence that the Duchess had several such operations. Despite this, the masculine appearance of parts of her face and body remained striking.[16]

So did the exhumation of 1966 clarify this at all? Apparently not. When Christina died in 1689, there was an autopsy, which makes no mention of her external genitals. When her grave was opened in the Vatican in 1965, it was found that the soft tissues had disintegrated, *and the undoubtedly female skeleton is consistent with a diagnosis of intersexuality*.[17]

A contemporary, the Jesuit priest Fr. Charles Manderscheidt, left a telling description of Christina, when he was instructing her in the Catholic faith, to which she ultimately converted: "There is nothing feminine about her, except her sex. Her voice and manner of speaking, her style, her ways, are all quite masculine. I see her on horseback nearly every day. Though she rides side-saddle, she holds herself so well and is so light in her movements, that, unless one is quite close to her, one would take her for a man".

When Christina abdicated in 1654, she was nearly twenty-eight, and after a reign of ten years, she left Sweden disguised as a man, but "her disguise was, in fact, more than anything, a revealing of her true inclination and her real personality…from now on, she would be reluctant to wear women's clothes or a woman's hairstyle…her speech would grow coarser, and her habits rougher, even her voice would deepen…for now there was nothing but the excitement of escape and the sublime exhilaration of freedom and movement. Formalities and responsibilities lay discarded along with her long hair and her high shoes, and her trailing, hindering robes".[18]

Of course, one might validly add that many women, or perhaps most women, perfectly female in every way, might also have welcomed such freedoms from restraint and constraint.

The last years of Christina in Rome have the tone of bathos. It was sad that she lived off the Pope's charity, neglected and forgotten. Her romantic and somewhat tragic tales were no longer relevant in the Europe of 1689, a tempestuous year of revolution and change. But, nevertheless, a post-mortem was carried out, which is now in the Austrian State Archives in Vienna. This provided some evidence that she may have died in a severe general infection with terminal heart failure, and/or vomiting with aspiration.[19]

This tentative diagnosis is compatible with the statements made in various connexions concerning symptomatology of the illnesses which affected the Queen during her lifetime. Thus began Professor Hjortjo's remarkable report which was made in 1966. In the previous December of 1965, the Vatican had given its permission for "a unique grave opening". The remains of Queen Christina were removed from the sarcophagus, which stands in the crypt of St. Peter's, in Rome. The main object of the opening was to take a casting of the silver mask covering the Queen's face. The initiative had come from the Vatican authorities, who wished to make a contribution in the form of the casting to the forthcoming Queen Christina exhibition to be held by the Council of Europe. Professor Hjortjo was commissioned to conduct the grave opening, but this led to the desire being expressed that the more detailed anthropological reports with their tables and photographs should also be made available.

Looking back on the Queen's life, a description given during her illness of 1666, when she was forty years old, seemed indicative of the suspected symptoms. At that time there was loss of weight combined with a pronounced thirst (she drank ten carafes of milk daily) and moreover, the series of temporary conditions of unconsciousness, combined with ulcerations of the legs reported from the last months of the Queen's life. All this undoubtedly suggests that her basic illness was diabetes.[20] The suspicion of this is not lessened when it appears that the Queen in general either improved or completely recovered after a change in diet. The post-mortem states: "The skeleton of the thorax gave insufficient space for the inner organs". This also confirms information found in the literature that Queen Christina had a certain "deformity in her body" probably caused by an accident in her childhood.

The author then goes on to examine the question already covered, and which has exercised so many writers during her lifetime and since her death, the much-debated point regarding the Queen's supposed intersexuality.[21]

The dead body of the Queen does not appear to have been embalmed, at least not in any effective manner. All external soft parts have completely disappeared. In the interior of her body, however, an amount of black-brown completely dried out and brittle remains of the inner organs were found. These had originally been placed in a separate sarcophagus[22] but had on a later occasion obviously been replaced in the body.

The Report continues: "Certain parts of the Queen's body with surviving funeral textiles were, for reasons of reverence, not subjected to anthropological investigation; other difficulties of local and technical nature also prevented this being done. Among other things, a rontgenographing of the contents of the coffin, of the cranium, and of the skeleton could not be made. Prevailing lighting conditions and lack of time prevented the retaking of possibly failed photographs; this meant that some of the pictures, especially of the extremities, were not satisfactory. The measuring technique used was that devised in R. Martin in 1928.[23] As comparison, the measuring results obtained at earlier investigations of the House of Vasa, who were related to Queen Christina, are given".[24]

This last remark is particularly interesting as it was evidence before the use of the major breakthrough DNA. The earlier investigations of the House of Vasa referred to were those of her great-grandparents, Gustav Vasa (?1496–1560) and Margareta, his queen (1514–1551), and her great uncle, John III (1537–1592), and her great half-uncle, Eric XIV (1533–1577). It may be recalled that Eric XIV, born the same year as Queen Elizabeth I of England, was also one of her suitors. Eric was a Renaissance prince, and not only commissioned the Swedish crown jewels from a Flemish goldsmith but built Kalmar castle. He was deposed and imprisoned, in another castle that of Orbyhus, rather in the style of what Henry VI suffered in England or Christian II in Denmark. When he died in 1577, rumours were soon circulated and it was said he died of arsenic in his pea soup. When his body was exhumed and examined in 1958, his body did indeed indicate the presence of an unusual amount of arsenic, as well as a laming blow from a guard's sword. Whether his half-brother and successor, John, knew or connived at this, or was in some way responsible, we cannot say.[25] Eric, who had been born the same year as Queen Elizabeth I of England (1533), was forty-three when he died. It should be noted that the death rumours started with Johannes Messenius, who was not born until two years after Eric died. He nevertheless became a great Swedish historian, who eventually died at Oulu in Finland in 1636. The rumours do seem to have been confirmed at last in the modern forensic analysis of arsenic poisoning, after the exhumation of 1958.[26] As John Butler observed, in 1995, when writing of the exhumation of the supposed bones of Becket, "Myths and rumours are of great importance as social facts".

The Report goes on to consider what Hjortso calls "The sexual constitution of Queen Christina", and recounts the various incidents in her life which might be germane to this question, that is, of intersexuality. The first doctor to attempt to clarify this problem was the professor in gynaecology and obstetrics in Lund, Elis Essen-Moller, in 1937.[27]

> ...he tried to collect all the available data of importance of the problem. The material was compiled, critically examined with regard to its reliability and

> analysed from various angles by a wise and experienced gynaecologist with a sharp eye for medical details. After thoroughly penetrating the problem, Essen-Moller's conclusion was that Queen Christina had been abnormal in her sexual constitution.[28] His phrase was significant: "Woman she truly was, but not completely; fate had made her a compromise between man and woman".[29]

Stolfe's opinion was that Queen Christina was a pseudohermaphrodite.[30] He added that the problem was at the same time complicated. "One cannot dismiss it with a few simple medical terms."

Queen Christina has left an account of her birth in her autobiographical notes. The assisting midwives thought at first that she was a boy because she was "completely hairy and had a coarse and strong voice". However, they discovered their mistake, and when the newborn child was shown to her father, he himself was able to see how things stood ("to find out for himself the nature of the matter").

To add to the above, the doctors whom Queen Christina, later in life, had reason to consult, judged her a woman, and it is documentarily certified that she had menstruations. If intersexuality had existed, this must thus have been either true hermaphroditism with an otherwise female *habitus* or feminine pseudohermaphroditism, both unusual forms. Regarding the combination of intersexuality and physical asymmetry, which was originally pointed out by Virchow, Hjortso was very sceptical about it. This combination is not mentioned in Overzier's large monograph either.[31]

Among other points, Hjortso adds the comment that the pelvis of the Queen had a construction that by itself would not have hindered a delivery.

In his summary, Hjortso emphasises on the moulding of the facial skeleton as extremely delicate and its entire structure gracile. Her jaws seemed atrophic or reduced; a considerable loss of teeth might have contributed to this. The result was that the mandible has taken on the appearance of a much older person that Queen Christina was (she was sixty-three at the time of her death). The structure of the skeleton was also recorded as fairly gracile. No sign of infirm changes or injuries to the skeleton caused during life could be found.

The author, Hjortso, came to the conclusion that objective criteria for the diagnosis of intersexuality was lacking. The anthropological investigation could not support the diagnosis.[32]

Of interest also are the comparisons of the previous exhumations of members of the House of Vasa, including Gastav Vasa, Christina's great-grandfather, whose grave was opened in 1945. The exhumation of his corpse revealed that he had suffered chronic infections of a leg and in his jaw.[33]

In 2016, the late lamented John Ashdown-Hill, so instrumental in the search for Richard III,[34] visited Clare Priory in Suffolk, in order to try and discover the bones of Lionel, Duke of Clarence. Had he found them, DNA might have been taken, which could be used in identifying the bones of Richard III. He used thermal imaging throughout the ground which had been the church of the priory, and especially just before the high altar, where it was recorded that Lionel, the third son of Edward III, had been buried, with his first wife, Elizabeth de Burgh, Countess of Ulster. Although no digging took place, John Ashdown-Hill recorded that "the ground had been disturbed". To him, as an archaeologist, this might have meant that other, previous attempts had been made to try to discover the burial places. To the Prior himself, Fr. David Middleton, who knew the history of the Priory intimately, it simply indicated that after the Dissolution in 1540 the ground of the chancel and church had been dug over for a vegetable garden! However, the six slabs of stone before the altar have never been identified, and it may very well be that Lionel was indeed buried there. The investigations of John Ashdown-Hill did, however, reveal the extraordinary story of Lionel's short life and how his body was exhumed from Pavia, where he had died in 1368, and returned to Clare to lay beside his first wife. But, like all of these stories or histories, things are never as simple as that.

John Ashdown-Hill published his investigations in 2016.[35] He recorded that in 1924, Mrs. K. W. Barnardiston, a local historian, had concluded during her investigations that Prince Lionel had first been buried in the city of Pavia in 1369 and was afterwards interred in the Convent Church of the Austin Friars in Clare, in accordance with the instructions in his Will that he should be buried in the Church *below the High Altar*. However, the will, variously published by John Nicols in 1770 and later by N.H. Nicholas in 1826,[36] simply does not appear to specify that location. He stipulated that while his heart and bones should be brought back to the Suffolk Augustinians, his flesh and entrails should be buried at Pavia, near to the tomb of St. Augustine of Hippo,[37] It seems clear that Lionel's flesh and entrails were buried in Pavia, for in 1392, Henry (the future Henry IV of England,) the son of John of Gaunt, made a pilgrimage to the Holy land. En route, he visited Pavia and prayed at the tomb of St. Augustine.

> He also saw the body of Lionel, the late Duke of Clarence, his uncle, who had been buried there. For this Lionel, just before his death, had given commandment to his attendants that his heart and bones should be conveyed to the convent of the Hermit Friars of St. Augustin, at Clare, in England, but that his flesh and entrails should be solemnly interred beside the grave of the distinguished doctor.

So far, so good. There is clear evidence that Lionel's heart and bones were brought back to England and buried at Clare Priory. Lionel's bequest to Clare Priory of embroidered black clothing and fabric was fulfilled, and Lionel's funeral expenses at Clare were settled. The sum of ten marks was paid to the prior and brethren in the chapter house on September 12, 1377, for their share in the funeral expenses. Moreover, John Newbury (or Newborne) esquire, one of the men who brought Lionel's remains back to Clare from Italy, was subsequently interred near Lionel's grave, a devoted follower perhaps.

The fact that only Lionel's heart and bones were brought back to England makes it likely that they would have been in one (or two) small container(s). This is consistent with the description of Lionel's grave at Clare Priory in *The Dialogue at the grave of Dame Joan of Acre*. The poem states that he was buried there "for such a Prince, to(o) sympilly" in "a small tomb...in the midst of the choir" (exigua...tumba/inque chori medio). Here is an example of words being lost, even in medieval English translation, for "medio, the midst", can mean anything from bosom, depths, heart, hub, and interior, as well as centre, so the search for the grave of Lionel might not be simply in the middle of the choir.[38] The burial site of Lionel's bones and heart may, therefore, be one of the small and rather shallow burial sites identified by the recent Ground Penetrating Radar (GPR) survey on the south side of the presbytery.

The first conclusion, nevertheless, of Ashdown-Hill, concerning the belief that the burial site in the centre of the presbytery site, before the high altar, which contains two bodies, male and female, is the tomb of Lionel and his first wife Elizabeth, was that it must be false. But it was false not only regarding Lionel but also regarding Elizabeth. A document dated 1364, just after her death, shows that she was buried at Bruisyard, in Suffolk. This document is in the National Archives, catalogued as E101/394/19, and is the account of her former chaplain, Nicholas de Flatbury and another of Lionel's officials bringing her body back from Ireland, where she had died, and taking it via Chester and Coventry to Bruisyard. The coffin was covered by a linen pall on which was a cross of red silk, and the funeral was conducted by the Bishop of Norwich.[39] Fr. Middleton confirmed that the detail of her burial are in the parish registers at Bruisyard Abbey near Saxmundham. The mix-up arose because Bruisyard was also a Poor Clare foundation. It was presumed that Elizabeth too was at Clare, whereas it was another Clare foundation. Lionel himself had had a hand in establishing the foundation at Bruisyard. He was a great benefactor, who greatly respected the Augustinians, and endowed the chair of theology at the cathedral school of Dublin.

The conclusion, therefore, of John Ashdown-Hill is quite convincingly that the bones were found in front of the site of the high altar by William St. John Hope in 1904 and recorded by Mrs. K.M. Barnardiston in 1924, as almost certainly those of Elizabeth de Burgh cannot actually have been the body of Lionel's first wife. So who were they?

J. Weever, in his *Antient Funeral Monuments*, suggests that the male body was that of Richard, sixth Earl of Clare, who was buried at Clare Priory, which he had founded. But, according to other accounts, Richard was buried at Tewkesbury Abbey. To be buried before the high altar indicates a person of high rank, and the other candidates in Weever's list include Joan of Acre, the Countess of Gloucester & Hereford, Lady Margaret Neville, Baroness Scrope, half-sister of Cecily Neville, Duchess of York, Dame Alice Spencer, and Dame Eleanor Wynkepery; while the male candidates include Edward Monthermer, the youngest son of Joan of Acre above, who was buried beside his mother, Edmund Mortimer, Earl of March, Sir John Beauchamp, Sir Thomas Gily (and his first wife), or Sir Thomas Clofton (and Ada, his wife). Presumably, from so many possibilities, if they were ever properly exhumed, there would be identifying jewellery or physical characteristics. This brings one round to the crux of the search for Lionel, for his nickname was "Long Lionel", because he was almost seven feet tall. When he was born, in Antwerp, in 1338, to Queen Philippa of Hainault, born in Flanders of a Flemish mother, and therefore a true Fleming, he already gave indications of the height and the huge frame he would attain as he grew to manhood. Agnes Strickland refers to him then truly as "an infant Hercules". But it was not only in size that gave Lionel his arresting looks. "He was a man of great strength and beauty of person, and exceedingly tall in stature."[40] He had inherited his height from his great-grandfather Edward I, whose nickname was "Longshanks", although he never attained more than six ft two inches in height. There was a Plantagenet gene which produced tall men, and sometimes tall women, which was to continue at least until the figure of Mary Queen of Scots, who at six feet was very tall for a woman in those times.

It is for this reason, among others, that Ashdown-Hill concluded that the bodies discovered in 1904 were those of Dame Joan of Acre and her son Edward Monthermer, who had also inherited the Plantagenet tall gene. Unfortunately, for them, both Lionel and his brother Edmund had also inherited something else, succinctly put by Agnes Strickland: "(They) were good-natured and brave; they were comely in features and gigantic in stature; they possessed no great vigour of intellect, and both were rather addicted to the pleasures of the table".[41] It would prove their undoing.

The slabs which were noted by Fr. Middleton, the Prior, when the author visited in January 2019, "paving slabs in the grass", are not recorded by William St. John Hope, or by Mrs. K. M. Barnardiston. They first appear on a plan in 1958 by Dickinson, who, however, seems to record their existence merely because they were paving slabs lying on the site in his day. It is therefore not certain that a real tomb site exists in this position. It is, therefore, possible, Ashdown-Hill concludes, that the Earl of March and Baroness Scrope were both interred in St. Vincent's Chapel, where two burial sites were identified by the recent (2016) GPR survey.

The final conclusion of John Ashdown-Hill was that the real location of the central burial site containing two re-interred bodies (one male and one female) is now incorrectly marked on site (as the slabs were probably moved between 1924 and 1958); that the genuine existence of a burial site on the north side of the presbytery is uncertain; and that as indicated in LC 03, the GPR survey suggests the existence of two small burial sites on the south side of the presbytery, towards the east, and one larger burial site a little further west on the southern side. It also suggests the existence of two burial sites in the Chapel of St. Vincent. When all this is further analysed, it does favour the "two small burial sites" as possibly those which contain the heart and bones of Long Lionel.

For the Prior, Fr. Middleton, it meant that the name of Elizabeth de Burgh had to be removed from the list of those buried at Clare. For him personally, entering what once was the hallowed site of the great Priory Church still recalled the day when he and his fellow seminary students made their profession on the same site as their forbears, kneeling or lying before the site of the original (and partly restored) altar in their white habits. This remembrance of a moving and seminal ceremony brought back the memory of the Abbey which Lionel knew so well and where he wished his bones to rest. His tumultuous life had led him as a mere youth to Ireland, where his first wife was the heiress of one third of the whole island, a third he could never bring to an efficient rule because of the failure of the English overlords to come to terms with what they called "the wild Irish". His first wife died soon after the birth of their daughter, Lionel's only child (who was later to marry into the Mortimer inheritance); he married Violante Visconti, niece of the ruler of Milan, thereby reviving the chimera of an English kingdom in Italy. This was doomed to failure like most of the others because the huge and life-loving Lionel behaved typically like the cartoon Englishman in Italy, taking no notice of the changes in diet and climate. Lovable and gentle as he was, he was his own worst enemy. On the other side, his in-laws, the Visconti, were anxious and ambitious to take their place in the higher society of the rulers of Europe, and the son of the English king (and such a king) was a major coup for them. The marriage took two years to negotiate. The Visconti had great wealth and local power. The dowry of Violante amounted to two million florins of gold, many Piedmontese towns, and castles, including Alba, situated in Montferrat, between Cherasco and Asti. On April 28, 1368, the marriage contract and treaty were signed at Windsor, and an instalment of the treasure paid down.

Lionel set out to fetch his bride, taking 457 men and 1,280 horses. He dallied in Paris, where he was sumptuously received by King Charles V, and the Dukes of Burgundy and Berri. Then at Chambery, he was magnificently entertained by the Count of Savoy, whose sister Blanche was the mother of the bride, Violante. The Count accompanied the bridegroom over the Alps to Milan. On May 27, they reached Milan, and the marriage was celebrated at the door of Milan cathedral on June 5, 1368. There were festivities of extraordinary magnificence; to the Visconti, this was their chance to display their wealth and culture to a wider world. Among those present at the wedding feast was the aged poet Petrarch, who sat among the greatest of the guests at the first table. Among others of future note was probably a page in Lionel's household, Geoffrey Chaucer, whose sister would later marry Lionel's brother. It was an extraordinary occasion. Another who was present was Lionel's confessor, Thomas Edwardstone, who died in 1396, and was afterwards a highly respected master at Oxford. He met Petrarch. On his return to Clare, he was chosen Prior, and by the time of his death was Archbishop of Nazareth, and, rather more realistically, a suffragan of Norwich.

Five months of continuous feasts, jousts, and revels followed, in the heat of an Italian summer. It is not surprising that Lionel's vast frame eventually rebelled against the strain and indulgence. In October, he was taken suddenly very ill "smitten by a sudden and violent sickness", when he was at Alba. Perhaps he knew quickly then that he would not recover, for he made a detailed will, already alluded to. On October 3, the will was drawn up, and on the October 7 he died (although accounts of the actual date differ).[42] There was, as was usual in Italy, suspicion of poison, but of this, his father-in-law could not have been complicit or guilty because he stood to lose so much by Lionel's death, and he was genuinely prostrated by news of his passing. Nevertheless, one of his devoted follows, Edward le Despenser, also distraught at the tragic end of the great adventure, declared opportunistically for the Church in the great contest going on between the Visconti and the Papacy and joined Hawkwood and his White Company in the war against Milan, until convinced of Galeazzo Visconti's innocence. It all ended in tears. More difficult to understand is the action of his widow, Violante, who finding herself without children, soon afterwards married Otto Paleologue, the Marquis of Montferrat, and with an ancestry older than that of Lionel, being of Byzantine stock. She, however, had been born under an unfortunate star, for shortly afterwards, he was assassinated. Perhaps Lionel was well out of this kind of ambiance.

It is as well to turn to the greatest contemporary chronicler, Jean Froissart, to consider what he had to say about these events. He was within the inner circle of the Plantagenet court, having been clerk to Queen Philippa and born the same year as her son Lionel. He was also present at Lionel's second, Italian marriage, and, he says, the guests danced to a vivelay "of his own composition". He describes the wedding feast,

> which had 30 courses, at the table, and betwixt every course presents of wondrous price intermixed; there were in one only course (presents of) seventy good horses, adorned with silk and silver furniture; and in another, silver vessels, falcons, hounds, armour for horses, costly coats-of-mail, breastplates glistering of massy steel, helmets, and corselets with costly crests, apparelled distinct with costly jewels, soldiers' girdles, and lastly certain gems of curious art set in gold and purple, and cloth of gold for men's apparel in great abundance. And such was the sumptuousness of that banquet that the meats which were brought from table would sufficiently have served 10,000 men.

One can almost imagine Froissart's pen dancing over the pages, as he recorded the word "costly" again and again.

But Froissart was there too to record the ending of it all. "But not long after Lionel, living with his new wife, which after the manner of his own country, as forgetting, or not regarding his change of air, he addicted himself overmuch to untimely banquetings, spent and consumed by a lingering sickness, (and) died at Alba." This last was in response to the question which hung in the air: "But as his death appeared extraordinary…". It is clear that this accounts very naturally for his premature end, without supposing it caused by treachery, as Stowe later recorded.[43]

Notes

1. Second Report of the Cathedral Committee (1888), pp. 46, 49.
2. Ibid., p. 58.
3. Memorials of the Cathedral & Priory of Christ Church in Canterbury, London (1912), p. 82.
4. Butler, John, *The Quest for Becket's Bones* (1995) quote.
5. Butler, John, *The Quest for Becket's Bones* (1995), p. 67.
6. Butler, op. cit., p. 73.
7. Butler, op. cit., p. 101.
8. Butler, op. cit., p. 102.
9. Ibid., pp. 104–5.
10. Ibid., p. 107.
11. L & P, Henry VIII.
12. Butler, op. cit., pp. 136–8.
13. Unpublished dissertation by Ann Newell (Northern Ireland) on Eileen, Countess of Kilmorey (2016).
14. Buckley, Veronica, Queen Christina, pp. 26, 97–8, 268.
15. Buckley, op. cit., n. 19. The most common form is Congenital Adrenal Hyperplasia (CAH), which accounts for about 60% of all cases of ambiguous genitalia in the newborn. CAH is the result of a biochemical defect which prevents certain steroids from being produced in sufficient quantities. As the body pushes the adrenal gland harder to increase the steroid level, more and more testosterone is made, encouraging masculinising traits in females. A female with CAH is technically a pseudohermaphrodite (organically female, but in appearance quite masculine). However, if Christina did suffer from CAH, hers would necessarily have been a mild case, since she would almost certainly have died in infancy, through salt wasting or insufficient cortisol. Other intersex conditions can also cause masculinising traits, in female sufferers, particularly after puberty. (Veronica Buckley acknowledges the help of Melissa Call of the UK Adrenal Hyperplasia Network for information in intersexual disorders.)
16. Sebba, Anne, That Woman (2011).
17. Buckley, op. cit., n. 20.
18. Ibid., p. 227.
19. Hjortson, Carl-Herman, Queen Christina of Sweden, A Medical/Anthropological Investigation into her remains in Rome, Lund (1966), C.W.K. Gleerup, Sweden, p. 2 et seq.

20. Bilt quoted (1897) and Stolfe (1960, 1961).
21. Essen-Moller quoted (1937).
22. Bilt (1897).
23. Martin, R. Lehrbuch der Anthropologie, Bd II (1928), Gustav Fisher-Jena.
24. Ingelmark (1956); Gejvall, Hjortso & Romanus (1962).
25. Scott, Franklin D., Sweden, University of Minnesota (1977), p. 143.
26. Erikson, lars, Johan III, ISBN: 91-85057-47-9.
27. Hjortson, op. cit., p. 14 et seq.
28. Essen-Moller, p. 68.
29. Ibid., p. 103.
30. Stolfe, S.; Drottning Kristina, Den svenska tiden (1960), Bonniers-Stockholm; Drottning Kristina, Efter tronavagelsen (1961), Bonniers-Stockhom.
31. Overzier, C., Die intersexualitat (1961), George Thieme, Stuttgart.
32. Hjortson, op. cit., pp. 14–16.
33. Vol. 101, National Archives of Sweden, concerning the exhumation of Erik XIV (1958) Konungahusens urkunder; Vasagraven I Uppsala domykyrka (1956), Gustav Vasa; Drottning Christina Gravoppningen I Rom (1965), Hjortson (1965).
34. Ashdown-Hill, John (1949–2018). He provided the funeral crown and rosary, to be placed on the tomb of Richard III in Leicester.
35. Ashdown-Hill, John, updated evidence in respect of the burial of Lionel of Antwerp, Duke of Clarence, and Others, in the choir of Clare Priory, Suffolk, 26 June 2016.
36. Nicols, J., Wills of all the Blood Royal (1770); Nicholas, N.H., (ed.) *Testamenta Vetusta*, London (1826), pp. 70–1.
37. Hingeston, F.C. (ed. Capgrave, J.) De Illustribus Henricis, 100 (sic. Actually 105), idem., Chronicle, 225–6.
38. Ashdown-Hill, op. cit., n. 5.
39. The Bishop of Norwich at the time was Thomas Percy (bishop from 1355–1369), although not consecrated until 1355. His successor was none other than Henry le Despenser (c. 1341–1406), an English nobleman known later as the "Fighting bishop", on account of his suppression locally in Norfolk of the Peasants' Revolt in 1381. He had fought in Italy with his brother Edward le Despenser, who took to the field against the Visconti after Lionel's death, in 1370. The brothers were cousins of Lionel, their grandmother being Eleanor de Clare, a grand-daughter of Edward I.
40. Hardyng, Chron. p. 334.
41. Strickland, Life of Philippa of Hainault, p. 352, in Lives of the Queens of England (1844).

42. Some authorities state the 17 October 1368. Sandford repeats that the way of life during the last five months of his life "probably cost the Duke his life by high living"; Sandford, The ceremonial of the marriage, p. 222.
43. Froissart, Sir John (c. 1337–1404), Chroniques, transl. from the French by Johns, Thomas (1839), Vol. I., pp. 382, 390.

CHAPTER 6

A Gothic Cult

On February 23, 1669, one Samuel Pepys was looking to celebrate his thirty-sixth birthday, and so set off for the theatre with his family. He ordered a conveyance, but then changed his mind, and decided, as it was Shrove Tuesday, to visit Westminster Abbey instead. His idea was to visit the royal tombs there. After Pepys and his family had seen the monuments, the Verger offered, for a small fee, to show them the body of Catherine de Valois, the wife, the widow of the famed Henry V, and then the wife of a Welsh adventurer named Owen Tudor. This lady had a famous story herself, and Pepys certainly wanted to see her body. Fortunately, it had become mummified. It was in a plain wooden box behind the altar, and had become "as leather" with mobile limbs. Pepys writes that he took the opportunity to take the lady in his arms and kiss her, so that he had this day, his birthday, "kissed a queen".

Today in England there would not be many who would kiss a corpse which was 232 years old, but Pepys's behaviour reflects how citizens of Charles II viewed such things, and during the next century such behaviour would reach proportions of which the solid, if mischievous Pepys, would have certainly disapproved. But how did the wife of a national hero and the daughter of the King of France, come to be in this invidious and less than appropriate condition?

When Catherine had died, in Bermondsey Abbey, in January 1437, she was the wife of a relatively obscure Welsh squire. She had only briefly been married to the warrior king, the young Henry V, and their only child, the

M. L. Nash, *The History and Politics of Exhumation*,
https://doi.org/10.1007/978-3-030-24047-9_6

future Henry VI, had been an infant when his father died. Catherine had been buried in Westminster Abbey in a plain tomb before the altar. It appears, however, that this was regarded as a temporary place, since the *Chronicles of Westminster Abbey* show that her son, the now reigning king, Henry VI, who was only fifteen when she died, later visited the Abbey with a view to deciding her proper resting place. The location, close to the high altar, was of the greatest importance, whilst the tomb appeared bare and unsightly. It was suggested that it might be moved a little lower down to make room for Henry himself. It could then be suitably decorated and inscribed. However, Henry VI, who is known to some historians as the "Holy Fool", because he was very pious and also very incompetent at governance, wished to be buried near to the tomb of Henry III, who had caused the present Abbey to be built. After his death, which occurred in the Tower of London, and is itself a mystery, in 1471, England was in the midst of a civil war, and it is not surprising, therefore, that a Yorkist king, Edward IV, or his advisers, thought that the wishes of a deceased Lancastrian sovereign held no importance, and his wishes were not respected.

Enter Henry Tudor, the grandson of Katherine of Valois and Owen Tudor, and the half-nephew of Henry VI. He twice visited the Abbey, with a view to arranging his own place of burial. These visits of kings intent on their burial tells us now a great deal about the mediaeval mind-set, which was about to radically change. He chose to be buried in front of the high altar, so Catherine was disinterred, and her coffin placed behind the high altar, probably with a view to her being placed in some other part of the Abbey at a later date. Henry VII intended to make her plain tomb something more resplendent, as he was always most anxious to impress his claim to the throne and used Catherine to strengthen that claim, even though he was descended from her second marriage. By an oversight, however, Catherine was left unburied. After the death of Henry VII, the responsibility rested with Henry VIII, but he had apparently little sympathy with the Abbey, and its contents, deciding to be buried himself at Windsor, which, unlike the wishes of his father, duly happened. He would not spare the money for a costly tomb for Catherine; and he even removed the silver from the tomb of Henry V, including the silver head. As we shall see in other chapters, Henry VIII, though outwardly pious and observant, became something of a grave robber.

Thus between 1509 and 1793, a period of nearly 300 years, the mummified body of Catherine of Valois could be viewed for a fee, and quite possibly handled, as Pepys had done, until she was at last decently buried, and placed again in a plain tomb, with an inscription, which she now occupies.

At the same period that Catherine's body was being dishonoured in this way, the public could see into the coffin of Richard II, whose portrait hangs so hauntingly in the Abbey, the first authentic portrait of an English sovereign. Richard had been buried by the Abbot of St. Albans in the Dominican Priory of King's Langley, after his mysterious death in 1400. This was the burial place of his elder brother Edward, so in this sense it was appropriate. Henry V, however, as if to make amends for the manner of his deposition and death, had the body exhumed and re-interred in Westminster Abbey. But the tomb was not well constructed, several side plates became loose, and it was possible to push items through the holes in the tomb and even to see the enclosed bones. Some of these, including the jawbone, were removed! One can only conclude that the holes were somewhat larger than "small". In 1880, somewhat late in the day, the tomb was repaired, and the various oddments which had been pushed through the holes, were removed. Not only that, but the missing jawbone was returned, perhaps by a guilt-ridden descendant of the original despoiler, and the tomb was at last firmly sealed and closed.

> In February, 1772, some workmen, digging among the ruins of the Abbey of St. Edmundsbury, in Suffolk, discovered a leaden coffin, supposed from some circumstances, to contain the remains of Thomas Beaufort, Duke of Exeter, the uncle of King Henry V. It has to be observed that the relatives of this king seem to be an unlucky lot according to this particular piece of research.[1] As it certainly was buried before the Dissolution of the Abbey, it must have been between two and three hundred years.

In fact, Thomas Beaufort, Earl of Perche and Duke of Exeter, had been born in 1377 and died on the last day of 1426, aged 49. He had been present at the death of the young king, Henry V, and was an executor of his will.[2] The discovery of the body in 1772 was therefore 346 years later. The body was, however, found "as perfect and entire as at the time of his death". How, therefore, had Thomas Beaufort died? He left no issue, as his only child, a son Henry, had died young. Thomas had married Margaret Neville, the daughter of Sir Robert Neville, Earl of Dorset, Lord of Lillebonne and Count of Harcourt (the mixture of French and English titles being normal at this time). But he was buried in Suffolk. Interestingly, when Thomas was enobled, in 1416, by his nephew Henry V, he was given the title Duke of Exeter *for life*.[3] Was this because there were no heirs, or did the young king fear his ambition?

But Dr. Collignon continues in his report: (The coffin) was found near the wall, on the left-hand side of the chapel of the Blessed Virgin; not enclosed in a vault, but covered over with the common earth. Upon examining the appearance of the body, the following circumstances were remarkable, as communicated to me, by an ingenious surgeon, on the spot, Thomas Cullum.

> The body was enclosed in a leaden coffin, surrounding it very close, so that you might easily distinguish the head and feet. The corpse was wrapped round with two or three layers of cere-cloth, so exactly applied to the parts, that the piece, which covered the face, retained the exact impression of the eyes and nose. The dura matter was entire. The brain was of a dark ash colour, with some remaining appearance of the medullary part. The coats of the eyes were still whole, and had not totally lost their glistening appearance. There was about half a pint of bloody-black water in the thorax; and a mass that seemed to be part of the lungs. The pericardium and diaphragm were quite entire. The abdominal viscera had been taken out very clean, and the integuments and muscles stuck very close to the vertebrae of the back. This cavity looked fresher than that of the thorax. I cut into the pfoas magnus, where there were evident marks of red muscular fibres. The other muscles had lost all their red colour, and were become of a dark brown. The tendons were still strong, and retained their natural appearance. The hands, which are preserved in spirits, retain the nails. There were some very small holes in the coffin, out of which had run some bloody water, of an offensive smell. All the principal blood vessels must have been cut through, in taking out the abdominal viscera; and if no ligature was made upon the vessels, their contents would escape, particularly as assisted by the pressure of the cere-cloth, which is of considerable weight, and doubtless put on hot. This fluid running out of the coffin, upon its being moved, might occasion the suspicion of the body being put in pickle.

Thus, continues Dr. Collignon, "so far Cullum's account, by which it appears, that the viscera of the abdomen had been taken out, so that the greatest part of the blood, he observes, did probably flow out, during that operation, from the mouths of the divided vessels, and whose diameter is considerable. This would greatly reduce the quantity of the fluids. The holes in the coffin, if purposely made, would seem designed to let out extravasated or transuding fluids; but are irreconcilable with the notion of the body being in pickle. If the holes were accidental, the notion of a pickle may still be allowed. Might not the cere-cloth, impregnated, perhaps, with gums or resins, and, from its taking so exact an impression, most probably laid on hot, preclude the external air; and, if done immediately after the party's death, obviate the deposition of eggs, or incapacitate them from ever hatching? The lead grasping close would co-operate with the cere-cloth, in the exclusion of air and insects.

We have undoubted accounts of bodies found very little changed, after long interment, where there was no appearance of any art having been used. And there is no doubt some constitutions are more prone to putrefaction after death than others; these circumstances may be dependent on the age, sex, and last disease; to which predisposing causes, thus attending persons to the grave, are to be added the soil and situation in which they are deposited. Could we be masters of all these particulars, in the few dead bodies hitherto discovered greatly free from the usual putrefaction, it would lead, perhaps, to the probable cause of the phenomenon, and point out a proper method of imitation. And till that is done, it is difficult to know how much merit is to be assigned to the art or mystery of embalming, and how much to the power of natural causes".

These observations added something to the canon of literature on the subject. Dr. Collignon's miscellaneous writings were published in 1785, the year of his death, but before this had happened, two other exhumations of great importance were recorded, one of them in Bury St. Edmunds (or St. Edmundsbury) itself. But two years after the discovery of the body of Thomas Beaufort, the Society of Antiquaries sought the permission of the Dean of Westminster to open the coffin of King Edward I. His body, interestingly, had been embalmed. Thus, on May 2, 1774, the honourable members found the body wrapped in a strong linen cloth, waxed on the inside, while the head and face were covered with a cloth of crimson sarsinet. The King was richly dressed in a red silk damask tunic with a stole of thick white tissue across his chest, set with filigree gilt metal, and semi-precious stones. Above these he wore a royal mantle of rich crimson satin. From the waist downwards, he was covered with a rich cloth of figured gold. In his right hand was a sceptre with a cross of copper gilt. In his left hand was a rod around five feet long, and a white enamel dove. On his head was a gilt metal crown. When they lifted the crown, his skull appeared bare, but his face and hands seemed intact. They measured the body at 6 ft. 2 in. long. Tall for the age he lived in, this had earned him the nickname "Edward Longshanks". Edward had died on his way to fight the Scots, yet again, on July 7, 1307. The symptoms, apparently, would suggest he died of cancer of the rectum. The attribution to "dysentery" was not the same as the modern understanding of it.[4] His body had then been embalmed, and brought south to be buried in Westminster Abbey, where it was enclosed in a tomb "starkly made in black Purbeck marble".

But why had the Society of Antiquaries specifically requested opening the tomb of Edward I? The answer is, apparently, because the members wished to look at authentic mediaeval costume, specifically royal attire. This was also the reason put forward for the opening of the tomb of King John at Worcester in 1797. However, Sir Joseph Ayloffe, a Fellow of the Society of Antiquaries, read a paper to the Society on May 12, 1774, concerning the opening of the tomb of Edward I. King Edward III, his grandson, aware of the reputation of his grandfather as being perhaps the greatest king England had had up to that point, repeatedly issued royal warrants, directed to the treasurer, and chamberlain of the exchequer, *De cera renovanda circa corpus regis Edward di primi*. His two successors, Richard II and Henry IV, both his own grandsons, continued to issue this warrant, so it had lasted at least from 1340 (the 13th year of the reign of Edward III) to 1415. But what exactly did this warrant entail, and why is such a warrant totally absent from the records concerning other sovereigns? What was this special treatment meted out to Edward I? Clearly, quite apart from an interest in mediaeval costume and regalia, Sir Joseph was interested, to a consuming degree, in the preservation and embalming processes of 1307, and what was done to reinforce this preservation. This all depended on the meaning of "*Cera*" in the warrant, and Sir Joseph spent no fewer than ten pages discussing the possibilities of its meaning, when applied to the preserved body of the dead king!

The will of the king, like most royal wills, and perhaps most wills, was both to cause trouble and to be ignored. The new king, Edward II, of a totally different character to his father, while at the same time possessing both his stature and his strength, had no appetite for continuing his military exploits. Edward I wanted his body to remain unburied and to be carried with his troops into battle until the Scots were finally subdued. Then he wanted his heart to be taken to Jerusalem, accompanied by 140 knights. However, in order to show some deference to the wishes of the great king, steps of an unusual kind were taken to preserve his body from putrefaction. Weever, in his *Funeral Monuments*, is the earliest writer to take notice of the warrants.[5] He says "Such was the care of his successors to keep his body from corruption, that the cearecloth, wherein his embalmed body was enwrapt, was renewed, as doth appear upon record".

Monsieur Rapin, following Weever, in his *History of England*, asserts that the body of King Edward was done over with wax.[6]

With these interesting questions in mind, it had been the Hon. Daines Barrington, also a member of the Society, who had proposed in 1770 that "the corpse of King Edward might be inspected, in order to examine the state of preservation in which it then was; and whether any remains of the composition, supposed to have been used to prevent its decay, were discoverable". He then, with some persistence, applied to the Dean of Westminster, Dr. John Thomas, through his learned friend, Dr. Blair, one of the prebendaries of that church, for leave to open the royal tomb.

These learned gentlemen were not of course motivated, as was the case in some of the other openings and exhumations, by morbid curiosity or Gothic frisson; this was, after all, their stock in trade. But nevertheless, the actual opening of the tombs and public knowledge being whetted, must have contributed to that stream of thought in some way.

The Dean, being a man of discretion and integrity, after some time decided to grant the request; after all, he may have been filled with curiosity himself, and certainly he was present on most of the subsequent occasions. His station and duty may of course have necessitated that, but he very likely shared the general interest. Nothing could be done, after all, without his permission. He fixed the second day of the month for its being opened; which was done, in the presence of himself and two of the prebendaries. The tomb was defended on the north side by a grating of strong ironwork. The upright bars of this grating terminated, at a height of five feet, with a fleur de lis; and the two standards, or end bars, finished in a busto of an elderly man with a long visage. Although rude in execution, this and two others clearly resembled the image of the king on his coins, his broad deal, and his statue at Caervarvon.

On opening the tomb…there appeared a plain coffin of Purbeck marble, laid on a bed of rubble stone, the coffin being six feet and seven inches long.…on lifting up the lid, the royal corpse was found wrapped up within a large square mantle, of strong, coarse, and thick linen cloth, diapered, of a dull, pale, yellowish brown colour, and waxed on its under side.

The head and face were entirely covered with a sudarium, or face-cloth, of crimson sarcenet; the substance whereof was so much perished, as to have a cobweb-like feel, and the appearance of fine lint. This sudarium was formed into three folds, probably in imitation of the napkin wherewith our Saviour is said to have wiped his face when led to his crucifixion, and which, the Romish church positively assures us, consisted of the like number of folds, on which the resemblance of the countenance was then instantly impressed.[7]

When the folds of the external wrapper were thrown back, and the sudarium removed, the corpse was discovered richly habited, adorned with the ensigns of royalty, and almost entire, notwithstanding the length of time that it had been entombed.

The innermost covering seemed to have been a very fine linen cerecloth, dressed close to every part of the body, and superinduced with such accuracy and exactness, that the fingers and thumbs of both of the hands had each of them a distinct envelope of the material. The face, which had a similar covering closely fitted thereto, retained its exact form, although part of the flesh appeared to be somewhat wasted.

It was of a dark brown, or chocolate colour, approaching to black; and so were the hands and fingers. The chin and lips were entire, but without any beard; and a sinking or dip, between the chin and underlip, were very conspicuous. Both the lips were prominent; the nose short, as if shrunk; but the apertures of the nostrils were visible. There was an unusual fall, or cavity, on that part of the bridge of the nose which separates the orbits of the eyes; and some globular substance, possibly the fleshy part of the eyeballs, was movable in their sockets under the envelope. Below the chin and under jaw was lodged a quantity of black dust, which had neither smell nor coherence; but whether the same had been flesh, or spices, could not be ascertained. (Could it have been the remains of the missing beard?)

One of the joints of the middle finger of the right hand was loose but those of the left hand were quite perfect.

Next above the before mentioned cere-cloth was a dalmatic, or tunic, of red silk damask upon which lay a stole of thick white tissue, about three inches in breadth, crossed over the breast, and extending on each side downwards, nearly as low as the wrist, where both ends were brought to cross each other. On this stole were placed, at about the distance of about six inches from each other, quatrefoils, of philigree work, in metal gilt, with gold, elegantly chased in figure, and ornamented with five pieces of beautiful transparent glass, or paste, some cut, and others rough, set in raised sockets. The largest of these pieces is in the centre of the quatrefoil; and each of the other four is fixed near to the angle, so that all of them together form the figure of a quincunx. These false stones differ in colour. Some are ruby, others a deep amethyst, some again are sapphire, others white, and some a sky blue.

The intervals between the quatrefoils on the stole are powdered with an immense quantity of very small white beads, resembling pearls, drilled, and tacked down very near to each other, so as to compose an embroidery of most elegant form, and not much unlike what is commonly called, The True Lover's Knot. These beads, or pearls, are all of the same size, and equal to that of the largest pin's head. They are of a shining, silver-white hue; but not so pellucid as necklace-beads and mock pearls usually are.

Over these habits is the royal mantle, or pall, of rich crimson satin, fastened on the left shoulder with a magnificent fibula of metal gilt with gold, and composed of two joints pinned together by a movable acus, and resembling a cross garnet hinge. This fibula is four inches in length, richly chased and ornamented with four pieces of red, and four of blue transparent paste, similar to those on the quatrefoils, and twenty-two beads and mock pearls. Each of these pastes and mock pearls is set in a raised and chased socket. The head of the acus is formed by a long piece of uncut transparent blue paste, shaped like an acorn, and fixed in a chased socket. (This motif of the acorn will have subsequent relevance.)

The corpse, from the waist downwards, is covered with a large piece of rich figured cloth of gold, which lies loose over the lower part of the tunic, thighs, legs, and feet, and is tucked down behind the soles of the latter. There did not remain any appearance of gloves.

Between the two forefingers and thumb of the right hand, the king holds a sceptre with the cross made of copper gilt. This sceptre is two feet six inches in length, and of most elegant workmanship. Its upper part extends unto, and rests on, the king's right shoulder.

Between the two forefingers and the thumb of the left hand, he holds the rod or sceptre with the dove, which, passing over his left shoulder, reaches up as high as his ear. This rod is five feet and half an inch in length. The stalk is divided into two equal parts, by a knob or fillet, and at its bottom is a flat ferule.

The top of the stalk terminates in three bouquets, or tiers of oak-leaves (hence the acorn?) of green enamel, in alto relieve, each bouquet diminishing in breadth as they approach towards the summit of the sceptre, whereon stands a ball, or mound, surmounted by the figure of a dove, with its wings closed, and made of white enamel.

The main stated purpose of the Society of Antiquaries in exhuming the king had been to see mediaeval costume and the regalia of the monarch at that time. This purpose seemed now almost to have been achieved, together with the other issue, which was to learn of the arts of embalming in the thirteenth century. The final piece of the regalia could now be viewed, although it must be remembered that even for a much venerated king, this did not mean that the actual crown, or real jewels, would actually be placed in the coffin. Sometimes they were, such as the sapphire ring of Edward the Confessor, but this had been extracted during one of his exhumations, and remains an important stone among the present crown jewels. "On the head of the corpse, which lies within a recess hollowed out of the stone coffin, and properly shaped for its reception, is an open crown or fillet of tin, or latton, charged on its upper edge with trefoils, and gilt with gold; but evidently of inferior workmanship, in all respects, to that of the sceptres and quatrefoils".[8]

The shape and form of the crown, sceptres and fibula, and the manner in which the latter is fixed to the mantle, or chlamys, exactly correspond with the representations of those on the broadseal of the king, as exhibited by Sandford, in his *Genealogical History of the Kings and Queens in England*".

In the seventeenth century, the engraver George Vertue made a series of portraits of what the former sovereigns were thought to look like; that of Edward I is clearly based on both the bustos on the grave railings and on the broadseal, and in that, it is reasonably accurate. There was of course, and still is, surviving, the effigy which adorned his catafalque during his funeral, before and after. This is said also to show traces of the stroke he suffered before he died.

No ring however could be found, and Sir Joseph assumed it had slipped off and could have been found among the folds of the robes. The feet, soles, and heels seemed to be perfectly entire; but again, whether they had sandals on he could not say, as the cloth was tucked all over them. This does raise the question of how he knew the feet were entire; perhaps he simply felt them through the cloth.

Then came another interesting question: the origin of the king's nickname, *Longshanks*. Many of the Plantagenets were tall, unusually tall for their times, which was a great advantage to a ruler.

> On measuring the body with a rod, graduated into inches divided into quarters, it appeared to be exactly six feet and two inches in length.(Some historians) tell us that he was taller by the head than any other man of his time. How far the appellation of *Longshanks*, usually given to him, was properly applicable, cannot be ascertained, since the length of the tibiae could not be truly measured, and compared with the femora, without removing the vest-

> ments, and thereby incurring a risqué of doing injury to the corpse…it has been conjectured that he obtained the nickname of *Longshanks* from a manifest disproportion of his thighs and legs to that of his body. But on inspection of the corpse, so far as could be done without removing the robes, no such disproportion was observable.

Interestingly, Sir Joseph does note that the height of the effigy placed on the tomb was six feet five and a half inches, but thought that this figure was "certainly made taller than the king". The cavity of the coffin was not capable of receiving a body of this length.

But why was Edward clothed in such grand attire? Sir Joseph thought this arose from the custom of exposing the corpse to public open and public view, either within the royal palace, or in some church, cathedral or monastery, until such time as they were deposited in their tombs. In Edward's case, this was doubly intended, because he was held in such esteem.

Sir Joseph then adds some interesting and important notes of previous royal exhumations. "Upon rebuilding the abbey church of St. Peter, Westminster, (Westminster Abbey) by Henry III, the sepulchre of Sebert, King of the East Angles, was opened, and therein was found part of his royal robes, and his thumb-ring, in which was set a ruby of great value".

In June 1766 (and thus within this Gothic period), some workmen, who were repairing Winchester cathedral, discovered a monument, wherein was contained the body of King Canute. It was remarkably fresh, had a wreath round its head, and several other ornaments of gold and silver bands. On his finger was a ring, in which was set a remarkable and fine stone; and in one of his hands was a silver penny.

In the reign of James II, upon searching the chest that contained the body of Edward the Confessor, there was found, under one of the shoulder bones of the royal corpse, a crucifix of pure gold, richly enamelled, and suspended on a golden chain, twenty-four inches in length, which, passing round the neck, was fastened by a locket of massy gold, adored with four large red stones. The skull, which was entire, had on it a list of gold or diadem, one inch in breadth, surrounding the temples; and in the chest lay several pieces of gold-coloured silk and linen.

In the year 1522, the tomb of William the Conqueror, in the Abbey Church of St. Stephen at Caen, was opened, and the body appeared as entire as when it was first buried, and royally cloathed; but were are not informed what the particular vestments were. There is an interesting addendum to this. A picture had been painted on what the royal corpse looked like and hung on the wall in the Abbey opposite William's monument, but it was removed when the Abbey was plundered by rioters under Admiral Chastillion. The picture then fell into the hands of one Peter Hode, the gaoler of Caen, and one of the rioters, who converted one part thereof into a table, and used the other as a cupboard door. These were discovered four years later, and reclaimed by M. de Bras, an officer of the town, and remained in his possession until his death; since then it is unknown what is become of them. A like fate overtook the wonderful portrait of Richard II, within the Abbey of Westminster itself, and was similarly discovered by John, Lord Lumley, being used as a basement door in the Abbey. He recognised it for what it was, and presented it to Queen Elizabeth I. Such is the treatment of those whose reputations wax and wane!

Forty years later, in 1562, the Calvinists broke open the tomb of William's wife and queen, Matilda, in the Abbey of the Holy Trinity at Caen, and discovered her body apparelled in robes of state, and having a gold ring with fine sapphire on one of her fingers. The Abbey had been founded by the Duchess, and was popularly called *L'Abbaye aux Dames*. The ring, inevitably, was taken off her finger, and given to the then abbess, Madame Anna a Montmorency, by whom it was presented to her father, the Baron de Conti, Constable of France, when he attended King Charles IX to Caen the next year, 1563.

In the reign of Charles I, the monument of William Rufus, second son of William and Matilda, in Winchester Cathedral, was opened, and therein was found the dust of that king, some reliques of cloth of gold (undoubtedly parts of the royal vestments) and a large gold ring. William II was named "Will le Rous" because of his red hair, but he was also later referred to as "The red dragon slain by a murderous dart", one of the prophecies of the Welsh wizard Merlin. Killed by an arrow while hunting in the New Forest, the main suspect, Walter Tyrrell, compounded the suspicions by fleeing to France. His body was brought to Winchester Cathedral in a cart, having been found by the charcoal burner Purkiss, and hastily buried. A year after his death, a bolt of lightning felled the tower of the cathedral, right onto the grave off Rufus. It was replaced by one "of very unroyal appearance". When the tomb was broken into by Parliamentary troops during the civil war, there was found a large gold thumb ring set with rubies, valued at £500, some of the remnants of cloth of gold in which he had been buried, and a small silver chalice, all found within his coffin.

His bones, and those of some of his royal predecessors, which had been rudely exhumed, had been collected on a previous occasion by Bishop Fox (c. 1448–1528), and carefully enclosed in a grey marble funerary chest, with those apparently of King Canute and Queen Emma. Strickland in the nineteenth century called this "a singular violation of royal etiquette, not to say propriety, to intrude the bones of the profligate bachelor king into the last resting place of so respectable a couple". "But", she went on, "It is so, and these ill-assorted relics of the royal dead, male and female, saint and sinner, remain packed up together in the same marble chest, placed on a low wall which separates the north side of the chancel from the aisle, in company with sundry other marble chests of the same fashion, containing (apparently) the bones of King Egbert and other Anglo-Saxon kings and prelates. This fear of "contamination by association" has lasted into the legal cases of the twenty-first century. Strickland ends this with a most memorable phrase, which could serve for all exhumations: "…suspended as it were between earth and heaven, a marvel and a moral to all beholders".[9]

The younger Henry, son of Henry II (often called "The Young King" because he was crowned in the lifetime of his father), but who died in 1183, six years before Henry II, was buried in the vestments that he had been consecrated in at that coronation.

When Henry II died in 1189, when prepared for burial, was dressed in royal apparel. He had a crown of gold upon his head, gloves in his hands, golden sandals, spurs on his heels, a great ring on his finger, the sceptre in his hand, and was girt with a sword. (Here, the learned Sir Joseph acknowledges that the historians Matthew Paris and Giraldus Cambrensis expressly contradict each other! But, he adds, "Giraldus does it in words that fully prove the general prevalency of the practice here spoken of". Sir Joseph should have been a politician).

The exhumation of King John, another truly "Gothic" incident, occurred in 1797, when the tombs in Worcester Cathedral were being repaired. Perhaps to atone for his rackety life, and scant attention to things spiritual, John insisted on being buried in a monk's cowl, denoting sanctity, something common to the Russian tsars. His body was exposed and one person, it is said, stole a finger bone from the coffin and had it encased in silver to keep as a memento.

When such things became known to the authorities, they took hurried steps to have the tomb re-sealed, but before these orders were carried out, much desecration had taken place, either from "mere curiosity or blatant vulgarism". One such incident almost defies the imagination. As Richard Haestier relates: "A particularly loathsome story is told regarding King John's body when it was exposed in 1797. It is to the effect that a native of the town (Worcester) baited his hook with a piece of the monarch's corrupt body. Having committed this almost unbelievable outrage, he caught a fish, whereupon he went screaming with delight through the streets, telling of what he had done".[10] While exaggeration and sensationalism must be considered here, nonetheless if the state of religion is remembered at this point, perhaps it should come as no surprise. On Easter Sunday, 1800, only six people took communion in St. Paul's Cathedral, whilst in Paris a prostitute was crowned goddess of Reason in the cathedral of Notre Dame.

Anticipating another important royal exhumation, that of Richard II, one hundred years later, Sir Joseph says that in reference to the above practice, that is, of dressing deceased sovereigns in royal robes and regalia, that Richard II, by his last will, directed that his body should be apparelled either in velvet or white satin, *according to royal custom*, and interred together with his crown and royal sceptre, but without any precious stones on them: and that likewise, according to royal usage, a ring, with a precious stone in it, of the value of twenty marks, should be put on his finger.

What is missing in the tomb of Edward I is the orb. After some dissertation on this, Sir Joseph concludes that in early coronations there is only the sword, the crown and the sceptre. By the eighth century this had expanded to include the armills, the pall, the ring, and the rod. Indeed, Thomas Walsingham is the earliest of English historians who mentions the orb as part of the regalia; but this may well have been because the sceptre and the orb were originally one. The practice of including gloves in the regalia, made of fine linen, was also part of the ancient coronation rituals and ceremonials.

The death wishes of Edward I, that his heart should be taken to Jerusalem, and his body with the troops to continue fighting the Scots, were not carried out. The corpse was removed from Burgh, where he died, with great funeral pomp; and many of the principal nobility, Peter, the Cardinal of Spain, and great numbers of the clergy, meeting it on the road, making processions, and assisting at the masses that were sung in all the churches where it rested. The body lay at Waltham was for seventeen weeks. At a parliament held at Northampton, fifteen days after Michaelmas (i.e. October 12th, 1307), the royal funeral was fixed for Friday, October 17. When it arrived in London, it was taken first to the church of the Holy Trinity, and on the second day, St. Paul's Cathedral. On the third day, it was taken to the church of the Friars Minor, and only after that was it brought to Westminster Abbey, in an open chariot. There, on the next day, when mass had been said by five bishops and the Cardinal of Spain, it was entombed in the chapel of Edward the Confessor. Anthony Beck, the Patriarch of Jerusalem, and Bishop of Durham, reading the last mass and the funeral service; the Bishop of Winchester, the gospel; and the Bishop of Lincoln the epistle. On the October 30, the young king, now Edward II, issued his writ to the Archbishop of Canterbury, commanding masses, dirges and prayers for the soul of the late king, in all churches and religious houses throughout his province.... At the same time, the Cardinal of Spain[11] granted one year's indulgence, and the Pope five, to all persons who should say a pater noster and an ave for the soul of the departed king.

This then brings one to the second question: how was the body of King Edward I preserved, especially remembering that he died in July in another part of the country and was now buried in Westminster until the middle of October? What is the real meaning of *cera renovanda*? This seems to indicate, through no fewer than eighteen times in the relevant warrants of Edward III, Richard II and Henry IV, after which they cease and no other sovereign is mentioned in this way. They relate either to the particular methods used to preserve the body from decay, or peculiar acts of devotion which were afterwards performed at the tomb of Edward I.

Weever and Rapin both say that the corpse was covered over with wax, when it arrived from Waltham to Westminster Abbey. Since it had been out of the grave for a long time (July to October) some extraordinary means must have been used for its preservation. It must have been necessary to renew the embalmment, but did this then proceed to "a yearly renewal of the antiseptic medicaments, and of the cerecloth in which the body was wrapped"? Was the *cera* the cere-cloth immediately next to the royal body, or the outermost wax wrapper in which it was found enclosed?

Wax had had used from earliest times for preserving bodies from putrefaction, but its later use involved not applying the wax like a plaster, but as one of the ingredients of the preservation process. Mixed and incorporated together, it was part of the antiseptic compound, wherewith the cere-cloths, used for wrapping up the corpses of kings and persons of high rank, were usually spread and impregnated. The other ingredients were a number of spices, sometimes very costly. There are many records afterwards of this being done, both in Plantagenet and Tudor England. When the coffin of Edward I was opened, Sir Joseph Ayloffe indeed noted that the vestments were strongly waxed on the underside and still had a faint aromatic smell. The idea that the cere-cloth itself could have been annually renewed, Sir Joseph rejected, because of the damage it would have done to the body. He came to the conclusion that *cera* meant no more than the frequent renewal of the wax lights which were kept burning about the royal sepulchre, and that a quantity of wax was delivered annually to the body on the anniversary of the king's *obit*. Henry IV had actually given lands to the keeper of the lamps about the tomb of the Duke and Duchess of Lancaster, his parents, for eight tapers to burn about that tomb, and to provide wax.

Thus concluded this particular exhumation. "After the spectators had taken a sufficient view, the top of the coffin, and the covering stone of the tomb, were restored to their proper places, and fastened down by a strong cement of terrace before the dean retired from the chapel".[12]

However, in a way there was a sting in the tail, as the biographer of Edward I, Michael Prestwich, relates: "The solemnity of the occasion was somewhat marred by fact that it proved necessary that one noted antiquary present 'should undergo a search for the embezzlement of a finger of the great Plantagenet'"![13]

The Gothic Cult had indeed infected even these "noted antiquaries".

But what had inspired the "Gothic Cult"? Not only in novels, but in poetry, a morbid interest had arisen inspired by the so-called "Graveyard Poets". An interest in decay, death, and morbidity; to achieve its effects, especially in the Italian Horror School, popularised by these poets, was added "Skulls, coffins, epitaphs, and worms". It was everywhere in Europe: not only in Italy, but in the French *Roman Noir* and the German *Schaueroman*. These poems and novels were read by an educated, or partly educated and moneyed elite and there were some surprising and to modern day mentality, reprehensible consequences. Moreover, the Gothic cult pushed out its frontiers until well into the nineteenth century, with Mary Woolstonecraft's *Frankenstein (1818)* and Edgar Allan Poe's *Fall of the House of Usher (1839)*, the latter full of the "Classic tropes of aristocratic decay, death and madness".

In 1782 perhaps the worst, and most reprehensible, exhumation of a royal body occurred. This was the body of Katherine Parr, who had been the last Queen of Henry VIII. Katherine had been married twice before she married the king, and, when he died, she left no time at all before she married the love of her life, Thomas Seymour, the brother of the Protector of her stepson Edward VI. Eighteen months later she died from the effects of childbirth, in a very similar way to the mother of Edward, Jane Seymour, sister of Thomas, and the third wife of Henry VIII. This was in September 1548. Her infant daughter Mary Seymour disappears into history. Her widower Thomas only survived her six months. The handsome and reckless adventurer was executed on orders of his own brother in March 1549. Tudor England was a dangerous place. Katherine Parr had died at Sudeley Castle, and she was originally interred on the north side of the altar of the then splendid chapel of Sudeley, and a mural tablet of sculptured alabaster was placed above her tomb. The chapel was afterwards despoiled, desecrated, and left in ruins, the roofless walls alone remaining.[14]

The scene in now May, 1782. Some ladies (in view of what was to happen we may use the term advisaedly), who happened to be at Sudeley Castle, presumably as guests, determined to examine the ruined chapel. One must take into account here the fever of Gothic excitement, which had been generated at this time by the novel of Horace Walpole, *The Castle of Otranto*, and the novels of Ann Radcliiffe, such as *The Mysteries of Udolpho*. These novels were of the school of "romance of terri or and curiosity, aroused by events apparently supernatural, but afterwards naturally explained".

Decay, death, and morbidity were associated with these early Gothic novels, along with corpses, skeletons and churchyards. The setting was that of convents, castles, monasteries, and abbeys, many of them in ruins. A picturesque and evocationive ruin was the perfect scenario. Sudeley subscribed to all of these.[15]

Observing a large block of alabaster fixed in the north wall of the chapel, they imagined that it might be the back of the monument that had once been fixed there. Led by this hint, they had the ground opened (presumably by a compliant servant or workman), not far from there, and not above a foot from the surface they found a leaden envelope, which they opened in two places, on the face and the breast, and found it to contain a human body wrapped in cere-cloth. Upon removing the portion which covered the face, they discovered the features, particularly the eyes, in the most perfect state of preservation. Alarmed with this sight, and with the smell which came from the cere-cloth, they ordered the earth to be thrown in immediately, without closing over the cere-cloth, and lead, which covered the face, only observing enough of the inscription to convince them that it was the body of Queen Katherine.[16]

It is just as if the "ladies" found they had gone far enough, and the curiosity suddenly became terror. Were they shamefaced at what they had done? Did they tell the owner of Sudeley, whose guests they were? How many women today would lead such an expedition, to find and inspect a dead body? However, they must have told someone, or the workman justifiably did, for in the summer of the same year, 1782, John Lucas, the person who rented the land on which the ruins of the chapel stood, removed the earth from the leaden coffin, which laid at a depth of two feet, or a little more, below the surface. On the lid appeared an inscription, of which the following is a true copy: "Here lyeth Quene Katharine, vith wife to King Henry VIIJth And after the wife of Thomas Lord of Sudeley high Admyrall of England and uncle to King Edward the vj. She died September MCCCCXLVVJ".

Lucas had himself the curiosity to rip up the top of the coffin, and found the whole body, wrapped in six or seven linen cere-cloths, entire and uncorrupted, although it had been buried upwards of two centuries and a half. He made an incision through the cere-cloths that covered one of the arms of the corpse, the flesh of which at that time was white and moist.[17] The perfect state in which the body of Queen Katherine was found affords a convincing proof that her death was not occasioned by poison (something in common with the discovery of the body of Thomas Beaufort), for in that case almost immediate decomposition would have taken place, rendering the process of embalming ineffectual, if not impossible.

In the Spring of 1784, the repose of the buried queen was again rudely violated by ruffians (as Miss Strickland calls them) when the royal remains were taken out of the coffin and irreverently thrown on a heap of rubbish and exposed to public view. An ancient woman, who was present on that occasion, assured my friend (says Miss Strickland) Miss Jane Porter, some years afterwards, that the remains of costly burial clothes were on the body, not a shroud, but a dress, as in life; shoes were on the feet, which were very small, and all her proportions extremely delicate; and she particularly noticed, that traces of beauty were still perceptible in the countenance, of which the features were, at that time, perfect, but, by exposure to the air, and other injurious treatment, the process of decay rapidly commenced.[18]

At last, in 1786, through the interference of the local vicar, the body was re-interred; but this was not before a scientific examination had been carried out by the Reverend Treadway Nash, historian of Worcestershire and Vicar of Eynsham, of Leigh, and erstwhile tutor at Worcester College, Oxford.[19] The following extract is from his report to the Society of Antiquaries:

"In October 14, 1786, having obtained leave of Lord Rivers (First Baron Rivers, 1722–1803), the owner of Sudeley Castle, with the Hon.

Somers Cocks, the writer,[20] proceeded to examine the chapel. Upon opening the ground, and tearing up the lead, the face was found totally decayed; the teeth, which were sound, had fallen. (One of these is on display in the twenty-first century). The body was perfect, but, out of delicacy, it was not uncovered. Her hands and nails were entire, of a brownish colour. The queen must have been of low stature, as the lead that enclosed the corpse, was just five feet four inches long. The cere-cloth consisted of many folds of linen, dipped in wax tar; and gums, and the lead fitted exactly to the shape of the body.

It seems, at first, extraordinary that she should be buried so near the surface; but we should consider that the pavement, and perhaps some earth, had been taken away since she was first interred. As she was buried within the communion rails, probably the ground was three feet higher than the rest of the chapel. I could heartily wish more respect was paid to the remains of this amiable queen, and would willingly, with proper leave, have them wrapped in another sheet of lead and coffin, and decently interred in another place, that at least her body might rest in peace; whereas, the chapel where she now lies is used for the keeping of rabbits, which make holes, and scratch, very irreverently about the royal corpse". Such fine sentiments interestingly are associated also with the innocence of other creatures!

He goes on: "The chapel seems a beautiful miniature of that belonging to Eton College".

The last time the coffin of Queen Katherine was opened, it was discovered that a wreath of ivy had entwined itself around the temples of the royal corpse, a berry having fallen there, and taken root at the time of the previous exhumation, and there had silently, from day-to-day, woven itself into this green, sepulchral coronal". There was nothing if not romance about the Reverend Treadway Nash. "A lock of hair which was taken from the head of Queen Katharine, after it had lain in the dust and darkness of the grave for nearly two centuries and a half, was kindly sent for my inspection by Constable Maxwell.[21] It was of exquisite quality and colour, exactly resembling threads of burnished gold in its hue; it was very fine, with an inclination to curl naturally. "The ruined chapel of Sudeley, with the very small remains of the castle, now a farmhouse, were visited by *Lawson, AD 1828*, and I am sorry to report that Queen Katharine's remains have not been re-deposited with the honour and historical respect due to the royal and noble lady; (thus wrote Agnes and Elizabeth Strickland) for instead of their being replaced within the walls in their own grave, and secured from further intrusion, they are buried in a lean-to building outside the north wall, in which divine service is sometimes performed, to preserve the right as a parochial church". How much better it would be to restore the chapel itself, for this purpose, and to erect a suitable monument to the memory of Katharine Parr. Surely some mark of consideration and grateful respect is due from this country to the memory of our first Protestant Queen (she clearly discounts both Anne Boleyn and Anne of Cleves, and it is true that the latter converted to Catholicism). Agnes and Elizabeth Strickland became almost too warm in their feelings of outrage: "…if the owner of the soil which covers her sacred dust does not endeavour to preserve her remains from further outrage, the Bishop of the diocese is called upon to devise some suitable protection, for the desecrated grave of this royal lady, to whom the Church of England owes the preservation of the University of Cambridge(!)".

Sudeley Castle has recently (it was 1844) been repaired, and some portion of it restored by Mrs. Dent the present possessor, who has also, we understand, placed a grated screen before Queen Katharine's monumental tablet, to preserve it from being carried away piecemeal, by the destructive and dishonest collectors of mementoes of celebrated persons and places; a species of relic-hunting which has caused of late years irreparable damage to many precious works of art, the ruin of some of the most venerable remains of antiquity, and in many instances, amounting to the crime of sacrilege. It is to be hoped that a practice of truly childish proportions and unconscientiousness, will be abandoned by all persons who imagine that they possess the slightest claims to good taste and good feeling. The time honoured memorials of historical facts are witnesses sacred to the cause of truth, and as such they should be venerated and protected from the outrages of ignorance and folly, in a nation whose greatest boast is the increase of refinement, which the increase of education is extending now, even to the humblest grades of life".

On reading this diatribe, most worthy as it is, one can almost feel the pen, or quill, becoming hotter by the minute, if it does not actually catch fire, but it is indeed the very antidote which was needed to correct and rectify the behaviour of what had gone on during the eighteenth century. However, among the "dishonest and destructive collector of mementoes of celebrated persons" was the greatest dilettante of the age, Horace Walpole, whose collection at Strawberry Hill not only contained a lock of the hair of Mary Tudor, Queen of France, but also a lock from the head of Edward IV, whose tomb had been opened in St. George's Chapel,

Windsor, in 1789. Ever since Stephen Langton had extracted some of Becket's bones during his first or second exhumation, it has, alas, been the practice of both high and low degree, and it still goes on.

But the rallying cry of the sisters Strickland was heeded, and when Agnes went to Sudeley in 1862 Mrs. Dent had by this time completed her restoration of the partially ruined buildings. Una Pope-Hennessey, who wrote Agnes's own biography in 1940, the biography of a biographer general, recounts how she describes the beautiful chapel with its splendid tessellated pavement, exquisite reredos, marble font, and the tomb and effigies of Katharine Parr, who can now boast the grandest tomb of any English queen, excepting Elizabeth. (One might question this, knowing that the whole of Peterborough Cathedral is the memorial of Katharine of Aragon). But for Agnes Strickland all had been put right. The raptures were now for the reparation. "it is well worth a pilgrimage to see it", she wrote, "and the beautiful Cotswold hills". But as Una Pope-Hennessey goes on, nothing could restrain Agnes Strickland once she had started. It was not the scenery, but the tomb, which caused her to versify. "…at Sudeley Castle are preserved some fragmentary notes (Una Pope-Hennessey writes that the current owner then, Major Dent-Brocklehurst, had been kind enough to copy the notes for her) entitled *Scenes & Tableaux for Sudeley Castle* and it is probable that Agnes was pressed by Mrs. Dent on her visit in 1862 to arrange a series of historical tableaux to celebrate the opening of the Castle once again".

Within the Abbey of Edmundsbury the main church contained the remains of the younger sister of Henry VIII, the elder Mary Tudor. Mary had married the ageing King of France, Louis XII, at her brother's insistence, in 1514, when she was eighteen and the king was fifty-two. He showered her with jewels of fabulous provenance and cost, and she was left a widow 82 days later.[22] Mary then married, firstly in Paris, and later in England, the man who had been sent to bring her back, Charles Brandon, the Duke of Suffolk, and Henry VIII's best friend. Henry was furious, because Mary was a valuable marriage pawn (she was also surpassingly beautiful), but Mary had escaped with a good number of the jewels, which she then gave to her brother, who was somewhat mollified. The rest of Mary's life was spent rather unadventurously, mostly at Westhorpe Manor in Suffolk; hence her burial in Bury St. Edmunds. She had been buried in the Abbey, as she had died in June 1533, at the age of thirty-seven, and before the dissolution of the monasteries; but in 1540, when all the monasteries, large and small, were being dissolved, Mary was exhumed and re-buried within the newly established Church of St. Mary.

In September1784, room was wanted for the communicants at St. Mary's altar, and the tomb was pulled down. This is in itself curious, because this was for most people a singularly unreligious age, and on Easter Day, 1800, for example, there were just six communicants in St. Paul's Cathedral in London; but perhaps the provinces set a better example. Everyone, apparently, had supposed that the tomb was a mere cenotaph, an empty tomb. But the queen's body was discovered, within the space formed by the stone slabs, lapt in a leaden case, somewhat resembling the human form. On the breast was engraved: "Marye, Queen of France, 1533, Edmund B". The body was in a wonderful state of preservation, a profusion of long fair hair…was spread over it; of this a handful was cut off by none other than a local baronet, Sir John Cullum, who, to give him his due, was also an antiquary.[23] Several of the other antiquaries present at the exhumation likewise possessed themselves of this abundant chevelure, which had resisted all the deforming powers of corruption. … at the beginning of the present century (wrote Agnes and Elizabeth Strickland in the 1840s) a lock of this queen's hair was advertised, lotted and puffed in the catalogue of the household furniture of a deceased Beccles antiquary, one of those who had taken it from her tomb; and it was knocked down to the best bidder, in company with chairs and tables, pots, spits, kettles, and pans. Very recently, continued the sisters, at the "utter desolation of Stowe" when the personnels of her descendants and representative, the late Duke of Buckingham, were sold, another lock of Mary Tudor's hair was publicly knocked down to a curiosity dealer.[24]

Each of these outraged ladies of the nineteenth century, writing of a more coarse and insensitive age, added something. They all agreed that an act of sacrilegious despoliation had been committed. It is true that in 1786, two years after the tomb was opened, hair from Mary Tudor's body was sold at public auction, and passed to the Marquis of Chandos and was sold, as the Misses Strickland had recorded, with the rest of the Duke of Buckingham's treasures in 1848. One of the locks of hair which was cut off was preserved in a locket and afterwards presented to Horace Walpole by Miss Farquier. Where are all these locks now? At least one of them is in the Museum of Bury St. Edmunds.[25] It is not, however, of that exquisite colour and quality which so enraptured the Reverend Treadway Nash in 1786. Now it seems grey and old, which indeed it is, but at least we have it.

Francis Ford, writing of the Funeral and after of Mary Tudor, in 1882, noted that when her hair was cut off in portions, it was nearly two feet long, and that one of these portions was sent to the Dowager Duchess of Portland by Sir John Cullum, who was present at the exhumation, and a paragraph published in the *Bury and Norwich Post* on July 5, 1786, states that this lock was sold for six guineas at the sale of the Duchess's effects that same year. The following remark appended to the paragraph is sufficient to show the extent of the spoliation committed, and the shocking indifference with which it was regarded in those days:

> The lovers of antiquity may deem it satisfactory to be informed that many persons in this town are in possession of the like relic, taken from the corpse at the same time, which, we have no doubt, they will gladly dispose of on such advantageous terms.

This particular lock referred to passed into the possession of the Marquis of Chandos, and was sold with the rest of the Duke of Buckingham's treasures at Stowe in 1848, as has been seen.

In addition to this, the tomb was removed, and the coffin was deposited just below the level of the pavement, where it still remains, beneath the slab of Petworth marble, marked with five crosses, which covered the original structure. For a time, Dr. Symond's inscribed tablet occupied a panel beneath the east window, but it was subsequently removed to its present position on the north side of the sacrarium, two or three yards west of Mary's last resting place.

Mary's Book of Hours of the Virgin, of the fifteenth century, with elaborate illuminations by a French or Flemish artist, formerly belonging to "Marye the Quene", was disposed of in 1874 at the sale of Sir William Tite's library, and is now in the library of Queen's College, Oxford.

The good writer concludes "the chief object (of the work) is to keep alive the memory of Mary Tudor in the neighbourhood with which she is so intimately connected, and in the town which has the custody of her mortal remains, nevermore, it is hoped, to be disturbed by the hand of man".

Agnes Strickland would have been proud to have found a fellow champion for the worthy cause of her reparation.

In 1788, Parliament passed a law to restrain the growing commerce in corpses, which gangs known as the "Resurrection Men" were engaged in, robbing cemeteries and churchyards of fresh corpses to supply the medical men who wanted them for dissection and for student demonstrations.

Inevitably, men like Burke and Hare later on would miss one step out, and go straight for convenient murder, rather than exhuming recent corpses.

The tomb of Edward IV was rediscovered in 1789, three years after the examination carried out by Treadway Nash on the remains of Mary Tudor. This was during restoration work on St. George's Chapel. When the coffin was opened, some long brown hair was found near the skill, with shorter hair of the same colour on the neck of the skeleton. In the bottom of the coffin was a dark liquid, which immersed his feet to a depth of three inches. A physician at Windsor analysed the liquid and concluded that it was from the dissolution of the body. After the discovery of the tomb, many relics were removed, including locks of the king's hair and a phial containing some of the liquid. One is tempted to conclude that this type of collection mirrored the relic collectors of pre-Reformation times; and that this was the Age of Reason, Georgian England. It seems that this is a pattern of human behaviour which will always be there in some form or other.

Edward's skeleton was found to measure six feet three inches and his long brown hair was still in perfect preservation.[26] It is interesting now to look at the will of Edward IV, which had been written on June 20, 1475, eight years before he died. Edward had issued Letters patent authorising the rebuilding of St. George's Chapel, Windsor, to Bishop Beauchamp (June 12, 1475). The Bishop was to be Overseer of Works to demolish all existing buildings on the site. The will was made just eight days after the authorisation, and must have clearly contained something concerning Edward's own burial and tomb, but unfortunately the original has not survived. A copy, however, had been made by Thomas Rymer.[27] The copy was shown to commemorate the Quintenary of the Chapel in 1975, and had been presented to the Society of Antiquaries by Bentley. The will provides for the completion of St. George's Chapel, and for the burial of Edward within it, "lowe in the grownde".[28] Edward followed the authorisation and the will with a Charter of Confirmation of privileges to the Dean and Canons on December 6, 1479.

The tomb of King John was next. In 1797, in Worcester, it was opened for an antiquarian study. A robe of crimson damask had originally covered his body, but most of the embroidery had deteriorated. This was not surprising, as John had been buried in 1216. The remains of a sword and parts of a scabbard lay at his side. His body was found to be five feet six and a half inches tall. The circumstances of his death were not conducive to good order, in company with his life. He had died during the night of October 18, 1216, at Newark Castle, and his remains were escorted, not by his own soldiers, but by a company of mercenaries, to be buried in Worcester Cathedral.

There has always been some controversy over the positioning of John's tomb in the cathedral, because he is flanked by the tombs of two saints, Wulfstan and Oswald, and King John was singularly irreligious in his life. The most interesting part of opening John's tomb was that he was also shrouded in a monk's cowl, worn to act as a passage through purgatory. This practice, interestingly, has often been practised in Russia, especially by the early dynasty of Rurik. It is said that the exposure rapidly turned the remains to dust, but this is at variance with other reports, some of them very local.

Richard Haestier states that John's body originally had been "wrapped in bull's hides". The monk's cowl was apparently at John's own request, as it was part of the insignia of a holy monk. Clearly, on the brink of death, John was hedging his bets. Like many irreligious persons, John was very superstitious. The placing of his body near to the two saints means that he probably shared the popular belief then that evil spirits would not venture near the grave of a man of sanctity, and here were two of them, on either side. Thus, the resting place offered protection, and ensured peace.

But, as has been seen, his body was exposed during the repairing of the cathedral in 1797. Someone, it is stated, stole one of the finger bones from the coffin. It seems inevitable that this was going to happen at this time. Security was lax; the exposed body was sometimes left alone. The thief had the finger encased in silver as a memento. Before the tomb was resealed, much desecration had taken place, either from mere curiosity or blatant vulgarism, as Haestier notes.[29]

The Gothic Age was certainly not over, and the worst instances of the trade in corpses and relics were still in full operation. "Romantic" figures of history came in for much interest among writers, historians and novelists. Among the leading figures were Mary Queen of Scots and her grandson Charles I of England. Both of them were executed, Mary in relative privacy but Charles in full public gaze. Thus, when the tomb of Charles I was found in 1813, during the construction of a tomb for George III (who, incidentally, was still alive, and living in another part of Windsor Castle) it attracted great interest. Workmen accidentally broke through to the vault of Henry VIII. The fact that the tomb was opened was reported to the Prince Regent, who agreed to examine the contents of Charles's coffin in the presence of the ill-fated royal physician, Sir Henry Halford.[30]

…on removing the pall, a plain leaden coffin, with no appearance of having ever been enclosed in wood, and bearing the inscription KING CHARLES 1648 (*) in large legible characters, on a scroll of lead encircling it, immediately presented itself to view. A square opening was then made in the upper part of the lid, of such dimensions as to admit a clear insight into its contents. These were an internal wooden coffin, very much decayed, and the Body, carefully wrapped in cere-cloth, into the folds of which a quantity of unctuous or greasy matter, mixed with resin, as it seemed, but had melted, so as to exclude, as effectively as possible, the external air. The coffin completely full; and from the tenacity of the cere-cloth, great difficulty was experienced in detaching it successfully from the parts which it enveloped. Wherever the unctuous matter had insinuated itself, the separation of the cere-cloth was easy, and when it came off, a correct impression of the features to which it had been applied were observed in the unctuous substance. At length, the whole face was disengaged from its covering. The complexion of the skin was dark and discoloured. The forehead and temples had lost nothing of their muscular substance; the cartilage of the nose was gone, but the left eye, in the first moment of exposure, was open, and full, though it vanished almost immediately; and the pointed beard, so characteristic of the reign of King Charles I, was perfect. The shape of the face was long oval; many of its teeth remained; and the left ear, in consequence of the interposition of the unctuous matter between it and the cere-cloth, was found entire.

It was difficult, at this moment, to withhold a declaration that, notwithstanding its disfigurement, the countenance did bear a strong resemblance to the coins, the busts, and especially to the pictures by Van Dyke, by which it has become familiar to us. It is true that the minds of the spectators of this interesting sight were well prepared to receive this impression; but it is also certain that such a faculty of belief had been occasioned by the simplicity and truth of *Herbert's narrative* every part of which has been confirmed by the investigation, so far as it had advanced. It will not be denied that the shape of the face, the forehead, an eye and the beard are the most important features by which resemblance is determined. When the head had been completely disengaged from the attachment which confined it, it was found to be loose and without any without any difficulty was taken up and held to view. It was quite wet, and gave a greenish tinge to paper and linen, which touched it. The back part of the scalp was entirely perfect and had a remarkable fresh appearance; the pores of the skin being more distinct as they usually are when soaked in moisture; and the tendons and ligaments of the neck were of considerable substance and firmness. The hair was thick at the back part of the head, and in appearance nearly black. A portion of it, which had since been dried and cleaned, is of a beautiful dark brown colour. That part of the beard was of a redder brown. On the back part of the head, it was no more than an inch in length, and had probably been cut so short for the convenience of the executioner, or perhaps by the piety of friends soon after death, in order to furnish memorials of the unhappy king.

On holding up the head, to examine the place of separation, the muscles of the neck had evidently retracted themselves considerably and the fourth cervical vertebra was found to be cut through its substance transversely, leaving the divided portions perfectly smooth and even, an appearance which could only be produced by the heavy blow inflicted with a very sharp instrument, and which furnished the last proof wanting to identify King Charles the First.

And so Charles was returned to his resting place. When this was done, the fourth cervical vertebra, which had been described, was found to be left out, most probably by design. Either the Prince Regent agreed to Sir Henry Halford retaining this as a memento, or Sir Henry Halford retained it without drawing it to the attention of those present. He then had it mounted to use as a salt cellar. (Truly, in this sense, he was a true Gothic Georgian, and a relic collector with the best of them).

In 1888, it was returned to the Prince of Wales (later Edward VII), who decided, with the permission of his mother, Queen Victoria, that it should be restored to the tomb. Accordingly, this was done, on December 13th, 1888. A small lead and wooden casket was made, and was engraved with details of its contents. This was lowered through a small hole in the floor of the chapel so that it rested on the velvet pall of the coffin.

This small but significant ceremony was recorded in detail in *The Annual Report of the Friends of St. George's, to 30th September, 1965.*[31]

December 13th, 1888.

This evening I witnessed, and took part in, a deeply interesting occurrence in St. George's Chapel. In the year 1813, the coffin of Charles I was opened and examined in the presence of the Prince Regent, the Duke of Cumberland, the Dean of Windsor and some others, including Sir Henry Halford, the Court physician.

The coffin lies in the same vault as Henry VIII, and of the Queen Jane Seymour and that of an infant of Queen Anne. (Her other infants were buried in the tomb of Mary Queen of Scots in Westminster Abbey). The vault is situated a few feet in front of the Altar steps at St. George's and the crown of it is close beneath the pavement of the Chapel. When King Charles's coffin was opened in 1813, Sir Henry Halford managed to extract the beard of the king, the vertebra of the neck which was severed by the executioner's axe, and a tooth from the jaw. These relics were subsequently preserved in the family of Sir Henry Halford and eventually came into possession of his grandson, who not long ago sent them to the Prince of Wales (the future Edward VII). It was the wish of the Prince that the relics should be replaced in the vault from which they had been taken 75 years ago, and he took the opportunity at Windsor this week to carry out his wish. (it is interesting to realise that the Prince would have been at Windsor to mark the melancholy anniversary of his father's death, which took place on each December 14th, the next day, and became an obligation placed on all by Queen Victoria. It was known to the family as "Mausoleum Day").

The relics were placed in the hands of the Dean, who had a suitable case of lead made for them with an inscription saying what they were, how they came to be taken away, and that they were replaced by the Prince of Wales. The Prince also himself wrote a few lines to the same effect on a sheet of notepaper, which was placed inside the case.

I saw the relics at the Deanery before the case was finally closed. The King's beard was of a brown colour, short and rather curled at the end. It was wrapped in a piece of paper which he apparently got from the Dean of Windsor, whose name was on it. (This was Canon Dalton).

The vertebra of the neck was cut clean through by the axe or sword of the executioner. The tooth was an eye tooth. These relics, as I have said, were placed in a leaden case, which was prepared for them, and the leaden case was then screwed down in a wooden box, about a foot square in size.

As soon as the 5 o'clock evensong was over in the Chapel (it was dark in December) and the lights were all put out, the work of opening the vault was commenced. The Dean, Canon Dalton, and myself were present, and three workmen, under the direction of Nutt, our chapter architect. (The workmen, always essential to these operations, are not named, as they will not be named at the opening of the Urn of the Princes in the Tower, in 1933). The doors of the Chapel were locked to prevent any intrusion and the work was carried out by the light of a few candles. (There is so often an air of skulduggery about these proceedings, lending a Gothic element to it, whether deliberately or accidental it is not possible to say).

A portion of the pavement having been removed, we came immediately to the crown of the vault, and in this, a square hole was carefully made. We then tied two candles to the end of a long stick which was put down into the vault. The four coffins were at once clearly seen. Henry VIII lay in the centre and on his left lay Queen Jane Seymour a little way off. On his right, quite close, was King Charles, and lying at the foot of his coffin was the tiny coffin of Queen Anne's infant.

We made a close examination of all we could see. The outer wooden coffin of Queen Jane had quite fallen away, but the leaden coffin was perfect and unimpaired. Henry VIII's coffin of wood was quite destroyed. The inner coffin of lead was all open at the top so that I could see into it, and there lay the bones and skull of the King as they had been lying for 350 years. I did not see the whole of the skeleton as it was partially covered by the pieces of the wooden coffin which had fallen across it, but I saw many of the bones and skull.

King Charles's coffin was quite uninjured (but then had it been restored somewhat in 1813?) and it was still covered with the black velvet pall, which had been placed over it at the time of the funeral. There was also a broad band of lead across it on which the date was clearly cut (1648).

At half past seven the Prince of Wales arrived, quite unattended. He first shook hands with us, and then going down on his hands and knees he looked into the vault while we held the candle for him and pointed out the different coffins to him. He spent some time looking in, and was greatly interested, as he could not fail to be.

The box with the relics was brought to him, and again going down on his hands and knees he let it down by a handkerchief, until it rested on the coffin of King Charles, where it was left. He then remained talking to us for a few minutes longer, and before he left he requested that we would see the vault securely locked again.

As soon as he was gone, the workmen, who had been sent away, were brought back, and the vault was then closed in our presence, after which the pavement was replaced over it. A short statement of what had taken place was then drawn up in order that, with the Queen's permission, it might be sent to the Newspapers!

This small and covert operation was in line with the tradition of royal funerals, which had always taken place at night, something not changed until the twentieth century. The replacement of the relics was of course only necessary because the royal physician had taken these things from the royal body.

But it was not only Sir Henry Halford who had his mind on a relic in 1813. An article in the *Sunday Telegraph of 20th September, 1987* confirmed not only the story of the salt cellar made from a vertebra of a dead king, but that also in 1813 a workman had removed a finger from the body of Henry VIII, nearby to Charles I, and had it made into the handle of a knife. Truly, the Gothic cult continued.

To conclude the exhumations during this period, one should include that of Henry IV, which occurred in Canterbury Cathedral in 1832.[32]

When the coffin was opened, the face of the deceased was seen in complete preservation. The nose elevated, the cartilage even remaining, though on the admission of air it shrank away, and had entirely disappeared before the examination was finished. The skin of the chin was entire, of the consistency and thickness of the upper leather of a shoe, brown and moist; the beard thick and matted, and of a deep russet colour. The jaws were perfect and all the teeth in them, except one foretooth, which had probably been lost during the king's life. The surveyor stated that when he introduced his finger under the wrappings to remove them, he distinctly felt the orbits of the eyes prominent in their sockets. The flesh upon the nose was moist, clammy and of the same brown colour as every other part of the face".

The age of sensitivity, to say nothing of squeamishness, had certainly not yet dawned (Figs. 6.1, 6.2 and 6.3).

Fig. 6.1 The coat of arms of Thomas Beaufort, Duke of Exeter, died 1427. Now in the Moyse's Hall Museum in Bury St Edmunds, Suffolk. (Courtesy of St Edmund's Bury Borough Council Heritage Service)

Fig. 6.2 The hair of Thomas Beaufort, Duke of Exeter, died 1427. Now in the Moyse's Hall Museum in Bury St Edmunds, Suffolk. (Courtesy of St Edmund's Bury Borough Council Heritage Service)

Fig. 6.3 A lock of the hair of Mary Tudor, sister of Henry VIII, now in the Moyse's Hall Museum in Bury St. Edmunds, Suffolk. (Courtesy of St. Edmund's Bury Borough Council Heritage Service)

Notes

1. *Some accounts of a body lately found in uncommon preservation, under the ruins of St. Edmundsbury, Suffolk; with some reflections upon the subject* by Charles Collignon, M.D., F.R.S., Professor of Anatomy at Cambridge (1725–1785); Professor from 1753.
2. Nash, Michael L: Royal Wills from 1509 to 2008, Palgrave (2017) in which mention of the will is made.
3. Dugdale's Baronetage, ii. 25.
4. Brewer, Clifford, *The Death of Kings*, p. 58.
5. Weever, *Funeral Monuments.*
6. Rapin, Monsieur, *History of England.*
7. Ayloffe, Sir Joseph, Society of Antiquaries, *Paper given on the opening of the tomb of Edward I*, 12 May 1774.
8. The "open" crown meant that there was now enclosure at the top with material, such as velvet.
9. Strickland, Agnes, *Lives of the Bachelor Kings of England* (1861), p. 95.
10. Haestier, Richard, *Dead Men Tell Tales* (1934), p. 47.
11. "Peter the Cardinal" was in fact Peter the Spaniard, Cardinal-Bishop of Santa Sabina, and Papal Nuncio to England. He had been Bishop of Burgos, and papal referendary, before being raised to the purple by Pope Boniface VIII. Castilian by birth, he was a man of intense loyalty, both at a time of a divided papacy and disputes among the Spanish dynasties. Late in 1306 Pope Clement V had sent him to England, where he was entrusted with the completion of peace between the kings of England and France. Edward I was happy to entrust his son, soon to be Edward II, to him, "as he (Edward) is of Spanish descent" (his mother being Eleanor of Castile, the first queen of Edward I). Edward the Prince of Wales obviously related well to Peter, and sent him a magnificent cope embroidered with pearls, which cost £60. He was there when consent was given for Edward to marry Isabella, the daughter of the King of France, a marriage ill-fated from the outset; and Peter was present at all the stages of the journeys and final interment of the body of Edward I. By far the best account is that given by Hilda Johnstone, of the University of Manchester, in her book on the apprenticeship of Edward II (1946), pp. 118–21.
12. Ayloffe, op. cit., *Archaeologica* (1775), pp. 376–413.
13. *Transactions of the Bristol & Gloucestershire Archaeological Society, iv. (1897–80)* quoted in Prestwich, p. 567.
14. Strickland, op. cit., *Lives of the Queens of England* (1844), pp. 131–5.
15. The "Gothic" novels, generally considered to have begun with *The Castle of Otranto: A Gothic Story* (1764) by Horace Walpole.
16. Quoted from *Archaeologica (Transactions of the Society of Antiquaries).*

17. Rudde, *History of Gloucestershire.*
18. Jane Porter was an historical novelist in her own right (1776–1850). She was fascinated, along with a legion of other women, by Lord Byron, the dark archetypal hero of the Gothic age.
19. *Archaeologica*, vol. ix (1787) which indicates a facsimile of the inscription, and a view of the exterior of the beautiful chapel.
20. *Cocks, John Somers (1760–1841)* married Margaret, daughter of Treadway Russell Nash, and so was his son-in-law.
21. *"Constable Maxwell"*, was probably Lady Matilda Maxwell, a contemporary of Agnes and Elizabeth Strickland. She was a Scot.
22. Nash, op. cit., *Royal Wills etc.* (2017) *The Jewels of the Kingdom.*
23. Sir John Cullum, 6th baronet (1733–1785).
24. Strickland, op. cit., *Lives of the Tudor Princesses* (1868); Green, Mary Everett, *Princesses of England* (1854) Vol. 5; Tytler, Sarah, *Tudor Queens & Princesses* (1896), pp. 192–3.
25. I am indebted here to Daniel Clarke, Heritage Officer, Moyse's Museum, Bury St. Edmunds, for sending me the pictures and the report by Dr. Collignon, on 7 April 2017.
26. Davies, Katherine, *The First Queen Elizabeth* (1937).
27. Rymer, Thomas, (1641–1713) *Foedera*, reprinted in Samuel Bentley's *Excerpta Historica* (1831), p. 367.
28. The will of Edward IV. See Nicols, J. (1780).
29. Haestier, Richard, op. cit., *Dead Men tell tales* (1934), pp. 23, 47.
30. A very good description of what followed is taken from an article by A.A. Mitchell in *History Today* (1966).
31. Article by Dr. Fellowes in a pamphlet entitled *Memoranda Concerning King Charles I.* The account was based on an eye-witness description by Dean Randall Davidson which is in the Chapter library. By the kindness of Commander C.J.M. Eliot, RN, it is now possible to make generally known a second description of what happened on this occasion; compiled by his grandfather, Canon Philip Eliot (Canon from 1886–1891) and then Dean (1891–1917).
32. *Archaeologica*, Vol. XXVI (1832), p. 444.

CHAPTER 7

The Odour of Sanctity

One reason for exhumation and removal of bodies is to honour the remains of someone considered illustrious. If that person was proclaimed a saint (not *made* a saint, there being no such thing), then the possession of the body in a more suitable location is all to the good. The founding of Venice, for example, necessitated the bodies of various saints being put into the foundations of the new city.[1]

> Bodies—more or less entire—were exhumed, purchased, or stolen, from scenes of fierce martyrdom, or from quiet resting places, and reverently conveyed in Venetian galleys to the Lido for distribution among the churches of the Lagunes. Each translation was an exhibition of manly abasement and womanly devotion: Doge and Dogaressa, no less than the poorest of the poor, took part in the ecstatic ceremonial. Each saintly personage had ascriptions of peculiar benevolence and became the centre of special devotions; indeed, many of the holy shrines were regarded as objects of perpetual pilgrimages.

A list of the bodies of saints enshrined in Venetian churches was published in 1519 by Giacomo Zoppi in Venice. They came from Chios, Alexandria, Acre, Samos, Constantinople, Roumania, San Paolo (head wanting!) Saragosa, Zara, Nicomedia, Ancona, Miraea, Sinai, Morea, Aste, Moravia, Armenia, and Aquileia.

But sometimes these intentions go awry.

The beatification of John Henry Cardinal Newman in 2014 was a case in point. Of course his body would have now to be moved to a more

M. L. Nash, *The History and Politics of Exhumation*,
https://doi.org/10.1007/978-3-030-24047-9_7

suitable location, where it could be venerated, and the shrine touched by the faithful. After all, he had been buried in 1890 in the Lickey Hills in Worcestershire, by his own express orders. It was a secluded rural cemetery, as John Cornwell relates in his revealing and reflective volume on Newman.[2]

Thus, in anticipation of his more elevated status, the grave was excavated with the utmost care on October 2, 2008. During the excavation, the brass inscription plaque which had been on the wooden coffin in which Newman rested was recovered from the grave. It read: (English translation, the original being in Latin) "The Most Eminent and Most Reverend John Henry Newman Deacon of St. George in Velabro Died 11 August 1890." Brass, wooden, and cloth artefacts from Newman's coffin were found. However, there was not a trace of his actual body. One may ask, how come cloth survived, but not bone, and what was this cloth anyway? Has it been subjected to testing? The wood presumably came from the coffin.[3]

More surprises were in store. It was explained by the Fathers of the Birmingham Oratory that on Newman's express orders his grave was filled with a rich mulch to hasten decomposition. When one takes into account that the graveyard was situated on saturated clay, "the mystery of the vanished remains is more or less resolved". "More or less" always gives room for some doubt.[4]

Newman, according to his own repeated wishes, shared his last resting place with a close friend, Fr. Ambrose St. John, who had died fifteen years before him. Nothing was found of his remains either, although the mechanical digger employed for the exhumation removed the soil down to eight feet. Because they had been buried together, there were inevitable rumours that the relationship might have been more than close, and, in today's terms (which of course they did not know), they were gay. Fr. Ian Kerr, who was a Newman scholar, was interviewed by Jeremy Paxman, and stated emphatically, that, on all the evidence, Newman was "heterosexual". Nevertheless, on the day of the exhumation, the graveyard was guarded by members of the local constabulary lest Gay Rights demonstrators should intrude upon the scene to cause an affray. No such insult occurred.[5]

Nevertheless, Newman was fulsome in his insistence on being buried with Ambrose St. John. A year after the latter's death, Newman wrote in his notebook on July 23, 1876, a notebook carefully kept by his devoted secretary William Neville:

> I wish with all my heart, to be buried in Fr. Ambrose St. John's grave—and I give this as my last, my imperative will.

This was not all. In February 1881, Newman added this instruction to the above: "This I confirm and insist on", to which he then added, "and command". He could not have been plainer: "confirm, insist, command, wish with all my heart".

Throughout history, there has been evidence of intense male relationships, which nevertheless stop short of the sexual. Reading now at this distance of the relationships of Newman to Hurrell Froude (the brother of the famous Professor James Anthony Froude), and to Ambrose St. John and others, one is bound, as Cornwell has done, to examine these in the light of this tradition, especially in academic and clerical circles, although the same evidence exists in the Navy and the Military and some other circles.

Froude was two years younger than Newman. "He was attractive to men", says Cornwell. He was tall and thin, with delicate features and penetrating grey eyes, "but bright with internal conceptions". He was "bold and volubly high-spirited, given to slang and irreverence". He sounds very much like Aubrey Beardsley, both in persona and in personality, at the end of the nineteenth century; and both were destined to die young: Froude at thirty-three and Beardsley at twenty-six. But the effect they both had on people they met and knew was indelible. Newman fell under his spell. Newman wrote that "the attachment developed into the closest and most affectionate friendship".[6]

It is not necessary, in a study like this one, to go into more detail, but when the other cases in this category are considered, the Sancti and the Beati, as well as those who are still neither, a somewhat alarming dimension emerges: that of anorexia and extreme fasting, which undeniably are linked with a sexual element. Cornwell says that in his journal, Froude anticipates the anorexic anxieties of twentieth (and twenty-first) century youth, recording his fasting in minute detail. "He connects fasting with the need to expunge feelings of pollution and self-disgust. A sense of sexual anxiety is suggested in at least one sermon several years later, when he spoke of the need for 'external purification' and the need to avoid 'all sinful pleasures'...Froude's obsession with food, fasting, excessive exercise, the desire to feel himself ever a child, low self-esteem, remarkable thinness, and pre-occupation with vomiting, suggest a form of bulimia."

To most of us now, these ideas of sexual repression of something which was in every way natural, and simply should have been channelled, are amazing and disturbing to the point of disbelief. But in this chapter, a list of people will be considered both in the light of their exhumation and the style and practices of their personal and communal lives. They bear extraordinary similarities. Into the category of self-denial and self-flagellation (what we now call self-harm) comes people as diverse as St. Theresa of Avila, Princess Diana, Emily Davidson, and Bobby Sands; the fact that they might have said they were doing what they did for particular purposes does not distinguish their very similar mindsets.

Froude was at one with Newman not only on the importance of fasting but the necessity of virginity and celibacy. Newman's decision, for the second time, not to marry (when he was 28) dates from the period when his intimacy with Froude deepened. There can be no doubt that of all Newman's male friendships, his attachment to Froude found him more loving than loved. With Ambrose St. John it was the other way round: St. John was entirely devoted not only to Newman himself, but to everything and anything Newman wanted or aspired to, always at the cost of his own.[7]

What Newman (and perhaps Froude and St. John) did not agree with, and emphatically rejected in 1848, only three years after becoming a Catholic, was that isolation and inner reserve that went with the culture of Catholic clericalism. This culture had become emphasised at the time of the Counter Reformation, and yet it was at this very time that there lived that most appealing of saints, Philip Neri, the latter-day apostle of Rome and a kind of Catholic Samuel Johnson, in that he treasured friendship, and invited response, which he received.[8]

There is no suggestion that when the exhumation of some male beati have taken place, there is a strange, sweet smell from their bodies: that phenomenon seems to be reserved for women, although the non-putrefaction of the body is something common especially to those considered to be saints or saintly. Nuri McBride, in a very important article on this subject, has written that "the foul and the divine were understood by how they smelt". The link between offensive odours, the body, and immorality is well established in the psyche of Western society. It was the West that invented the aphorism "Cleanliness is next to Godliness". Two popular plague preservatives, the lemon and the lavender, live on in many cleaning products in the West. As Nuri McBride says: "It's not really clean until it smells clean". The use of pomanders, scent and then at last, the surely Heaven-sent fixative of Coco Chanel in the early twentieth century, all testifies to the importance of perfume and sweet smell. If things stink, they are earthly and therefore wicked; if it smells nice, it is connected to the abstraction of the spiritual world, and therefore good. The conundrum is then, if smells of corruption denote a corrupt nature, what happens when a holy person dies? It is in this Western mind-body dualism that the concept of the Odour of Sanctity is born. This logical thinking is at the basis of the Assumption of the Blessed Virgin Mary and the obligatory doctrine which was formulated as recently as 1950. As the Mother of the Redeemer, her body could not corrupt or be capable of corruption, and therefore was assumed into Heaven. Newman's homily "On the fitness of the Glories of Mary" contained the line "Who can conceive that that virginal frame, which never sinned, was to undergo the death of a sinner? Why should she share the curse of Adam, who had no share in his fall? Dust thou art, and unto dust that shalt return, was the sentence upon sin; she then, who was not a sinner, fitly never saw corruption." One can almost sense Newman's mind working itself to this logical conclusion. Newman's orders to mulch his coffin, extraordinary as they were, was (thinks Cornwell) evidently an acknowledgement of his own sinfulness, deserving of final physical corruption. How could he have known, that his burial instructions would result, paradoxically, in a circumstance parallel with the fate of Mary's assumed body. The sermon continues: "Pilgrims went to and fro; they sought for her relics, but they found them not." Of course, Newman's body was exhumed, not only to place it somewhere of greater honour, but, who knows, as a repository of relics. The present writer has seen a minute fragment of the elbow of St. Theresa of Lisieux, placed in a monstrance, and given to a merchant seaman (also a librarian) as a reward for his unstinting transatlantic service during the Holy Year of 1950. Such dismemberment might have awaited Newman, and he was aware of it.

Somehow there has to be both a mental leap, and an attempt to bridge the gap between the mediaeval mentality concerning death and the final four things (Heaven, Hell, Death, and Judgement) and the mentalities of six or eight centuries later. Facial features on mediaeval tombs were often composed, as they had been in life, depicted either asleep, or with eyes opened; awaiting the Final Judgement with equanimity and bearing no visible reference to death's actuality. This was the sculpture known as the *gisant*. The figure showing death's actuality was the *transi*, which had fully entered into death and was not going to portray things otherwise. Although a few *transi* figures seem locked in rigor mortis, the transitory state between death and decomposition, usually the flesh of the partially nude, often partially enshrouded body was altered from a life-like configuration to one that foretold the decay and mortification of the grave. The psychological point of reference had shifted from an image of the dead body as whole and incorruptible to a *memento mori* that unsparingly reflected upon the inevitable end of all living matter.

The *transi* was sometimes depicted with flesh hanging off the skeleton, eyes and nose gone, lank hair, ribs exposed, worms and toads feasting on the remaining flesh and entrails. An early example, in relief, was on the tomb of Cardinal Jean de la Grange, who died in 1402, fragments of which are now in the Musee Calvet, Avignon. The epitaph reveals the intention and philosophy of such a representation: "Wretch! Why art thou proud? Thou are naught but ashes and soon will be like me a food for worms".[9]

But it is not only a double mental take on the subject of death and dissolution; it signifies the last defiant throw of that dual mentality in the fifteenth century. The first glimmers of the light of the Renaissance were already detectable on the horizon.

The Odour of Sanctity, formally known as Osmogenesia, is a supernaturally pleasant odour coming from the body, or wounds, usually after death. It was presented as a physical sign of the spiritual superiority of the person. It is, primarily, a Western phenomenon. It was not recognised as a part of the beatification process until 1758, when Cardinal Lambertini, who later became Pope Benedict XIV, was in charge of these matters, and it has since been downgraded as a favourable sign of holiness. To begin with, it was strongly associated with the incorruptibility of the body and a sign of it, but it was not limited to the officially venerated saints of the Catholic and Eastern Orthodox rites. Modern theologians will say that the Odour of Sanctity is metaphorical, but that is not how persons viewed it, or indeed experienced it, when there was a saintly exhumation.

The scents can be brief or persistent, attached to the body, grave, water the body was bathed in, or objects the person touched. In the case of the modern saint Padre Pio, his spectral scent of roses and pipe tobacco visited people after his death and was considered a sign of his saintliness. All Odours of Sanctity are sweet, and are described variously as notes of butter, honey, roses, violets, frankincense, myrrh, pipe tobacco, jasmine and lilies being the most frequently reported accompaniments. The scent is also always culturally specific and deeply intertwined with symbolism. The comparison with wine tasting is unfortunately irresistible.

Nuri McBride compared the examples and experiences of five saints from the twelfth, thirteenth and fourteenth centuries; seven from the fifteenth to eighteenth centuries; and a further six from the nineteenth and twentieth centuries, making eighteen in all. To these could be added the uncanonised Therese Neumann, who died in 1962. They had much in common. Firstly, they were all women. Fourteen of them were mystics, that is, they had visions and went into ecstasies. Fourteen of them were cloistered nuns. Fifteen of them were also Ascetics, that is, they fasted and ate little. Nine of them committed self-harm, as we would know it today. Four of them (five, if Therese Neumann is included), were stigmatics, that is, the five wounds of Christ appeared on their bodies, or, in their minds, they thought these wounds were there. Eight of them seriously restricted what food they took; and ten of them suffered from what would now be called anorexia mirabilis. Six of them were Carmelites; four were Dominicans; two were Poor Clares; and one each from the Franciscans, Beguines, Good Shepherd, and Holy Family Orders. It is not known to which Order, if any, Lydwine of Schiedam belonged.

There is, apparently a medical explanation of all the wondrous odours which emanated from the coffins and bodies of these saintly women over a period of ten centuries.

The explanation is that it is nothing more than ketoacidosis. Ketosis is a natural process that occurs when the body runs out of glucose and starts to metabolise fatty acids. This progression volatises acetone, which produces a mildly sweet smell, unrecognisable to most. Should this devolve into the pathological metabolic state of Ketoacidosis from alcohol abuse, *starvation*, or diabetes, the acetone becomes detectable, even overpowering. Someone engaged in long fasts, or dying while in an advanced state of ketoacidosis would have a strong, sweet smell.

As Nuri McBride comments: "These women's lives were dedicated to transcending their physical forms, and nothing is more corporal than the haze of human decomposition".

One of the most popular of the fragrant saints, St. Therese of Lisieux, smelt of lilies, violets and roses upon her deathbed. Her most often attributed quote is: "The splendour of the rose and the whiteness of the lily do not rob the little violet of its scent…If every tiny flower wanted to be a rose, Spring would lose its loveliness". Following on the previous comments concerning perfume and the fixative found by Coco Chanel, in St. Therese's own lifetime, violet absolute was synthesised, making a material which was the once the most expensive fragrance component in the world, affordable to all, and the de rigueur fragrance for respectable women. This is the point: before 1875, however, the scent of violets would not have been readily identifiable to the general population, and no Odour of

Sanctity is associated with violets in any primary sources before that time. So the implication is that the odour of violets appealed to suggestible imaginations. Again, McBride has a telling phrase: "the discarded bodies of these perfected souls should already be touched by a whiff of Paradise". "While the worldly woman's corpse corrupts by its nature and stinks, so the heavenly woman's body remains pure and fragrant." However, concludes McBride, the conversation is still about a *woman's* body (not a man's).

St. Teresa of Avila lived in seclusion, practised tri-weekly self-flagellations and didn't wear shoes (this is why this body of Carmelite nuns is termed "Discalced" or without shoes; it is something shared in common with the Jain nuns of India, although they are the opposite of secluded, being wandering).

The moment St. Teresa died, her bedroom attendants said the room was filled with the scent of roses that grew to saturate the building. The convent smelt like it had erupted into bloom and cascades of invisible blossoms poured from the windows. Her grave held the smell of roses for eight months. But these stories come, like so many stories, with warnings. "the nose, like any of our senses, can be fooled especially when primed. In a time of sorrow and acute stress, a smell that was imperceptible moments earlier can become overpowering. One could rationalise the sickly sweetness of early decay or illness as divine honey." Stories, as we all know, and have perhaps contributed to ourselves, grow in the telling. All raconteurs know this.

The earliest saint in modern times to be associated with the Odour of Sanctity is Marie of Oignies (Nivelles in modern Belgium), who died in 1213. Her life was written by her confessor, and, like those histories often written by disaffected monks, one has always to be careful of those who will write hagiography or the reverse, and who may have an agenda.

Angela of Foligno, who died in 1309, was eventually beatified by Pope Clement XI on July 11, 1701, and canonised by none other than Pope Francis on October 9, 2013, the first year of his pontificate. There may curiously be something political here, reflecting the great struggles of the past between the temporal authority of Emperors and the spiritual authority of the Popes, bolstered in later times by the acquisition of territory as well. Angela was born in the Holy Roman Empire but died in the Papal States.

Columba of Rieta, who died in 1501, was declared Blessed by Pope Urban VIII in 1625; while Lydwine of Schiedam is a most interesting case, because she was the unfortunate victim of multiple sclerosis, and one of the first to be documented. She died in 1433, and in 1615, her relics were taken to Brussels, but in 1871, they were returned to her hometown, and in 1890, she was declared Venerable.

St. Catherine of Siena is one of the great saints of history, a major political figure of her times, who died in 1380. Her case will shortly be examined at some length.

Rita of Cascia died in 1477, but one of the most fertile periods for this phenomenon is during the Counter Reformation. It was as if during this time, extraordinary saints who did supernatural things were the order of the day. To this period, between c. 1560 to c. 1730 belongs such figures as St. Teresa of Avila, the Venerable Catalina of Cardona, Catherine of Ricci, Rose of Lima, Mary Magdalen of Pazzi, Marianne Fontanella (Mary of the Angels), and Veronica Guiliani.

Catalina of Cardona had been the governess of Don Juan of Austria, the illegitimate half-brother of Philip II of Spain, a glamorous figure of imperishable memory and the Christian victor of the Battle of Lepanto in 1571. This is a battle forever associated with the practice of saying the Rosary.

Catherine of Ricci and Rose of Lima were contemporaries, but in very different places, Rose being the first canonised saint of the New World. Both seemed to fulfil some kind of need to those who must be missionaries and so had to lead lives very much on the edge. Sometimes, these holy women came from very different backgrounds, and so those who came afterwards, or those who had known them, had, necessarily, access to very different source material, some plentiful and some sparse, and all of it motivated by some passion or purpose.

Marianne Fontanella was the daughter of a Count and Countess. She died in 1717, but already in 1778 Pope Pius VI was proclaiming her virtues; and in 1865, under Pope Pius IX, she was declared Blessed. Her body is kept in Turin.

Veronica Guiliani, who died in 1727, was canonised by Pope Gregory XVI in 1839, and, in addition to the Odour of Sanctity, her body remained incorrupt.

The most recent period for the phenomenon is that of the nineteenth and early twentieth centuries. Again, one is tempted to theorise that the Church was under great threat during these two periods from all manner of rival creeds, both religious and political. The first fragrant saint to emerge was Mariam Bouardy. She was born of Greek Catholic parents from Syria and Lebanon who belonged to the Melkite rite of the Catholic Church. Declared Blessed in 1983, she was canonised in 2015, again by Pope Francis, who, unlike Pope John Paul II, has been much more sparing in his declarations of sainthood.

Blessed Maria Droste zu Vischerung, another from the upper echelons (she was a Countess herself), was born in 1863 and died in 1899, so was a contemporary of the famed and much better known Therese of Lisieux. However, the great contribution of this holy woman was that through her devotion, the world was consecrated to the Sacred Heart of Jesus. This was, and is, a cult within the church which many of these women adhered to. Blessed Jeanne-Germaine Castang, whose dates almost completely coincided with Therese, came from Bordeaux, and was declared Blessed in 2007 by Pope Benedict XVI. She is known as the "Saint of the Perfumes", so strong was the phenomenon with her.

Mariam Thresia (1876–1926), at least, lived until the age of fifty, and again was a holy woman from a far distant rite of the Catholic Church, the Indian Syro-Malabar. She was declared Venerable in 1999, Blessed merely a year later, in 2000, and her canonisation date is set for 2019. She is linked to St. Therese of Lisieux because as a mystic and stigmatic, she spoke of the intercession of Therese in 1925, just before her own death.

St. Maria Maravillas, who died only in 1974, was the daughter of the Spanish ambassador to the Vatican, and was canonised in 2003.

Finally, there is Therese Neumann, who lived from 1898 to 1962. She has so far not been declared Venerable or Blessed, but, during her lifetime and after had a cult following. She was a stigmatic, and it was said she ate nothing but the Blessed Sacrament and drank only water.

These extraordinary lives, of devotion and self-denial, are following a certain stream within the Christian and other faiths, which has been there from the beginning and the hermits in the Egyptian desert and the land of stones and saints in Celtic Ireland, Iona, and the Farne Islands. Because there are modern medical explanations for their asceticism does not detract or invalidate their undoubtedly holy lives. St. Therese is of course known for her autobiography *The Journey of a Soul*; while St. Teresa of Avila was also known for a wicked sense of humour. These were not ordinary people.

St. Catherine of Siena deserves a section of her own, because not only was she one of the fragrant saints and a great political figures, but, after her death, she was exhumed, and the subject of extraordinary treatment of her body.

After a short lifetime, during which she advised and castigated Popes, Catherine, a Sienese born, died in Rome on Sunday, April 29, 1380, at 12 noon, the time of the Angelus. "We did not bury her until the Tuesday, at the hour of Compline, that is, at dusk. And there was no smell to be perceived, her body remained pure, unharmed, fragrant, the neck and legs could still be bent, as if she were still alive. During those three days, her body was visited by the people, who came in great numbers, and those who could touch her thought themselves fortunate. God worked so many wonders at that time, and her grave was visited by the faithful like the graves of the other saints in Rome."[10]

The death chamber was moved later to the Dominican Church of S. Maria sopra Minerva. Only the ceiling of the room remained in the house in Via del Papa, now 44, Via Santa Chiara, where it is still shown (in 1938) in room now transformed into a chapel. The house belonged (in 1938) to the Roman Congregazione di Carita. Catherine's first dwelling in Rome was pulled down in the sixteenth century, when the Piazza San Pietro came into existence.

Italy has always been, and is now, a country of fierce local rivalries, and nowhen more so than during the lifetime of Catherine. She was canonised by a Sienese Pope, the great Pius II, the traveller and diplomat, one of the first Renaissance Popes. Her biographer, Raymond of Capua, was elected General of the Dominican Order in 1380, the year Catherine died, and it was from this exalted position that he decided to fulfil the wish, not only of himself, but of many others, the cherished wish, to bring back her body from Rome to Siena. If this were not possible, then at least he would bring her head.

Thus, when he was in Rome, in October, 1383, he had Catherine's coffin opened, and her body exhumed. With the Pope's permission, he detached the head, and entrusted it to two friars who happened to be going to Siena, one of them being Fra Tommaso della Fonte, and the other Fra Ambrogio Sansedoni. The silken bag in which the two Dominican friars carried the head the long way from Rome to Siena, is still preserved in the house of Santa Caterina in Siena. This was not yet Catherine's triumphal entry however into the town which had so often murmured against her. She (or rather her head) arrived secretly, yet no-one knew that her head, enclosed now in a reliquary of gilded copper, was standing in the sacristy of San Domenico.

In the following Spring, that is, 1384, Raymond came to Siena himself, and everything was prepared for the solemn translation of the relic. On April 23, a course of sermons began in San Domenico (the Dominicans being the preaching Order), and on Sunday, May 1, the great feast day which marked the beginning of the best time of the year, it was announced from the pulpit that a procession would be held the following Thursday. The government of Siena, recognising the international reputation of its native daughter, resolved that Catherine's feast (day) should be kept with every solemnity, and invited all bishops, abbots, prelates within the borders of the State to be present. There was also a circle of Catherine's disciples, who would also be there.

The relic was secretly taken out the evening before to San Lazzaro, the leper hospital in the Via Romana, that road which had seen so often Catherine going on her errands of mercy to the sick, now was also to witness her triumph.[11]

The morning of May 5 witnessed a procession which contained, inter alia, two hundred little boys and two hundred little girls, all carrying large bouquets of roses and lilies, in memory of the nosegays that Catherine used to tie in her garden. Then came the baldachino, under which Catherine's head was carried in a casket.

More extraordinary, then came Catherine's own mother, Mona Beincasa di Piagenti di Puccio, known as Lappa, now more than eighty years old, who had outlived so many of her children, perhaps her original brood numbering nearly twenty. Some said that Catherine was her twenty-third child, when she was born in 1347. During her lifetime, Catherine had prayed that her mother would come out of her illness in 1370, and so she had.[12] Lappa would live until 1412. She had lived longer than she wished to. "I think my soul must be stuck crosswise in my body, so that it cannot get out", she usually said; an interesting insight into the mediaeval mind. But after her illness in 1370, she became a Mantellata, a disciple of her own daughter, and a tertiary order of the Dominicans.

"Like Bernard," said David Hugh Farmer, "Catherine had prophetic visions and personal intransigence; these led both of them to identify God's cause with their own", a perceptive statement.[13]

One male body which apparently did survive in a very good state of preservation was that of the English king and saint, Edward the Confessor. In 1089 (*Another authority says 1102), only twenty three years after his death, the Abbot of Westminster decided to open his tomb, following a dispute concerning the preservation. Some stated that the body would have crumbled away; others, seeing that the king was a saint, that it was incorruptible. The Abbot therefore decided to open the tomb in the presence of a senior cleric as witness, namely, Gundolf, Bishop of Rochester.

The chronicler, Ailred of Rievaulx, described the events on the opening of the sepulchre:

> there issued out such aromatic odours as filled the church with their fragrance. In the first place, the burial cloths were clean, and substantial: next, unfolding his vestments, they found his underhabit and ornaments in the same state. They stretched out his arms, bent his fingers and found the whole body sound, and flexible; (this flexibility was found later in other saints, such as St. Catherine of Siena) they next examined the flesh, which was firm and pure as crystal, whiter than snow. But when, after a long suspense, none dare venture to touch his face, the Bishop Gondolphus laid his hand upon the forehead cloth and stroking it over the face, drew it over the beard, which was white as frost. Surprised at this, he attempt to draw a hair from the beard, but that adhered strictly. For which, being reproved by the Abbot, he owned his fault which excess of love occasioned. After this, they preserved the grave dressings and clothed him anew, reinterred him.

What is particularly interesting about this first exhumation is the use of similes: "pure as crystal.....white as snow......white as frost". The monkish chronicler seems determined on the sense of the immaculate; but how literally should such statements be taken?

The second exhumation took place in 1163, that is, nearly a century after Edward's death. Although regarded as saintly, there had been no formal canonisation. Already, in 1138, in the troubled reign of King Stephen, an attempt was made to obtain formal Papal canonisation, supported by a new *Life*, written by Osbert of Clare. Pope Innocent II delayed making a decision and encouraged the monks of Westminster to collect more information. During the time of the Abbot Gervase, who was an illegitimate son of the late King Stephen (who had died nine years before) he, the abbot, applied to the English pope, Adrian IV, to have Edward formally declared a saint. If anyone was going to do it, surely the English pope would canonise an English king. Adrian, however, refused, which is surprising. Was it the subject or the applicant which displeased him? It might well have been the applicant, being the son of the dead king. Adrian was very anxious to please the new Plantagenet king, Henry II, making him, among other titles, Lord of Ireland.

However, later in 1160, Abbot Laurence made a much greater effort, this time supported by Henry II himself and Thomas Becket. This is particularly significant in the light of Henry's later relations with Becket. He was also friendly with the new Pope, Alexander III, supporting him against an anti-Pope. A bull of canonisation duly resulted, the next year, 1161.

The net result of all this was that Edward's body now had to be honoured in a new and advanced way, so the second exhumation took place on October 13, 1163. Edward's body was to be transferred to a new tomb. The translation of the body was a national event, the sermon being preached by Ailred of Rieuvaulx, who by this time had also written another *Life of Edward.* The day of the translation, October 13, was henceforth kept as the principal feast of St. Edward.

The body was again found to be in a wonderful state of preservation. But this time, the legendary sapphire ring was removed from his finger by Abbot Lawrence and placed with the Abbey's treasures. The legend of this ring was that the king had, during his lifetime, given it to a beggar, when he found that he did not have alms sufficient to give him. Two pilgrims to the Holy Land then received the ring from a figure of St. John, who appeared to them (presumably in a vision) and charged them to take the ring back to Paradise in six months' time. Edward was buried with the ring (again, presumably within the six months) and also with a gold crucifix around his neck.

Following Edward's death, pilgrims began to come to his tomb, when St. Wulfstan, Bishop of Worcester, sought his intercession. Wulfstan had been the only Saxon bishop present at the coronation of William the Conqueror in 1066.

In 1163, Abbot Laurence also removed the vestments from the body and made three copes from the burial clothes.

In the new shrine, it now became possible for pilgrims to make contact with the saint's coffin, and thus to feel it was possible to be healed from their ailments.

In 1245, during the reign of Henry III, the great benefactor of the Abbey, who caused it to be reconstructed, work began on a new shrine for St. Edward, work which was to continue all the way to 1504, during the reign of Henry VII. In the meantime, other relics had been added to the shrine, including a crystal phial of the Holy Blood presented by the Knights Templar, which Henry III carried in procession in 1247, and a marble stone, added in 1249, which carried an impression of the Saviour's foot. Yet another translation took place in 1269, when the new shrine was ready. It had taken over twenty-five years to build and decorate; the most skilled Italian workmen were employed, and the shrine was of unparalleled magnificence.

During the reign of Henry VIII, in 1538, the pedestal of the shrine was pulled down, and the Confessor buried beneath it. Henry's treatment of his royal predecessor did not amount to that meted out to Thomas Becket and others. Perhaps he recalled that he had, after all, been crowned with the crown of St. Edward.

In 1554, Henry's daughter, Mary Tudor, while not restoring the shrines removed and destroyed in 1538, made an exception of two. One was that of St. Edward, having the pedestal re-erected and the saint's coffin placed within the upper part of the pedestal. It is possible to see that during this operation some of the slabs were not placed or replaced in their correct positions. Queen Mary had restored the working Abbey, with Abbot Feckenham at its head. She also restored the shrine, and the gilded wooden feretory, usually attributed to him, dates from the reign of Henry VII, and may be the work of the great Torrigiano.[14]

The next viewing of the saint's body was the result of a spectacular accident. Preparations were being made in 1685 for the coronation of James II. A large amount of scaffolding was erected so that as many people as possible could have a view of the occasion. When the scaffolding was pulled down, much of it collapsed, bringing the pedestal and coffin with it. The coffin was broken, and the head of the king could now be seen "firm and whole", and with its jaw full of teeth.

A Mr. Henry Keepe wrote that he put his hand into the coffin and, in turning over the bones, drew from under the shoulder bones a gold crucifix, richly adorned, and enamelled with a gold chain some twenty-four inches long. This had obviously remained in the coffin all the time since 1066. The impunity with which this was done, with no apparent criticism being made, is in line with how Samuel Pepys kissed the corpse of Katherine of Valois in 1669, a mere sixteen years previously. It was indeed a very different age.

Mr. Keepe showed the crucifix to the Archbishop, "who looked upon them (apparently other relics too) as great pieces of antiquity". Mr. Keepe was then introduced to King James II by the Dean of Westminster, and he presented the crucifix to the King "who was pleased to accept the gift". Did he know it had been rifled from a royal tomb?!

James II kept the crucifix, and had it with him, together with other treasures, when he fled down the Thames from the advancing William of Orange, his own son-in-law, in 1688, nearly four years later. The Faversham fishermen who took him across to exile in France are said to have pillaged his possessions, and they stole the crucifix; it must still lie somewhere.

The pious James, known to his detractors as "Dismal Jimmy", however, had had Edward's coffin repaired during his brief reign, with heavy plates, some two inches thick. These were bound with iron and the body lies in this coffin today.

As for James, his own body would be examined for signs of sanctity and relics taken before its burial in St. Germain in 1701. At the time of the French Revolution, it would suffer the indignities visited upon many royal bodies during such turbulent times.

It does seem a characteristic of some saints that their bodies are frequently exhumed, or, euphemistically, "translated", quite frequently. This has usually been to keep them from falling into the wrong hands. Typical was another saintly king, namely King Edmund of East Anglia, who was certainly a martyr, and as much the patron saint of England at one time as St. George, who, of course, was not English at all, coming from what is now Turkey. But he was the favourite saint of soldiers, which ensured his invocation at the beginning of battles. Of Saxon stock, and brought up as a Christian, Edmund became King of the East Angles some time before 865. Fighting the Vikings five years later, Edmund was defeated and captured. He refused to recant his faith, or to rule as the vassal of the Viking leader, an early stand for local independence. He was then killed, although the manner and consequence of his death has been the subject of many legends. He may have been beheaded, but it is also quite possible he suffered the Viking death of being spread-eagled, that is, his lungs were pulled through his back, and spread out, in what the Vikings called the "bloody eagle", as they then resembled wings. This atrocity took place at Hellesdon, in Norfolk, and his body was buried in a small wooden chapel nearby. In c. 915, his body was discovered, like Edward the Confessor's later on, to be incorrupt, and was translated to Bedricsworth (later renamed Bury St. Edmunds, or St. Edmunds Bury).

The landing of another Danish army at Ipswich in 1010 again placed the body in danger, and so it was moved to London, where it remained for three years. Despite local protests, it was then moved back to Bury. Everyone, it seems, wanted to keep a holy body.

In 1095, the body of Edmund was translated yet again, to a large new Norman church; and in 1198 it was re-shrined. This event was vividly described by Jocelin of Brakelond. Although a cult had now grown up around the shrine, this is the last date where it can be certain what happened to the body. After the battle of Lincoln, in 1217, the defeated French soldiers claimed to have taken it to France. This set of relics, located at Saint Sernin, Toulouse, was offered to Westminster cathedral in 1912, perhaps as a goodwill offering. M.R. James and other scholars protested that these relics were not authentic, and the translation did not take place. The better consideration was that the body of St. Edmund had been re-buried within the precincts of the Abbey during the Dissolution in 1538. Its present whereabouts are unknown, and a matter of speculation. The finding of the body of Richard III under a car park in Leicester in 2013 has prompted a new book named *Edmund: In Search of England's Lost King*, by Francis Young, in 2018. Three times after the death of Edmund (which resembled a latter-day St. Sebastian's) his body was found to be incorrupt: when it was examined in 956 by Bishop Theodred of London; in 1095, when it was confirmed as being still incorrupt; and in 1198, when Abbot Samson of Bury St. Edmunds touched the incorrupt body. But in 1538, at the Dissolution of the Monasteries, no mention is made at all of his body or his relics. Did something happen to it between 1198 and 1538?

This reluctance to accept relics was not present in 2018, however, when an extraordinary story broke on BBC News. On June 19, 2018, it was reported that a fragment of bone, purporting to come from the body of St. Clement, had been retrieved from a rubbish tip.

In February 2017, Mr. James Rubin, the owner of Enviro Waste, spotted an unusual looking object on a desk in the company's warehouse, in east London, where staff had been sorting waste to see what could be recycled or refurbished. Mr. Rubin asked, "Where has this come from?" But apparently no-one knew (of course, someone did). It was very hard to pinpoint the place exactly where it had come from, as the company's trucks clear up to 30 premises a day. But Mr. Rubin was curious, took it back to his office, and began to enquire online. He recognised the Latin inscription on it, which was "Ex Oss St. Clementis", from the bones of St. Clement. He thought of giving it to a museum or a university, hoping they would be able to work out what it was. He appealed online for suggestions on the company's blog. There were hundreds of answers, including ones from Hungary and the United States, asking to take the relic. Rather sensibly, Mr. Rubin decided to give it to Westminster cathedral.

It was at this point, that the relic's owner decided to come forward, but to remain anonymous. He said that it had been stolen during a car break-in, but agreed that it should go to the cathedral on a permanent loan basis, as part of its Treasures Exhibition. Legally this is interesting in itself, because the ownership remains with this anonymous man.

The deal was brokered by the historian and Catholic expert, Sophie Andreae. She said "It's a really happy outcome to this particular extraordinary story. These objects are of very great significance. Catholics feel that they have not just a link with a very holy person, but also a link with the divine."

But who, especially to non-Catholics, was St. Clement? Everyone, believing and non-believing, knows the name of St. Christopher, patron saint of travellers, and a lesser number will know of St. Nicholas, his fellow patron, though they may know of him under "Santa Claus", Santa Nicholaus. Like St. George, St. Nicholas came from present day Turkey, and was bishop of Myra, but, like St. Christopher, virtually nothing is known about him, but he was, and is, the patron saint of sailors (he is also the patron of children, unmarried girls, merchants, pawnbrokers, apothecaries, and perfumiers; but this is simply to show how much in demand he was). Prayers to him were composed by St. Anselm and St. Godric, among others. However, the significance of Clement becomes marked when his fellow saints as patrons of travellers reveal such insubstantial histories. Indeed, St. Christopher, perhaps, with St. Francis, the most favoured universal saint, was demoted by the Vatican in 1969 to the status of a local cult, following close investigation into the origins of his legends. This led to a sharp reaction in many countries, almost of outrage, especially in Italy. As travel has become more dangerous, devotion of St. Christopher has increased.

Out of this ménage, St. Clement emerges, especially as patron of travel by sea, or water, with (technically) somewhat better credentials.

Clement is considered to be the third pope after St. Peter, and may have occupied this position between AD 91 and 101. He certainly knew not only St. Peter, but "had seen, and conversed with, the Blessed Apostles", according to St. Irenaeus. His chief claim to fame is his Epistle to the Corinthinian, c. 96, which emphasises the collegiality of the early church, before any monarchical episcopate. Long counted as a martyr, the colourful story of his martyrdom and subsequent history of his tomb and body must be considered something else. The aphorism of John Butler, in his *Quest for Becket's Bones (1995)* is apposite in this, and many other such stories: "Myths and rumours are of great importance as social facts". In other words, they assume a life of their own, and, although, to use a modern expression, they may be fake news or history, they cannot be dismissed, because of the effect they have had, and do have still, on many people and issues. Myths have long been thought to have some core of truth, however small.

The story of Clement's death, related in his *Acta* of the fourth century, has little historical value, but they say that he was thrown overboard from a ship, with an anchor tied to him, having been a successful, perhaps too successful missionary in the Crimea. This was after he had been compelled to work in the mines. Angels were then said to have made a tomb for him at the bottom of the sea, which was uncovered at an exceptionally low tide. The low tide at least is possible.

Fast forward seven centuries. The missionaries Cyril and Methodius, beloved of the Orthodox faith, and apostles of the Slav countries, miraculously recovered the body of St. Clement, piece by piece, together with the anchor. These relics were translated to Rome, c. 868, and buried in the Church of S. Clemente, which is itself on the site of first- and third-century Christian places of worship. J.D.N. Kelly is very sceptical about these stories, in his *Dictionary of the Popes (Oxford, 1986)*. He says "The claim that he died a martyr should be rejected in view of the silence of the earliest authorities; the story, too, that he was banished to the Crimea, successfully preached the Gospel there, and was killed by being drowned with an anchor round his neck, is without foundation".[15]

The story goes that by a miraculous ebbing of the sea, a shrine was revealed, containing his bones. Almost 800 years later some of the bones are said to have been brought to Rome and enshrined in the Basilica di San Clemente. A monastery in Ukraine is said to have his head and other relics.

Dr. Tessa Murdoch, Deputy Keeper of Sculpture, Metalwork, Ceramics and Glass at the Victoria & Albert Museum in London asked the question on many lips: "How can we be sure?" of any of this. Her answer is simply: "It purports to be (that) and it has been treasured as that". So objects also achieve a life on what they purport to be, but maybe not what they actually are. She says that the inscription on the red wax seal in the case which includes a cardinal's hat and tassels could give clues about when the relic was endorsed by the Catholic church. "A part of a relic was representative of the whole. So even though this is a tiny piece, purporting to be a bone of St. Clement, it represents the whole saint and martyr. Because these things are cherished and kept in sacred places, sometimes under altars, the general public is not perhaps aware of their potency and so its very rare that something like this comes into the public domain in such extraordinary circumstances, and it kind of reminds us all of the extraordinary power and association of such a small object."

She went on to say that "the best way to comprehend their significance is to think of gifts between loved ones, such as locks of hair. We can relate to things like that but if you actually translate those sort of special gifts between loved ones into the life of faith and sacred gifts, I think it helps understand the depth of power that these objects have".

Sophie Andreae commented that it is not possible to know now how and when it came into England. It may be a survivor from the iconoclasm of the Henrician Reformation; but more likely it came into England in the nineteenth century once persecution had ceased (after Catholic Emancipation in 1829) and wealthier Catholics could travel abroad and bring artefacts from Italy back with them.

Whatever the relic is that is now in the treasury of Westminster cathedral, it has been revered as a holy object, and was doubtless given originally as one, though not necessarily the bone of St. Clement.

Sometimes men in holy orders (although not necessarily holy themselves) are buried in consecrated ground as figures of some consequence, and then forgotten. The exact location of royal bodies is sometimes forgotten or deliberately concealed, to say nothing of lesser mortals. So it should have come as no surprise when the remains of no less than five former Archbishops of Canterbury were found, beneath a mediaeval parish church in Lambeth, next to Lambeth Palace, the London residence of the Archbishops.

Deconsecrated in 1972, St. Mary's was due to be demolished before becoming a Garden Museum. In October 2015, the museum was closed for eighteen months to undergo a redevelopment project.[16] In the crypt, which being near the Thames, the excavators had expected to be flooded, they made the remarkable discovery. There were thirty lead coffins, and one of them had a gold crown on top of it, so the searchers knew they had found something of significance. The remains had dated back to the 1660s, the decade which saw both the great plague and the great fire of London, although Lambeth being on the south side of the river it escaped the flames. The site manager, Karl Patten, and his team used a mobile phone camera on the end of a stick to search the void below. The Garden Museum Director, Christopher Woodward, was contacted, and they then saw that the "golden crown" was an Archbishop's mitre, glowing in the dark. The red and gold mitre rested on top of one of the coffins. Harry Mount, from the *Sunday Telegraph*, was the first outsider to be granted access, and found the discovery "spine-tingling". The coffins have been left undisturbed, but the builders have installed a glass panel in the chancel floor above them for visitor to catch a glimpse.

Two of the coffins had nameplates, those of Richard Bancroft, Archbishop from 1604 to 1610 (covering the period of the Gunpowder Plot and the King James version of the Bible), and one for John Moore, in office from 1783 to 1805, someone less remembered. There is also a nameplate for Catherine Moore his wife.

According to Christopher Mount, the Lambeth Palace records have since revealed that a further three Archbishops were probably buried in the vault, namely, Frederick Cornwallis (in office from 1768 to 1783, a longish period, taking in the time of American Independence), Matthew Hutton (who was archbishop for only one year, 1757 to 1758), and

Thomas Tenison (in office from 1695 to 1715, taking in the reigns of William III and Queen Anne, and lasting long enough to see George I). There were some remains of a sixth Archbishop, Thomas Secker (in office 1758–1768), who had his internal organs buried in a canister in the churchyard.

Also identified from coffin plates was John Bettesworth, the Dean of Arches, and therefore an authority on the Canon Law of the Church of England at the time, who lived from 1677 to 1751. He presided over the ecclesiastical court of the Archbishop of Canterbury.

But as for the others, Christopher Woodward admitted that for the moment they were anonymous. Further clues, however, may lie in the history of the church. It was once one of the most sacred and precious site in London, built in the eleventh century along the Embankment, opposite Westminster Abbey and the tomb of St. Edward the Confessor, and built by none other than the Confessor's sister. Over the centuries, a number of the archbishops chose both to worship and to be buried there.

The mechanics of exhumation depend initially on whether this is a spiritual or secular matter, that is, is it in the realm of Civil Law or Canon Law? Both of these are part of the Law of England and Wales, but the jurisdiction, judges and courts are different. If the matter is a secular one, then an application for exhumation must be made under S. 25 of the Burial Act, 1857. An application is made, and this is either granted or refused; there is no statutory right of appeal against either decision. However, in the twenty-first century there is of course Judicial Review, that is, if consideration is given to whether the Secretary of State acted unreasonably or irrationally in reach a decision.

Such a case came to the fore in the extraordinary case involving the exhumation of a Polish priest, Fr. Jarzebowski, in 2011. Permission to exhume his body from the churchyard, where it had been buried nearly fifty years previously, in 1964, was granted by the then Secretary of State, following a request by the priest's religious Order, and endorsed by senior members of the Catholic Church. The Order was now in possession of a defunct property, Fawley Court, the mansion, situated in Henley-on-Thames, and, incidentally, the house which had inspired *Toad of Toad Hall*. Fr. Jarzebowski (1897–1964) had been buried in the grounds of this mansion. The new owners, who were the Iranian heiress, Aida Hersham, and her partner, the Marks & Spencer heir Patrick Sieff, did not want a burial ground on their property. They were paying £16.5 million for it. The Order were bound by the terms of a charitable endowment, and in selling the property, they were contractually bound to remove the remains of the deceased. Under the conditions of sale; Fr. Jarzebowski would be re-interred with other members of the same religious Order in Fair Mile cemetery, and where people could still visit the grave—an important factor, given that this particular priest had achieved a saint-like status among Polish Catholics, both in the UK, and abroad.

The exhumation was therefore for purely practical, legal reasons. A clause in the sale agreement included a condition that the Marian Fathers could lose up to £3.5 million of the sale price if the remains, not only of the priest, but of the founder of the Order, Prince Stanislas Radziwill, a member of the former Polish royal family, were not removed.

Prince Stanislaw Albrecht Raziwill had died in London on June 27, 1976. His name had become well known in high circles in both Britain and America because he had become the brother-in-law of President John Fitzgerald Kennedy, when he married Jacqueline Kennedy's sister, Caroline Lee Bouvier. Thereafter she was known as Princess Lee Radziwill. They had two children: Prince Anthony Radziwill, born in 1959, and Princess Anna Christina Radziwill, born in 1960. President Kennedy stood godfather, and at the insistence of his wife, was personally present in Westminster Cathedral, when the baptism took place in 1960. But when the Prince died, he was buried in the crypt of St. Anne's Church, at Fawley Court. As of 2010, the Marian Fathers were seeking authorisation to exhume the body following the closure of the Divine Mercy College in 1986, and the sale of Fawley Court in 2010.[17]

But the case of Fr. Jarzebowski raised issues other than those purely legal ones considered in the court. The Polish Catholic community did not see it like that, and challenged the permission to exhume, under the name *R. (on the application of Rudewicz) v. Ministry of Justice (2011) EWHC 3078 (admin.)* Mme. Rudewicz was a distant but nonetheless the closest living relative of the dead priest.

Looking at the exhumation controls imposed by S. 25, the High Court accepted that there should usually be "some proper reason" for disinterment, and that a Secretary of State who granted permission "for a frivolous reason, or for no reason at all", would be acting unreasonably and irrationally. The Appeal Court was presided over by Lord Neuberger.

The Court decided that the decision could not be impugned in the present case. The Secretary of State had been entitled to decide that relocating the priest's remains (a specific course of action favoured by the Catholic Church) to a burial site where he would be re-interred/re-united with his colleagues, and where the public would have unrestricted access to his grave, favoured the grant of a S. 25 licence, regardless of the opposition from the applicant and others. The fact that the deceased had wanted to be interred in his original resting place was deemed irrelevant since the constitution of the religious Order which had bound the deceased in life, clearly stated that the Head of the Order had the final say on a priest's burial place. Human rights arguments were rejected by the High Court, but one is bound to ask why the priest's wishes were observed in the first place. There remains from this case a feeling that the deceased was bound in life, and his body continued to be bound after that life had ended.[18]

The Secretary of State in 2011 was Ken Clarke, being Justice Secretary. The back story to this exhumation is rather interesting. The applicant to the court, appealing against the exhumation, was one Elizabeth Rudewicz. She thought it would be disrespectful to the dead priest, with whom she had had a close connection. Two thousand people joined her in this protest.

As has been seen, the exhumations, of which there had to be a number, included Prince Stanislas Radziwill, who had died in 1976, and been interred in the crypt of the chapel, and Fr. Jarzebowski, and a Mexican boy of saintly repute, of which more later.

The chapel was now deconsecrated but the building itself is a Grade II listed building.

During his lifetime, Fr. Jarzebowski had set up a school. In the 1950s, a Polish woman arrived at the school to work there, bringing from Mexico, where she had lived for many years, the remains of her son, who had died, aged fourteen, in 1944. The woman and the boy had escaped from Poland after the invasion of Poland at the beginning of World War II, and made their way to Mexico. Whilst they were there, they met a priest who had also come from Poland, Fr. Jarzebowski. The priest had fallen in what seemed a mortal illness, and the devout boy prayed to God to take his own life rather than that of the priest. This is what happened. The boy died, and the priest lived. Eventually, Fr. Jarzebowski moved to the United Kingdom, living in Hertforshire. The story of the boy, Witold, however, became something of a legend and a cult among the Polish Catholic faithful. The presence of the boy's body, now in England, could only add to it. He was buried in the former St. Raphael's Convent in Bullingham, Hertforshire. His mother, Zofia, eventually moved herself to Henley-on-Thames, and the question of Witold's body then again became important. Although she then died in 1995, aged 90, Fr. Jasinski, however, mindful of the importance of the boy's body, moved it to Henley, so that it could be re-interred with his mother. The priest, however, now found himself the subject of a prosecution, for moving a body without all the requisite permissions. Judge Toby Harper, QC, even put the case back, for Fr. Jasinski to carry out missionary work in the Ukraine, so clearly it was not considered a case of paramount importance, or one in which the final outcome was predictable. Thus it was, that on July 28, 2011, a judge at Worcester Crown Court decided that there was insufficient evidence to convict him. Fr. Jasinski returned to Rome, where he still lives.

It is perhaps worth noting that in 1940, presumably just before he escaped from Poland, Fr. Jarzebowski had met the famous Polish spiritual director, Fr. Michael Sopocko. He has since been beatified, and another of his charges, Sister Faustina, has been canonised by the Polish pope, John Paul II., on April 18, 1993. Clearly, this heady air of holiness is infectious. Pope John Paul II has since been canonised himself.

Notes

1. Staley, Edgcumbe, *The Founding of Venice, in The Dogaressas of Venice* (c.1915), New York, Charles Scribner's Sons, pp. xvi–xxi.
2. Cornwell, John, *Newman's Unquiet Grave* (2013), pp. 1–3, Prologue.
3. Similar to the excavation of the ground in which (Sir) Roger Casement's body was interred after his execution at Pentonville, on August 3, 1916. The difference there was that lime had been used, and he was buried without a coffin, being executed as a traitor. Nevertheless, recognisable remains were still identified.
4. The tomb of Margaret Audley, Duchess of Norfolk (1540–1564), resided in the Church of St. John the Baptist, Maddermarket, in Norwich, she having died in that city; her husband's first wife, Lady Mary Fitzalan Howard, lay in the tomb with her. Together they had a splendid tomb, on which were heraldic quarterings, and the two effigies, shown in their robes of state. When Lady Margaret was exhumed, in anticipation of being moved to the family tombs in Thetford or Framlingham, it was discovered that the tomb was empty, except for dust and, intriguingly, some red hair. See Williams, Neville, Thomas Howard, *4th Duke of Norfolk* (1964) Barrie & Rockcliffe.
5. Cornwell, op. cit., pp. 1–2.
6. Ibid., pp. 1–2.
7. Ibid., pp. 39–42.
8. Ibid., chapter 19, passim.
9. Meyer, Barbara Hochstetler, *The First Tomb of Henry VII of England*, The Art Bulletin, p. 361, and n. 22.

10. Gigli, *Opere I.*, 484–9; quoted in Jorgensen, Johannes, *St. Catherine of Siena* (1938), translated from the Danish by Ingebord Lund, Longmans, Green & Co., p. 393. Gigli edited St. Catherine' Letters, in Vols. I & II of the *Opere di Santa Caterina*, published in Siena in 1713, For this edition, Gigli made use of ms. T, III, 3, of the Municipal Library of Siena; a ms. Which is none other than a volume of the famous collection of the Saint's writings made in Venice, before 1412, by Nicolo Guidiccioni of Lucca, who had a great devotion to the saint. See Jorgensen, pp. 403–4. This means that, by descent, it can be relied upon as an authentic source.
11. Jorgensen, pp. 398–400.
12. Ibid., op. cit., pp. 131–2.
13. Farmer, *Oxford Dictionary of Saints* (1978, 1992). He was Reader in History at Reading University, retiring in 1985.
14. Farmer, ibid., op. cit., pp. 149–51.
15. Kelly, James D., *Dictionary of the Popes*, pp. 8–9.
16. *BBC News Daily*, April 16, 2017.
17. *New York Times*, June 29, 1976; *London Times*, June 28, 1976.
18. Conway, Heather, *The Law and the Dead*, Rutledge, (2016), p. 189.

CHAPTER 8

Royal Requiem

In the summer of 1965, a young novice monk at Quarr Abbey on the Isle of Wight was summoned from his routine to attend an extraordinary service in the neighbouring St. Cecilia's nunnery. The future Fr. Gregory Corcoran did not feel like going. It was a hot, close day, and the idea of attending a Mass during the afternoon in a crowded church did not appeal; but it was to be something memorable. Indeed, his memories of that day are still as green as ever.[1]

Abbot Aelred had come to celebrate a requiem Mass for Mother Adelaide, who had been at the Nunnery for eight years before her death. But this was 1965, and Mother Adelaide had died in 1909. The situation was that the Portuguese government had adopted a policy of bringing all the bodies of Portuguese royal persons who had died abroad, back home to Portugal. Behind this was a longer term plan of restoring the Portuguese monarchy, which had come to a somewhat abrupt end in 1910, the year after the death of Mother Adelaide. In her previous life, Mother Adelaide had been Her Highness Princess Adelheid of Lowenstein-Wertheim-Rosenberg, born in 1831. When she was twenty she became the wife of the former King of Portugal, Dom Miguel, who had reigned as *de facto* King from 1826 to 1834. He had then renounced all claims to the throne in favour of his niece, Dona Maria da Gloria II, and retired to Germany. His body was also being returned to Portugal, from Braunbach in Bavaria, where their bodies would be re-united.

M. L. Nash, *The History and Politics of Exhumation*,
https://doi.org/10.1007/978-3-030-24047-9_8

After the exhumation of the former nun's body (at which the young novice was not present), a grand Requiem Mass was held in the church of the nunnery. The body was enclosed in a coffin of English oak. The Portuguese ambassador, Senor Manuel Rocheta, and his wife were present. The Portuguese consul in Southampton, Senor Martin de Almeida, had been present at the exhumation, the Roman Catholic bishop of Portsmouth, Monsignor Derek Worlock being represented by Fr. P.J. O'Connell, the Bishop's chaplain. The exhumation took place with a simple service in the cemetery, as the nuns sang.

The oak coffin was placed on trestles in the sunlit cloister at the front of an altar bearing crucifix, candles, and flowers. It was then carried into the sanctuary of the nunnery church, accompanied by sixty nuns singing a canticle from Isaiah.

The hot afternoon then proceeded with Vespers of the Dead being sung, followed by the Requiem Mass celebrated by Dom Aelred Sillem, the Abbot of Quarr, in the presence of the Portuguese ambassador and his wife, the Portuguese consul, and Lady Bernadette Smeyers, the Abbess of St. Cecilia's.

The young novice watched the Requiem intently, and noticed that during the Mass the Ambassador's wife was telling her rosary beads, something forbidden by the strict rules; and the ambassador himself turned over two pages at once. It was just as if, thought the novice, they were not fully conversant with the Mass at all. Another odd thing was that no one communicated during the Mass, that is, no one received holy communion, under either wafer or wine.

The next day the body was flown to Lisbon from Bournemouth airport by military aircraft, where a State funeral awaited, before being transferred to the Royal Pantheon, together with all the royal bodies gathered from abroad.

The story of the former German princess, who had become the wife of the exiled Portuguese pretender, was that of a young girl who had been married to a much older man; their marriage, however, does not appear to have been unhappy, and after his death in 1866, she devoted herself to the upbringing and education of their children and grandchildren. At the age of sixty-four she became a Benedictine nun, at St. Cecilia's at Solesmes, in France, in 1895. As Mother Adelaide of Braganza (the dynastic name of the Portuguese royal family), she came to England when the community was threatened by anti-religious feeling in France, and was exiled in 1901.

Dom Miguel had compromised his own position for his present and his future when, as *de facto* ruler of Portugal, he had given support to the Infante Carlos, Count of Molina, and Pretender to the Spanish throne. Going into exile in Germany, he died whilst out hunting at Bronnbach, in the Grand Duchy of Baden, on November 14, 1866. He his body was buried in his wife's family vault in the Franciscan monastery of Engelberg at Grossenbach in Bavaria. From there in 1967 it was transferred to Lisbon to be re-united with that of his wife.

An interesting consequence of their marriage was that their daughter Maria Antonia married Duke Robert of Parma and the grandmother of the Empress Zita of Austria. If Adelheid had lived a few more months she would have learned of the marriage of this grand-daughter to the Archduke Karl of Austria, destined to be the last Habsburg emperor, in 1911. Maria Antonia had been born in 1862, and died in 1959, aged 97. She gave this longevity to Empress Zita, who died in 1989, aged 97, and her eldest son, the last Crown Prince of Austria, Archduke Otto, who died in 2011, aged 98.

At the Abbey, she was visited by the King, Edward VII, and the Queen, Alexandra, on a number of occasions.

It is of some interest that the local report of the exhumation and requiem was followed by a letter, wishing to correct some of the report. This letter read as follows:

> I have just read your account of the exhumation of Mother Adelaide of Braganza, and am very surprised that you should refer to her as a "Portuguese Queen"...by no stretch of the imagination was she ever Queen of Portugal. Dom Miguel was never legitimate king, and in fact renounced all claims in 1834, when he settled in Germany.

However, to balance this, Dom Miguel was indeed Regent, as the dynastic quarrel was in full spate, the King of Portugal, his brother, having decided not to return from Brazil, preferring it there, and having gone there to escape Napoleon. Moreover, he had left his daughter, aged seven, as the infant Queen of Portugal. It is not surprising that her uncle seized power. His niece, in the meantime, had been taken by the British to Windsor, where she became a playmate to Princess Victoria, who was exactly the same age. Eventually, Maria returned, aged fifteen, to successfully reign over Portugal until she died in 1853, after the birth of her eleventh child. Her second husband had been a Coburg, like Prince Albert, and then became Regent. Victoria had much better luck in most circumstances.

The grandson of Dom Miguel and Dona Adelheid was Dom Duarte, born in 1907, two years before his grandmother's death in England. In 1942 he had married a relative, Dona Francoise of Orleans-Braganza, who was seven years his junior. Their son was Dom Duarte, Duke of Braganza, born in 1945, who married Isabel de Heredia in 1995. This of course was in the future. In 1965 Dom Duarte was a rather young twenty-year-old, but nevertheless in the sights of Salazar, the dictator of Portugal, as a future king. This was very much in the pattern of what was happening in Spain. In 1969 Franco, the Spanish dictator, named Don Juan Carlos, as the Prince of Spain and future king. The advantage in Spain was that the monarchy had ended later, in 1931.

Another relevant dimension to all this is that Portugal, while deposing its own king, had become a haven for many others. Salazar was well acquainted with all the heads of the exiled royal families living then within the triangle of Cascalis-Sintra-Estoril. Among these were King Simeon of Bulgaria, the Count of Barcelona (official pretender to the Spanish throne), the Count of Paris (pretender to the Bourbon throne of France), and King Carol of Roumania, as well as the Archduke Joseph of Austria-Hungary.

Salazar, moreover, was in love with Carolina Asseca, whose father, the Viscount Asseca, had been a very relevant character in the household of the late King Manoel II of Portugal, who had died at Twickenham in England, in exile, in 1932. The Assecas were part of an important group of the nobility and the Viscount had been very close to Queen Amelie, the last queen of Portugal, and the mother of Manoel II.

The Portuguese royal family, like some other royal families, was not known for its brains or intellect, but, inevitably, there was one who was indeed of some intellect. This was the Infanta Filippa, who was the brains of the Portuguese royal family; Carolina Asseca was a very close friend of the Infanta. One can see how all the pieces of the mosaic might so easily have fallen into place. Old Dom Duarte did not share the intellect of his sister, and neither did the other sister, the Infanta Adelaide.

The claim of this branch of the Portuguese royal family, the Miguelists, can be seen to be somewhat shaky, and therefore, the marriage was arranged between Dom Duarte and his cousin from Brazil, which then strengthened the claim. She also had some rights to the Portuguese throne. Unfortunately, whilst being very pious, she lacked the charm and the glamour of her sister, who had married the Count of Paris.

Salazar was very much influenced by both Carolina Asseca and the Infanta Filippa, and therefore, had the Braganzas brought back from their exile in Switzerland to Portugal, and begged old Queen Amelie to stand as godmother to Dom Duarte's eldest son, the present Duke of Braganza. Queen Amelie left him some legacies in her will, such as the tiara the present Duchess of Braganza wears nowadays. Queen Amelie, understandably, did not much like the Miguelists, as they were the junior branch of the family, but, her own line having died out, she agreed to do all this for the sake of the monarchy.

The main problem with Salazar's great plan (and the plans of the moving spirits Carolina Asseca and the Infanta Filippa) was that their candidate was a rather poor one, not very intelligent, who had, in addition, a drinking problem. Thus, when the old Duke Duarte arrived back in Portugal, Salazar had transferred to the State many properties having belonged to the Braganzas in Portugal, and granted Dom Duarte a pension, and put at his disposition and that of his family an old convent palace at Coimbra where they lived in a state rather beneath their royal status.

Bringing back to Portugal the remains of Queen Amelie and other members of the former royal family was part of a *mise en scene* that might have paved the way for a restoration of the monarchy. However, in the end, Salazar was not all that sure and nothing came of his scheme.

In Spain, however, the candidate proved to be of some mettle, and later became a very successful King, at least for most of his reign.[2]

It may have been these plans of Salazar and Franco, which were the catalyst for many more exhumations resulting in a string of royal requiems across the globe in the next three decades. There was undoubtedly a movement after the fall of the Soviet Union in 1989 for a return of some kind to the monarchies which had formerly existed in Eastern Europe. One of the exiled kings, Simeon II of Bulgaria, even returned to his own country as Prime Minister, leading the Simeon II Party, thus, echoing the prophetic George Bernard Shaw's play *The Apple Cart* in 1929. Shaw was thinking almost certainly of the fidgety Prince of Wales, the future Edward VIII, and his prediction of the abdication and its aftermath was somewhat uncanny; but it could equally be applied to the events of sixty years later. The state of Yugoslavia, which was an artificial construct, fell apart in its constituent provinces, as was predictable, but those now in power wished to recover the bodies of royal persons who had died abroad in the interim, perhaps not so much to restore their heirs to power, but to put together the dynastic mosaic again, which had been an integral part of their history. Histories are bound by their very nature to be good, bad and indifferent, and to remove or obliterate the past is also bound to reverberate on those who do it.

Interestingly, the Portuguese exhumations and repatriations were followed by royal bodies being returned to Brazil in the 1970s and 1980s. The kings of Portugal in the early nineteenth century, having fled before Napoleon to South America, decided they liked it better there, and declared themselves Emperors of Brazil, leaving Portugal to another branch of the family of Braganza. But their bodies were returned on death to the Royal Pantheon in Lisbon. Then, in 1965 and 1966, when Braganza bodies were being returned from England and Germany to Lisbon, the Brazilians wanted the bodies of their Emperors and their families back again in Brazil; so the imperial remains made another journey across the Atlantic. A restless family continued its life even after death in constant motion.

The bodies, therefore, of the Emperors of Brazil, Pedro I and Pedro II, which had been interred in the monastery of Sao Vicente de Fora, were removed from there to Brazil in 1972, to the Petropolis Cathedral in Rio de Janeiro. The body of the imperial princess, Maria Amelia, only child of Emperor Pedro II from his second marriage, was also moved to Brazil in 1982, but to the Convento de Santo Antonio in Rio.

The body of King Carol II of Roumania and his wife Maria Lupescu (the former mistress the notorious Madame Lupescu, whom he had married in exile after his abdication in 1943) were not returned to Roumania until 2003. They were then re-interred in Curtea de Arges, alongside other Roumanian royals. At the same time, or a little later, former royal properties, including palaces, were returned to the former King Michael and his family. Michael was the son of Carol by his first marriages to Queen Helen and reigned briefly as a very young man, until his forced abdication and exile by the new Communist regime in December 1947. One of his last royal acts had been to attend the wedding of his cousin, Princess Elizabeth, in Westminster Abbey, in the November of the same year.

Two years later the Danish authorities and Queen Margrethe II allowed the body of the Tsarina Maria Fyodorovna, who had died in Denmark in 1928, and been buried among the royal tombs in Roskilde Cathedral, to be returned to Russia, to lie with her husband, Alexander III. The ceremonies for her re-interment lasted three or four days, from September 23 to the September 26, 2006. After a service in the very impressive St. Isaac's Cathedral, she was laid to rest again next to her husband, her son Nicholas II, and her grandchildren, in the fortress of Peter and Paul in St. Petersburg. All the tsars are now buried there from the time of Michael Romanov, with the exception of the infant Ivan VI, who died in 1761.

Two of those grandchildren were missing also in 2006. Although the bodies of Tsar Nicholas, his wife, the Tsarina Alexandra, and three of their five children had been found in a mass grave in the Urals in 1991, and identified by DNA testing in 1998, the remains thought to be those of the third daughter Maria, and the Tsarevich Alexis were not found until 2007. They were also found some distance away from the other bodies, and this was one reason why the Russian Orthodox Church questioned their identification, and asked that the remains be re-examined ahead of re-burial with the rest of the family.

The senior investigator was Vladimir Solovyov, who headed the investigating team. He told the Russian TASS news agency:

> The exhumation was done in the presence of representatives of the Russian Orthodox Church. The necessary samples were taken from the remains of Nicholas II and of the Tsarina Alexandra Fyodorovna. Also, samples of blood were taken from the stains on the full-dress uniform of the assassinated Tsar Alexander II, the grandfather of Nicholas, who had been killed on March 1st, 1881.

The remains of the last two children were then taken to the crypt of St. Catherine sacrarium in the fortress of Peter and Paul in St. Petersburg.

The involvement of the Orthodox Church was crucial in these exhumations, and in the year 2000 the Church had already canonised Nicholas II, the Tsarina Alexandra, and the three daughters who had been buried there in 1998. The question remained as to whether the Tsarevich Alexis and the remaining daughter Maria would also be canonised; but until their remains were confirmed as authentic, they were kept at the Russian State Archives.[3] Ironically, it was Maria who had been the most religiously observant of all the five children.

Three of the royal personages of the former Yugoslavia were also repatriated and given a final royal requiem in 2013. These were King Peter II, his mother Queen Maria, and his wife Queen Alexandra. Peter had been king from the assassination of his father, King Alexander, in 1934, to his final deposition in 1945. He had reigned as a child and youth, under the regency of his mother, the former Princess Maria of Roumania. After an exile spent in tragic and wasted years, mostly in America, he died in Denver, Colorado, on November 3, 1970, aged 45. At his own wish he was buried in the St. Sava monastery church in Libertyville, Illinois. To date he has the distinction of being the only European monarch to be buried in the United States.

In January, 2013, his remains were exhumed and returned to Serbia, to be buried in the Royal Family Mausoleum in St. George's Church at Oplenac. In April, 2013, his mother, Queen Maria of Yugoslavia, was exhumed from her grave at Frogmore, Windsor, where many royal persons since the time of Queen Victoria have been buried. It was necessary to obtain the permission of the Queen for this exhumation and removal. Her body was first removed to the Serbian church in London, to await the flight to her adopted homeland. She had gone into exile in 1941, and died in 1961. Her grandson Crown Prince Alexander then flew to Belgrade, accompanying her body. Alexander himself had been born in Claridge's Hotel in London. The room where he was born was declared by King George VI to be Yugoslav territory for the day of his birth!

The three royal persons were to be re-interred in Topola, Serbia. For the exhumation of the third body, that of Queen Alexandra, born a Greek princess, the permission of the Greek Foreign Ministry had to be obtained, as she had been first buried in Tatoi, outside Athens., on February 7, 1993, although she had died in Britain. The repatriation of her body took place on May 9 and 10, 2013. Again, her son Crown Prince Alexander, accompanied her body back to Belgrade, but also accompanied by Princess Katherine, and Katherine's son Mr. David Andrews, as well as high representatives of the Foreign Ministry of Greece and the Serbian ambassador to Greece. Princess Irene of Greece, sister of the exiled King Constantine of the Hellenes, and of Queen Sofia of Spain, was also among those who accompanied the party, together with Mrs. Alison Andrews, daughter of Princess Katherine.

To the cries of "Welcome home, Mother! Eternal glory to her!" Queen Alexandra's body joined those of King Peter and Queen Maria for a triple State funeral on May 26, 2013.

2017 had been proclaimed *The Year of Maria Theresa* in Austria, for it marked the tricentenary of her birth in 1717. The Empress Maria Theresa is one of the most iconic personages in Austrian and Hungarian history; Empress because she was married to the Emperor Francis of Lorraine, and crowned and anointed Queen of Hungary in her own right. She had been the subject of a famous, or infamous, piece of legal pragmatism, named aptly, the *Pragmatic Sanction*, to enable her to succeed her father, the Emperor Charles VI, in his hereditary dominions. It was a legal document more noted in the breach than in the observation, but the charisma and strength of character of Maria Theresa led her ultimately to triumph and acclaim, as well as being the mother of twelve children, among them the ill-fated Marie-Antoinette.

Interestingly, in the present context, it was her father, Charles VI, who ordered the vault in Konigsfelden in Switzerland to be opened, and its contents surveyed in 1739, one year before his own death. Konigsfelden monastery had been the final resting place of many of the Habsburg dynasty because Switzerland had been also their place of origin. Perhaps the Emperor intended the bodies buried there to be brought to Vienna, but died before he had achieved his objective. Perhaps Maria Theresa knew this. As the elder of two daughters, she was close to her father, much in the way that Queen Elizabeth II of Britain had been close to her father George VI. The monastery, moreover, had fallen into some disuse, and was being used as a barn.

Whatever the reason, thirty-one years later, on September 10, 1770, Maria Theresa made a special request to the Cantonal authorities to allow all the remains there to be removed. This was eventually permitted and they were taken for re-burial in a splendid new mausoleum at St. Blasien in the Black Forest. This was not, however, to be the end because again in 1807 the mausoleum no longer fell under Habsburg domain and jurisdiction, and Maria Theresa's grandson, the new Emperor Francis I of Austria ordered that the remains be moved again to St. Paul in Laventhal. The remains still rest there today, in front of the high altar. What had caused the second exhumation was the extinction of the Holy Roman Empire of the German Nation by Napoleon in 1806. The Emperor had to abandon his, by now, empty title, and became instead Emperor of Austria, a title of much more substance, which would last another hundred years.

The bodies moved from St. Blasien were those of Elizabeth of Carinthia, Queen of the Romans (King of the Romans was the subsidiary title given to the heir of the Holy Roman Emperor, something akin to that of Prince of Wales); Leopold the Glorious, Duke of Austria; his wife Catherine of Savoy; Henry the Friendly and his wife; Elizabeth of Virneburg, Countess of Ottingen; Elizabeth of Austria, Duchess of Lorraine; and Jutta of Austria. They were relatively minor royals, but the Habsburgs usually looked after their own, with almost pathological concern, as if they were a special race, which, indeed, they considered that they were.

Both the Habsburgs Maria Theresa of Austria and of Hungary, and Carlos II of Spain, had a fascination with the exhumation of distant ancestors, considering them "The dust from which we came".[4]

But it was not only the Habsburgs and the House of Braganza which would have royal repatriation. The last king of Poland, Stanislaus Augustus, as great an art patron as Charles I and George IV of England, was repatriated to Poland from Russia, where his body had lain since his death in exile in 1798. He had had an extraordinary life. There were a number of pivotal dates in this life. The last one (in his living life) or the most important one at the end, was his abdication, on November 23, 1795, of the Polish throne. It would never be revived for another king. "I do so", he said, "for the sake of my unhappy country". Then he burst into tears, and had to be helped from the throne, a broken man. The abdication was the final confirmation of the third partition of Poland, which swept it altogether from the map: one third to Prussia, one third to Austria, one third to Russia, although, to use an Irish analogy, the thirds were bigger or smaller than each other. The ruler of Russia was still the Empress Catherine II, to whom history, rightly or wrongly, would give the title "The Great". In return for this final act of submission, Stanislaus was confirmed in his private estates. In a not unkindly letter, she advised him to spent his final days in Rome, as this would be best suited to his political situation and his predilection for Art. She permitted him also the choice of route to the Eternal City, so that he might avoid all those places "most likely to evoke painful recollections". But Stanislaus preferred to remain at Grodno and took up botany as an additional diversion.[5] But the central character in all this was Catherine II, the Empress of Russia, called The Great. Three extraordinary exhumations, that of her husband, and two of her lovers, Grigori Potemkin ("The Prince of Princes") and the last Polish king, Stanislaus Augustus Poniatowski, were to follow their deaths.

Catherine died first, on November 17, 1796. Her death affected him profoundly, although ironically it benefited him considerably, for she was succeeded by her son, the Emperor Paul I. Mother and son had thoroughly disliked one another, to put it mildly, and, as a final riposte to his mother's policies, Paul released all the Polish prisoners-of-war, and, in a letter full of sympathy and affection, invited Stanislaus to settle in St. Petersburg, and assigned to him a pension of 100,000 ducats. The three petitioning powers had already agreed to pay his debts between them. Dethroned kings are not always treated so well, although one author referred to Paul's conduct as "cranky behaviour"[6] (see note 6(i)). The Marble Palace was given to him as a residence, and his first visitor there was the Emperor himself, attended by his whole court. From henceforth the former king lived in ease and comfort occupying himself for the most part with his books, of which he now began to make a complete catalogue.

Stanislaus died, rather suddenly, on February 12, 1798, of an apoplectic seizure, in his sixty-sixth year. On hearing of the last illness of his guest, the Emperor Paul at once hastened to his side, and never quitted him until it was all over. At eight o'clock on the night before he died, the Papal Nuncio, Lorenzo Litta, arrived to bestow absolution on the unconscious monarch.[7] The funeral of a crowned head was generously accorded to his remains, by the Russian Emperor. Paul himself rode in front of the hearse, at the head of the Life Guards with his drawn sword reversed. The Ministers and Dignitaries of the Russian court followed in parade carriages adorned with the royal arms. The White Eagle standard, embroidered with the escutcheons of Poland and Lithuania, was borne before them by a herald. The Metropolitan of St. Petersburg conducted the funeral service, together with the Papal Nuncio and the French Bishop of Rennes, on March 8, 1797, after his body had been embalmed, and had lain in state for nine days.[8] All the regiments of the Guards were drawn up on both sides of the Nevsky Prospect, from the Marble Palace to the Catholic Church, where the relics of Stanislaus were reverently laid within a mural niche. By the Emperor's special command, two stately standards were placed over the tomb to mark the last resting place of the last King of Poland.[9]

When Nisbet wrote these words in 1909, the phoenix of Poland had not yet risen from the ashes, and would not do so until 1918. The last Emperor of Russia had then also disappeared, but what was then to happen to all the royal and imperial remains in a Bolshevik and Radical Russia? For twenty years the grave of Stanislaus remained quiet. Then, in 1938, when the Soviet Union planned to demolish the church of St. Catherine, where he lay, he was exhumed, and his remains transferred to the second Polish republic, and re-interred in a church in Wolcyzn, his birthplace. This was done in secret, and caused controversy in Poland when the issue became known. On July 11th, 1938, the coffin containing the earthly remains of Stanislas arrived at the small railway border crossing of Stolpce in an ordinary goods waggon attached to the end of a passenger train. The wagon was uncoupled and shunted into a siding. It was unsealed and the coffin opened for inspection. This must have caused something of a shock because, during the nineteenth century, the crypt of St. Catherine's had been flooded twice, and the remains were described as "insubstantial". The inspection was carried out not by customs, but by a three-man commission from Warsaw. They certified that

> the coffin contained "the very insubstantial remains" of Stanislas Augustus. When he was re-interred in Wolczn, the parish priest was sworn to secrecy as he was laid in the crypt, in the company of many generations of Poniatowskis and Czartoryskis. As the king's coffin was too large for the crypt, it was placed in a niche, which was promptly walled up. "The whole operation", wrote Adam Zamoyski, "had resembled more the burying of stolen treasure than of a royal body".[10] But then so many royal bodies have been viewed like this.
>
> In 1990, due to the poor state of the church in Wolczn, which was then in Belarus, his body was once more exhumed, and brought to Poland, to St. John's cathedral in Warsaw, where, on 3rd May, 1791, he had celebrated the adoption of the Constitution that he had co-authored. A final funeral ceremony would be held on 14th February, 1995.[11]

On that day the final requiem of Stanislaus took place in the Cathedral of St. John the Baptist in Warsaw, presided over by the Cardinal Primate of Poland. This, as Butterwick says, in something of an understatement, "no ordinary royal funeral", although perhaps no royal funeral could be so classed. The king had been dead for 197 years.

Because he remained in some ways a controversial figure in a very convoluted Polish history (and during that history Poland has not been short of controversial figures), his remains did not seem to unduly interest the reborn Poland of Jozef Pilsudski in 1918. By the Treaty of Riga in 1921, Poland recovered many of her cultural and historical treasures plundered during the period of partition. However, in 1938, when that fragile independence was again threatened, Soviet Russia planned to bulldoze the Catholic church of St. Catherine in St. Petersburg, where Stanislaus was interred in 1798. Enough respect was shown for the Russians to unilaterally hand back the coffin to Poland which contained the remains of their last king. Now a conundrum lay ahead, for tradition demanded a royal funeral on Wawel Hill in Cracow; but it had been just three years since Pilsudski had been buried there. But at that time the authorities in Poland decided that Stanislaus had forfeited his right to be buried there or in Warsaw because of his controversial behaviour at the end of his life and reign. So Stanislaus was buried quietly in the parish church of Wolczyn, where he had been baptised in 1732. Nevertheless, this led in turn to a public debate on the merits and demerits of the long dead king, something then postponed for sixty years, due to the circumstances which now overwhelmed not only Poland but engulfed the whole of Europe.

When Poland had its frontiers drawn yet again, in 1945, it had been "shunted west", and Wolczyn now lay in Belarus. Every request for intervention was turned down until 1987–1988, when, under pressure from writers and historians, the Ministry of Culture appointed a commission to travel to Wolczyn. When it reached the devastated church in December, 1988, it found only bits of his coffin. (Interestingly, when the present writer visited St. Petersburg and the Church of St. Catherine, in 2005, he was told by the lady in charge that bits of his original coffin there still survived). It returned to Warsaw with some fragments of the royal robes found by some Belorussian academics a year before. Six frustrating years of delay and procrastination followed, six years in which Polish life was transformed, following the fall of the Soviet Union.

Stanislaus's scanty remains, mixed with earth from Wolczyn, were finally interred in Poland. Nationalist politicians grumbled about the funeral. Cardinal Glemp almost apologised for his homily (something Cardinal Wyszynski would not have done, although he did agree to the burial in his cathedral). When Adam Zamoyski wrote his biography of Stanislas in 1992 the last line was "As this book goes to print, the coffin lies under a dust sheet on the landing of a back staircase in the Royal Castle".[12] It had been a long journey for this royal body. The press showed little interest, but this might have been because of so many years of repression and suspicion. Only one publication mentioned the sympathy Varsovians seemed to feel for the king. The truth was that the Poland of 1995 was very different in makeup from that of 200 years previously. The population was much more homogenous; that of Stanislaus's time had been multi-ethnic. Stanislaus and his enlightened compatriots looked towards France, England, and the Netherlands for their exemplars, and he had visited all of them and learned much which contributed to the Constitution of 1791. But for Stanislaus the times were wrong. Then it could not be sustained. In 1995, there was a perception that the former Soviet occupation had made Poland and other occupied states "backward". But, whatever these perceptions, Poland had at last buried its last king. A line could be drawn.

But what of Potemkin and Peter III of Russia, lover and husband of Catherine? How Tsar Paul I dealt with them on beginning Tsar in 1796 is instructive. It had been a coup which had brought Catherine to power in 1762, a palace coup of those who envisaged more advantage in Catherine, who had become Orthodox and Russified, whereas her husband was pro-

Prussian and Lutheran in outlook. It would be the Baltic-born Catherine who would come to personify Russia.

Paul was in some ways a complex character. This is not surprising, as he had to endure the removal and murder of his father, Tsar Peter III, at least with the knowledge of his mother, who then assumed power as the Empress Catherine II, better known to history as Catherine the Great. Peter III made the mistake, made by some rulers of Russia both before him and after him, of not appearing entirely Russian. Peter had actually been born Karl Peter Ulrich in Kiel, in Holstein, in 1728. Nevertheless, although seemingly born a German prince, his father claimed descent from Rurik, the founder of the original Russian dynasty. But it was his mother, Anna Petrovna, who was the daughter of Peter the Great and his second wife the Empress Catherine I. On his father's side, Peter also had a claim to the Swedish throne because his father's mother Hedwig was a sister of the childless Charles (Karl) XII of Sweden. But it was not only these conflicting dynastic claims but the different religions involved. Peter had been brought up as a Lutheran and educated in the Prussian military style. In Russia of course he and his children were expected to be strict Orthodox. When he arrived in Russia in 1742, therefore, at the invitation of the Empress Elizabeth (also a daughter of Peter the Great), he was instructed in the Russian language and converted to Orthodoxy. Three years later, in 1745, he was married, perhaps unwisely, to a German princess, Sophia Fredericke Augusta of Anhalt-Zaerbst, who took the name Ekaterina(Catherine) when she also converted to Orthodoxy; but herein lay the genesis of what later happened. Catherine embraced the new situation with all the fervour she could muster, whereas Peter was forever hankering back to his Prussian military education and the Lutheran faith.

Catherine suffered a miscarriage in 1753, but was pregnant again in 1754, and Paul was born in the September. Immediately rumours circulated that Sergei Saltykov was his father, a Russian nobleman who was Catherine's lover. Even if this was the case, Paul still had Romanov blood because Saltykov was also descended from one of the sisters of Michael Romanov, the first Tsar of the Romanov dynasty. But this showed the state of the marriage of Peter and Catherine. Peter, who was not good-looking to begin with, had his complexion ruined by the smallpox. As it turned out, Paul seemed in every way to be a carbon copy of Peter, so perhaps he was his father after all. Interestingly, the 1722 Law on the Succession of Peter the Great did not require a blood link, but only that the "worthiest" should be nominated by the reigning Tsar or Empress.

Although nominated twenty years before his accession, his neglect of Orthodoxy meant nothing could save Peter when he succeeded briefly in 1762. A palace coup by Catherine, the guards regiments and Catherine's lover Grigory Orlov meant that Peter was compelled to abdicate on June 29, 1762. Placed under house arrest on his estates in Ropsha, he died only a week later, between July 3 and July 6. Officially he died of "haemorrhoidal colic", but various rumours hinted at poison, strangulation, suffocation, beating or shooting: any of these lethal choices. The officer in charge of the former emperor's escort reported "an unfortunate scuffle". No-one was charged.[13]

During all this, Prince Paul was still only seventeen, and overwhelmed by events. He is one of those few royal persons in history both of whose parents become reigning sovereigns. There have been few of them: the children of Ferdinand and Isabella of Spain, the children of Peter the Great and Catherine I, and Paul himself, the child of Peter III and Catherine II. Paul would not forget this, when it was his turn to rule. Meanwhile, during the reign of his mother, which lasted for thirty-four years, mother and son would grow steadily apart. It was not his mother's lovers he resented, but the fact that some of them, Grigory Potemkin in particular, abrogated so much power and privilege to themselves. Stanislaus Poniatowski, the erstwhile lover and Catherine and last king of Poland, he actually had a great affection for, while conscious that Poland's extinction as an independent state had benefited Russia.

Thus it was, when Paul succeeded his mother at last in 1797, he set himself to undo as many of Potemkin's reforms as he could, and ordered that the favourite's body be exhumed and his remains scattered. But before this, he set himself a much more important task: the exhumation and rehabilitation of his father Peter III.

He was afraid that his mother, using the Law of 1722, might have disinherited him and nominated someone else, although that someone else might have been his own sons, whom Catherine loved. He could find nothing among her papers. Paul emphasised that he had succeeded to "the throne of our forefathers which we inherited", thus avoiding the word nomination. He was determined to remind people of his paternity by now according Peter III rites that he had been denied after his murder in 1762. On November 9, only three days after his mother's death, the new emperor issued an edict.

> On the occasion of the death of our beloved mother, …we have appointed a Commission of Mourning to organize the transfer of the corpse of our beloved father, Sovereign Emperor Peter Feodorovich, of blessed memory,

> from the Holy Trinity Monastery of St. Alexander Nevsky, to the Cathedral of St. Peter & St. Paul, and the burial of the body of Her Imperial Majesty in that same church.[14]

Peter's remains were exhumed from their vault in the monastery, where assembled relatives were obliged to kiss them. (There are shades here of course of the exhumation of Ines de Castro, to say nothing of the conduct of Samuel Pepys with the mummified body of Katherine of Valois.) On November 25, 1797, Paul enacted a posthumous coronation for his uncrowned father, by placing a crown from his own head onto Peter's casket, which, to quote Wortman, "symbolically and posthumously dethroned Empress Catherine", creating "a symbolic fiction of continuity and hereditary right".[15]

On December 2, 1796, Peter's casket was brought to the Winter Palace, to the sound of canon fire in a solemn parade of army units, among whom walked Aleksei Orlov, the sole survivor of the conspiracy of 1762, holding a crown over the coffin in an act of penance. The coffin was placed beside Catherine's catafalque for a joint lying-in-state, to which crowds were admitted, "without any regard for station, apart from badly dressed peasants".[16]

A double funeral was held on December 6, 1796, in the Peter-Paul cathedral. There followed two weeks of vigils and requiem masses, after which, on December 18, the coffins were lowered side by side into a double vault, in front of the iconostasis, although at floor level separate sarcophagi mark the graves.[17] For Paul, honour had been duly paid to his father, and, as for his mother, she was now in a sense re-united with the husband she had despised.

Paul altered the Law on the Succession, the subject of his third edict issued in 1797, after his coronation, which had taken place on April 5. Paul read out the manifesto on the Succession after taking communion, during the coronation ceremony, emphasising its importance. The drawback with the freedom of nomination which Peter the Great dictated in 1722 was that it left the future unsure and unstable. Paul restored the rule of male primogeniture, based on German statutes. In the event of the disappearance of a male line, the succession would pass to a male of the female line (something experimented with in England in 1553, on the death of the last male of the direct line); since to "avoid complications of the transfer of one dynasty to another (*iz roda v rod*) a male person is to be preferred to a female". However, in the last resort, a female ruler of the blood is to be preferred to an outsider; her husband was not eligible to become sovereign. The subtext of all this of course was to ensure that someone like his own mother could never again assume power, although this was to rule out *realpolitik*. The phrase "a female ruler *of the blood*" seems a direct reference to Catherine, who was of course by birth not a Romanov. There are purists who argue that since the death of Paul's father, Peter III, who was a male member of the House of Gottorp-Holstein, then that house, and not the Romanovs, had ruled since 1762, but the name of a dynasty and all it implies cannot be easily dispensed with, something Habsburgs and Windsors have learnt well.

But the Act achieved its purpose: it would ensure that the State is never without an Heir. The Heir is appointed always according to the law. So that there is not the slightest doubt who should succeed. "Interestingly, the Act was signed by both Paul, and his second wife, the Empress Maria" (original name Sophia Dorothea Augusta Louisa of Wurttemberg).[18]

Destiny decreed that the short and pug-nosed Paul should almost exactly follow the fate of his father, whom he so much resembled. On March 11, 1801, conspirators broke into Paul's bedchamber to place him under arrest, as he had so much alienated the aristocratic elite with his new reform for other classes. They could see their privileges slipping away. "What have I done to you?" inquired Paul, but moments later he was dead, killed even sooner than his father, in a "scuffle". Officially he was dead of "an apoplectic stroke", inflicted apparently by Divine Providence. Paul, it seems, had begun to argue, one of the panicking conspirators (probably Nikolai Zubov) struck him over the head with a heavy snuffbox, he fell, and the conspirators piled on top of him. The guilt was collective; no-one admitted to the fatal act, which may have been one of strangulation. They woke Alexander, Paul's eldest son, and told him he was Emperor. The assassins did not stand trial because officially no crime had been committed; but they were dismissed from service.[19]

As for Potemkin, in life as in death, a different fate awaited his remains that that anticipated. Paul's revenge, of that is what it was, was visited not only on his body but his earthly possessions. The Tauride Palace (Potemkin had been Prince of Tauride) was turned into a barracks, and the city of Gregoripol, which had been named in Potemkin's honour, was renamed. But his grave survived Paul's destruction order. His remains or his grave were eventually displayed by the Bolsheviks. His remains now lie in his tomb in St. Catherine's Cathedral, in Kherson. The exact whereabouts of some of his internal organs, however, including his heart and his brain, which were first kept at the Galia Monastery in Jassy (near where he died), remain unknown.

It is instructive here to recall the circumstances of Potemkin's death. He had fallen ill in the fever-ridden city of Jassy, where he had gone to conclude the Treaty ending a war with the Ottoman Turks. Although he kept busy, overseeing the peace talks, planning in the meantime an assault on Poland, and preparing the army for renewed war in the south. He fasted briefly, but refused medicine and recovered some strength. He then consumed a feast once again (this was something he certainly shared with Stanislaus Poniatowski, another lover of Catherine, whose Thursday dinners were legendary, and to which invitations were eagerly sought) and ate "a ham, a salted goose, and three or four chickens". To later readers it does not seem surprising that on October 2, 1791 (Old style, October 13, New style) he felt better, and dictated a letter to Catherine, but then collapsed once more. Later he awoke, and dispatched his entourage to Nikolayev. He then left Jassy in his carriage, but, after 60 kilometres, he asked for the carriage to be stopped, as he realised he was dying. He asked to be taken out of the carriage, so that he could die in the field. He was lifted out, and laid on a piece of carpet in the field out in the open steppe, and died on October 5 (Old style, October 16, New style). When he had died, his attendants sought for a gold coin to place over his good eye (Potemkin had had only one eye for some years, the cause of its loss being something of a mystery). They could not find one, so placed a copper kopek instead. Contemporary rumours have been picked up by some historians, such as the Polish Jerzy Lojek, suggesting that Potemkin was poisoned because his madness (or rather, recklessness) made him a liability, but this has been rejected by Montefiore, who suggests he succumbed to bronchial pneumonia.

Eight days after his death he was buried, but of course there were other consequences than the grief and vacuum felt by Catherine, who ordered the suspension of all social events when hearing of his end. He had been planning an assault on Poland, but with a clear purpose. He was in contact with the prominent Polish noblemen, Felix Potocki and Francisek Ksawer Branicki, and if Potemkin's niece, Alexandra, who was married to Branicki, is to be believed, there was now worry for the fate of Poland because behind the planned assault was another plan, to revitalise the Polish state with himself as its king.

Potemkin was hugely powerful and in the regions he controlled he ruled autonomously for Catherine. He had used the state treasury as his own personal bank (something common to almost all who wield great power) and this prevented the resolution of his financial affairs on his death to this very day. Catherine stepped in to purchase the Tauride Palace and his art collection (something else he shared with the ill-fated Poniatowski) from his estate, and paid off his debts. Consequently, he left a relative fortune.

As for Poland, now left in something of a vacuum itself, Potocki and Branicki were not the best of confederates for Potemkin to have chosen. "His whole life was a series of light adventures and serious scandals", was how the historian Nisbet Bain described Potocki.[20] In spite of this seemingly frivolous lifestyle, or perhaps because of it, Potocki was responsible for the second partition of Poland.

As for Branicki, he was one stage to the worse, if that were possible: "Only eighteenth-century Poland could have produced such a fantastic specimen of decadent humanity" was Nisbet Bain's verdict. This was only diluted by his subservience to his uncle-in-law Potemkin, which was of the most servile description.[21]

Two years before Potemkin's death, in 1789, Catherine herself had declared her intention not to violate Polish territory (it was by then a rump state) and she did this by skirting the long border, but even at the time this action was accompanied by an astounding letter from Potemkin, her chief Satrap, apologising for the damage done in Poland by Russian troops. But Potemkin was many things to many men, particularly he was many princes. In his capacity as a Polish magnate (he had obtained his *indigenat* or patent or nobility some time before) he expressed his sympathy with the (Polish) Republic and begged it to accept from him a gift of twelve cannon and 500 carbines. This extraordinary letter was actually, moreover, written in Polish, and in it he blamed the Poles gently, almost tenderly, for having previously addressed him, a Polish citizen, in French!. Interestingly, Potemkin's father, Alexander, was of Polish origin, and a middle income, noble landowner. His son had gone far beyond any of his father's aspirations: Prince of the Russian Empire, "Prince of Tauride" in 1783, Prince of the Holy Roman Empire, in 1776, on Catherine's insistence. It extended, as it would, to other members of his family: one of his sisters, Maria, married the Russian senator Nikolay Samoylov, and one of her grandsons was General Nikolay Raevsky. But there had been a darker side to Potemkin's multi-faceted personality. Another sister had married Vassily Engelhardt, and had five daughters. These young women came to the Court in 1775, looking perhaps for husbands. They were Potemkin's nieces, yet it is possible that he seduced at least two of them, and one Varvara, who after married Galizine, certainly had an affair with her uncle which lasted some time.

Modern writers have explored the death, funeral, and various exhumations of Potemkin in considerable detail. In fact, like several others, their life *after* death has offered almost as many dramas as life itself. For a number of them, the journeys of their bodies through revolution and upheaval tells themselves the history of the countries they passed through.

Potemkin's body returned Jassy after his death on the steppes of Bessarabia. There a most interesting post-mortem was carried out by the French doctor Massot and his assistants. This was probably done in the very apartments which had been occupied by Potemkin in the Ghika Palace. It was followed by an embalming. Slicing open his belly, the good doctor took out his organs, extracting them one by one, and examining them. The entrails were fed out, like a hosepipe. They found the innards "very wet", awash with bilious fluid. The liver was swollen…there was not the slightest evidence of poisoning, despite the rumours.[22] It is most likely that Potemkin was weakened by his fever, whether typhus or malaria, haemorrhoids, drinking and general exhaustion, but these did not necessarily kill him. His earaches, phlegm, and difficulties in breathing mean he probably died of bronchial pneumonia. In any case, the stench of the bile was unbearable. Nothing, not even the embalming process, could cleanse it.

During the embalming Massot sawed a triangular hole in the back of the skill and drained the brains out of it. He then filled the cranium with aromatic grasses and potions to dry and preserve the famous head. The viscera were placed in a box, the heart in a golden urn. Then the corpse was sewn up again like a sack, and dressed in its finest uniform. It is of course these very things which would help identify Potemkin's body in the fate which awaited it.

Catherine II decided that Potemkin's funeral should be held in Jassy, although he had asked apparently to be buried in his own village of Chizhova. The Empress believed he belonged in one of the great cities he had built, Kherson or Nikolaev. One of the reasons she chose a grave so far away was to make it more difficult for Prince Paul in the future to wreak his retribution on Potemkin.

So, on October 11, 1791, Potemkin began his lying-in-state, probably in the hall of the Ghika Palace. The catafalque was enclosed in a chamber of black velvet, trimmed with silver tassels, and help up by silver chords.

The dais was decorated in rich gold brocade. Potemkin lay in an open coffin, upholstered in pink velvet, covered by a canopy of rose and black velvet, supported by ten pillars, and surmounted by ostrich feathers. Its colour and ostentation were somehow a commentary on Potemkin's conspicuous consumerism during his life.

His many orders and batons were laid out on velvet cushions, and on two pyramids of white satin which stood on either side of his coffin. His sword, hat and scarf lay on its lid. Nineteen huge candles flickered, while sixteen officers stood guard. Soldiers and local Moldavians were alike in their sorrow for their "lost protector". In front of this magnificent mise-en-scene, as Montefiore has it, was a black board inscribed with Potemkin's titles and victories. This too will appear in later scenes of the long drama which would unfold. Two hundred years later, in 1998, Montefiore would find this black board, assisted by a Rumanian priest and two professors, in the Golia church in Jassy. The board lay under a piano, behind a pile of prayer books. It was dusty but undamaged.[23] Thus some extraordinary memorials to an age survive. It was reminiscent of Lord Lumley finding the iconic and priceless portrait of Richard II in the crypt of Westminster Abbey, where it was serving as part of a door!

The black hearse, bearing the coffin, drawn by eight black-draped horses, was carried then into the Church of the Ascension, where canons fired a final salute.

But not all of Potemkin's body arrived in Kherson to be finally buried, on November 23, 1791. His viscera were buried separately. The resting place of his heart was especially significant. The viscera were said to be buried in their golden box in the Church of the Ascension at the Golia monastery in Jassy, under the carpet and flagstone and before the ruler of Moldavia's red velvet mediaeval throne. When the body actually reached Kherson, it was not buried. It was simply laid in an unsealed, specially constructed tomb in a crypt, in the middle of St. Catherine's church. Catherine had intended a marble monument to be designed and erected over his tomb, but when she died herself, five years later, in 1796, the marble was still not ready. So the Prince, whom Montefiore describes as "a parvenu who was somehow royal", remained interred but somehow unburied.

Two years later, in 1798, Emperor Paul issued his decree, which was sent to the Procurator-General, Prince Alexander Kurakin, stating that "the body was unburied, and 'finding this obscene', His Majesty orders that the body be secretly buried in the crypt, in the tomb designed for this, and the crypt should be covered up with earth, and flattened as if it had never been there...." Paul gave his real orders only orally to Kurakin, that he should smash any memorial to Potemkin, and scatter his bones in the nearby Devil's Gorge. Under cover of darkness the tomb was filled in and covered up, but the oral part of Paul's retribution was not carried out.

Thus, in the nineteenth and twentieth centuries there were no fewer than five exhumations of the body of the Prince, in 1818, 1859, 1873, 1930, and 1984. It records, in brief, the history of Russia from Potemkin's death for 200 years afterwards.

Firstly, in 1818, it had been Potemkin's cousin, Archbishop Iov Potemtkin of Ekaterinslav, who conducted another midnight grave opening. He had the church floor lifted, opened the coffin and discovered the embalmed cadaver of his cousin, still there. Unable, as has been seen in so many of these cases, to leave without a souvenir, the archbishop probably took some artefact from the grave, and carried it in his carriage when he left. Was this, as Montefiore opines, "an act of familial and episcopal grave-robbing?" Could it have been the golden urn containing the heart of Potemkin?

The exhumation of 1859 was rather more official. Another commission decided to open the grave to prove that Potemkin was still there and that the archbishop had not taken away his entire body. The searchers discovered a large crypt, when they opened the tomb, a wooden coffin and inside a lead one, and a gold fringe to go round it. Milgov, a local bureaucrat, tidied up the crypt and closed it again.

In 1873 yet another commission excavated and found the wooden coffin again, containing a skull with a triangular hole in the back, left by Massot's embalming, and tufts of dark-blonde hair, the remains of the coiffure that was said to be the finest in Russia, as well as three medals, clothes, and gold braid scraps of uniform. They sealed it up again, and this time constructed a fitting gravestone approximately above the tomb.

Then the Revolution came, and all its iconoclasm and upheavals. In 1930, a young writer, Boris Lavrenev, returned to Kherson to visit his sick father. On a walk through the fortress he saw a sign outside St. Catherine's Church which read: "Kherson's Anti-religious museum". Inside he saw a pyramid glass case. "There was this brown thing inside it", he wrote. When he got closer he saw that it was a skull. On the table next to it was written: "The skull of Catherine II's lover, Potemkin". In the next case there was a skeleton still with shrivelled muscles on the bones. A sign read: "The bones of Catherine II's lover, Potemkin". In a third case, there were remains of a green velvet jacket, white satin trousers and rotten stockings and shoes: Potemkin's clothes.

Lavrenev must have been shocked, for he sent a telegram to the Ministry in charge of protecting Art. When he returned to Leningrad a friend wrote to him that the "museum" had been closed. Potemkin had been gathered up, put in a new coffin in the vault, and bricked up, yet again.

On May 11, 1984, almost on the eve of the end of the Soviet system, the chief of Kherson's Medical department, L.G. Boguslavsky, opened the tomb for the fifth time. He found "Thirty-one bones...belonging to the skeleton of a man of 185 m...of about 52–55 years old, who had probably been dead for about two hundred years". Potemkin had been reduced to statistics. But now some surprises. There were in the coffin too some epaulettes, said to belong to a British officer of the time of the Crimean war (1854–1856), so the very time just before the exhumation of 1859. The coffin this time was more modern (1930), but it had a Catholic as well as an Orthodox cross on it. The analysis decided that it was definitely Potemkin.

In July, 1986, Boguslavsky wrote to Professor Evgeny Anisimov, the distinguished eighteenth century scholar, who was however unconvinced by the evidence. If it was Potemkin, why the Catholic cross and the British epaulettes? The size, age, and dating of the body were right. The old coffins, leaden, gilded or wooden, as well as the medals, any remaining icons and clothes, had all disappeared during the Revolution. The Catholic coffin, shorter than the skeleton, was probably supplied in 1930, and it should be remembered that Potemkin's family had come from Catholic Poland, and Potemkin, in his last days, was constructing arguments to make him ruler, if not king, of Poland. The English epaulettes are from another grave, the relics of "ignorant Bolshevik pilfering". So, in 1986, the Prince was once again buried, for, if one counts the viscera of Jassy and all the other excavations, for the eighth time, and promptly forgotten.

Now, after the year 2000, there is, in St. Catherine's Church in Kherson a wooden and iron rail around a solitary flat marble gravestone, seven feet long and three feet wide, that lies in the middle beneath the cupola. Inside, beneath a large gilded crest, set on the stone is the inscription. Around the edge of the marble are seven gilded rosettes, each engraved with his victories and the cities he founded...no-one has opened the tomb for a few years now and no foreigner had ever seen it. But, in 1998, Montefiore became the first. Led down a wooden trapdoor concealed in the middle of the floor, steep steps and a narrow passageway, he and the Orthdox priest who took him, Fr. Anatoly, reached a small chamber. It was said it was once lined with icons, and contained the silver, lead and wooden coffins of Potemkin, "all stolen by the Communists". Now, the simple wooden coffin, with a cross on it, stands on a raised dais, in the midst of the vault. The lid of the coffin is opened. Inside there is a small black bag containing the skull and the numbered bones of Potemkin. That is all. But one question remains: where is the golden urn containing his heart? The most probable scenario is that it was indeed the artefact which his cousin the archbishop took in 1818, and that it now resides in Chizhova, Potemkin's own village, where he had wished to lie all along. In this church he had learned to write and to sing.

Perhaps the most notable of exhumations at the end of the twentieth century was that of Princess Alice, the widow of Prince Andrew of Greece, and the mother of the Duke of Edinburgh. She had let it be known before she died, in Buckingham Palace, in 1969, that she wished to be buried in Jerusalem, near her beloved Aunt Ella (Princess Elizabeth of Hesse, the sister of the last Tsarina of Russia, who had married the Grand Duke Serge). Inevitably, this means of course that the finding of the Grand Duchess's body, along with six others, in September 1918, her own exhumation after summary execution by the Bolsheviks, two months before, is always linked with that of Alice.

Elizabeth of Hesse always comes over as a much more cheerful and resilient character than the unsmiling and neurotic sister who was the last Empress of Russia. Indeed, Prince Frank of Teck, who was her cousin, when he saw her at Balmoral, wrote in a letter to his mother, Princess Mary Adelaide, that he thought she was "an actress". He then added, "when you have read this, burn it!", perhaps thinking that he had been indiscreet. Elizabeth's husband, Grand Duke Serge, was a deeply unpopular Governor of Moscow, and it must have come as no surprise when he was assassinated on February 17, 1905, the year of the first attempt at Revolution in St. Petersburg. He knew that he was unpopular, and that an attempt might be made on his life, and for this reason, forbade Elizabeth to accompany him on his forays around the city. She arrived at the scene of his murder but it was already too late to do anything. Elizabeth then did something which was characteristic of her, but raised disquiet in some quarters. She went to see his assassin, Kaliaev, in prison, and asked him to pray with her for God's forgiveness for his crime. She obviously got through to him because he did not die himself unconfessed.[24] It is difficult to imagine her sister, the Tsarina, doing this.

Elizabeth decided to spend the rest of her life in good works and entered the religious life in a convent in Moscow, a Fr. Mitrophan being chaplain of the Order. It was from here that she was taken about April 1918, and imprisoned at Alapaievsk in Siberia. Also removed with her was Sister Barbara, the most loyal of the sisters at the convent, and five other members of the Russian Imperial family shared her imprisonment. The Grand Duke Serge (a younger one), Prince John, and his younger brothers Constantine and Igor, and Prince Vladimir Palev.

On the evening of July 17/18, 1918 (the same date the entire family of Tsar Nicholas II was also murdered), all the prisoners were taken from the schoolhouse, where they had been living, and were thrown down the deepest mineshaft in the area, one that was already disused. Elizabeth knelt at the very edge of the mine, and said very clearly and loudly in German: "Thou, Dear God, forgive them, they don't really know what they are doing". They did not die at once. They were heard singing psalms, and Elizabeth (or Ella, as she was always known to her family) actually tore part of her dress off to make a bandage for Prince John, who had broken his arm in the fall. The soldiers then threw a grenade into the mineshaft, which brought all suffering to an end. There is, however, another version of this story, as inevitably there would be. According to this, the chanting of the psalms heard by the local peasants went on all through the night and the next day. It had been very clear and firm at the beginning but then it grew blurred, and eventually there was silence. The White Army had brought equipment with them, when they came to Alapaevsk. They brought the bodies out of the mine one by one. Prince John, Elizabeth, and Sister Barbara had the three fingers of their right hand folded as though they were about to make the sign of the cross. The inquiry established that all of them, with the possible exception of Grand Duke Mikhaylovich, had died of starvation, and that the order for their liquidation had come from Moscow.

But now someone else enters the story: Fr. Seraphim. His father, a merchant in Moscow, had greatly respected Elizabeth. He had a son who had become a monk. Fr. Seraphim happened to be in the area of Alapaevsk just at the time the White Army wrested it from the Red. He remembered the Grand Duchess's great affection for the Holy Land, the interest taken by her in the activities of the Russian Palestinian Society, and her constant regret that her own activities prevented her from going there on pilgrimage. Fr. Seraphim made a vow that he would bring the bodies of Elizabeth and Sister Barbara to Palestine. He got hold of two coffins and decided to make for the Chinese border in order to reach Pekin (Beijing).[25]

Fr. Seraphim was not Siberian-born, which would have helped matters. He had little if any knowledge of the terrain or of the vast distances to be covered. But this was no ordinary priest. It took him two years, but he accomplished his mission. The two coffins were placed in the crypt of the Russian Church in Beijing. It had been necessary to exchange the travel-worn coffins for new ones, and so the bodies were seen when the coffins were opened in the presence of the Russian clergy in Beijing, together with a number of emigres. The body of Elizabeth was incorrupt. She looked asleep. The three fingers of her right hand were folded, as had been noted when she had been taken out of the mine.

When her brother and sisters heard of Fr. Seraphim they made arrangements for transfer of the two bodies to Jerusalem. The Marchioness of Milford Haven commissioned a Russian artist in Rome to decorate the walls of the chapel in the Church of St. Mary Magdalene, which had been consecrated in 1889, in the presence of Elizabeth and her husband Serge. All the expenses were met jointly by the Marchioness, and by Princess Henry of Prussia and the Grand Duke of Hesse.

Elizabeth and her faithful little "Varia" (Sister Barbara) reached Jerusalem in January, 1921, where the coffins were met with high honour and all the officials; the funeral was sung by the Patriarch Damianus.

Three times a year now a requiem is sung: on September 18, St. Elizabeth's day, in the Orthodox calendar, round about Christmas, and on the July 18, the date of the martyrdom. The Abbess of the Monastery there was Abbess Tamara, but she was the Princess Tatiana, the daughter of the Grand Duke Constantine, a first cousin of the Grand Duke Serge.

The news of their murder (unlike that of the senior Romanovs) was not made public until four months later, in November 1918, ironically one day before the Armistice.

The bodies of the Tsar and his family of course were not found for several decades, but it so happened that the White Russians, under the command of General Smolin, occupied Alapaievsk in September 1918, and at a dinner an engineer became intoxicated, and revealed that the bodies of Ella and her companions were buried nearby "in the deepest shaft". Work to clear the mine of debris took several days and a great deal of water had to be pumped out, but eventually the searchers were rewarded. The bodies were found and brought to the surface, the six royal victims, the physician, the valet, and Sister Barbara: not unlike the company which perished at Ekaterinburg.

General Smolin recorded: "The sight of the dead bodies was dreadful… all except Ella and the nun (Barbara) were in travelling clothes. Ella was in a grey dress with a white neckerchief: a cross of cypress wood hung on her breast. The nun was dressed in the same manner, and on her breast were a gold cross and a watch. When the other bodies were examined, some valuable gold and silver objects were found on them. It was obvious that the executioners were in such haste to fulfil their ghastly task that they had not sufficient time to rob the victims".[26]

The royal victims were given a solemn burial Mass in the local church, which was attended by an enormous throng of local people; but what then? The Revolution was far from over, and the outcome was uncertain. Ella's body began an extraordinary journey, ending in Peking (Beijing) where it was re-interred in the Russian Orthodox cemetery there. But the travels of Ella's body were not over yet.

One day in London Princess Beatrice spotted a picture of the cemetery in the *Illustrated London News*, and in January 1921 Ella's youngest sister, Victoria, arranged for the coffins of Ella and of Sister Barbara to be brought to Jerusalem (then under the British Mandate of Palestine) and buried on the Mount of Olives, at the Russian Orthodox Convent of St. Mary Magdalen. Princess Victoria, her sister Princess Louise, and their brother Prince Louis of Battenberg, were all there for the service.

In 1984, in very different times, Ella was recognised as a saint by the Russian Orthodox Church abroad, and by the Russian Orthodox Patriachate (i.e. within Russia itself) in 1992, when it was deemed safe to do so. In July 1998, a symbolic reparation was even made in Britain, when the Queen and the Duke of Edinburgh attended the dedication of effigies of Christian martyrs of the twentieth century in Westminster Abbey. These effigies are above the great West Door.

It is sometimes strange when the events of history interweave themselves, for when the royal party returned from Jerusalem after the re-burial of Ella in 1921, Princess Alice told them that, after seven years, she was once again pregnant. This late child was her only son, Philip, one day to be the husband of Elizabeth II, and who was to return to the same church to re-inter his own mother next to Ella, as she had wished.

The Church of St. Mary Magdalen in Jerusalem had been built in 1885 in memory of the Empress Maria Alexandrovna, the wife of the Tsar Alexander II. Tsar Alexander had been assassinated in 1881 (the seventh attempt to kill him) but the Empress had been dead some time, and her place taken by the mistress of the Tsar, which had caused much grief and dismay within the Imperial family. The children of the Empress took particular exception to the Tsar's new wife. In 1888, one of Empress Maria's sons, the Grand Duke Serge, attended the consecration of the church in honour of his mother with his wife, who was of course Ella (the Grand Duchess Feodorova). It was after this visit that Ella decided to convert from Lutheranism, in which she had been brought up in Hesse, to Russian Orthodoxy.[27]

The church was built, predictably, in the Muscovite style, in white stone with blue roofs. It is perched on a hillside and its seven golden domes can be seen a long way away. It looks across the Kidron valley towards the walls of Jerusalem, the Temple Mount, and the Dome of the Rock. The painting on the ceiling above the iconostasis is of Mary Magdalen in front of the Emperor Tiberius.

Thus, it was that when Princess Alice died in 1969 she left verbal instructions that she wished to be buried in Jerusalem near her Aunt Ella. The 1967 war between the State of Israel and the Palestinians had not long taken place, and it was no time to think such a thing was now possible. The British had relinquished their Mandate in 1948, and a state of war was unfortunately now the norm within this area of the Middle East.

There was a touch of humour when Princess Alice made this request. When her family protested that it was a long way away, and that it would be difficult to visit her grave there, she replied:

> "Nonsense. There is a perfectly good bus service!" But, for the time being anyway, she had to be buried in England. The funeral took place in St. George's Chapel, Windsor, on December 10th, 1969. Alice had come full circle, for she had been born in the Castle in 1885.[28]

Seven years later, one of the most notable of Deans of Windsor came into office. This was Michael Mann, and he at once began to try to fulfil the wishes of Princess Alice. He opened negotiations with the relevant authorities in Jerusalem. Anyone who has visited the holy city will know at once the sensitivities of the various religious groups there, verging on the paranoiac. The church of St. Mary Magdalen is Russian Orthodox; Alice had been married to Prince Andrew of Greece, and had become Greek Orthodox. Not only that, she had founded her own Order of Nuns, in the habit of which she had attended the marriage of her son to the then Princess Elizabeth in Westminster Abbey in 1947, to the astonishment and mystification of many onlookers. But, as has been seen by her comment above, Alice was an engaging and unpredictable character. She was indeed *sui generis*. No-one was like her. One of her cousins said "I don't know what kind of a nun she is, who chain smokes and plays canasta!" She did do both of these things, and was known in Buckingham Palace for being preceded and succeeded by clouds of cigarette smoke, just as her daughter-in-law was preceded by yelping corgis.

But it was not only that the church of St. Mary Magdalen was Russian; it was *White* Russian, that is, the church abroad, the church before the Revolution of 1917. Moreover, it was a convent which contained its complement of nuns and its archimandrite.

In Windsor, Alice's coffin lay on one of the two catafalques in the royal vault of St. George's Chapel. Her eventual removal would not be technically an exhumation from burial in the earth, but it was removal from a vault to another country. Michael Mann had been told by the Lord Chamberlain that it was one of his tasks, now that he was the Dean of Windsor, to bury Alice in Jerusalem. Prince Philip gave him permission to proceed.

The man in charge in Jerusalem was the Archimandrite, Anthony Grabbe, someone of disquieting personality, being both disarming and difficult in equal measures. The progress which had been made was put back by the State Visit of the Queen and Prince Philip to Jordan in March, 1984. The difficult archimandrite was dismissed in January 1986. The situation was saved from a rather unexpected quarter. In New York one Prince Theimouraz Bagration Moukhransky, a Caucasian prince, who was the President of the Orthodox Palestine Society in the United States; related to both Ella and Alice, was, in Hugo Vickers' words "An aristocrat of the old school", who knew situations could sometimes be ameliorated, and problems solved by courtesy and tact. By September 1987 the proposed burial of Alice had been approved by the Greek Patriarch in Jerusalem, the Bishops of the Russian Church in exile, and the Supreme Council of the Orthodox Palestine Society: all sides of a thorny problem brought together by one man.

There was then a new question as to who actually owned the church of St. Mary Magdalen. The indefatigable prince then engaged two lawyers, one in Washington, and one in Jerusalem, and finally came to a satisfactory solution between the Russian Orthodox Church in exile and one of its dismissed clerics.

But the old sensitivities lay only just under the surface. The Greek Patriarch in Jerusalem said all would be well if there was a full burial Mass in the Greek Orthodox Church, and then the burial in the Russian Church. That is not quite what happened.

Alice's coffin was now taken privately from the royal vault at Windsor on August 2, 1988, where it had lain for nearly nineteen years. Fr. Gregory came to say some prayers and then the small group took off from Heathrow. The group consisted on the Dean, Michael Mann, and his wife Jill, who was acting as lady-in-waiting to Princess Sophia, one of the sisters of Prince Philip, who was also one of the party. Christopher Kenyon, the undertaker, also went with the party. On arrival in Jerusalem, they were met, among others, by an Israeli undertaker, and taken to the Mount of Olives.

The coffin was taken straight to the Greek Church and the Requiem Mass began immediately. The Patriarch then invited the party to an enormous breakfast which seemed unending, during which the Dean presented the Patriarch with a signed photograph of Prince Philip.

At 10:30 am the party set off for the Garden of Gethsemane. Christopher Kenyon, on the advice of the Israeli undertaker, had hired several strong-arm men to see off the paparazzi, but at the gate of the Garden it seemed there would certainly be a scuffle among the pressmen and photographers. Fortunately, the gate could be closed against them.

The nuns of the White Russian convent then began the Russian Orthodox liturgy for the dead, and, as they started, the Greeks rushed in and started singing: the old rivalries died hard. Again, fortunately, the Russians behaved immaculately. They simply stopped until the Greeks had sung themselves out.

Princess Sophia was obviously very moved by the beautiful singing of the liturgy and felt that her mother's wishes had at last been fulfilled. The small party then attended a very long lunch. When it was all over, and he was back in England, the Dean wrote gratefully to Prince Bagration.

There was to be one final footnote, and it was a very important one. On April 11, 1993, Alice received a posthumous award from the Israeli state as "Righteous among the nations", which was approved by the Holocaust Memorial, Yad Vashem. The truth was that, underneath the humorous, caustic and sometimes eccentric exterior, Princess Alice was a saviour of the persecuted Jews in Athens. During World War II, and the German occupation of Greece, she had sheltered several of them in her own house, and enabled others to escape. She had risked her own life to help persecuted Jews, and for this she received the highest award given by the Jewish state to a non-Jewish foreigner. Other recipients included Archbishop Damaskinos, the Regent of Greece, and Queen Helen of Roumania.

The final act, therefore, was on October 31, 1994, when Alice's two surviving children, Princess Sophia and Prince Philip, went together to Jerusalem to receive the award on her behalf. In a ceremony they jointly laid a wreath in the Holocaust Museum and planted a tree at Yad Vashem.

The exhumation of the former Emperor of Ethiopia, Haile Selassie I, took place on February 17, 1992. According to different reports his remains had been buried beneath the office of the man who overthrew him in 1973, Mengistu; or they were buried beneath the bathroom; or beneath the toilet. For a man who had been so venerated, and had been used to glorious ceremonies and almost complete power for most of his life, this was a fall indeed.

Workmen found Haile Selassie's body after three days of digging under the office or bathroom at the Grand Palace, which has been the residence of the Emperor before he was deposed. "The reason why Mengistu chose this site was to see that the body did not rise from the dead", the state-run Ethiopian radio said.[29] The exhumation began when police received information from a military officer who claimed that he had buried the emperor, together with a palace engineer and a grave digger, the Ethiopian radio reported. Mengistu himself had fallen in May, 1991, after eighteen years of a rule which had sought to turn the 3000-year-old monarchy into a Soviet-style state. There was now an interim government which sought to make amends for the past. It was indeed also a case of Retribution and Reparation. But Mengistu's superstitious fears about the resurrection of Haile Selassie immediately tell of the life of a very extraordinary man indeed.

The interim government approved the exhumation so that the former Emperor could be buried in the presence of his family, and the Mo'a Anbessa Society, which seeks a restoration of the constitutional monarchy.

The emperor's remains were kept in a church until the burial ceremony, which was planned for July 23, 1992, the centenary of his birth. It was a fitting date to choose. But his was not the only exhumation at this time. The remains of sixty-two senior officials who had served Haile Selassie were exhumed from a mass grave at the capital's main prison. The bodies of twelve generals who were executed after trying to overthrow Mengistu in May, 1989, were also on the list for exhumation.

The official explanation for Haile Selassie's death in 1975, at the age of 83, was that he had died of some illness, but Mo'a Anbessa say he was smothered with a pillow as he slept. The state radio said that he had been buried on August 27, 1975. Next day the New York Times reported that the state radio in Ethiopia had said the former Emperor had been found dead in bed by a servant, and that cause of death was probably related to the effects of a prostate operation. After his exhumation, strangulation was also considered as a cause.

Now, his body was to lie in the church to which it had been taken after the exhumation for almost a decade, as the Ethiopian courts tried to find out the circumstances of his death. His coffin rested in Bhata Church, near to the resting place of his great uncle, the Emperor Menelek II. At last, on November 5, 2000, Haile Selassie was granted the Imperial style funeral which he had always merited, conducted by the Ethiopian Orthodox Church, a branch originally of the ancient Coptic Church of Egypt. However, the post-communist government of Ethiopia refused calls to declare the ceremony an official Imperial funeral. Haile Selassie's real name was Ras Tafari; the former was the name he adopted after his wonderful coronation ceremony in 1930, meaning *Holy Trinity*. The Empress Zawditu, with whom Ras Tafari has shared power since 1916, actually crowned him herself in a ceremony on October 7, 1928, during a period when she had at first suspected him of treason, and then relented. It was then that Ras Tafari was given the title *Negus* for the first time, meaning king in Amharic, the native language of Ethiopia. Thus, this first coronation had been controversial. When the empress died suddenly on April 2, 1930, a second coronation was planned. This took place exactly seven months later. The new emperor was crowned in the cathedral of St. George in Addis Ababa. Among those who attended "this most splendid affair" were the Duke of Gloucester (the third son of King George V), Marshal Franchet d'Esperey of France, and the Prince of Udine, representing King Victor Emmanuel III of Italy. The British author Evelyn Waugh was also present, and penned a report in his inimitable style; as did the American travel lecturer Burton Holmes, who shot the only known film footage of the event. The New York Times thought that the ceremony and its aftermath may have cost three million dollars in the currency of 1930. During his lifetime a worldwide cult grew up, the Rastafarians, centred in the West Indies, believing that this king was the re-incarnation of Jesus Christ. There was a prophecy that the new messiah would come out of Africa; thus, the fears and superstitions of Mengistu. Perhaps the most prominent believer of this cult was Bob Marley. He attended the funeral with some other followers; but the strength of the belief meant that many Rastafarians rejected the event, and refused even to accept that the bones were the remains of Haile Selassie. There remains some debate within the Rastafarian movement as to whether Haile Selassie actually died in 1975. Interestingly,

Haile Selassie himself said, enigmatically, during his lifetime: "Who am I to disturb their belief?" He cannot have gone unmoved by the scenes of wild hysteria when he landed in Jamaica, on April 21, 1966, and, as he emerged from the aircraft, with his cape swirling round him, 100,000 people knelt on the tarmac when they saw him. This day is now celebrated by Rastafarians as their second holiest day, the most holy being November 2 (1930) the Emperor's coronation day, when the movement really began.

During his colourful and chequered life, the Emperor had established very close links with Britain, and he and Queen Elizabeth II exchanged state visits. On his visit to Britain in 1924 he presented King George V with two lions, and, in return, received the Imperial crown of the Emperor Tewedros II, and return it safely to his joint ruler, the Empress Zawditu. The crown had been taken by General Sir Robert Napier during the 1868 expedition to Abyssinia (as it was then called).

It is instructive that when Haile Selassie fell in 1973, the immediately interim government was sufficiently still awed by the ancient monarchy to instal a temporary head of state, General Aman Mikael Andom, an Eritrean Protestant. This was only meant to serve until the return of the Crown Prince, Asfa Wossen, who was then receiving medical treatment abroad. However, when the sixty executions took place, Wossen condemned them; and in response the new government by revoking its acknowledgement of his Imperial legitimacy, and announcing the end of the Solomonic dynasty. The recorder of the fall of Haile Selassie was none other than Ryzard Kapuscinski, the brilliant and irreplaceable writer, who was possibly the greatest journalist of the twentieth century, a time in which there were many. His book in the words of an excellent reviewer, "was hard to put down and hard to forget".[30] It seems fitting that an extraordinary man should attract another extraordinary man to chart his end and downfall. This reviewer covers what was "an ossified and ritualised autocracy, with layers of bureaucracy, preventing information reaching the centre or action being carried out….(for)all eyes turned to the centre and everyone scrambling to catch the attention and favour of the monarch". Truly, it has never been said better.[31]

Notes

1. Interview with Fr. Gregory Corcoran, at Quarr Abbey, Isle of Wight, May 25, 2018.
2. I am indebted here to Ricardo Javier Mateos Saniz de Medrano, who provided most of the above information, and who is the author of *Estoril: los*

anos dorados, Reyes, principes, millionarios y exilados: una cronica de la alta sociedad de la posguerra europea (1946–1969) laesfera de las libras (2012).

3. *Sky News Report*, September 24, 2015.
4. Wheatcroft, Andrew, *The Habsburgs: Embodying Empire, Viking (1995) Penguin (1996) The Folio Society (2004)*, pp. 207–9.
5. Nisbet Bain, R., *The Last King of Poland, & His Contemporaries* (1909), G.P. Puttnam's Sons, Methuen & Co., p. 291.
6. Zamoyski, Adam, (i) *The Last King of Poland, Jonathan Cape* (1992); (ii) *Treasures of a Polish King, catalogue from Dulwich Picture Gallery* (1995).
7. Zamoyski, Adam, op. cit., p. 451.
8. Ibid., pp. 451–2.
9. Nisbet Bain, op. cit., p. 292.
10. Zamoyski, op. cit., p. 456.
11. Michalski, Jerzy, *Stanislaw August Poniatowski*, Polski Biographiczy, T. 41 (2011), p. 368; Butterwick, Richard, *Poland's Last King & English Culture* (1998), Clarendon Press.
12. Zamoyski, op. cit., p. 462.
13. Hughes, Lindsey, *The Romanovs: Ruling Russia 1613–1917*, Hambledon Continuum (2008), pp. 101–4.
14. Hughes, Lindsey, The Funerals of the Russian Emperors & Empresses, in M. Schaich, (ed.), *Monarchy & Religion: The Transformation of Royal Culture in Eighteenth Century Europe*, Oxford (2007), p. 414. The reference for the edict is PSZ, XXIV, no. 17.557, p. 2.
15. Quoting Wortman, R., *Scenarios of Power: Myth and Ceremony in Russian Monarchy, 2 vols.*, Princeton (1995), Vol. I, p. 173.
16. Hughes, op. cit., quoting Gendrikov, V.B., S.E. Sen'ko, *Petropavlovskii sobor, Usypal'intsa imperatorskogo doma Romanovykh*, St. Petersburg (1998), pp. 42–3.
17. Hughes, op. cit., p. 134.
18. Ibid., pp. 137–8.
19. Ibid., pp. 143–4.
20. Nisbet Bain, *The Last King of Poland* (1909), p. 153.
21. Ibid., p. 154.
22. Montefiore, Simon Sebag, *The Life of Potemkin* (2000), p. 487 et seq.
23. Ibid., pp. 480, 492, 498, 499–502.
24. Vickers, Hugo, *Princess Alice*, New York (2000), pp. 72, 153–6.
25. Almedingen, E.M., *An Unbroken Unity: A Memoir of Grand Duchess Serge of Russia (1864–1918)*, The Bodley Head (1964), pp. 128–31.
26. Vickers, Hugo, op. cit., p.136, n. 29, quoting Smolin, *Alapaievsk Tragedy.*
27. I am indebted to Katrina Warne for this and other information about the Church of St. Mary Magdalene in Jerusalem, and for the photos she took during her visit there. Information given on November 1, 2018.

28. Vickers, Hugo, op. cit., p. 399.
29. Associated Press Report, Abebe Andualem, February 17, 1992.
30. Kapuscinski, Ryzard, *The Emperor: Fall of an Autocrat (1978) Penguin (2006)*. Translated from the Polish.
31. Yee, Danny (2007). Accessed April 1, 2019.

CHAPTER 9

Law Sacred and Secular

The lacunae in the secular law was made glaringly obvious when, during a case of body snatching in 1788, it was found that the accused had committed no offence as such, although he had breached the ecclesiastical law.

Both sources of the English Common Law had existed in tandem for many centuries, even though in 1533, during the Reformation Parliament, the old Canon Law of the Catholic Church in England had been gradually replaced by the Canon law of the new Church of England. The situation now seems complex, looking back, but basically the authority of Rome over the Canon Law had been replaced by a new *Ordinary*, now the Head of the Church of England, the sovereign. The old law of the Catholic Church of course remained for the Catholic Church now going underground, but from now on, it had become, in England, simply the rules of a theocracy, and would even come to be classified as "Foreign Law". That is still the case today. The new National Church gradually in time developed its own Canon Law, but for the most part, it remained as it had done since the Middle Ages, always constrained of course by the secular law, which could overrule it. Scholars now consider that the National Church became the Established Church, as it is known today, during the Revolutionary Settlement of 1689.[1]

Further light has been cast on these issues by a complaint brought to an Anglican tribunal under the *Clergy Discipline Measure of 2003* by the Venerable Peter Rouch against the Reverend Dr. Andrew Hawthorne. The complainant avowed that the Respondent had breached clergy

M. L. Nash, *The History and Politics of Exhumation*,
https://doi.org/10.1007/978-3-030-24047-9_9

discipline by retaining fees which should have been remitted either to the Diocesan Board of Finance or the Parochial Church Council. The Respondent challenged the jurisdiction of the tribunal on a number of grounds, one of which was that he was now "…a member of the Personal Ordinariate of Our Lady of Walsingham established by Pope Benedict XVI in 2011, and…therefore argues that he is no longer a member of the Church of England, and is no longer subject to its authority".

The riposte to this was that when he was ordained within the Church of England, the Respondent became subject to the ecclesiastical law of that Church and proceeded to quote from the judgment of *Edes v Bishop of Oxford (1667) Vaugh 18 at 21, and Mackonchie v Lord Penzance (1881) 6 App. Cas 424 at 446* that "The ecclesiastical law is as much part of the law of the land as any other part of the law, whereas the Roman Catholic canon law is technically a foreign law although no doubt consensually binding amongst its members".

The Tribunal chair then made reference to the provisions of the *Clerical Disabilities Act 1870* which relate to the formal deed of relinquishment available to a person to the office of minister in the Church of England, after having relinquished any and every preferment held by him. He further explained the present somewhat complex application of this provision. The Church Discipline Act 1840 had been repealed, and the *Ecclesiastical Jurisdiction Measure of 1963* had been included within the Schedule to the 1870 Act, but the Clergy Discipline Measure of 2003 had not been included in it.

These somewhat arcane arguments meant simply that the Respondent had not properly left the Church of England, as required by law, and was still technically subject to its discipline. It is tempting to see this case as a spat between two rival priests, who are goading each other on. The writer of an article on this case commented "Whilst the cavalier approach of Dr. Hawthorne—'You can't touch me, I'm part of the Ordinariate'—did not cut any ice with the legal deliberations of the Tribunal, the penalty imposed certainly reflects the limited ecclesiastical sanctions that can be imposed".[2] It is only fair to add that in *Mackonochie v Lord Penzance (1881)* on page 438, reference was made to the judgments of the famous Nicholas Lyndwood, Dean of the Arches in the reign of Henry V, thus confirming that the Church of England considered then that its Canon Law was simply a reformed continuum of the pre-Reformation Canon Law, also claimed by the Catholic Church in England. It seems some accommodation has been made, some mutual recognition, by both parties, since

1881. In that case, the charges brought against the priest concerned involved practices considered to be too Catholic and High Church for the Church of England. The priest concerned ignored all threats and strictures and was declared contumacious and excommunicated, or, in case the actual word "excommunication" itself appeared Catholic, then "the procedure thereby substituted for excommunication". Truly, there are nowhere persons like theologians for getting into a Byzantine tangle!

Thus it was that in 1788 one Lynn was convicted on an indictment, charging him with entering a certain burial ground and taking a coffin out of the earth, from which he took a dead body and carried it away for the purpose of dissecting it.[3]

Was it only a crime in ecclesiastical law? Only the Act of 1 Jac. 1 c.12 (1604), which had it a felony to steal dead bodies for the purposes of witchcraft, would have made it a crime in the secular law, but, as the judge pointed out, that clearly could not affect the situation in 1788.

Coke was quoted, in his Institutes Third Volume, on page 203, "the monument and the sepulchre and burial of the dead", that the burial of the cadaver is ***nullius in bonis*** and belongs to ecclesiastical cognizance, but as to the monument, action is given at Common Law for defacing thereof. In non-legalese, it was not an offence in secular law to steal a body, but it was an offence to deface a monument. There may be "injury in taking the shroud" and Trespass in digging the soil. But the act of carrying away the dead body was not criminal. *Preventing* the burial of a dead person may be an offence.

The Court must have been away that this splitting of hairs and quoting of ancient Latin might well have rendered the Law itself an ass, as the saying was. Therefore, the judge said that

> ...common decency required that the practice (of carrying away cadavers) should be put a stop to. The offence *should* be cognizable in a criminal court, as being highly indecent, and *contra bonos mores*; and the bare idea alone of which nature revolted. That the purpose of taking up the body for dissection did not make it less an indictable offence...but inasmuch as this defendant might have committed a crime merely from ignorance no person having been before punished in this Court for this offence, they only fined him five marks. Taking a body from a churchyard was not a felony, but a misdemeanour; but a newly emerging and higher code of ethical behaviour, at least nominally, on the part of the legal establishment, is apparent.

It is an interesting exercise too of the continuing authority of Canon Law in some areas that John Holmes and Peter Williams had been publicly whipped "from Holborn to St. Giles", just eleven years earlier, in 1777, for unearthing cadavers. These are, of course, early examples of bodysnatching, which became a lucrative trade during the time of the so-called "Resurrection M".

When the relatives of Edward Lee came to see the body, they were told it had already been buried…the defendant went clandestinely through the ceremony of burying *a coffin*, but it was filled with rubbish; and that he was seen at nightime removing a heavy package from his own house (into) a hackney coach; and that the body was afterwards found at the surgeon's, in the process of dissection and identified as the body of Edward Lee.

It was perhaps such cases that encouraged Burke and Hare to pursue their ghastly careers just five years later, in 1827. This also led to the Anatomy Act of 1832, acknowledging the need of surgeons to practice dissection upon dead bodies.

Another case, *Foster v Dodd (1867) LR3 QB67*, dealt with the continuing question of whether burial grounds are protected in perpetuity. Unless there is such a dedication, a burial place may simply cease to be a burial place and become a former burial ground.

One of the judges in this case, Byles, J., then asked the pertinent question: "So, that the freeholder might dig up the bodies buried there?" He answered his own question by saying that would be a Nuisance at Common Law, for *salus populi suprema lex.* It must lie in consecrated ground and then it has ecclesiastical protection; "but whether in ground consecrated or unconsecrated, "indignities offered to human remains in improperly or indecently disinterring them, are the ground for an indictment".

A dead body, by law, belongs to no-one ("res nullius") and is therefore under the protection of the public.

Of course, by 1867, the Victorian cult of death and everything associated with it was well under way, with all its ensuing industries, but a big step forward has been taken from the often callous and insensitive treatment of corpses during the eighteenth century and Regency times.

The Law Sacred, or Canon Law, had of course its own rules associated with exhumation, but, as Canon Law is part of the Law of England, the Burial Act 1857 brought the two together, especially in Section 25, which is still in forces today. This section provides, inter alia, that

> Except in cases where a body is removed from one consecrated place of burial to another by faculty granted for that purpose, it shall not be lawful

> to remove any body, or the remains of any body, which may have been interred in any place of burial without licence under the hand of one of Her Majesty's Principal Secretaries of State, and with such precautions as such Secretary of State may prescribe as the conditions of such licence....

There is thus absolutely no doubt as to the strict rules of exhumation. Moreover, even today, the interpretation of this Statute is such that it only refers to the holy or consecrated grounds of the Church of England. When Queen Maria of Yugoslavia was exhumed in 2013 to be repatriated in Serbia, this was made quite clear, when she had been buried in the Orthodox Church of St. George in Oxford. "Consecration according to the Orthodox rites is not the same as the consecration required by the Burial Act of 1857." The required consecration is that under the laws ecclesiastical of England, and *Re Talbot (1901) p. 1*, was quoted. In that case, Dr. Tristram, the Diocesan Chancellor, said (pages 5–6):

> In this case a very important question of practice has been raised. I am asked by the Petitioner to grant a faculty for the removal of the remains of the deceased from the consecrated place of burial where they are now interred to ground which is not consecrated in the sense in which the law understands consecration. I have not been able to find any precedent prior to the date of the passing of the Burial Act 1857, of any Ecclesiastical Court having granted a faculty for the removal of remains from consecrated to unconsecrated ground, although it is clear that up to the date of that Act the Ecclesiastical Courts were not precluded from granting such a faculty either by Canon or by Statute law. The practice of the Ecclesiastical Courts, previous to the passing of this Act, was to decline to grant a faculty authorising remains buried in consecrated ground to be reinterred in unconsecrated ground, as by so doing they would whbe sanctioning the removal of remains from a place of burial under the special protection of the Ecclesiastical Courts, to a place interment under the protection of no Court...provided the remains when placed there were not treated either with indignity or so as to create a nusisance...Such being the state of the law prior to 1857 as to the protection of bodies buried in consecrated ground, s. 25 of the Burial Act 1857 placed for the first time bodies buried in unconsecrated ground under the protection of the statute law of this country...The ground on which the Court would formerly have refused to grant the faculty prayed for in this case having been removed, the Court having regard to the circumstances of the case, has come to the conclusion that in the exercise of its discretion it ought to grant the faculty, but being of opinion that it is not to be acted upon until a licence has been obtained from the Home Secretary under the above section approving of the place of re-interment.

Dr. Tristram continued:

> (Graves) are to be encouraged. They express family unity and they are environmentally friendly in demonstrating economical use of land for burials. Normally the burial of family members in the family grave occurs immediately after the death of the particular member of the family, whereas in this case (the) remains will have to be disturbed after many years in order to inter them in a new family grave. Nothwithstanding this, we have concluded that there are special factors in this case which make it an exception to the norm of permanence…Faculties have been granted in the past for the bringing together, or accumulation of, family members in a single grave after many years provided special reasons were put forward for the lapse of time since the burial. Mr. Hill drew, attention to a decision of Newsom QC Ch in *In Re St James's Churchyard Hampton Hill (1982) 4 Consistory & Commisary Court Cases*, Case 25 where he granted a faculty over 50 years for remains to be exhumed and transported to Canada to be reburied in a family plot in Woodstock, Ontario…We therefore allow this appeal. In doing so it should not be assumed that whenever the possibility of a family grave is raised a petition for a faculty for exhumation will automatically be granted. As in this case it is to be expected that a husband and wife will make provision in advance by way of acquisition of a double grave space if they wish to be buried together. Where special circumstances are relied upon in respect of a child who has predeceased his or her parents, it will be insufficient if there is simply a possibility of establishing a family grave. As in this case, there would have to be clear evidence of the legal right to such a grave, if no family member was already buried in it.

In the current case of Queen Maria of Yugoslavia, the Chancellor of the Consistory Court of Oxford stated: "In my view there cannot be a better example than here of the exercise of the comity of nations relied upon by my predecessor, Chancellor Boydell, in the case of *In Re St Mary the Virgin, Hurley (2001) WLR 831*, In addition it is difficult to imagine a better family grave than a royal mausoleum".

The difficulties currently being encountered in Highgate cemetery in North London are centred around a problem going back to the nineteenth century, namely that at that time many people reserved plots and never used them. So in 2019, there are 400 unused plots. Before the nineteenth century, it was common practice for old graves to be regularly exhumed to make space for new burials, with remains removed to charnel houses; but in such cases as Highgate, an Act of Parliament will now be necessary to be able to use these 400 spaces.

Archaeology and anthropology have often been the reasons put forward for exhumation applications and the legitimacy of historical research. The case of *Re Holy Trinity, Bosham (2004) 2 AllER, Consistory Court pp. 820–834* considered the issues in a serious light. The immediate matter in hand was an application to continue a search begun in Victorian times for the body of King Harold II, famously killed by an arrow at the Battle of Hastings in 1066. Several places have been claimed to be his burial place, or rather the burial place for most of the pieces of his dismembered body. It has even been claimed that he was buried on the seashore. It was a case of course for the calling of expert witnesses. Dr. Elders thought that there was "An overwhelming case for the necessity of research", but the Consistory Court judge, the Chancellor Hill, thought that Dr. Elders may have been placing the test too high. "A cogent and compelling case must be proved for the legitimacy of the research". The general norm creates a presumption *against* exhumation. However, that has to be balanced against great national, historic, or other matters of importance. In this instance, the judge felt that the petitioner had failed to come near to the standard required. But each case is decided on its own facts.

The chief factor in all of these cases is the answer to the question: what is the underlying purpose of the request for an exhumation, whether from the secular or ecclesiastical authorities, and is there enough real evidence to support it?

Remains may be exhumed in order to be cremated, for a variety of reasons.

Appeals against refusal to grant a faculty may be heard either in the Chancery of York or in the Court of Arches, which are two divisions of a single appellate court, representing the two provinces in England of the Church of England, York, and Canterbury.

Interestingly, the Head of a Religious Order may stand in the place of the next-of-kin, something which happened in the case of the Polish priest, Fr. Jazebowski, in 2011.

The recent case of Shadrach Smith, a deceased Catholic, in 2011, is instructive in the continuing sensitivity over those of different faiths being buried in the same graveyard. Permission to exhume is usually sought by one of the surviving relatives; however, anyone can apply, as long as they explain why they are making the request. In this case, a Muslim family wanted to exhume the remains of a Catholic man (Shadrach Smith) interred beside one of their dead relatives in a multi-denominational cemetery because Mr. Smith was a non-believer, that is, not a Muslim. The

Ministry of Justice confirmed that it would not allow exhumation without the full written consent of Mr. Smith's family, which had been refused here.[4] It is extraordinary that what seems exactly similar to the furore raised in 1557 over the burial of the Protestant wife of Peter Martyr in Cambridge in what had been a Catholic Church should be repeated in 2015.

Exhumation requested for historical or scientific reasons must be supported by some public benefit being established if it is granted. This was the case in *Re St Mary, Sledmore (2007) 3 All ER 75 (see n.15)* where a faculty was granted to exhume the body of the Yorkshire baronet, Sir Mark Wright, who had died in 1918, during the Spanish flu pandemic. It was thought that examination of his body, buried in a silver casket, and therefore well preserved, might help in the fight against Asian bird flu in 2007.

This case can be compared to *Re St Nicholas's, Sevenoaks (2005) 1 WLR 1011, and Re Holy Trinity, Bosham (2007) 1 WLR Fam. 125*, where petitions were refused because the evidence tended to be based on rumour, myth, and speculation, rather than hard facts.

A Section 25 licence was required in 2008 to exhume what was thought to be the remains of John Henry, Cardinal Newman; he had been buried in grounds consecrated by the *Catholic* Church. The same thing happened in the exhumation of Queen Maria of Yugoslavia in 2013, as she had been buried in grounds consecrated by the *Orthodox* Church. In this instance, the return to a secular authority, because the religious one is only valid if it is *Anglican*, is the same as in the ceremonies of marriage. Other religions may be allowed to go through their own ceremonies, but only the *Anglican* ceremonies are legal in themselves.

Ensuring that the relevant consents are in place is a vital part of the process. The initial emphasis is on the deceased's next of kin, as "identified and prioritized by standard probate principle". This was emphasised in the case of *R (on the Application of Plantagenet Alliance Ltd) v Secretary of State for Justice (2014) EWHC 1662 (QB) (107)*. This was one of the cases which were a consequence of the discovery and exhumation of the remains of King Richard III in Leicester in 2012. The final resting place of the king was disputed, and as all his lands had been in the north, as well as his place of birth (Middleham), the Plantagenet Alliance wished him to be buried in York Minster. The weight of the evidence, as well as the fact that no-one in the Alliance could plead to be next-of-kin, meant that they lost the case. The king now has a splendid white marble tomb in Leicester cathedral.

Disinterment without a faculty (permission being granted) was always an offence against ecclesiastical law. In committing the common law offence (misdemeanour), the underlying motive was irrelevant. An individual could be convicted of unlawfully disinterring a corpse, where the intent was to sell it for dissection purposes. Clearly, the disinterment of Queen Katherine Parr in the eighteenth century was not only an ecclesiastical offence but also a common law misdemeanour; the fact that it was done out of a fashionably Gothic curiosity would have been irrelevant. Whether the "ladies" concerned realised quite what they were doing is another question.

The continuing vexed question of the medical world's need for dissecting fresh bodies had only been dealt with in a piecemeal, and totally inadequate way, over the centuries at least since 1500. It was further complicated by the fact that the physicians were looked upon as the professional men, and the surgeons, who actually did the dissecting of both living and dead bodies, belonged to the Guild of Barber-Surgeons and were looked upon simply as artisans. Their status in society was quite different, right up until the eighteenth century. Eventually, the barbers were separated from the surgeons, who at last in 1829 received their own royal charter and professional recognition. One of the last significant Acts of Parliament before this happened was the Murder Act of 1752, which stated that the only bodies that could be used for medical dissection were those of executed murderers. Interestingly, this was in line with similar practices from ancient times, when condemned criminals were used for actual killings during theatrical performances, a grisly practice indeed. The Anatomical Society had been formed in 1810 as a pressure group, which at last saw its purpose realised. The practice also of using unclaimed corpses had been sanctioned in Scotland as far back as 1694. James IV of Scotland had permitted four executed criminals to be used for medical dissection, as had Henry VIII. Elizabeth I confirmed this as six, and Charles II expressly said six. These were trifling numbers compared to the necessity of medical practitioners needing a thorough knowledge of the human body. The emergence of criminologists, such as Cesare Lombroso, who examined the bodies and skulls of executed Corsican brigands, further brought the matter to public attention and scrutiny. His compatriot Guiseppe Beccaria placed issues on a more rational basis later.

The position and continuing authority of the Established Church in England has been seen in 2019 during the ongoing excavations for the HS2 project in London. As archaeologists continued their immense task of dealing with the exhumation of 60,000 bodies buried in St. James's Gardens, next to Euston station in North London, the Church retained a vigil over proceedings. Although no-one has been buried there since Georgian and early Victorian times, the Church told the archaeologists that any and all human remains must be treated with the utmost care and dignity.

When the skeleton of Matthew Flinders was found (see Chap. 10 on Investigation & Identity) in January 2019, at the request of the Church, the chief archaeologist, Helen Wass, said they were not releasing images of any of the remains, though they were filmed for a BBC Documentary to be released later in 2019.

A Church of England spokesman said Ecclesiastical law required all bodies disinterred from an old graveyard to be reburied together, as close as possible to their original home. The Church does not usually make exceptions for significant historical figures. The Church was still looking for a suitable place, ideally one that is already consecrated ground.

Though the remains (and here reference was made particularly to Matthew Flinders) do not need another funeral, "it's usually the case there is some sort of blessing or service", he said. When one considers the number of bodies or remains in this exhumation, it is a very daunting task.

Church law considers anything above ground to be the property of descendants, and anything below ground counts as part of the remains that must be reinterred. However, the spokesman continued, the law was "less rigid" on this, and the Church had been more likely to make exceptions for something like a plaque. It would be up to the bishop of the diocese—in this case the Bishop of London—to rule on who should take possession and who should care for the artefacts recovered with the body or remains.

The Church would not, in the case of Matthew Flinders, rule out allowing Australia to have some artefact from the discovery. Helen Wass said that the breastplate would probably be replaced with a replica for the reburial.

HS2 was in discussion as to where things may go. It may give them to the Museum of London, which would put some artefacts in storage for posterity, whilst leaving others on display.

The Australian High Commissioner, George Brandis, said that the remains should be reburied with a "fitting tribute to his (Matthew Flinders') place in history. I hope that, when they are, an appropriate form of memorial will be erected over the final resting place of Captain Matthew Flinders to mark his significance both in Australia's story and his heroic place in the great age of adventure and navigation".[5]

Notes

1. Such as Diarmaid McCullough, Lecture in the Temple Church, November 7, 2018, before the Ecclesiastical Society of the Church of England, and The Canon Law Society of Great Britain & Ireland (of the Catholic Church).
2. Pocklington, David, *Clergy Discipline, Former Clergy and Parochial Fees*, posted on January 29, 2015.
3. R v Lynn (1788), 2 Term Rep. 733, Nisi Prius, 13; English Reports (1788) 171, pp. 900–1.
4. Conway, pp. 187–8; Rayner, G., Grave of Catholic Shadrach Smith will NOT be exhumed, family told in row over Muslim burial plot next door, *The Daily Telegraph*, London, February 11, 2015.
5. Miller, Nick, *Matthew Flinders Found: London Dig Unearths Grave of Great Explorer*, January 25, 2019. Sydney Morning Herald & The Age, Europe correspondent.

CHAPTER 10

Reasons Many and Various

The exhumation of Sir Mark Sykes in 2007, prompted by the Bird Flu epidemic of that time, disclosed a most extraordinary story, or back story as the current media will have it. Sir Mark was the only child of an unhappy but very aristocratic marriage, between his forty-eight-year-old father, Sir Tatton Sykes, and the eighteen-year-old Christina Anne-Jessica Cavendish-Bentinck, a relative of the lady who would become known as Queen Elizabeth the Queen Mother. The marriage, it is said, had been arranged, or insisted on, by the mother of the bride. Some accounts say that, in essence, Sir Tatton was trapped into marrying Christina.

The facts are interesting in themselves. Sir Tatton owned a 34,000-acre estate in the East Riding of Yorkshire, with its heart at Sledmere House. This was described as "like a ducal demesne among the Wolds, approached by long straight roads and sheltered by belts of woodland, surrounded by large prosperous farms…ornamented with the heraldic triton of the Sykes family…the mighty four-square residence and the exquisite parish church".[1] Sir Tatton also had a stud, where he bred his prize Arabs.

This sounds an idyllic setting, and it is easy to see how the mother of the bride realised what a good match in material terms this was; and it is just as easy to see how this would quickly have bored a sprightly young girl married to a man thirty years her senior. Her spending became reckless. At first, her husband paid out a large amount of money covering her debts, but then he had had enough. He inserted a message in the papers disavowing his wife's future debts, and obtained a legal separa-

M. L. Nash, *The History and Politics of Exhumation*,
https://doi.org/10.1007/978-3-030-24047-9_10

tion. In both Canon and Civil Law, he would have been entitled to an annulment.

It was into this marital melee, that Tatton Benvenuto Mark Sykes was born on March 16, 1879, in Westminster, London, where the Sykes had their London house; and it was here that Lady Sykes lived apart from her husband, presumably enjoying the delights of the capital. When Mark was three, Lady Sykes converted to Roman Catholicism and took her son with her. He was educated at the Jesuit Beaumont College and at Jesus College, Cambridge, although he never took his degree. The fact was that his unusual and probably lonely childhood left him very much to his own devices, and the vivid imagination he developed was not accompanied by the corresponding self-discipline which would have made him a scholar. But his personality would have been enough, and it was. An old friend, Aubrey Herbert, would later say of him: "(He was) an effervescent personality. He could turn a gathering into a party, and a party into a festival. He bubbled with ideas, and he swept up his listeners with his enthusiasm. In addition he had a remarkable talent for sketching caricatures and for mimicry…Mark Sykes had vitality beyond any man I have ever met. When one had been in his company one felt almost as if one had been given from the fountain of life".[2]

This was the charismatic personality who was thus launched into public life, and inter alia, was a Captain with the Green Howards, saw action in the Second Boer War, became Parliamentary Secretary to George Wyndham, the Chief Secretary for Ireland, became friends with Balfour when he was Foreign Secretary and worked closely with him, and finally something which really changed the course of his life (and was the cause of his death) he became honorary attache at the British Embassy in Constantinople, during the last years of Ottoman rule. Sykes had travelled to the Middle East with his father every winter as a young man, and already knew it well, but now he was involved in an official capacity.

In the meantime, he married Edith Gorst, also a Roman Catholic, who was the daughter of the Conservative Party manager, Eldon Gorst. Unlike his parents, this was a happy marriage and produced six children. In 1913, he succeeded to the baronetcy and the vast estates of his father.

In 1911, he became a Member of Parliament as a Unionist for Hull Central. Most of the illuminati of the day were known to him, some well, including T.E. Lawrence, Gertrude Bell, F.E. Smith, and Hilaire Belloc. When World War I began in 1914, he was Lieutenant-Colonel Sykes, Commander of the 5th Battalion of the Green Howards, but he was needed in the Intelligence Department of the War Office under Lord Kitchener. Kitchener placed him on Sir Maurice de Bunsen's Committee advising the Cabinet on Middle Eastern affairs, which quickly became his province and his forte. He quickly became the dominant person on the Committee, and it is arguable that he came to understand the Arab mentality better than his more idealist contemporaries. Having failed to keep Turkey entering the war on the German side, the issue became clearly what was to happen to the vacuum in the Middle East when the Ottoman empire finally guttered out?

It became Sykes' special role to hammer out an agreement on this issue with his French counterpart, Francois Georges-Picot. From 1914 to 1918, Sykes had become the principal expert on Turkish affairs and in 1915 arrived at Downing Street to advise the Prime Minister on the state of affairs within the Ottoman empire. Eventually, in 1919, he was at the peace negotiations in Paris, and was the joint author of the Sykes-Picot Agreement. His charisma was as potent as ever. A young Harold Nicolson described Sykes' effect: "It was due to his endless push and perseverance, to his enthusiasm and faith, that Arab nationalism and Zionism became two of the most successful of our war causes".

Sykes had personally designed the flag of the Arab revolt, a combination of green, red, black and white. Variations on this design later served as the flags of Jordan, Iraq, Syria, Egypt, Sudan, Kuwait, Yemen, the United Arab Emirates, and Palestine, none of which existed as separate nations before the First World War (and Palestine has still not achieved separate sovereign status).

Authorities differ, indeed clash, over what was the approach and the achievement of Sir Mark, and whether his legacy, the Sykes-Picot Agreement, over the division of spheres or areas of influence in the Middle East, divided between France and Britain (and, interestingly, originally, Tsarist Russia) might have been re-thought if he had lived. The biography written by his grandson Christopher Sykes is predictably going to be in his favour. Christopher Sykes entitled it *The Man who created the Middle East*,[3] which must be something of an exaggeration. The review of this in *The Guardian*, by Anthony Sattin, had who had written a book about that other iconic figure of the Arab revolt, T.E. Lawrence. The reviewer was always going to see it through Lawrence's eyes, rather than those of Sykes. They had been at Oxford together, and Lawrence did apply himself, and did get his degree; but there could be fewer stranger characters than Lawrence, and few who were so devoted to their own agenda. Whether that is good or otherwise, is another issue. Lawrence did not have a high opinion of Sykes and his approach. He called him "the imaginative advocate of unconvincing world movements", a man who carried "a bundle of prejudices, intuitions, half-sciences" and "would take an aspect of the truth, detach it from its circumstances, inflate it, twist and model it". The civil commissioner for Basra, now in Iraq, thought Sykes "a genius for happy but not always accurate generalisations". But surely generalisations, of their very nature, cannot be accurate. In 1918, just before Sykes died, another visionary who could be in an ivory tower, President Woodrow Wilson, said that Arabs should be given "an absolutely unmolested opportunity of autonomous development". That was never likely to happen to peoples whose first loyalties had been to their own tribes and religion and in the not so distant past, to the Caliph in Constantinople.

Sykes was absolutely not, as Sattin suggests or states in his review, an anti-semite. He may have had a damascene conversion, but he worked with Balfour and his declaration in favour of a homeland for the Jews in 1917, and on news of his death, Nahum Sokolow, a Russian Zionist colleague of Chaim Weizmann, who was in Paris at this time, wrote that he "…fell as a hero at our side".

It is also very arguable that, despite his romantic and perhaps unstructured enthusiasm, he really did understand both his own contemporary Arab mentality and even what it is now. The writers Kedourie and Townsend both endorse the fact that Sykes remained a purist, who shunned democratic progress, instead investing his energy in an indomitable Arab spirit. He was a champion of Levantine tradition, of a mercantile trading empire, finding the progress modernisation in the West totally unsuited to the desert kingdoms. This take on Sykes' own mentality is borne out by the mercantile success of Turkey, Syria, Lebanon, and Jordan, perhaps even Egypt and Cyprus, before the debacle which began after the failure of Suez in 1956.[4]

But fate or destiny was now to catch up with Sykes. While travelling in the Middle East he had contracted the so-called Spanish influenza, then its second wave. He died in the Hotel Lotti, near the Tuileries Gardens in Paris, on February 16, 1919. He was thirty-nine years old. His remains were transported back to Sledmere for burial, where, interestingly, although he died a Catholic, he was buried in the Anglican cemetery.

The scene now moves, eighty-eight years later, to the laboratories of Professor John Oxford, Professor of Virology at St. Bartholemew's Hospital in London, and the Royal London Hospital, Queen Mary's

School of Medicine and Dentistry. Professor Oxford needs tissue from human bodies who have been contaminated with the avian flu of 1918–1919, in order to understand its genetic structure and so combat the threatening bird flu of 2007. He and his team have already obtained lung material from frozen coal miners who were victims, in Spitzbergen, from victims in Alaska, and from two victims in London, but the material so far available to the team has provided only low-quality samples which have been of insufficient quality to enable the necessary scientific experimentation to take place. Consequently, they have been searching for some time for victims of the virus who were buried in sealed iron or lead coffins. They believe that such bodies may be better preserved than those so far made available to them. They have identified the body of Sir Mark Sykes, as someone who was so buried and so whose body may provide material of the quality they seek.

The six grandchildren of Sir Mark and his wife have all given their written permission. The case now moves before the Consistory Court of York and before its Chancellor Peter Collier QC, on January 10, 2007.[5]

The Faculty requested of the Court was for the exhumation of Sir Mark Sykes and then re-interment of the remains after samples had been taken from the body. There had to be benefit proved for medical and scientific research, evidence of public benefit, and the issue before the court was whether this public benefit that might ensue from the proposed research displaced the presumption against exhumation, as Christian burial in consecrated ground was final.

The principle of proportionality also applied here. Was the disturbance of a Christian burial justified in the light of the above? Professor Oxford had an additional ground for his research, which was the question "Was the outbreak of encephalitis lethargica in 1920 triggered by the influenza?"

Cases quoted in the judgement are of interest both here and elsewhere in this study. *Norfolk County Council v Knight and Caister-on-Sea Burial Committee*[6] and *Re St. Nicholas, Sevenoaks*[7] are cases in point. In the beginning, Chancellor Ellison was not persuaded. The County Council considered a point in the road dangerous to traffic, and wanted to widen it. This would have necessitated the exhumation of 400 sets of human remains to create this road-widening scheme. The Chancellor opined "That such weighty reasons exist on the grounds of danger past, present and potential, or for that matter any sufficiently weighty ground which would justify my granting a faculty to permit the large upheaval which would follow" did not convince him. This case now has implications for the HS2 plans in

2018, which will involve the removal of more than the 400 bodies of the Norfolk case.

In the second case, there was speculation and family tradition at the core of the petition. This was brought by one George Locock, who wanted to exhume the remains of his grandfather, to take Deoxyribonucleic acid (DNA) samples, in an effort to prove that he had been the illegitimate child of Princess Louise, one of the five daughters of Queen Victoria. The doctrine of proportionality and the weight of convincing evidence applied, and the request was refused.[8]

Chancellor Peter Collier reminded the Court that "It is accepted within the Church that human osteology (the scientific study of human remains) is capable of benefiting the public by contributing to medical history and to forensic science. In theological terms: "There may be every justification for arguing that a corpse has no more external significance than an empty shell, but it continues to be the vestiges of a once loved and loving human being". This quote came from the Church Archaeology Human Remains Working Report, at para. 153. "Consistent with this approach", continued the Chancellor, "is the essential requirement that skeletons made available for investigation are treated with respect and re-buried in a dignified manner at the conclusion of the investigation". It has been said that "A Society that cares for its dead demonstrates that it values life", again quoting from the Report at para. 153.

The Court decided that the Sykes Petition was an exceptional case and the faculty to exhume would be granted. The caveat was that because the coffin of Lady Edith, the wife of Sir Mark, who had died after him, had to be removed first, was not otherwise disturbed. Twelve months were granted for completing the work, and, in the language of the Consistory Court "A faculty (should) pass the seal to permit the exhumations prayed for".

In the wider sense, the use of Sir Mark's body to promote medical research was also seen by some to be some kind of redemption for the harm perceived to have been done by the Sykes-Picot Agreement; and indeed, the indelible effect of that Agreement is seen in frighteningly recent terms when the followers of Isis ploughed up the Sykes-Picot boundary between Syria and Iraq, ordered to do so by Abu Bakr al Baghdadi, who saw himself as the new Caliph.

Occasionally the Government admits the possibility of a mistake, or at least uses exhumation as a way of mollifying a political situation or a domestic disquiet. Two cases which share this in common are those of the

Irish patriot (and to the Southern Irish, martyr) Sir Roger Casement, executed for his part in the Easter Rising of 1916; and Edith Thompson, a suburban housewife, who possibly connived at the murder of her husband, and was executed in 1924. In both of these cases, the Government very much later allowed their bodies to be exhumed: in the case of Roger Casement, in 1965, and in the case of Edith Thompson not until 2018.

Both of these cases are in their separate ways extraordinary and both became causes celebres, over which much ink has been spilt, and much print expended. They both might equally qualify to be considered under Retribution and Reparation.

The scenario which came to fruition, in the case of Casement, in 1965, had a further extraordinary factor to contend with. When the Labour Party in Britain won the General Election of October 1964 the Prime Minister, Harold Wilson, lost no time in addressing the Casement affair, because it gave his party an opportunity to present its own dimension on Irish affairs in a most positive way. Thus the change of government heralded a change in policy, and already on January 14, 1965, a secret deal had been concluded with Dublin to exhume and return the body of Roger Casement. There was an important rider to this, voiced by the new Home Secretary, Sir Frank Soskice. It was he who pointed out that it would be unacceptable to Northern Ireland and its government for his (Casement's) body to go there, as he had wanted in his will. He must be interred in Republican territory and not be subsequently moved. The very next day Britain's wartime leader, Sir Winston Churchill, suffered a stroke, the eighth of a long series, and the one from which he would not recover.

Fate now intervened in a somewhat dramatic way, for on January 24, 1965, Sir Winston died in London, at the age of ninety. A state funeral loomed, which was exactly what the Irish government had in mind for Casement. Two state funerals then took place, one in London and one in Dublin, both in snow and bitter weather. Neither of these elements deterred the massive crowds which followed and witnessed the funeral corteges. Obviously, in Britain, the one eclipsed the other; and in Ireland, it was the other way round.

Even before the death of Churchill was announced, and before the news of Casement's exhumation had also been made public, Casement's body had been exhumed. No time was lost. It had been exhumed by prison warders, "with a great deal of humanity, and even reverence", being placed overnight in the Catholic chapel of Pentonville prison. Some prisoners were observed by the Irish officials watching the operation by means of extending mirrors from their cells and examining the reflection.

Identification was based on the grave's location, number twenty-seven (between one for a man named Kuhn, and one for a Robinson). Thus are the criminal dead further robbed of their identity. The size of the femurs also helped in the identification, as did Casement's black hair and a portion of the scalp, which were clearly visible on an otherwise very white skull, while one tibia showed signs of having been broken and re-set. Along with his disarticulated bones, calcified remnants of the shroud and several teeth with lead fillings were taken from the grave, and placed in a lead-lined casket. British officials insisted on paying for all this. All of the principal members of the skeleton were apparently uncovered, although in 1916 Casement had been buried without a coffin, with quicklime being laid down.

On January 26, 1965, through a decree of the Queen, Elizabeth II, the lying-in-state of Churchill began in Westminster Hall, and four days later, on January 30, the state funeral took place in St. Paul's Cathedral. The writer himself was present during some of these ceremonies. He queued for many hours in the winter weather with his then-girlfriend and another friend, and as the long queue crossed the Albert bridge, a particularly vicious wind blew through the openings in the ironwork of the bridge, causing the friend to say that he was going to re-design bridges. Later, watching the funeral cortege wend its way from Westminster to St. Paul's, he watched from a vantage point in Whitehall, and when it turned the corner of Trafalgar Square to enter the Strand, a girl watching and leaning out from a floor high above, crossed herself. When we returned home to Southampton, we found that my girlfriend's mother had pulled all the curtains in the windows of her house for the whole day, as her own tribute to Churchill.

After the funeral, the coffin crossed the Thames on a barge, and as it did so, thirty-six cranes dipped their jibs in salute, perhaps the most moving movement of the whole day. After it had arrived at Bladon cemetery, near to Blenheim Palace, where Churchill had been born in 1874, my parents, my brother and I went to view the grave, still freshly dug and piled high with flowers. We were four of over 100,000 people who visited the grave in the first week.

Meanwhile, in Dublin, preparations had been made to receive the body of Casement. On February 23, 1965, the remains were flown from RAF Northolt into Baldonnel military airbase near Dublin, soon to be renamed

Casement Aerodrome. The British ambassador stood dutifully, if incongruously, in the welcoming party, alongside Frank Aiken, whose dogged persistence had at last paid off.[9]

1965 was the date of the writer's first visit to Ireland. Among other memorable experiences was meeting a lady of hundred in Akill, who could speak only Irish (Gaelic) and who kept repeating, in Irish, "God is good"; learning that Fermanagh, one of the six counties in the North, might defect to the South; and visiting family of my friend in Dublin, where two of the men were hotly disputing the life and death of Michael Collins. When the news came on the radio in any bar we were in, it was the first broadcast in Gaelic, and the hubbub in the bar did not diminish one iota; when it continued in English, there was a noticeable drop in the noise while people listened. This was a very different Ireland of today. Unspoilt and undeveloped as it was, it was also an ultra-conservative Catholic and Gaelic Nationalist state, an artificial construct, which lasted perhaps until the visit of Pope John Paul II in 1979, when a third of the population greeted him and attended his great Mass. The struggle within Southern Ireland was between this state and a more secular democratic and republican ideal. Since then the second state has prevailed, with certain gains, but also certain losses and sacrifices. The choice always involves sacrifice. It is certainly arguable that Casement had the first state in mind when he made his own choice and sacrifice. It brings to mind the immortal words of *1066 and all that*, that like Cromwell and his republican and repressive view of personal morality, the republicans in Ireland were "Right but Repulsive", and those who preferred and fought for the original Catholic and Gaelic nationalist state were "Wrong but Romantic".[10] It seems impossible to escape the impression that Casement was wrong but romantic.

It was the year before the fiftieth anniversary of the Easter Rising. Harold Wilson called it "a satisfactory end to an unhappy chapter", although the re-burial would not be at Murlough Bay, as Casement had wanted in his will. This might have been somewhat of an understatement. Casement was instead to have a memorable state funeral in Ireland's capital. The President of Ireland, the same Eamon de Valera who had escaped from prison in England, spoke on behalf of those few of his contemporaries still surviving by saying: "Now thanks be to God he is back here".

The colossal figure of 665,000 people, pretty well then the population of Dublin, came to pay their respects to Casement during the five days of his lying-in-state at Arbour Hill, the last place he had been in Ireland before being shipped out through Kingstown. (Was it five days, one wonders, in order to trump the four days of Churchill?) No relatives travelled from Magherintemple, the Casement family home in Co. Antrim, but his two surviving nieces, the daughters of Casement's brother Charlie, were brought from Australia, to which Charlie had emigrated. They were in their seventies and seemed bewildered and overwhelmed by all the ceremonies. They had never actually met their uncle, but had always felt that they had loved him at a distance, because he had sent them letters and presents when they were little girls. Now, one of them Mrs Nina Ayers, in an old-fashioned fur coat, and the other Mrs Kathleen Vaughan (the unmistakable classic Casement long jaw came to bury their Uncle Roddie. (It is interesting that Roger Casement used his other names in family and intimate connections, Roddie and David). There was one other relative, Katje, the widow of Casement's brother Tom, the last Casement of his generation. She alas could not attend because she was in no fit mental state to travel from her English hospital.

But Murlough was not forgotten. The Glens *Feis* Chairman, P.J. O'Clery, brought a sod from the Murlough gravesite to Glasnevin cemetery and laid a wreath. To the relief of the Irish government, and that of the British one too, there were only the most minimal of semi-military demonstrations from the Republican movement, by one notorious Irish Republican Army (IRA) dissident, Richard Behal.

On Monday, March 1, after a solemn Requiem Mass in the pro-Cathedral of Dublin, Casement set off on his final journey (*to date*).[11] A national day of mourning had been declared and the event was televised by the fledgling RTE (Radio Teilifis Eireann (Irish News) The national public service media of Ireland). The state funeral proceeded with Casement's tricolour-draped coffin on a gun carriage. Accompanied by ranks of soldiers in Irish Army green, it wended its way through the centre of Dublin to Glasnevin cemetery. As the cortege moved into O'Connell Street, amidst enormous crowds and swirling snow, there was a flash of lightning and a roll of thunder…Ireland's last hero, so long dishonoured, in an unmarked grave in an English gaol, passed by. Sadly, Nina and Gertrude, Casement's cousins, who never ceased to further his cause and his memory, were never to know of this event, not in this life at any rate.

Though old and blind, a hatless Eamon de Valera, eighty-two, could not be dissuaded from delivering the graveside oration, in a blizzard at the cemetery. "Casement deserves better", he reportedly said. Speaking first in Irish (Gaelic) and then in English, he declared to his wide audience, "I do not think it presumptuous on our part to believe that a man who was so unselfish, who worked so hard for the downtrodden and the oppressed, and who so died, is in heaven". Then, through sleet and heavy wind, he recited the burial places of the men of 1798 (Wolf Tone's rebellion) many themselves hanged.

Later that year de Valera presented the original of Casement's last letter to Gertrude (July 20, 1916) to the National Library. It mentions William Orr, executed in 1797, and asks his cousin "to defend my honour and my name…in all this tangled web". Both his cousins, and many others, did just that for many years.

The return of Casement's remains, although a patriotic rather than an irredentist affair, was the harbinger of the next year's fiftieth anniversary celebrations of the Easter Rising. It was to spark off a renewal of nationalist fervour over the partition, and presage another round of conflict, beginning in 1968, seven years before the death of de Valera, the last 1916 leader.

The exhumation and subsequent events had, of course, started a fresh interest in the life and career of Casement, as such events often do. In a way, he had had the last word: "In all this tangled web…" In him, as Shakespeare so eloquently said, "the elements were so mixed". That was the essence of his fateful fascination, both of him and for him. Interestingly, perhaps as a last gesture of reconciliation, the government archive which records the authorisation for the exhumation does indeed refer to him as "Sir" Roger Casement; or it may simply be a bureaucratic, if fortuitous, slip.

Sir Roger Casement had been born in Dublin, of an Anglo-Irish family and baptised an Anglican. His father was a picaresque character, who became Captain in the King's Own Regiment of Dragoons and had served in the 1842 Afghan campaign, before travelling to Hungary to be a volunteer in the Revolution of 1848. Unfortunately, he arrived there after the surrender. His mother, Anne Jephson, purportedly had the infant Roger baptised again as a Catholic at Rhyl, North Wales, when he was three years old, that is in 1867. After living in England in genteel poverty, Anne Casement died when Roger was nine years old. When Roger was thirteen his father also died, at Ballymena, and being looked after by relatives for three years, he left school at sixteen, and went to work for the Elder Dempster Line, a Liverpool shipping company. These early circumstances, being a Catholic, being left to his own devices, and working in a maritime environment, shaped his coming extraordinary life. It seemed to be in the stars that he would meet a fellow kindred spirit in Joseph Conrad, in the Congo in 1890. Casement had been working since 1884, when he was twenty, for Henry Morton Stanley and the African International Association. This was a front for the takeover of the Congo as a personal fiefdom by the King of the Belgians, Leopold II, and so Casement became an employee in this sense of the Belgian government.

While in the Belgian Congo, Casement met Joseph Conrad, whose short novel, *Heart of Darkness*, was the result of his visit, published in 1899. Casement and Conrad at that time agreed that "European colonisation would bring moral and social progress to the continent, and free its inhabitants from "slavery, paganism and other barbarities". But both in this respect were ingenues, and "both would learn the gravity of his error".[12] For Casement, he joined the British Colonial Service, and his talents ensured his rise from clerk to progression to the Foreign office, and in 1901 at the age of thirty-seven, he became British consul in the eastern part of the French Congo. This then progressed to a commission from the British government to investigate the human rights situation in the Belgian Congo, which was being treated as a private fief by Leopold II, the King of the Belgians. Eventually, the truth of the *Casement Report* of 1904 was acknowledged by the Parliament of Belgium, which transferred the management of the Congo from Leopold to the Parliament itself.

Riding now on the crest of his reputation, the British government sent Casement to Brazil in 1906 as consul, and promoted him soon afterwards as Consul-General. While there he exposed the sufferings of the Putamayo Indians in a report similar to that of his Congolese days, for which he had been appointed a Companion of the Order of St. Michael and St. George in 1905. This new report exposed the crimes of the Peruvian Amazon Company repeated by Casement in his 1910 report. In 1911, he was rewarded with a knighthood.

About two years later, although it must have been in his mind for a long time, Casement came to a fateful decision concerning his fractured loyalties, both religious and political, or rather the two inextricably wound together, like the caduceus. He decided to espouse openly the cause of Irish independence and nationalism, even though he must have known only too clearly that the nation which had given him his honours was on the verge of war. Taking the well-known aphorism "My enemy's enemy is my friend", he manipulated the German antagonism to the potential advantage of Ireland, by recruiting to the Irish cause in Germany itself. By these actions, both before and after war was actually declared, in 1914, he became legally a traitor to Britain under the Treason Act of 1351, which was still operative.

Arriving in Ireland by German submarine in 1916, in order to lead Sinn Fein and the planned Easter Rising in Dublin, he was captured by British agents and escorted via Kingstown to the Tower of London. His subsequent trial, conviction, appeal, and execution, in Pentonville goal, became the stuff of Irish legend and much controversy. It may be difficult to quite recapture now the figure that Casement had become. His tireless work for the underdog both in the Congo and among the Putamayo Indians in South America was of course remembered. Casement was seriously good-looking and had a large and devoted female following of admirers. His image also coincided with the ultra-puritan Catholic representations of Jesus Christ, dark, bearded and inscrutable, the explosive combination of good looks and religious fervour. There was an undeniable sexual appeal in Casement's image and pictures, of which there were many, and of which he must have been aware. It was not only an appeal to women.

Suddenly this hero and icon had fallen from grace, and from a great height. The icon had feet of clay, after all. But his appeal was so strong that something had to be found to finally discredit him, so that his execution would not only make him a martyr, but a tarnished one. It mattered not at all that so many saints and martyrs were also tarnished characters, for this was within the First World War and at a desperate time for Britain in 1916. It was easy to make out that the landing in Ireland, with German assistance and collaboration, was a stab in the back.

The agent of this policy of blackening Casement's character came, appropriately, in the form of the so-called *Black Diaries*. These, the meticulous civil and colonial servant that Casement was, had been kept for a number of years, and enumerated not only his notes on the oppressed and his social calendar, but his numerous, indeed addictive, sexual exploits, in London, Paris, and especially in South America. Homosexuality had been criminalised in Britain as a secular offence originally by Henry VIII, but the actual physical offences had been listed in an Act of 1861. Since that time many men had been ruined, in reputation and every other way, by the discovery of homosexual practices. The Government and Courts of Britain now seized its chance and publicised the Diaries, although they were never accessible in full until 1999. That is how explosive they were in the minds of the British establishment. The Diaries which caused the most concern were those of 1903 and 1911, the latter the very year that Casement received his knighthood, which was of course, on his conviction, rescinded. (He afterwards returned his insignia). The authenticity of the diaries has of course been questioned many times, both before, during and after the trial of Casement. Singleton-Gates has been the traditional provider of vital material for almost all researchers into Casement's life, and it is only right that the final proof of the authenticity of the diaries should come from him. In an interview which has had no publicity, he solemnly testified that, not very long ago, in his presence and in the presence of a well-known witness, the ultra-violet ray machine was used. This was a secret and highly unofficial exercise, but it established that, *without any doubt at all*, the diaries are entirely in Casement's own hand.[13]

Casement mirrors in his own person the contemporary Irish uncertainty as to its/his own identity and divided loyalties. "(There were) many shades of ambivalence: familial, physical, religious and political; and in all of these areas, even the physical, he seemed to reflect, in an unusual way, the problems of identity suffered by Ireland as a whole".[14] In another part of his book, Sawyer says: "His sexuality was just one areas of his many-sided ambivalence".[15]

To begin with, he was both an Irishman and an Imperialist. During his re-union with his old and faithful friend, Richard Morten, in Brixton prison, he said: "…all this (the change of direction) has come by sure and certain stages—an irresistible destiny appointed since I was a little boy. I felt it then and have often felt sure of it in later days".[16] He now felt he was in an "Elsewhere Empire", a memorable description.

The Easter Rising was suppressed, and most of its ringleaders executed. De Valera was one of these ringleaders, and was imprisoned in Britain, but managed to escape. Casement's chances of a reprieve were compromised by the publicity given to the diaries, although even in the Court of Appeal the judges did not fail to emphasise his former good works. Just before he was executed, he became a Catholic in his cell in Pentonville, and received his first, and only, communion, on the day of his death, which he met courageously. His conversion confirmed to the Catholic Irish his status not only as a hero but a martyr to the cause of Irish independence. Casement had within his own personality the confusion and dichotomy of loyalties which affected so many Irish as to their true identity, but at last, he had chosen.

His status after his death was, of course, stronger and more enduring even than during his lifetime. He was not forgotten. Frank Aiken was the long-time External Affairs Minister of the eventual Irish Republic, which came into some kind of inchoate being in 1932 (although the actual declaration was not until 1937). He kept the campaign alive, to bring Casement's body back to Ireland. During the 1940s and 1950s, the

Conservatives in Britain maintained their prohibition on his exhumation. But the Wilson government, as we have seen, was determined to use it to mend what fences they could with Southern Ireland.

In July, 2018, the British government had a change of heart over another very controversial execution, in 1923, and allowed the exhumation of Edith Thompson. This trial, and verdict, which along with another, taking place at exactly the same time that of Marguerite Alibert, was held at the Central Criminal Court in London, the Old Bailey. The trial of Edith Thompson and her lover Frederick Bywaters, did not of course have the same heavy and indelible political tones of that of Casement, just seven years earlier, but it did very much concern the concepts of British justice and the interference with that justice. It also concerned wider issues, including the impartiality of the judiciary, much- vaunted when compared with other judicial systems, and what has been aptly described as "a seed planted in the fertile soil of English prejudice".

Edith Thompson was the daughter of William Grayson, who worked as a clerk for the Imperial Tobacco Company, and who taught dancing freelance with his other daughter Avis. When she was fifteen, Edith began to be courted by Percy Thompson, a shipping clerk. He was nineteen and apparently keen to marry Edith. She appears, as time went by, to have been less keen, but nevertheless married him in St. Barnabas Church, Manor Park, in 1916. She was then twenty-three and Percy was twenty-seven. By this time Edith was on her way to becoming manageress of a milliner's, where she had been a buyer. The trouble really began when Percy brought home a friend who then became a lodger. This was Frederick Bywaters, who was a steward on board ship, and was eighteen. Edith, who was by this time twenty-seven, had fallen out of love (if it had ever been there) with Percy, and transferred her affections to the young Freddy, who was a willing accomplice. Something was emphasised at Edith's trial which may, or may not, have been a deciding factor, but certainly operated against her, and this was her apparent obsession with current pulp fiction, which, alongside the developing cinema, opened up a world of fantasy for many. It can have been no coincidence that one Alfred Hitchcock was one of her father's dancing pupils in 1919, and his sister became a close friend of Avis, Edith's sister. Indeed, they eventually became church wardens together.

A novel had been published entitled *Bella Donna*, prefiguring *The Sheikh*, the silent film starring the iconic Rudolph Valentino. It is possible that in her daydreams Edith imagined that she was the heroine of *Bella*

Donna, one Ruby Chepshow. By this time the book had been adapted for the theatre, and played to packed houses. Edith began composing passionate love letters to Freddy, and, by the time of the trial, they had passed 90,000 words. She refused her husband in bed and desired to be free. One of the letters to Freddy contained the words: "Do something drastic". Edith claimed in her letters that she had become pregnant by him and carried out her own abortion. She then told him of her lack of periods, and of the orgasm, she had experienced when they had open-air sex in Wanstead Park on the morning of Saturday, September 30, 1922. The poor and possibly by now demented Freddy took her at her word. When Edith and her husband were walking home from Ilford station on October 3, four days later, Freddy jumped out from behind some bushes, and stabbed Percy to death. Edith screamed, apparently hysterically, "No! Don't!" But it was of course too late. The fantasy had become reality.

There seems strong evidence that Edith was pregnant, or pregnant again, by Freddy. In one letter she had told him of meeting a woman who had lost three stone. "I can't even lose one", she told Freddy. Her tales of trying to poison Percy were proved however to be fantasies in the autopsy which followed Percy's murder.

Freddy and Edith were both found guilty of murder on December 11, 1922. During the trial, Freddy maintained that he had acted entirely alone. What does Edith's family think today? Graham Syms (who is a great-nephew of Edith's brother) and his wife Sue, and their side of the family think that this action of Freddy, in accepting sole responsibility, made the public warm to Freddy as "a gentleman who was chivalrously protecting his lover". Whatever the truth of this, when a petition calling for mercy attracting nearly one million signatures was launched, it was for Freddy and not for the hapless Edith.

What is all too clear here is that the positions of men and women in society in Britain, and of how they treated each other, was being paraded before the public, the press and the world.

What was the evidence against Edith? She had written the letters, which certainly went way beyond what would have been appropriate in a married woman at that time, perhaps at any time. She had committed adultery, not a crime in England, though a sin in the eyes of the church (of which her family were certainly members). Had been an accessory before the fact? She had seemingly encouraged Freddy "to do something drastic", but did that mean murder? The judge, Sir Montague Shearman, coming to the end of his time on the bench, unwell, and from another age, steered the jury into believing that it did. The highly coloured novels had poisoned her mind. Although when the guilty verdict was given against her, many believed then it was a serious miscarriage of justice, even three decades later, into the time when Ruth Ellis was hanged (and she had certainly killed her lover, with malice aforethought), "there was a lingering sense of awkwardness, even shame" in Edith's family, and children were ushered out of the room if she was mentioned. She had become truly a skeleton in the cupboard.

What was as reprehensible at the time was that she was not examined physically, which might have found that she was pregnant, and this would have saved her from the scaffold. But surely she knew that pregnant women were not hanged? Between the time of the verdict, December 11, and the execution, January 9, she had hardly eaten anything, and yet she had put on a stone in weight.[17] When the execution took place, on January 9, 1923, it was in circumstances which could not have been more distressing or gruesome to all concerned. It is possible she had a miscarriage on the scaffold. Certainly, she began haemorrhaging and according to one report "her insides fell out". The hangman declared that he would never hang another woman. The Home Office experienced serious disquiet as to whether she had been pregnant, and her execution was therefore illegal.

In 1971, due to the extended building which was then going on at Holloway prison, some of the bodies were moved from the prison graveyard, among them Edith's, and four of them were buried together, in a new grave at Brookwood cemetery. Edith's sister Avis was still alive then, but was not informed. In the 1980s the history of Edith attracted the notice of Professor Rene Weis, a professor and Shakespeare scholar in the University of London. It became something of a cause celebre to him personally, as it had been at the time of her death. He was determined that posthumous justice should be done, and in 1983 was allowed to purchase her grave; but it was not until July 2018, that the Home Office agreed to the exhumation.

Early on the morning of Tuesday, November 28, 2018, the body of Edith Thompson was exhumed from Brookwood cemetery. For the first time, runs a somewhat emotive report, since October 4, 1922, she was in the hands of people who really cared for her.[18]

Her departure from the cemetery was witnessed by Professor Weis, his wife Jean, and Nicki Toay, a grand-daughter of Edith's cousin. A private ambulance was used for the first part of the three-day journey to her parents' grave in the City of London cemetery (where, ironically, her husband,

Percy Thompson, also lies). The ambulance conveyed her remains to the premises of Frederick Paine, funeral director at Kingston. Later that day she was transferred to a private chapel of rest in their head office in Old London Road. This was to enable a select number of visitors to pay their respects, the funeral taking place on Thursday, November 22. The cortege left Kingston mid-morning, and crossed the Thames via Southwark bridge. On arrival at Manor Park, the cortege passed the church where she had been married, and paused outside 231 Shakespeare Crescent, where she had grown up. It then passed her old school in Kensington Avenue. On arriving at the Anglican chapel in the City of London cemetery the funeral service was conducted by Fr. Brian Creak, a high Anglican clergyman. A recording of her sister Avis's voice was played. Edith was then buried in the grave of her parents, William and Ethel Grayson, who had died in 1941 and 1938 respectively.

Kate Colquhoun has called Edith's story "a dark parable of society's vilification of women", but to balance the equation it is as well to remember that the petition which collected nearly a million signatures was for Freddy and not for her. Even at this distance, she does not appear a sympathetic character: self-absorbed, distracted by a phantasmagorical world engendered by the superficialities of the pulp novel and the silent screen. But this, of course, does not make her a murderess, or justify her execution.

By an extraordinary coincidence, another hapless woman was being tried almost at the same time at the Old Bailey, and the ending of the trial was very different. One needs to examine the question of why it was such a very different ending, and the answers are as unsatisfactory and disconcerting as those at the end of the trial of Edith Thompson.

Marguerite Alibert was a courtesan in Paris, during and after the First World War. As Andrew Rose says in his extraordinary book *The Prince, the Princess, and the Perfect Murder*,[19] quoting Balzac, "A courtesan is a monarchist at heart". This was certainly true of Marguerite. Her most high profile lover during the First World War was the green and impressionable Prince of Wales, quite possibly then a virgin. She was his first great love, and of course, letters were exchanged. Edward, never literary or cultured in any other way, was a great and imprudent letter writer to all his loves, Wallis Simpson, all of them. Marguerite kept the letters. Edward returned to Britain and his erstwhile duties as heir to the throne.

Marguerite in due course met an Egyptian aristocrat, Fahmi Bey. He was considerably younger than she was, but Marguerite's career had not differentiated the ages of her clients or her lovers. But this time it was different: Fahmi wanted to marry her. This she had to consider. Like the fabled Marguerite of *La Dame aux camellias*, Marguerite spent wildly. She was always short of money, and like all in her way of life, was not getting any younger. Fahmi Bey's family was extremely rich and well- positioned in society, both in the Arab and the French worlds. She decided to marry him and went through a civil marriage in Cairo on December 26, 1922 (if one runs the stories of the two women, Edith Thompson and Marguerite Alibert, in parallel, this was one day after Edith's twenty-ninth and last birthday in Holloway gaol). Cairo was en fete, not just because of the season, but because one month before Howard Carter and Lord Caernarvon had discovered the tomb of Tut-an-khamoun.

The city was in a ferment over the discovery, but Marguerite had more immediately pressing matters on her mind. As part of the marriage contract, she was required to convert to Islam. Despite the remonstrances of a Catholic priest, she did this on January 11, 1923 (two days after Edith's execution in England). She made her oath in Arabic and took the name Munira, after her new mother-in-law, who held the purse strings in the family. One might say it was a tactical move to secure her future, even a diplomatic one. But from now on, Marguerite would not be tactful or diplomatic in all her other moves. She quickly reverted to what she had been in Paris, and her behaviour became (rather like Edith's) not befitting a married woman, and most certainly not a Moslem and Oriental woman at that time. A month later the inner chamber of the tomb of Tut-an-khamoun was opened, and people flocked to the Valley of the Kings to see it. Among them were Fahmi Bey and Marguerite, who made two trips, the second on March 10, 1923.

Unfortunately, by this time both were quickly realising that the marriage was a mistake, and that the yawning gaps between them could not be bridged. Nevertheless, for the next four months they continued the endless rounds open to the idle rich, and on July 1, took up residence at the Savoy Hotel in London, in order to enjoy the season. The year 1923 was to prove to be one of quite exceptional heat and drought in England. The heat only added to the fevered atmosphere which existed between the two.

During the evening and night of July 9 to 10, a great altercation took place between Marguerite and her young husband, and verbal and then physical exchanges took place. Fahmi had a revolver, which he had pointed at Marguerite, and at one point, during a scuffle, with the doors of their suite open into the corridor, she picked up the gun and fired it at the back of his head. The night porter heard three shots, and returning along the corridor saw Marguerite throw down the gun, and Ali Fahmi Bey lying on his right side, crumpled against the wall. "He was unconscious, breathing stertorously, and bleeding profusely from a head wound from which protruded fragments of brain tissue and splintered bone. Alongside him lay a pool of blood in the corridor".[20] During this night the most tremendous thunderstorm hit southern England, accompanied by four or five hours of continuous thunder and forked lightning. As day dawned, it became clear that the heat had not abated.

In St. James's Palace the Prince of Wales was preparing to host a large dinner party, the hostess being his sister Princess Mary, as he was still a bachelor prince.

Ali was removed to Charing Cross Hospital but was already clinically dead, and did actually die at 3.25 in the morning. Marguerite was taken to Bow Street Magistrates' Court and charged with his murder. On the afternoon of July 10, she was taken to Holloway prison.

When the trial began, on Monday, September 10, 1923, the great Edward Marshall Hall agreed to be the defending lawyer for Marguerite, at a fee of 652 guineas, a sensational amount of money at that time. He helped that he spoke fluent French. During his defence he uttered these memorable words:

> She (Marguerite) made one great mistake, the greatest mistake any woman can make: a woman of the West married to an Oriental…I dare say the Egyptian civilisation is and may be one of the most wonderful civilisations in the world. (Obviously alluding to the recent discoveries, which had set the world alight). I don't say that among the Egyptians there are not many magnificent and splendid men, but, if you strip off the external civilisation of the Oriental, you get the real Oriental underneath and it is common knowledge that the Oriental's treatment of women does not fit in with the idea the Western woman has of the proper way she should be treated by her husband….

But it was not only this that Marshall Hall emphasised. He proceeded to blacken Ali Fahmi Bey in every sexual way he could, imputing that he was "a monster of Eastern depravity and decadence, whose sexual tastes were indicative of an amoral sadism towards his helpless European wife".[21] Among other imputations was his practice of anal intercourse and his alleged questionable relationship with his chief servant, Said Enani, a quite shameless character assassination.

This blackening, or demonising of Ali has close similarities as to that which happened at the trial of Roger Casement. Any imputation of unorthodox sexuality, anything different from the received orthodoxy, could serve the purpose. With Casement, albeit it was wartime, imputations of homosexuality implied in the Black Diaries were enough. With Ali, it was "common knowledge" of the Oriental, and reports and suggestions made by Marguerite herself or her sister Yvonne or anyone else who could serve this purpose. This demonisation is balanced on the other side by a deification of the alleged victim, something the life and character of Marguerite could never have sustained.

But once launched on his "Eastern theme", there was no restraining the great advocate.

"Picture this woman", he invited the jury, "inveigled into Egypt on false pretences, by a letter for which adulatory expression could hardly be equalled and which makes one feel sick…At first, all is honey and roses. He shows her his beautiful palace, his costly motor cars, his wonderful motorboat, his retinue of servants, his lavish luxuries, and cries "I am Fahmi Bey; I am a Prince" This European woman became more fascinated and attracted to this Oriental extravagance…"

And then, perhaps most extraordinary of all:

> "The whole sex question is one of mystery," he announced, as if solving a crime. "Nature gave us the power to get morphia from the seed of the poppy, gave us alcohol, and cocaine from the seed of the coca plant in Peru. Probably there are no better things than these in their proper places. Probably thousands in the War had come to bless them. Just as they are the greatest boon to men and women, so probably these three things taken together are three of the greatest curses that are in the world at the present moment. It is not their legitimate use; it is the abuses of morphia, alcohol and sex that give all the dreadful trouble in the world". The barrister seems to have become the musing philosopher. But then, remembering his brief, "Fahmy had developed abnormal tendencies and he never treated Madame normally".[22]

But then the letters had emerged (unknown to the general population), the question of the letters written by the Prince of Wales to Marguerite and which she still had. If this emerged, the Prince, currently the cynosure of high society, would be irretrievably disgraced. It would be, to the somewhat puritanical King George V., an echo of the worst scandals surrounding his own father and his uncle the Duke of Argyll. Something had to be done. If Marguerite were found guilty, the letters would cause the most unwelcome publicity. The King intervened. Word had reached the Royal Household that the letters might soon be on the market. Lord Stamfordham, the King's Secretary, had been shown some of the letters and considered them to be "very bad", particularly the references to Queen Alexandra when Princess of Wales. The King was anxious, naturally, to protect his mother from ridicule, and commanded his Private Secretary to resolve the matter without publicity. The astonishing thing is that Stamforham had done this before, with regard to compromising letters kept by Daisy, Countess of Warwick, which had been sent to her by the King's father, Edward VII, and this only in 1914–1915. Now, only eight years later, he was being asked to do it again. Through a series of contacts, the letters were retrieved by the middle of August. The scene was set for what was to be a show trial, but one with a difference. The authorities wanted Marguerite to be acquitted. A murder conviction would—quite simply—have been catastrophic for the Crown.[23]

Marguerite Alibert was acquitted on September 14, 1923, and on September 23 she went to Victoria station, caught the boat train to Paris, and resumed her former life. She died on January 2, 1971, aged eighty, almost fifty years since the traumatic trials of herself and Edith Thompson in London. The Prince of Wales, the exiled Edward VIII and Duke of Windsor, died in Paris eighteen months later, aged seventy-eight.

Thus, the lives and ends of two women run in parallel in their historical and legal context. For one, the end is death by execution. For the other, it is an acquittal. It is the same court, in the same year, in the same legal system.

Andrew Rose considered the two cases and the two women. What particularly joined them together, and perhaps many other women, at least in their fantasies, was the mushroom growth of a new genre of Romantic Gothic novels, beginning in the 1890s, that is almost precisely one hundred years since the first rush of Gothic novels. These new ones, of course, would be able to further the fantasies through the escapism of the early cinema, particularly in times of great flux and instability. Robert Hitchens had begun this genre with his novel *The Green Carnation* in the mid-1890s, and followed it with *Bella Donna (1909)*. This was the story of Ruby Chepstow, a woman with a past, who, married to a virtuous but unexciting man, is suddenly confronted with all the glamour of the Orient in the form of a fascinating Arab when aboard a ship on the Nile. But Hitchens had compounded the genre with his novel *The Garden of Allah*, which between 1904 and 1929 went through forty-three editions, and in

1917 it had been filmed. It is highly probable that both Edith and Marguerite saw this film. But Hitchens was not the only author in this highly charged and hothouse genre. Elinor Glyn, the mistress of George Nathaniel Curzon, the Viceroy of India, had her own contribution to make, particularly in her novel *His House (1909)*, and she was joined by another, Katherine Rhodes. But perhaps the most potent of all was *The Sheikh (1921)*, by one E.M. Hull. This author turned out to be Edith Maud Hull, the wife of a Derbyshire pig farmer. It is difficult to underestimate the influence of this book. It had all the pulp fiction potency of *Fifty Shades of Grey*, and a similar appeal to women.

Obviously, these writers had tapped a very productive vein in the female psyche, or at least, of many women. *The Sheikh* engendered a wildly successful dance tune, *The Sheikh of Araby*, and by the time of Marguerite's trial in September 1923 the vampish actress Pola Negri was negotiating the filming of the book. During the trial, the Prosecuting Counsel, Sir Thomas Inskip, K.C., who was also the Solicitor General, referred to the influence of *Bella Donna*. The character of Ruby Chepstow was much more Marguerite than Edith was. The age of the husband in the one case and the lover in the other was remarkably similar: they were both women who had taken much younger men as lovers. But the difference was this. To Edith, the romantic gothic novels were her fantasy; to Marguerite, it had all become reality. "Edith had gone to the gallows with remarkably little public sympathy", wrote Rose,[24] while Marguerite had escaped.

A major figure in the Nazi Party and the wife of a dictator in South America were both the subject of sensational exhumations long after their deaths. These exhumations served to re-examine not only their own histories, but also how they came to be famous or infamous, and also questioned the systems that produced them. They both changed the course of history, not only in their own countries but because they became universal figures, instantly recognisable.

Rudolf Hess, the Deputy leader of the Nazi Party and Eva Peron, the indispensable right hand of her husband, President Juan Peron of Argentina, shared this in common. Both their lives and their deaths were passing extraordinary.

In July 2011, the British Broadcasting Service (BBC) reported that the Lutheran Church in Wunsiedel, Bavaria, had decided to terminate the graveyard lease of the burial plot of Rudolf Hess and members of his close family. Since 1987 the grave had become a site of pilgrimage for the German Far Right (and not only from Germany). The remains were therefore exhumed, disinterred, and, according to the report, subsequently cremated and scattered at sea. As part of the above process, the gravestone bearing the names of Rudolf and Ilse Hess, his wife, were also taken away, leaving no physical record of the original burials (although presumably they were still recorded in the church registers, for legal reasons). The world has now lived into, and become disturbingly familiar with, the obliteration of former cultures, leaving if possible no physical trace. This has however been going on at least since Roman times. Thus there was another reason for obliterating the names on the gravestone; for not only were the names and dates of the deceased engraved thereon, but the stone also carried a quotation, recorded as being from an Ulrich von Hutten, who, rather like Rudolf Hess, had performed one life-defining act. He had chosen to attack the Archbishop of Trier (the Catholic bishop), in 1522, to advance the cause of the Lutherans. He failed, and spent the rest of his life in exile on an island in Lake Zurich. Nearly 500 years later, the apparent comparison with the life and exile of Rudolf Hess is obvious. Ulrich von Hutten had marked his endeavour with a motto, which started with the words *Ich hab's gewagt*. Because this resonated so much with Rudolf Hess, it was precisely these words which the Hess family had used on the Wunsiedel gravestone: "I have dared".

But what was it that Hess had dared to do? He had flown solo from Germany to Scotland on one of the fastest aircraft in the world, in May 1941. This was an aircraft which normally required a pilot and a navigator, but Hess had done it alone. What had motivated him to do this? For in doing this, he had left behind his Fuhrer, Adolf Hitler, his family, his position and all that meant something to him in his life. Why did he do this? It was as much a sensation and an astonishment to the British Government as it was to the Nazi Party in wartime Germany.

Perhaps to his wife Ilse, who had considerable influence over him from the time they first met, the mission, if that what it was, came as no surprise, as there is a letter from Hess to Ilse of November 1940, telling her of his intention to make a flight. Whatever the motivation was, the flight in the Messerschmitt Bf 110 which ended up over Eaglesham in Scotland, and Hess parachuting out, meant that from that day he had entered lifetime captivity.[25]

Was Hess lured to Britain by British Intelligence, or was it a mission so unusual and so unexpected by almost all, that two warring nations suddenly drew a deep breath and paused? As is often the case with such singular events, there were other significant persons involved, and the scene for the beginning of these strange events is the Berlin Olympics of 1936, which, inevitably Hitler utilised, not entirely successfully, for propaganda purposes. It was here that the British Duke of Hamilton met Albrecht Haushofer. Between them, they hold many of the clues which may explain the flight of Hess. But the much-quoted French expression *cherchez la femme* is also apposite here, for the connecting woman is one Mrs Roberts, the wartime intermediary between Albrecht Haushofer (who influenced Hess, and whose father, Karl, had been the geopolitics professor of Hess), and the Duke of Hamilton. The nephew of Mrs Roberts was an important member of S01, the wartime black propaganda department. Hess landed in Scotland on May 10, 1941, and by some quirk of fate, the prime minister of pre-war Poland, Sikorski, now a government in exile, landed at Prestwick airport on May 11, 1941, one day later. The family of the Duke of Hamilton owned the site of Prestwick airport.[26] The Finnish art historian, Tancred Borenius, also had a role in the affair. Hess had never met the Duke of Hamilton, but Haushofer had put them in touch with each other. The Duke was chosen as the first contact, because it was (probably mistakenly) believed that he was one of those opposed to Churchill. In fact, it seems unlikely that the Duke would actually do this. When Hess landed he was on duty as wing commander at RAF Turnhouse near Edinburgh; and after meeting Hess, travelled to talk to Churchill and members of the War Cabinet.

Another book, *Double Standards (2001)*, suggests that Hess was to be met by the Duke of Kent. There is a bizarre twist to this, if both Hess and Sikorski are considered together, for the Duke and Duchess of Kent had been offered the throne of Poland in the 1930s, something not altogether fantastic, and reported in the New York Times.[27]

It is not the brief of this book, which is specifically on why people are exhumed, to go into great detail on the mission of Hess to Britain, but an outline is necessary. It seems without doubt that, particularly in the early days of the war, Churchill, who was of a bellicose nature and certainly would never have compromised with Hitler, was still of a relatively unknown quantity. There were those who wished for a brokered peace. Most of these were likely to be of very right-wing opinions, and among them were Nazi sympathisers. Knowing how obdurate Churchill would be to any suggestion that there should be negotiations with Hitler, a prime issue became his removal from office. There remained another largely untried personality: the reluctant king, George VI. Any part of an Anglo-German peace plan would have constitutionally to involve the king.

There is the possibility that there was another dimension to all this: that the British Military Intelligence (M16) had sent someone to Geneva in January 1941 to take a message to Hess, in what would have been a last-ditch stand to obtain some kind of peace deal and stop the war. There is certainly evidence that this happened, and that the "someone" was Tancred Borenius, a Finnish art historian, who had settled in Britain, but whose history qualified him for this extraordinary task. Borenius had been born in Vyborg, which was then in the Grand Duchy of Finland, the Grand Duke being the Tsar of Russia. The two parallel careers of Borenius, as art historian and diplomat, both reached the highest levels. He became the first professor of art history in the University of London, and a prolific author on his subject; and, as a diplomat, he served as a liaising officer between Finland and Britain. Borenius may very well have been a spy for the British Government and in this role, may indeed have been instrumental in persuading Hess to fly to Britain in 1941. Not only that, but Borenius had a very interesting social network. Among those he knew very well was the Earl of Harewood, who was married to the Princess Royal. Thus Borenius was a consultant at Sotheby's, and advisor to the Earl of Harewood, who had a fine art collection. He even accompanied Queen Mary, who had a known interest in artistic matters, on her visit to Yorkshire when visiting her daughter Mary, the Princess Royal. The only one of Queen Mary's children who showed real cultural interests was the Duke of Kent, and it also seems likely that he knew Borenius.

Borenius flew to Portugal in January 1941, and then took the train across technically neutral Spain, and then Vichy France to Switzerland, a journey of some peril. On arriving in Geneva he met the art historian Carl Jacob Burckhardt, of the well-known patrician family of Basel.[28]

In the original German diaries, von Hassell states that Borenius was sent by the English *stellen*, an interesting German word which could be translated as "those in authority", while leaving identity open.[29] Throughout the 1930s the royal connections of Borenius had flourished, as has been seen. Did Borenius gain an entrée to even more powerful circles through them? As for Carl Jacob Burckhardt, who would become a controversial personality, he clearly acted on the information given to him by Borenius, and by March 10, 1941, at the latest, Albrecht Haushofer, the intermediary of Rudolf Hess, was aware of the meeting, and what was discussed. Albrecht travelled to Geneva on April 28, 1941, and a fortnight later Hess was in Scotland.[30] There is a final twist to this tale, and while it is sad, it also raises other questions, for Borenius died on September 2,

1948 in Laverstock House, Salisbury, Wiltshire, to which he had been admitted in 1946, from St. Andrew's Hospital, Northampton. Both of these hospitals specialised in the treatment of mental disorders. Could it have been, like Hess himself, that the stress of all these ventures and connections had disturbed the balance of his mind?

Trying to put a bold front on the inexplicable, the German government issued a press release on May 12, 1941, which read: "Party member Hess had got hold of an aircraft and taken off against orders. As yet he has not returned. A letter was left behind unfortunately showing signs of mental derangement which gives rise to fears that Party member Hess was the victim of delusions". Hitler then sent Joachim von Ribbentrop, the Foreign Minister (who had been the ambassador in London before the war) to break the news to Mussolini.

The response of Churchill at the beginning was certainly muted, saying only that Hess had landed by parachute near Glasgow, but when he was more confident of his position, he stated in the House of Commons that (Hess's plan) was that he, Churchill, "be thrown out of power, and a Government set up with which Hitler could negotiate a magnanimous peace. The only importance attaching to the opinions of Hess is the fact that he was fresh from the atmosphere of Hitler's intimate table."

That freshness of course quickly became stale, and the problem then became "What to do with Hess?" So his long, long captivity commenced, first in Britain, where, in the first aftermath of his flight he was taken to Buchanan castle, and then to the Tower of London, and then to Mytchett Place in Surrey, afterwards referred to as "Camp Z". There he stayed for the next thirteen months. Hess had already showed signs of paranoia and neurosis while still in Scotland, when he realised his mission seemed to have failed; but one can imagine his extreme stress after the flight and trying to make himself understood, although he spoke good English. Major Frank Foley, the leading German expert in M16 and former British Passport Control Officer in Berlin, now took charge of a year-long debriefing of Hess and his motives.

If Hess was not deluded, or indeed insane, at the time of the flight, the conditions now conspired to make him so. It is indeed reminiscent of other top-flight prisoners throughout history who have suffered similar incarcerations, mainly through the agenda of others.[31] Like all such prisoners, there is a constant fear of being poisoned. His first of many attempts at suicide was not long in coming. On June 16, 1941, he rushed his guards and attempted to jump over the railings of the staircase at Mytchett Place.

He did fall on the stone floor below and fractured his left leg. It was eighteen weeks before he could even walk with crutches. About this time he began to complain of amnesia, which would last at least until the Nuremberg trials in 1945. From 1942 to 1945 he remained at Maindiff Court Hospital. Here he was allowed considerable latitude as a prisoner, but attempted suicide again on February 4, 1945, when he stabbed himself with a bread knife.

Facing charges as a war criminal (even though the invasion of Russia and the "final solution" of the Jewish issue, did not take place until after his flight) and transported to Nuremberg on October 10, 1945.

The chief psychiatrist at the Nuremberg trials, Douglas Kelley of the US Military, gave the opinion that Hess suffered from "a true psychoneurosis, primarily of the hysterical type, engrafted on a basic paranoid and schizoid personality, with amnesia, partly genuine and party feigned", but found him fit to stand trial. Hess admitted on November 30, in a statement to the tribunal, that he had faked memory loss as a tactic.

His defending counsel argued that he could not be responsible for anything that occurred in Germany after May 1941, although Hess admitted that he had signed the decrees before that, including the Nuremberg racial laws, and the incorporation of Polish territories into the Third Reich. Judgement was not passed until September 30, 1946, and Hess was personally sentenced on October 1. He was found guilty of crimes against peace, and of conspiring to commit crimes; but he was not found guilty of war crimes and crimes against humanity. He received a life sentence, together with seven other prominent Nazis. The seven were transported by aircraft to Spandau prison in Berlin on July 18, 1947. The Soviet member of the tribunal had wanted the death penalty.

Although a minimum of visits were allowed, Hess refused to let his family visit until 1969. He continued to say his food was being poisoned and that he had amnesia. Another suicide attempt occurred in 1977. Gradually the other six prisoners were released: the most famous, or infamous, Admiral Doenitz (who had succeeded Hitler very briefly as Fuehrer), in 1956, Schirach and Speer in 1966. Hess became the lone prisoner of Spandau, but conditions were now far more pleasant. Numerous appeals were made for his release, but they were always vetoed by the Soviets, because Spandau was located in West Berlin, and after the airlift of 1948–1949, and the division of the city into four sectors became something more than the spoil of the victors, this gave the Soviets a toehold in that sector. Even Willy Brandt was not successful in his appeals.

On August 17, 1987, when Hess was ninety-three years old, he successfully committed suicide, in a summer house in the garden of the prison, which had been used as a reading room. He had taken an extension cord from one of the lamps, strung it over a window latch, and hanged himself. The Four Powers in Berlin did not release a statement confirming this until September 17.

Hess was initially buried in a secret location to avoid media attention or Nazi sympathisers. Thus he was re-buried in the family plot in Wunsiedel on March 17, 1988: this was the first exhumation. In 1995, Ilse died and was buried with him. But the town became a scene of Nazi pilgrimages every August, on the anniversary of his death, and so the second exhumation took place. The grave was re-opened on July 20, 2011. His remains were cremated and scattered at sea by family members. His gravestone was destroyed. Spandau prison was demolished in 1987 to prevent it, too, from becoming a neo-Nazi shrine.

Something very similar, but not quite so long drawn out, with all the same signs of cultural obliteration, took place in the case of Eva Peron.

On January 9, 1950, the wife of the President of Argentina, Eva Peron, was inaugurating the new seat of the Taxi Drivers' Union, when she fainted in front of the Minister of Education, Dr Oscar Ivanissevich, who was also her personal physician. Three days later, the Minister, also a surgeon, operated on Eva, and removed her appendix. In doing so, he also diagnosed cancer of the uterus, and recommended an operation. This was the first knowledge of the illness which would kill her; but Eva instead on continuing with her gruelling schedule, and refused the operation.

But who was Eva Peron? Born in 1919 into a poor family, she became entranced by the cinema and attempted to become an actress. Success seemed to come her way when she signed a contract with Radio Belgrano to play some of the great women of history: an extraordinary portent. Among these women were Empress Carlotta of Mexico, Elizabeth I of England, Sarah Bernhardt, the Tsarina Alexandra Feodorovna, Empress Josephine, Isadora Duncan, Madame Chiang-Kai-Shek, Eleonora Duse, Empress Eugenie of France, Lady Hamilton, Anne of Austria, and Catherine the Great of Russia. It was a formidable line-up. Could Eva Duarte have had any inkling that she would one day join this list? In Paris, in 1947, the Papal Nuncio, Monsignor Angelo Roncalli (the future John XXIII) could not help exclaiming, when he saw her: "E tornata l'imperatrice Eugenia!" (The Empress Eugenie has returned); although, in truth, the two women were rather different. Eugenie had been tall and dark and Eva small, fragile, and blonde; but it was all about image and impression.[32]

This same Pope John received a letter from Eva's mother, Dona Juana, in 1959, asking him to help find Eva's remains, which had then disappeared, and pouring out her distress over the ill-treatment of the body of her son, Juan, by their mutual enemies. But it would be John's successor, Paul VI, who would arrange for an Italian priest to lead the searchers to her remains in Milan, where he had long been the respected Archbishop.

On Christmas Day, 1943, a rising politician, one Juan Domingo Peron, arrived at the Radio station to give a broadcast. He was forty-eight years old and a widower; he was looking for a pretty girl on his arm. Eva was looking for someone with power and personality who would further her ambitions. They met. The rest is part of not only Argentinian history, but world history. But it would be Eva who would ultimately further Peron's career. This is how it all began. Peron was elected President; he married Eva. The civil ceremony took place on October 22, 1945, and the religious one on November 26.

Once she was the President's wife, she enjoyed the trappings of state, particularly jewellery, for which she had "an insatiable appetite". But for her, it was said jewellery was reassurance. Beneath the façade was she a fragile girl, unsure still of herself. How true this was of both Queen Mary of Britain, and of the renowned Duchess of Windsor, Wallis Simpson. Both of them had known poverty, or being poor relations. "We were in short street", was how the future Queen Mary put it. All of them developed this insatiable appetite for jewellery. When, in 1947, the dictator Franco was shocked by the gold and jewels she wore to meet the Spanish workers, she would retort: "The poor like to see me be beautiful. They do not want to be protected by a poorly dressed woman. You see, they dream about me. How can I let them down?" But, nevertheless, Ricciardi, the jeweller used to hide his most beautiful pieces from her when he knew she was coming to his shop, just as the good nobility of Norfolk would hide their best pieces when they knew a visit from Queen Mary was in the offing. If she liked a piece, one had to give it to her. Eva knew intuitively the company she had risen to. But on her deathbed, she also said: "If God gives me my health back, I will never wear jewels or beautiful dresses again".

At the fall of the Peron regime in 1955, the *Revolocion Libertadora* exhibited and auctioned her possessions, including dresses, furs, shoes, hats and jewels. Between December 9 and 19, 1957, the liquidating commission sold, or tried to sell, 65 kilograms of gold and as much of silver, a

48-carat emerald, 3 platinum ingots, 1,650 diamonds, 120 gold bracelets and 100 gold watches. Before the auction, the commissioner's special account contained 11 million pesos; after the auction, it had 100 million pesos. These funds disappeared without a trace. A report stated that this sale could not even be compared with that of King Farouk of Egypt (who had been deposed in 1952). The assets of Juan and Eva Peron had all been frozen in 1955. By the Law 20503 after 1973 the assets were unfrozen. Half of the assets were to go to Isabel, the widow of Peron then, and a half to Eva's sisters.

Her death was long drawn-out and she was visibly dying in public, like the kings and queens of old. On May 7, 1952, she passed her thirty-third birthday, and on June 4 her husband, Juan Peron, began his second presidential term. Eva had been the light and the driving force behind the success of both her husband and the Peronist Party. Now that light was fading, was guttering out. On July 26, Eva uttered her last words: *Eva se va, Eva is leaving*. At 8.25 in the evening, she died.

Actually, this was not the time she died. She died at 7.40, but 8.25 was the time she had married Peron, and this was the time she chose for her death. The mythology of Eva Peron was complete. Beginning on that evening, and on every evening henceforth, until the fall of the Peronist regime, the evening news would be interrupted with the words "It is 8.25. pm., the time when Eva Peron entered immortality". National mourning was decreed for one month.

But Eva knew she would be exhibited. Now her poor, wasted body would receive the kind of treatment reserved for the royalty of old. She would be made incorruptible. The manicurist arrived at dawn the day after her death. Her hair was dyed, her chignon restyled. The manicurist and the hairdresser would give her a beauty that would last one hundred years. She would be the sleeping beauty of Argentina, forever guarding her people.

Dressed in a white shroud, and the blue and white flag of Argentina, she was laid in a clear glass casket. Between her fingers was placed the rosary given to her by Pope Pius XII, the same pope who would later excommunicate her husband. She was then exhibited in the hallway of the Secretaria. The hallway was flanked by staircases, so that the mourners came in by one and left by the other, a procession which could have been choreographed by Florenz Ziegfield. The event was filmed by Edward Cronjagar, the cameraman from 20th Century Fox. The resulting film was entitled *And Argentina's heart stopped*. This continued for thirteen days.

Not even the later funeral of Diana, Princess of Wales, could compete with it, though it ran it a close second. Mourners queued for ten hours to see her. The powerful myth had commenced; when the sky cleared, it was claimed her face could be seen in the full moon.

On August 9, 1952, the casket was placed on a gun carriage and taken to Congress, and then to the CGT (Confederacion General del Trabajo, the umbrella trade union movement head quarters, and the office of Eva Peron) building, where it lay while the monument, a new building, was being constructed. During these processions, there were two million spectators. Some commented, and it was one of those enduring comments, that her remains were more political than human.

The embalmer awaited her, Dr Pedro Ara. He was known throughout the world, and was said to have been involved in Lenin's mummification. It was said that he had mummified a young teenager from Cordoba whose father, crazed with grief, had dressed her every evening and sat her at the dinner table (a resonance of Ines de Castro, all those centuries hence).

During the thirteen days of the exposition, the workers had taken off the glass case to clean the inside of the glass. Anticipating the emission of gases, they had the air circulating to prevent the glass from fogging up. Ara was not pleased when he heard. He knew, of course, that exposure to the air might cause irreparable damage to the body. Eventually, in his laboratory (to which only he and Juan Peron had keys), Eva's body would be submerged in boiling pools of "God knows what mysterious liquids".[33]

Dr Domingo Tellechea later revealed that the procedure followed the ancient arts of Spanish mummification. This involved sending preserving liquids all the way through the circulation system, even to the capillaries. Some areas of the body were filled with wax, as has been seen in previous exhumations and burials. Then the entire body was covered with a layer of hard wax. This procedure took an entire year.

In July 1953, the body was at last ready, but the monument was not. So she was kept at the CGT, where a kind of chapel was built. Eva had always said that she wished to lay among the workers. Eva lay under a glass bell, on a tiny bed of silk. She wore an ivory tunic with wide sleeves, designed and sewn by Thala Palud, a Spanish lady who was friends with the embalmer. "She seemed to sleep", as Peron said when he saw her. The carefully constructed illusion was complete. Only selected persons were allowed to see her; she assumed a religious aspect, as if she were a Madonna. Elizabeth I of England had carefully fostered this façade or replacement also.

During this time the front of the CGT building remained covered in flowers, but on September 16, 1955, Juan Peron was overthrown. Without

Eva, his regime appeared for what it was, a brutal dictatorship. Juana Larrauri had the integrity, in the midst of indescribable confusion, to pay the embalmer at last his fee of 50,000 dollars.[34] Now Peron went into exile for twenty years, but Ara, the embalmer, remained with his creation, like some latter-day Pygmalion.

The new regime saw, not unnaturally, the body of Eva as some kind of political threat or legacy. Even those most opposed to her life and image were affected when they saw her embalmed body. Captain Francisco Manrique, the leader of the military, described her as follows:

> She was the size of a twelve-year-old girl. Her skin looked like wax, artificial. Her lips were painted red. If you tapped her finger, it sounded hollow. Ara, the embalmer, did not part from it. He loved it.[35]

But, whatever the effect the body had on its viewers, or, indeed, *because* it had this effect, it had to go. Isaac Rojas expressed this fear when he said: "the cadaver had to be excluded from the political scene". But where? Juan Peron himself had no time, and perhaps no inclination now, to decide anything. He went into exile, firstly in Paraguay, then Panama, and finally Spain, where he remained nearly twenty years, until 1973. The Franco regime in Spain, which had given him a home in Madrid, was itself now coming to an end. Perhaps he sensed this. But Eva's body now began a long odyssey which would not end until about the same time.

On November 24, 1955, one Moori Koenig (the son of a German soldier who had been killed in World War I) was put in charge of operations. Pedro Ara was there when he arrived. He wanted to make sure the rules were followed. The body would be placed in the same casket that had held it during the exhibition in the Secretaria. Moori Koenig had hired a welder to solder the cover. But the welder did not turn up, and this meant that they would not be able to transport Eva in the sealed casket. Her body would be touched. Koenig removed the Peronist flag which covered her remains. Ara recollected: "Eva's body appeared dressed in her new tunic, which covered her bare feet. I signalled to two workers who came over to help me. Without touching her as such, one of them took her by the ankles over the tunic. The other worker and myself took her by the shoulders. And this is how we covered her thin body, slowly, very carefully, from the platform to the bottom of the casket, without disturbing her hair or her dress. My assistants were pale, and covered with perspiration due to the respectful emotion and fear that they felt. More than one tear fell, and not only from the eyes of fanatic Peronists".

The truck driven by Captain Frascoli left the CGT garage with the open casket. It remained parked until dawn in the courtyard of the navy's First Infantry Regiment. Moori Koenig admitted much later that when morning came, they lit a candle and laid a bouquet of flowers next to the truck. In order to shake off the Peronists, who were searching for their Senora, the truck was driven to a number of locations, parked in the streets of the capital, behind a cinema screen in Buenos Aires, and inside the city's waterworks. Eventually, Koenig took it to his office in Military Intelligence. Wherever it was, candles and flowers appeared "as if by magic". There it would remain in a wooden crate, labelled anonymously, until 1957. Koenig did not follow his orders to bury Eva secretly in a dignified manner; he kept Eva, he contemplated her. Could it have been that this embalmed body exuded some strange hold upon those who saw it? Koenig might even have buried her in a random field near General Paz Avenue (similar to what had happened to Thomas Paine in New York). He would only say "I buried her standing up, because she was a man!" (Could he have possibly heard of the legendary burial of Queen Maeve in Ireland?) Did he later have the woman, whom he thought he was honouring as a soldier by not laying her in a tomb, disinterred, or exhumed? Did he keep her in his office for a longer period of time in order to have her near "his thoughts", as Ara had done? To meditate on a woman's courage that had made his soldiers even more masculine? The second man to fall in love with the corpse would end up murmuring "She is mine. That woman is mine".

The next stage of this extraordinary drama was now to take place. When Francisco Manrique came to see Koenig, thinking that he had carried out the order, and that Eva was secretly buried, and then discovered the truth, Manrique reported to General Aramburu, who considered Koenig mentally ill and replaced him.

Manrique himself now called Major Hamilton Diaz and Colonel Gustavo Ortiz, and these two soldiers would accompany the mummified body to Europe in collaboration with an Italian priest introduced to the *Casa Rosada* by an Argentinian priest, Fr. Roger. Besides these, no-one knew where Evita was, except that the operation was being carried out with the connivance of the Vatican. This was 1957.

A few weeks later, the Italian priest returned to Argentina, bearing a sealed envelope, containing the details of Eva's next resting place, and gave it to President Aramburu. He refused to open it and gave it to a notary, telling him to give it to the next Argentinian president, four weeks after his death (presumably the death of Aramburu). This too shows the potency of a mummified body as a political and cultural icon.

In 1970, a Peronist guerrilla group, the *Montoneros*, captured and killed the former president, Aramburu. They had targeted him because he had overseen the disappearance of Eva's body; but Aramburu had not wanted to know where she was, did not, in fact, know. The notary now kept his word, and four weeks later handed over the envelope to the incumbent President, General Alexandro Augustin Lanusse. Lanusse had wanted to strike a deal with the exiled Peron for some time, and now the wandering body played a part in this reconciliation. A Colonel Caand two prbanillas then flew to Milan with the same Fr. Rotger who had intervened during the first journey of Eva's body.

In the meantime, the Italian priest had died. There was only one solution: to look through the registers at the cemetery for the women who had been buried there since 1957. They came upon a certain Maria Maggi de Magistris, Italian, widow, emigrated to Argentina, dead for five years before finding a tomb in Milan. Colonel Cabanillas introduced himself to the authorities as the dead woman's brother. He requested authorisation to remove his sister's remains to Spain. On September 2, 1971, a group of men found themselves before the neglected plot, 86, section 41. It was Eva. She was exhumed.

The coffin was transported back to Spain in the funeral parlour's truck, and crossed the French–Italian border; but from the moment she arrived in Spain, where of course she had been seen during her state visit in 1947, had addressed the crowds in Madrid, she was accompanied by many cars. Juan Peron was not informed until the last minute.

At Puerta de Hierro a party met the coffin, which included Peron, his third wife Isabel (Maria Estela, known as Isabelita), Lopez Rega, Jorge Paladino, the Argentinian ambassador Rojas Silveyra, Colonel Cabanillas, and two priests from the Merced. This time Eva's body was not in a hearse, but in a bakery truck. Peron tried to open the casket, and hurt himself on the zinc cover. Lopez Rega drew appalled glances when he suggested using a blow torch. Finally, the rusty cover was opened with a crowbar. Eva's body reappeared once more.

When he saw her, Peron exclaimed "Those bastards!" and began to cry. When he signed the form for the body's identification, Isabel undid Eva's chignon, which had become wet. She refused to sign the document. "If I did not know her when she was living", she argued, "how would I recognize her now?" For all three of them, Peron, Eva, and Isabel, the immediate future still held much of drama and destiny, for their stories were not yet over.

Why did Peron exclaim in this manner? Did he know something of the treatment of Eva's body or was it just shock? Pedro Ara, who had moved also to Madrid, was summoned to assess the damage/According to him, everything was reparable. However, Eva's sisters, Blanca and Erminda, who had come to Madrid also to see her body, issued a statement much later, in 1985, saying: "We cannot allow history to be distorted. That is why we are testifying to the gross mistreatment inflicted on our dear sister Eva's remains". Among these observations they claimed was that her body had been covered with quicklime and occasionally showed burns.[36]

In 1973, Hector Campora was elected President of Argentina, but it was generally considered a pretext for the return of Peron, and return he did after one month, where one million people lined the street on the way to the airport. But by this time the Peronists had divided into right and left-wing factions, and the day ended in a massacre, with right-wing mercenaries picking off the young intellectuals, workers and peasants. Peron had not organised this but his entourage had, and he was now old and senile. However, the enormous posters now featured three faces: Peron, Eva, and Isabel. Peron and Isabel had left the "problematic cadaver" of Eva behind in Madrid. He said he would bring it back to Argentina, but he never alluded to it again. Isabelita, however, wanted to re-invent the myth of Eva; she herself adopted the bulging chignon, although she would never be Eva.

The Montoneros wanted their beloved Eva back again, and in frustration, they desecrated the tomb of Aramburu and removed his corpse, which they vowed to keep until the body of Eva returned.

The next act in the drama was that Peron died, unexpectedly, in 1974. He had been elected President, with Isabelita as Vice-President, and she now took over. Isabelita's real name was Maria Estela Martinez de Peron; the task of bringing Eva home was now her responsibility.

On November 17, 1974, a charter flight brought Eva's body from Madrid to Buenos Aires. She was taken to the Olivos residence, where Dr Domingo Tellechea began the repairs which Peron had neglected in the three years that had passed since her body had been rediscovered. Tellechea's report confirmed the damage observed by her sisters, and also corroborated the story that Moori Koenig had had her buried standing up, for her feet were ruined by being in the vertical position that had to support her body: it was a bizarre detail in a story not short on the bizarre.

Now a brand-new Eva, her hair restyled, dressed in the same white tunic that Isabel had put on her, her nails freshly polished, was yet again thrown out of the Olivos residence on March 26, 1976, the day that Isabelita herself fell from power.

At last, on October 22, 1976, Erminda and Blanca received the casket and deposited it in the Arrieta vault (that of Elisa Duarte's husband's family) in the Recoleta cemetery. On the Ricoleta vault there was placed a small plaque which announces her presence. A few nostalgic old women come to light candles from time to time.

The very dictator who had cautioned Eva against wearing jewellery when visiting the poor, Generalissimo Francisco Franco, was himself the subject of an exhumation debate of some moment in the autumn of 2018.

When the Socialist Pedro Sanchez came to office as Prime Minister in June 2018, he pledged that he would remove the body of Franco from the Valley of the Fallen *(Valle de los Caidos)*, where he had lain since his death in November 1975. That pledge fuelled a political, social, and cultural debate, which threatened to re-open the wounds of the Civil War in Spain between 1936 and 1939, and is akin in Britain to the divisions of its own civil war in the seventeenth century, which still resonates even today.

This was not an easy thing to promise. By November, the body of Franco was still there, and the visitors to the basilica had risen to 1,500 a day. A spokesman for Vox, the far-right party, said: "Franco, for all his faults, kept Spain from the threat of communism. He was not a genocidal dictator like Hitler. We must not make a monster of a man who died over 40 years ago". However, there is indeed another side to this, because half a million people died in the Civil War, and many more in the years afterwards who opposed Franco. Only Cambodia has more mass graves than Spain. But the split is everywhere apparent; this seismic line through the nation. On the forty-third anniversary of Franco's death, on November 23, 2018, there was a torchlight procession from Madrid to the Valley of the Fallen. Sympathisers are unlikely to pay any attention to the thousands of Republicans also interred there. Their bodies were plucked from graves around the country on the orders of Franco, without the permission of their families. Today, with crypts crumbling, those remains have merged into a mass grave, making it impossible for investigators to know who is there.[37]

The family of Franco would prefer the body to stay where it is, but suggests that, if it is moved, it should go to Almudena Cathedral in Madrid, where his family already have a tomb. Perhaps it should have been there in the first place. But the government is fearful that if it is there it will be a rallying point for the far right, and makes it all the more sensible now that figures like Rudolf Hess have been exhumed and their remains scattered at sea, rather than continuing focal points for the divide. The government of Spain is suggesting that Franco and his wife should be re-buried on the edge of the capital. Outside the cathedral, however, some said the cathedral was the only alternative place, as Franco was a Catholic and deserves a Christian burial.[38]

Previous to this, a close friend of the writer wrote to him from Spain concerning the proposed exhumation. His grandfather was assassinated by the Republicans in 1936, but he never felt a great sympathy for Franco or his family. He highlights something else which has emerged. Franco married his grand-daughter into the Carlist branch of the Spanish royal family, whose present spokesman is Luis Alfonso de Borbon. He protested against the exhumation at the Valley of the Fallen, and his radical supporters had cried: "You are our king", thus compromising the position of King Felipe VI. At the same time, the government is trying to extinguish the Dukedom of Franco, which upon the death of Franco's daughter is now in the possession of Carmen, his grand-daughter, and the mother of Prince Luis. In point of fact, the dukedom was conferred not by Franco himself but by King Juan Carlos, for the contribution of Franco's daughter to the restoration of the monarchy. Franco's widow also received a title from Juan Carlos. There is now a fear in the nobility that the government is seeking to extinguish all titles, an indelible part of Iberian history.

But did Franco himself want to be buried in the Valley of the Fallen, or was it simply an idea of the government of 1975, when he died? In the end, my friend's fears, Franco will indeed be exhumed, and he will be buried with his wife in the quite large pantheon he had built for the family in Mingorrubio, which is a tiny place near the El Pardo palace.[39]

Another iconic Spaniard was actually exhumed in 2018 because the court had ordered it, following a request by a lady who claimed to be his daughter, and therefore entitled to share in his estate. Salvador Dali, one of the greatest exponents of the Surrealist movement in the early twentieth century was exhumed in order to collect samples for use in this paternity claim. Experts confirmed that the body of the enigmatic artist still sports the trademark moustache thirty years after his death in 1989. Narcis

Bardalet, who embalmed the body of Dali after his death helped with the exhumation, and told Catalan radio that he had been delighted to see that the best-known feature of Dali was still in place, like clock hands "at ten past ten, just as he liked it. It's a miracle".

Dali was buried in the crypt he had designed for himself in the museum of Figueres, Catalonia. His remains were disinterred to help settle a long-running paternity claim from Maria Pilar Abel, who claimed to be his daughter, from a liaison Dali had had with her mother in 1955. She insisted that she was his only child.

When Bardalet saw the body of Dali again he said: "His face was covered with a silk handkerchief—a magnificent handkerchief. When it was removed, I was delighted to see the moustache intact…I was quite moved. You could also see his hair". He continued: "Dali's body resembled a mummy; it was just like wood," adding that it was so hard that the experts had to use an electric saw rather than a scalpel to collect bone samples. He predicted Dali's body would last a good while longer. "The moustache is still there, and will be for centuries". Obviously, his embalming was of the best.

Once the last visitors of the day had left the museum, the 1.5 tonne slab was lifted from the grave so experts could get to the body to take hair, nails and two large bones. The DNA recovered from the remains were then compared to samples from the claimant. Under Spanish law, she would be heir to a quarter of Dali's fortune if the DNA supported her contention. The Gala-Salvador Dali Foundation, which controls the artist's lucrative estate, had sought to fight the exhumation order by appealing against the judge's decision to let it go ahead. Since Dali had bequeathed his properties and his fortune to the Foundation and to the Spanish state, Abel had brought her claims against both.

In 2007, she was granted permission to try to extract DNA samples from skin, hair, and hair traces found clinging to Dali's death mask; however, the results proved inconclusive. Another test was attempted the same year using material supplied by the artist's friend Robert Descharmes. His son Nicholas has said it was negative.[40]

When the results of the exhumation were released two months later, they too proved negative. The answer may lie in Dali's paintings themselves, which often contained coded messages. Dali had always feared, perhaps knew, that he was impotent.

The dominant theme of the 1929 painting *Dismal Sport*, for example, was a deep sexual anxiety. Dawn Ades. In her book, *Dali* examines this.

"The potential remedy or alternative to masturbation, sexual relations with another, has its own attendant threat of impotence, which Dali expresses through a number of images, the psycho-analytical weight of whose symbolism must be fully conscious…in *Dismal Sport* there is a subtlety in such symbolism which suggests a real personal authenticity…the oppressive size of the staircase springs from the theme of impotence, and expresses a fear of sexual intercourse".[41]

From royal and famous bodies to lesser mortals, but the act of exhumation is the same. On August 4, 2018, The Times reported an extraordinary case. Before he died in Stockholm, Miguel Angel Martinez requested in his will that he be buried in London beside his former girlfriend. However, when his body arrived in the United Kingdom, there was a problem: his heart was missing. Much of his liver was also gone and there was no sign of water in his lungs to suggest he had been drowned, which a report had indicated; that he had committed suicide by throwing himself into the waters of the Swedish archipelago.

Now, thirteen years later, his Spanish family have been given permission to exhume his body from Gunnersbury cemetery in London. Bianca Martinez Santamaria, his sister, believes that her brother, who was forty-five when he died, in 2005, had been killed and his heart removed. The speculation is that his killers were organ traffickers, or that his heart was stolen after he died.

Martinez had lived in the United Kingdom for two years and had worked at the Royal Brompton Hospital in Chelsea. He had left his home in Bilbao, Spain, in April 2005, to travel across Europe by train. Five months later his body was washed up on the island of Lidingo. After a post-mortem examination, it was concluded that he had thrown himself from a ferry and drowned. Because of his will, his body was brought to the United Kingdom. A mix up in paperwork when his body arrived two months later meant that inconsistencies in the account of his death were raised. Because some documents were missing, a second post-mortem was ordered. According to this report, for Westminster coroner's court the body "had been previously eviscerated", and "both lungs were present and had been dissected and showed no signs of changes other than the changes of decomposition. At the time of the post-mortem it was not possible to identify a specific cause of death due to the absence of the heart" the report concluded. The Swedish authorities, however, have insisted that the heart was in situ when it left their custody and suggested that it might have putrified, but other experts have doubted this.

The last sighting of the hapless Martinez, who had mental health problems, was on August 1, 2005, after he had been interviewed by police about an altercation at a bank in Karlstad. His sister thinks that something happened at the police station and that some police officers know things that they hid. She obviously believed that someone killed her brother to remove his organs.[42]

Yet another bizarre case involved an exhumation seeking exoneration of a convicted criminal. On February 19, 2019, The Times also reported that the Church of England had given rare permission for a grave to be dug up for DNA testing which could clear a convicted rapist, and prove that his own father was the real attacker.

Eric McKenna, who is now sixty years old, is serving a twenty-three-year sentence after being convicted in 2018 of raping a twenty-one-year-old woman in Gateshead in 1983, and raping an eighteen-year-old woman at knifepoint in Newcastle in 1988. He was traced when police were cautioning him for harassing a neighbour and matched his DNA with the cold case.

Jurors at McKenna's trial at Newcastle Crown Court were told that DNA from the same man was found at both scenes and there was a "billion to one" chance of it belonging to someone else. His family have now tried to cast doubt on that claim, suggesting that the crime may have been committed by his own father. Documents from a Church of England consistory court state that McKenna's estranged sister, Eileen Hutton, came forward to claim that she believed her brother to be innocent. She alleged that "her father may well have been the perpetrator". She alleged that her father, Thomas McKenna, who died in 1993 of a heart attack, aged sixty-two, was "a violent person, particularly towards women", and had served time in prison.

Erick McKenna's wife, Moira, applied to the Church of England consistory court to ask for the remains to be exhumed from a churchyard in Newcastle to obtain a DNA sample from his bone fragments. Both of his children, including the convicted man, have agreed to it.

Euan Duff, Chancellor of the Diocese of Newcastle, granted the request. He said: "Even if there is even a slight, but real possibility that there has been a serious miscarriage of justice, then it is wholly proper that everything is done to ensure that is not the case".[43]

Truly, whether for royal persons or lesser mortals, exhumation continues to raise a multiplicity of issues.

* * *

In October 2016, a decision was taken by the Polish government to exhume the bodies of a former President, Zaczynski, and his wife, who were killed, along with ninety-four other people, in a sensational air crash on April 10, 2010. This crash occurred near Smolensk in Russia. Eighty-eight of those on board had been flying to events to commemorate the massacres at Katyn in 1940. The other eight were crew members, but all on board died.

There had been a state funeral for the former president and his wife, eight days later, on April 18, 2010. Now their remains were removed from their marble sarcophagus in the alabaster tomb in Wawel Cathedral in Krakow. What was the reason for this exhumation? Apart from serious and international questions relating to the disaster itself, the exhumation sought to identify who or what was actually in the tomb of the president and his wife. The remains were taken to the Jagiellonian University in Krakow, for tests, including computer tomography and DNA tests.

Of the ninety-six people killed in the crash, no less than eighty-three were to be exhumed before the end of 2017. Four bodies had been created, while nine others had already been exhumed in 2011 and 2012. What was the reason for this mass exhumation? Basically, it was to answer two questions: had the victims been correctly identified, and had the crash been an accident? What evidence was there in both cases?

Lech and Maria Zaczynski had belonged to the Law and Justice Party, which was led by the late President's twin brother, and the Prime Minister of Poland at the time was one, Donald Tusk, since famous or otherwise notable (depending on who was talking) member of the Commission of the European Union, receiving much publicity for his part in the Brexit negotiations of the United Kingdom.

Tusk's team had neglected to have each of the bodies examined out of disregard for the late president, a political rival, or so it was alleged. What was undeniable was that six of the victims had been buried in the wrong graves. Quotes from the relatives included: "The forceful examinations constitute a violation of the taboo existing in our culture that calls for respect of the bodies of the dead", and "It also shows the lighthearted approach to the feelings of the families".[44]

Of course, Poland, being until relatively recently, a deeply Catholic culture, viewed the disturbance of the Christian dead as a taboo, unless for very good reason. One of the daughters of a victim of the Smolensk crash, Marta Kochanowska Hodder, said "It is very difficult to go through exhumation. Questions and issues arise which are difficult to face the first time, let alone the second time after so many years. For example, how to bury a beloved person? How to explain to yourself why your beloved one was not buried properly the first time. Everything is caused by failure to comply with legal obligations before the first funerals. However, it is the family who bears this burden".[45]

Temperatures in Poland allowed exhumations only between mid-October and mid-April, which of course caused a delay. Another factor to be considered was that the autopsy document arriving from Russia was incomplete. The bodies had also arrived from Russia in sealed coffins.

But there were other developments. On Tuesday, June 21, 2016, a Polish court convicted and handed down a suspended sentence of eighteen months' imprisonment to Pawel Bielawny, a former deputy head of government security over the circumstances of the crash.

Eventually, it was reported on June 1, 2017, that in the coffin of the late president and his wife remains of two other people were found. The report was citing the Polish Deputy Prosecutor General, Marek Pasionek, at a press conference in Warsaw. According to him, the Prosecutor's office was now checking the possible fault of Russian doctors in connection with the burial of the remains of the tragedy in different coffins.

"A separate investigation was being conducted on the responsibility of Russian doctors. We sent a request to Russia for legal assistance", said Pasionek; who also stated that the exhumations would be completed in April 2018.

Someone, somewhere, was bound, sooner or later, to speak what had remained unspoken, and had been causing such disquiet and suspicion across the Polish nation since the crash. This happened on January 12, 2013, in Toronto, Canada, when the widow of the late Deputy Minister of Culture, Tomasz Merta, voiced her thoughts and feelings:

> What I am about to tell you now are suspicions—and not even my own—but rather the suspicions of the individuals in the inner circles of the Polish military—I heard a statement that was made—but I am not taking any responsibility for how credible, or not credible, it is. I heard that, had the generals and journalists not been re-assigned to different aircraft, it wouldn't have been the Tupolev (Tu-154M) but rather the Casa (transport aircraft) that would have been taken out.

Because the generals were no longer onboard the Casa, there was no reason for it to get airborne. And for this reason, it was the Yak (-40) that flew off to Smolensk. This Casa (transport aircraft) was never examined in any way. It was not subject to any examination. Aside from a single note in the deposition given to the military, no-one was interested (in) why this aircraft didn't fly (to Smolensk). Perhaps this is someone's crazy phantasy, but perhaps it isn't.

Some Polish military personnel had suggested that if the Casa had to stay behind at the Okecie military tarmac, so that the explosives could be removed from it,—because they were no longer needed, I am only repeating what I was told.

It is worth for us repeating the entire process of "disarming" the case of explosive substances at the crash site. It all started with the publication of CesaryGmyz, in *"Rzeczpospolita" on October 30, 2012*, and information that the detectors, which were used by experts in Smolensk (in late September and October), showed traces of TNT (Trinitrotoluene, the standard measure of bombs) and nitroglycerine.

As it turned out, the journalist was also reporting about the indication of hexogen. The storm broke.

The Prosecution denied the publication, and, ultimately, the editor-in-chief of *Rzeczpospolita*, Cesary Gymz, and two other journalists, lost their jobs. The entire editorial staff of one of Poland's most popular weeklies, *Uwazam Rze*, was also silenced.

This appears on the surface to be yet another conspiracy theory, but there are facts in it. The editor did lose his job. The staff in a popular weekly journal were silenced. It is all summed up in the simple but stark phrase: "The storm broke". What was in the background, the ongoing fallout from the Katyn massacre, the inevitable suspicion when so many high ranking people were killed in one crash, the fracturing of the Polish democracy from without and within, continues, and will continue to rumble on. The exhumations in one way solved nothing. They established negligence and disquieting haste on all levels. The Polish people have a long history of tragic incidents and suppression of news and evidence; but to quote an oft-quoted phrase "You can deceive some of the people some of the time, but you cannot deceive all of the people all of the time". Exhumation has many faces. The wrong people were in the wrong coffins, but why were the coffins sealed when they arrived?

The massacres at or near the forest of Katyn then entered the psyche of the Polish people. It consisted of a series of executions of Polish officers and intelligentsia carried out by the then Soviet Union. Specifically the NKVD (Narodnyy Komissariat Vnutrenikh Del, The People's Commissariat for International Affairs) under Beria, in April and May 1940. 2010, when the air crash took place, was the fiftieth anniversary of Katyn, and was meant to be a reconciliation. It proved not only to be the opposite, but in many ways exacerbated it. Katyn accounted for 22,000 victims, a horrific figure even during wartime. It had been ordered by Beria, who eventually was to be shot in the melee after Stalin's death in 1953. This included 8,000 officers, 6,000 police officers, intelligentsia whom the Soviets identified as "intelligence agents, gendarmes, landowners, saboteurs, factory owners, lawyers, officials and priests". It also included not only Poles, but Ukrainians, Belarussians, Polish Jews (including the Chief Rabbi of the Polish Army. Baruch Steinberg).

The discovery of mass graves in the Katyn forest in 1943 led to their exhumation.

In the aftermath after the War, and the eventual fall of the Soviet Union in 1989, an investigation, at last, took place, conducted by the office of the Prosecutors General of the Soviet Union (1990–1991) and of the Russian Federation which followed it (1991–2004). These investigations confirmed Soviet responsibility for the massacres, but there was a refusal to classify them as war crimes or as an act of genocide.

When the air crash took place in 2010, Ben McIntyre, writing in *The Times* said, "In dark times Poland needs the sunlight of truth",[46] This referred not only to Katyn but to the air crash itself.

Those killed in the crash reads like a death toll of everybody who was important in Poland in 2010, or had been important, and it is more than surprising than they should all have travelled in one airliner. They included the former President of Poland in exile, Ryszard Kaczorowski, the chief of the Polish General Staff, and other senior Polish military officers, the President of the National Bank of Poland, Polish Government officials, eighteen members of Parliament, senior members of the Polish clergy, and, most poignant of all, relatives of victims of the Katyn massacre. All were wiped out in a moment. Attempting to land in thick fog, the plane struck some trees, rolled inverted and crashed to the ground.

Exhumations answer some questions, but they can raise many more. Nowhere was this more the case than in two of the exhumations of Presidents of the United States, Zachary Taylor and James Knox Polk. A number of American presidents have had uneasy or unquiet graves, meaning they have been moved a number of times, but this does not mean they were exhumed. James Knox Polk, eleventh President (1845–1849), was in many ways a very underrated and understated man, responsible for the implementation of *Manifest Destiny*, by which the USA reached the Pacific Ocean. His portrait shows a strong, determined, and soulful face, with deeply set thoughtful green eyes. He has been interred in three different places since his death in 1850, and now faces the prospect of being moved yet again. Teresa Elam, a distant relative of the president, said a proposal to disinter their remains would be an act of desecration. Polk and his wife are currently buried in the grounds of the Capitol in Nashville, Tennessee. A new proposal making its way through the Tennessee legislature calls for digging up the bodies of Polk and Sarah Childress, his wife, both of whom have been buried where they are now for more than a century. They would then be relocated to a final resting place in a Polk family home, in the small city of Columbia. Supporters say that this would *justly honour an unjustly overlooked President*, a man who expanded United States territory by a third, signed a law establishing the Smithsonian Institute, and created the Naval Academy (among other things).

The relative Teresa Elam calls it nothing short of macabre and an unsavoury effort to promote tourism in Columbia. (These are both common objections to the exhumation, which have a certain ring of truth about them). However, the relocation of a presidential body is not unheard of in the USA. In 1858, the remains of James Monroe, the fifth President, and the author of the famous *Monroe Doctrine*, was moved from New York to his native Virginia, and the coffin of Abraham Lincoln has been moved around his burial spot in Springfield, Illinois, at least seventeen times, by one count, including a bizarre thwarted effort in 1876 to steal his body and hold it for ransom (again, not unheard of, as has been seen during the Eva Person saga, and again in Switzerland, with the theft of the body of the actor Charlie Chaplin).

Disinterring the grave of Polk and his wife would require the approval of the state's House of Representatives, the Governor, the Tennessee Historical Commission and a local judge. Something much in favour of moving the bodies is seen in Polk's own wishes. He drew up a will five months before his death, Polk being a lawyer himself, stipulating that he and his wife should be buried in Polk Place, his home.[47]

General Zachary Taylor, a Whig, was elected President in the election of 1848, and took office in April 1849. His predecessor, Polk, did not think much of this ageing general, who was a Whig. "Gen'l Taylor, is, I have no doubt," he wrote, after the inauguration of Taylor as President, "a well-meaning old man. He is, however, uneducated, exceedingly ignorant of public affairs, and, I should judge, of very ordinary capacity". Polk had also been shocked, riding up Pennsylvania Avenue in a carriage with Taylor, the Mayor of Washington, and the outgoing Speaker, Robert

Winthrop, to hear Taylor express the view that California and New Mexico were so far distant from the rest of the United States that it would perhaps be better if they were to become independent states. Taylor's speech in the Capitol had a mixed reception. The *Union* said it consisted of "common-place, non-committal generalities" and gave off a whiff of being "Ultra Whig". In truth, its greatest mark of distinction was its lack of any mention of the slavery crisis that was engulfing the nation.[48]

His term was brief, for perhaps celebrating too well during Independence Day, on July 4, 1850, he ate copious amounts of raw fruit and iced milk. Over the course of several days, he became severely ill with an undiagnosed digestive ailment. His doctor said it was *cholera morbus*, which was a flexible term then intestinal ailments as diverse as diarrhoea and dysentery, but not related to Asiatic cholera, the latter being widespread at the time of Taylor's death. Several of his suites went down with a similar illness. Fever ensued, and the President's chances of survival considered small. Zachary Taylor himself said, "I should not be surprised if this were to terminate in my death". Despite, or perhaps because of, treatment, Taylor died at 10.35 pm in the evening of July 9, 1850, at the age of sixty-five.

Almost immediately after his death, rumours began to circulate that he had been poisoned by pro-slavery Southerners, and similar theories persisted into the twenty-first century. In 1978 Hamilton Smith based his assassination theory on the timing of drugs, the lack of confirmed cholera outbreaks, and other material.[49]

In the late 1980s Clara Rising, a former professor at the University of Florida, persuaded Taylor's closest living relative to agree to an exhumation, so that the remains could be tested. The remains were exhumed, and transported to the Office of the Kentucky Chief Medical Examiner, on June 17, 1991. Samples of hair, fingernails, and other tissues were removed, and radiological studies were conducted. The remains were returned to the cemetery and re-interred, with appropriate honours, in the Mausoleum.

Neutron activation analysis conducted at Old Ridge National Laboratory revealed no evidence of poisoning, as arsenic levels were too low. The analysis concluded that Taylor had contracted *cholera morbus or acute gastroenteritis*, as Washington had open sewers, and his food and drink may have been contaminated. Any potential for recovery was overwhelmed by his doctors, who treated him with "ipecac, calomel, opium, and quinine", at forty grains per dose (approx...2.6 grams), and "bled and blistered him too". It is no wonder he succumbed. Political scientist Michael Parenti questions the traditional explanation for Taylor's death. Relying on interviews and reports by forensic pathologists, he argues that the procedure used for arsenic poisoning was fundamentally flawed.[50]

A 2010 Review concludes that "there is no definite proof that Taylor was assassinated, nor would it appear that there is definite proof that he was not".[51]

As for Abraham Lincoln, his unquiet grave has been relocated no less than seventeen times. This has been mostly due to reconstructions of the Lincoln tomb and fears for the safety of the President's remains. There was an attempt, which was thwarted, to steal his body in 1876. The coffin itself has been opened five times, so in that sense, five exhumations: on December 21, 1865; on September 19, 1871; on October 9, 1874; on April 14, 1887, and on September 26, 1901.[52]

The most significant of these was the last one. Lincoln had been buried in a red cedar coffin. When this exhumation took place in 1901, it was found that this coffin had been itself within a pine box, and this had to be broken away. The initiative for a new burial had come from Robert Lincoln. He decided that this time the burial would be once and for all, and that the coffin would be buried ten feet down in a huge cage, and then encased in concrete. (However, it may be recalled that in Napoleon's case, this also had been done in some way, but the concrete was nevertheless penetrated).

The reconstruction of the tomb took fifteen months, and during that time Lincoln's coffin was in a temporary grave close by. Robert Lincoln's idea had come from the burial procedure employed for George M. Pullman, the inventor of the Pullman sleeping car. A discussion then arose as to whether the coffin should be opened to make sure it was actually Lincoln, and not a substitute body, a perennial fear with the famous. There always seems a sense of reluctance to do this. In a way, the viewers think it is a kind of macabre voyeurism, but they usually still do it. Some still thought it would be a violation of privacy. Two plumbers, Leon P. Hopkins and his nephew, Charles L. Willey, chiselled an oblong piece out of the top of the lead-lined coffin. This was just over Lincoln's head and shoulders. When the casket was opened, a harsh, choking smell arose. Twenty-three people slowly walked forward and peered down. Many of the men removed their hats out of respect. Lincoln's features were totally recognisable. His face had a melancholy expression; but his black chin whiskers hadn't changed at all. The wart on his cheek and the coarse black hair were obvious characteristics of Lincoln's. The biggest change was that his eyebrows had vanished. The President was wearing the same suit he had worn at his second inauguration in 1865, shortly before his assassination. It was now covered with a yellow mould. Additionally, there were bits of red fabric, possibly the American flag buried with him. All twenty-three people were unanimous in their agreement that the remains were indeed those of Abraham Lincoln.

After viewing the body, the oblong piece was soldered back into place. The coffin was lowered into the cage, and 4,000 tons of cement were then poured down covering the cage and casket.

One of those who viewed the body was J.C. Thompson, who in 1928 said: "As I came up (to the coffin) I saw that top-knot of Lincoln's—his hair was coarse and thick, "like a horse's" he used to say-and it stood up high in front. When I saw that I knew it was Lincoln. Anyone who has ever seen his pictures would have known it was him. His features were not decayed. He looked just like a statue of himself lying there".

Another who viewed him was the only child to do so, a thirteen-year-old boy, Fleetwood Lindley. He was the last person living who had seen the face of the dead Lincoln, when he died on January 31, 1963 (the year of another assassinated president). Three days before he died, he had been interviewed, when he said: "Yes, his face was chalky white. His clothes were mildewed. And I was allowed to hold one of the leather straps as we lowered the casket for the concrete to be poured. I was not scared at the time, but I slept with Lincoln was the next six months".

Fleetwood Lindley was buried in Oak Ridge Cemetery not far from Lincoln's tomb.[53]

To balance the passage of the bones of Thomas Paine from New York to England, the story of the exhumation of John Paul Jones fully fills the void.

Jones became one of the heroes of the War of American Independence, an iconic and charismatic figure, whose real life has been almost lost under the layers of propaganda and fiction. Born on a Scottish island in Kirkcudbrightshire, in 1747, the son of a gardener, he early determined to seek his fortune in the wide world. Only the bones of his story can be covered in a work like this, but suffice that he threw in his lot with the American colonists in their struggle against the government in Britain. In the course of this, with a tiny squadron of ships he managed to terrorise the British coast during the War, and among his wilder exploits was his raids on his native Scottish coast, for which, presumably he had remembered with some precision. On one of these, he managed to take the inhabitants of a country house as hostages. He comes over, at this stage of his life, like the highwaymen of the period, striking a delicious terror into the hearts of those who met him, especially the women of his acquaintance. Like Francis Drake, two centuries before, he used a desperate situation to legitimise his exploits. Like Drake, he acted no better than a corsair or a pirate, but this suited his masters at the time. He was rightly described as "A hero of liberty in America, a dashing heart-throb in Paris, and a despicable pirate in England".

He recognised his own charismatic qualities in others, and on meeting Prince Potemkin in the Russia of Catherine the Great, he wrote: "You would be charmed with the Prince Potemkin, than whom no one could be more noble-minded". But there was a question whether even Russia was big enough for the two of them, when Jones arrived in 1788, the American War had ended. Looking for employment, the fledgeling American state not able to afford a peacetime navy, Empress Catherine was pleased to have him in her own force, and made him a Rear Admiral, hoping he would defeat the Ottoman Turks in the Black Sea. "Paul Jones has arrived", wrote Catherine, "I saw him today. I think he'll do marvellous things for us". Catherine needed sailors, and could never resist a Western celebrity.[54] Jones was not the only American working for Potemkin. Lewis Littlepage, from Virginia, has been working for none other than Poniatowski, the last king of Poland, as his agent in Russia. Jones, it was rightly said, generated both excitement and resentment. There were also British Naval officers in Catherine's navy, including Admiral Samuel Greig and his officers, and they absolutely refused to serve under Jones, and only in extreme emergencies would they work with him. Potemkin, who was adept at settling disputes, found Jones difficult and eventually fell out with him, but the nemesis of Jones was not Potemkin, but another officer who resented him, the Prince of Nassau-Siegen. It was almost certainly him who set a trap for Jones in St. Petersburg, among the seedier side of that city. Jones was accused of raping a young girl, and although it was proved by Jones's friend, Segur, that the girl's mother was a procuress, denounced by her own husband, Potemkin remained silent. The best that could be done was Jones was not reinstated but neither was he charged. He was received by Catherine one more time on June 26, 1789, and he then left for Paris, on the verge of Revolution. He wrote to Potemkin: "Time will teach you, my lord, that I am neither a mountebank nor a swindler, but a man loyal and true". It was, alas, too late.

His American compatriots had not forgotten him, and Washington and Jefferson now commissioned him to defeat the Algerian pirates off the Barbary Coast. But his life had wearied and aged Jones prematurely, and on July 7 (18),1792 he died in Paris aged forty-five, from kidney disease and pneumonia.

At that time the American minister to France was one Governeur Morris, who was no admirer of Jones. He thought him reckless and self-indulgent. With something akin to a puritanical attitude, he thought Jones should be buried "in a private and economical manner". But he was obliged to apply to the French government for the burial plot, and lost interest. Fortunately, the French thought otherwise, and gave him a state funeral, recalling his heroism for liberty, the first state funeral given, it was said, to a Protestant in France. Morris found he was too busy to attend. But now the horrors of the French Revolution took over, and with them total disarray. The cemetery where Jones was buried was closed six months later, and soon covered over. Over time it was turned into a garden, and then became part of a slum known as *Le Combat*, due to the animal fights waged atop the graves. By the time people thought of repatriating his body, in the 1840s, no-one could remember exactly where he was, even the name of the cemetery in which he had been buried.[55] During the Paris Commune, another period of disarray in 1870–1871, Jones's death certificate even was burned, along with many other documents, so that when, in 1899, an enterprising journalist, Julius Chambers, claimed to have discovered his grave, it turned out to be incorrect; but this gave momentum to others to start the quest for his body.

By this time General Horace Porter was ambassador to France, someone very different from Morris in 1792. He made it his mission to find Jones. There had been a reprint of Jones's birth certificate, in an 1859 article written by an antiquary. The certificate stated that Jones had been buried in "the cemetery for foreign Protestants", which the antiquary believed was the old St. Louis cemetery. Porter's researches confirmed this.[56]

Thanks to a letter written by one of Jones's friends, Porter knew that he had been buried in a lead coffin, and lead coffins were expensive and rare in that part of the city. There was now a gap of two years before Porter could finance a dig at a price he could afford. A top Parisian mining engineer led the excavations, which began on February 3, 1905. The soil, which had been variously used as a dump, and an animal burial ground, was very loose, and the men had to build a network of timber around themselves to keep them from being crushed.[57] As Porter described the conditions: "slime, mud, and nephitic odours were encountered, and long red worms appeared in abundance". Bodies were stacked two and three deep, which he then says indicated the poverty of the inhabitants. That is not necessarily true, as space was the prime objective, and this had been done, for example, in the rather upmarket Highgate cemetery in London.

Jones's body was not the only one in a lead coffin, so a coffin with an inscription was sought. One lead coffin was better constructed than the others, but had to wait a week before being opened, because of the air at the site being so bad, so that the men could create better ventilation. At the appointed hour, workers removed the coffin's heavy lid, and were greeted by a strong alcoholic odour. The French had pickled the corpse in spirits. But now identification began. A corpse of roughly Jones's height lay inside the coffin, wrapped in a winding sheet that still felt moist. Carefully, the men lit half a dozen candles, and unravelled the sheet. To their surprise, the body inside was remarkably well preserved, its greyish-brown skin entirely intact and only slightly shrunken. The curls of the hair were still tightly wound into an eighteenth-century coif. Porter bent into the candlelight and compared a copy of Jones's Constitutional gold medal, which was engraved with his portrait, to the corpse. The broad forehead, the curve of the brow, the high cheekbones, all added up. "Paul Jones!" the men exclaimed in unison, and took off their hats.

The next night the body was taken to the Paris School of Medicine, for a complete examination. When the scientist unwrapped the sheet, they found the limbs partially covered in tinfoil, yet another aid to preservation. The scientists also found, importantly, a linen cap embroidered with a curly letter "J", which became a "P" when turned upside down, a further sign of identity.

But it was the well-preserved internal organs that provided the most convincing proof: the lungs showed signs of pneumonia, and the kidneys evidence of the interstitial nephritis that has helped kill Jones. The conclusion of the examination was that it would take "a concurrence of circumstances absolutely exceptional and improbable" for the corpse to be that of anyone but Jones.

Now, in an act which Montefiore has called "Necro-imperialism", President Theodore Roosevelt sent four warships to Cherbourg in order to bring Jones home to the United States, although "home" surely would have been Scotland, or even France, where he was. Officers carried Jones's remains, encased in a new coffin, to an American church in Paris, for a patriotic service filled with flags and flowers. The service was held on July 5, 1905, one day after American Independence Day, but exactly 158 years after Jones's birth. After a grand procession along the Avenue de l'Alma (which one day would focus the world's attention on an exiled princess who was killed in Paris), the remains travelled by special train to Cherbourg, and then steamed "home" in the USS *Brooklyn*, to the Naval Academy in Annapolis. Horace Porter, whose brainchild the whole search and exhumation was, was offered the chance to go with the coffin, but said he would make his own way home. He must have felt that the whole enterprise had been hijacked by Roosevelt, and wished to retain his own dignity; but no less could be expected from such a flamboyant president. After all, this was the man who swam naked in the Potomac, and invited all the ambassadors to America to join him (which, incidentally, the French ambassador, a man of some wit, certainly did).[58]

Congress eventually reimbursed Horace Porter for all the money he had spent during his search, but, typically, Porter then donated the funds to build a memorial to Jones. It must be true that some of these exhumations become personal obsessions, right up to the time of the search for Richard III, and of course beyond. It took years for the memorial to be completed, but Jones was finally interred in the crypt of the U.S. Academy chapel in 1913. He now rests inside a twenty-one-ton sarcophagus of donated French marble, carved by a French sculptor, and modelled on Napoleon's tomb. It is interesting to think that when Napoleon had been born in 1769, Jones was already twenty-two years old, and well into his picaresque life. An honour guard stands watch whenever the crypt is opened.

Two of the most important figures in Africa and the world during the twentieth century were Nelson Mandela and Haile Selaissie. The first the leader of a revolutionary movement, the other the living embodiment of a 3000-yearold dynasty, and to some something more than that. Yet in some ways, they both represented the extraordinary and enigmatic face of Africa. Haile Selassie ruled Ethiopia for nearly sixty years; Nelson Mandela was supremely triumphant as a leader and the first black President of a united rainbow nation of South Africa. One ended well, despite all that was stacked against him; the other ended badly and sadly, after a lifetime of drama and glory. Nelson Mandela was not exhumed, but his story resulted in the very controversial exhumations of a number of his family members in 2018. Haile Selassie was indeed exhumed.

Ndaba Mandela, one of Nelson's grandsons, threw some interesting sidelights on his grandfather in an article in the London Times in 2018.[59] He tells a story of how once, when the family was sitting down to lunch, the Queen herself called by telephone. Someone handed Mandela the phone and he began chatting happily away with her, calling her "Elizabeth", and never once employing any deferential protocol. After the call had ended, his wife, Graca, chided her husband for being so informal. "What are you talking about?" he replied, grinning, "she calls me "Nelson". We always call each other by our first names. Don't forget. I'm royalty. I'm a Thembu prince". This gem of a story tells the reader everything he or she ever wanted to know about the true faces of Nelson Mandela and Queen Elizabeth II.

But there was a sad side to the story. After Mandela's death, his family disintegrated. It was large, complicated and tarnished by feuds. Mandela had six children by two wives: Evelyn Mase and Winnie Madikizela. He had seventeen grandchildren. Mandla Mandela was the eldest son of Magatho Lewanika, Nelson's son by his first marriage, who died of HIV/AIDS in 2005. Mandla has positioned himself as the heir of the dynasty. He caused outrage when he had the remains of three family members, including his father, exhumed, and moved to the village of Mvezo, where he is the tribal chief. His aunt Pumla, the only surviving one of four children Mandela had with Evelyn, and fourteen other members of the clan took him to court to have the bones returned to Qunu, Mandela's home town.

As for Haile Selassie, his long reign in many ways defied description or forecast. Born into the glory of the Solomonic dynasty, of Biblical tradition, the descendant of Menelek, the son of King Solomon and Baucis, Queen of Sheba, he became Regent in 1916, for the Empress Zawditu. They shared joint sovereignty until she died in 1928. Haile Selassie then had his own coronation in 1930, according to the elaborate rites of the ancient Ethiopian Coptic Church.

In 1935, the Italian Army invaded Ethiopia, seeking to add it to its late disparate attempts at Imperialism, to match the British, French, Spanish, Belgian, and Dutch empires. Albania and Libya formed the other parts. The invasion caused outrage in the League of Nations, based in Geneva, and there the exiled emperor rose and protested in his native Amharic language, only to be mocked by the Italian delegates. They were seeking revenge for the humiliation of Italy in 1896 at the Battle of Adowa, where they had been trounced by the Ethiopians. Now, armed with modern weapons and gas, the native army stood little chance. The emperor went into exile in England, but returned when Ethiopia was liberated by white South African troops in 1941.

Thereafter, for a long period, the emperor regained his former position and prestige. Queen Elizabeth II paid him a state visit, during which they were photographed together gazing at the thundering waters of the Nile. Addis Ababa became the Headquarters (HQ) of the new African Union.

Then in 1974, the ageing emperor began to lose control of the situation. The empire was being run still as if it was a mediaeval fiefdom.

Falling into the category of things expected but still surprising, are the many exhumations connected with the current enterprise known as HS2. HS2 stands for High-Speed Train, Mark 2, a project to bring a fast service from London into the Midlands. No fewer than 45,000 bodies will have been exhumed before excavations are finished. Hundreds of archaeologists are now employed in projects including a Roman temple in Northamptonshire and Grim's Ditch in Buckinghamshire. There are also future exhumations possible and to be considered at Edgcote, the battleground of the Wars of the Roses, on July 26, 1469; and the Park Street burial ground in Birmingham, where the bodies or remains may tell the archaeologists of the quality of life during the Industrial Revolution, as burials took place here between 1810 and 1873, roughly contemporaneous with north London. The largest dig, however, is at St. James's Gardens, a Georgian and Victorian burial ground that abuts Euston station in north London. Although the headstones were cleared as long ago as 1889 when the area became a park, many of the skeletons will be identifiable because their names were written on metal plates attached to their coffins. Helen Wass is the Head of Heritage for HS2, and was looking forward to identifying the coffins of, among others, Matthew Flinders, the first person to circumnavigate Australia, James Christie, an officer in the Royal Navy, before he held an auction of chamber pots and pillowcases in Pall Mall in 1766, which led to the famous auction house of today; Lord George Gordon, infamous for inciting the anti-Catholic Gordon riots of 1780; and Bill "The Terror" Richmond, the most famous pugilist, or bare-knuckle fighter of his day and a favourite of King George IV. Among others, he had enthralled Lord Byron, because he was so nimble in the ring. This may have been because he had an odd knee, but he may have had osteoporosis. He may have other evidence of his trade on his body. Born a slave, he escaped bondage when the British captured Staten Island in 1776, and his fighting prowess came to the notice of officers during a brawl in a tavern, where he took on three soldiers who had goaded him about the colour of his skin and "easily payed them in full for their merriment". By the next year, 1777, he was bound for Britain to become a professional boxer.

The first of these to be found was Matthew Flinders. The discovery has been described as "Australia's version of the recent discovery of Richard III", and experts hope that Flinders' skeleton will yield new insights into his life and work. After a long forensic examination, the remains will be reinterred, with the blessing of the Church of England, in a new site in or near London. Australia's High Commissioner, George Brandis, has called for a "fitting" memorial to be raised over his final resting place.

Under a white tent, the size of a football field, Wass's team was patiently scraping away soil to uncover the old graveyard which took an estimated 60,000 bodies. Flinders is just one of them. When he died, Flinders had just returned from years in a French prison in Mauritius and in failing health, not surprisingly. He was preparing his seminal *A Voyage to Terra Australis*, the story of his extraordinary adventures (with his cat, who, in the feline world, is as famous as he is), meticulous mapping and discoveries around the continent. It was published the day before he died, in 1814. He was just forty years old.

On January 15, 2019, the coffin of Matthew Flinders was found. The ornamental cursive inscription on the lead coffin breastplate read: "Capt. Matthew Flinders, RN. Died July 19, 1814. Aged 40 Years". The lead in the plate had helped preserve parts of the wooden coffin, though the rest had crumbled away under the pressure and moisture of the earth. The complete skeleton of Matthew Flinders, though "not the best preserved", lay underneath.

Flinders' bones, now washed and cleaned, now rest in a forensic archaeology laboratory, where researchers will spend the next two years uncovering the secrets of the skeleton and others selected from the site. It is hoped that the remains will give new insights into Flinders' life, and possibly the cause of his death, which history relates was from kidney failure after a long illness.

It is now known that Flinders was 1.6 metres in height, or 5 feet and 3 inches. Cutting-edge techniques can now tell us perhaps the type of water he drank and his medical history. His life at sea may certainly have left traces on his skeleton.

The breastplate can also be analysed, including its inscription and artwork, which may tell something of his burial. There are other interesting consequences too: where should the artefacts go? Probably to the Museum of London, where they would be partly on display and partly in storage for posterity.

The story of HS2 and its phenomenal number of exhumations does hark back to the lines by Thomas Gray, written when the burial ground was first in use:

> Some mute inglorious Milton here may rest (and)
> Full many a flower is born to blush unseen, and waste its fragrance on the desert air (and, perhaps most significantly and oft quoted)
> The path to glory leads but to the grave.
> The Graveyard Poets knew what they were writing about.

Notes

1. Shane, Leslie, *Mark Sykes: His Life and Letters*, New York (1923), p. 6.
2. Herbert, Aubrey, *A Tribute Given to Sykes at His Memorial Service, SRO/HP DD/HER/53.*
3. Sykes, Christopher Simon, Sir, *The Man Who Created the Middle East* (2016).
4. Townsend, Charles, *When God made Hell: The British Invasion of Mesopotamia and the Creation of Iraq, 1914–1921*, p. 236; and Kedourie, E., *England and the Middle East, Chapter 3, and Townsend*, p. 267.
5. Re St Mary Sledmere, York Consistory Court, 3 All E R, 75.
6. (1958) 1 All ER 394n.; (1958), 1 WLR 309 Consistory Court nd Re St Nicholas, Sevenoaks.
7. (2005), 1 WLR 1011.
8. See article in Royalty Digest Quarterly by Charlotte Zeepvat, *Thirteenth Grandchild of Queen Victoria?*
9. Dudgeon, Jeffrey, *The Black Diaries*, 3rd edition (2018).
10. Yeatman, R.J., and Sellar, W.C., *1066 and All That* (1930), *Methuen* (2005).
11. Dudgeon, op. cit., says this (my italics), "*As, Who Knows, a Final Burial in Murlough May Yet Happen.*" It may also be significant that the Mass took place on March 1st, St David's Day. David was one of Casement's names which he used; and also because his first Catholic baptism took place in Wales, when he was a child, arranged probably by his Catholic mother.
12. Schillinger, Liesel: Traitor, Martyr, Liberator. *New York Times*, June 22, 2012.

13. Dudgeon, op. cit., Chapter *Diaries and Death*, p. 140.
14. Sawyer (1984), p. 1.
15. Ibid., p. 92, n.
16. Ibid., pp. 142–3.
17. Professor Rene Weis took medical opinion on this, and it is uncertain where the truth lies.
18. Clarke, John (online article), retrieved February 20, 2019.
19. Rose, Andrew, *The Prince, The Princess, and the Perfect Murder* (2013), Coronet.
20. Ibid., p. 133.
21. Ibid., p. 247.
22. Ibid., p. 249.
23. Ibid., p. 181.
24. Ibid., p. 254.
25. Conyers Nesbit, Roy, *Rudolf Hess: Myths and Reality* (1999), Sutton.
26. McBlain, John, *Rudolf Hess: The British Conspiracy.*
27. Nash, Michael L., *A King for Poland, Royalty Digest.*
28. They were a prolific family, both in numbers and talent, who had produced the famous art historian, Jacob Burckhardt (1818–1897); the sculptor Carl Burckhardt (1878–1923); the film maker, Rudy Burckhardt (1914–1999); and some very eminent surgeons and psychiatrists, such as Johann Gottlieb Burckhardt (1836–1907), and Orientalists, such as Titus Burckhardt (1908–1984) and the author Andreas Burckhardt, who was not only a leader of the International Red Cross, but a spy as well.
29. Von Hassell, Ulrich, *Diaries*, quoted in John Harris's book on Hess.
30. See also article in *Daily Telegraph*, October 25, 2010.
31. See Fleming, G. B., Juana I. (2018) Palgrave Macmillan. Juana, Queen of Castile, fated to become Juana la Loca, is one of them.
32. Ortiz, Alicia Dujovne, *Eva Peron* (1997), p. 64, n. 33.
33. Ibid., pp. 319 et seq.
34. Ibid., p. 347.
35. Ibid., pp. 348–9.
36. Ibid., pp 371–2.
37. Keeley, Graham, Report in the Times, November 19, 2018.
38. Ibid.
39. Medrano, Ricardo Javier Mateos Sainz de, September 1, 2018.
40. Jones, Sam: report in the Guardian, *A Surreal Sight: Dali's Moustache Is Still in Place, Says Embalmer after Exhumation* (2018).
41. Ades, Dawn, *Dali* (1995, reprint 2002), Thames & Hudson.
42. Simpson, John, Crime correspondent, *The Times*, August 4,2018.
43. Burgess, Kaya, Religious Affairs correspondent, *The Times*, February 19, 2019.

44. *CBS News*, 12 November 2016.
45. Smolensk Crash, *News Digest*, May18, 2018.
46. McIntyre, Ben, *The Times*, April 13, 2010.
47. Faussetmarch, Richard, *New York Times*, March 24, 2017.
48. Merry, Robert J., *A Country of Vast Designs: James K. Polk, The Mexican War and the Conquest of the American Continent* (2009), Simon & Schuster, p. 469.
49. Hamilton Smith, The Interpretation of the Arsenic Content of Human Hair. *Journal of the Forensic Science Society*, Vol. 4, summarized by Stan Forshufvud & Ben Weider: *Assassination at St. Helena (Napoleon)* Vancouver, Canada, Mitchell Press (1978).
50. Parenti, Michael, The Strange Death of Zachary Taylor: A Case Study in the Manufacture of Mainstream History. *New Political Science* 20 (2), pp. 141–58.
51. Willard & Marion, *Killing the President* (2010) o, 189.
52. Sanders, Gerald, *Abraham Lincoln Fact Book*, p. 61.
53. Kundardt, Dorothy Meserve, *Life Magazine*, February 15, 1963; Lewis, Lloyd, *The Assassination of Lincoln: History and Myth*; Craughwell, Thomas, *Stealing Lincoln's Body* (2007); chapter 8, pp. 181–97; all of this put together by Norton, R.J.
54. Montefiore, Simon Sebag, *The Life of Potemkin* (2000).
55. Lovejoy, Bess, *Rest in Pieces* (2013), op. cit.
56. Porter, Horace, *The Recovery of the Body of John Paul Jones, in "Paul Jones, Founder of the American Navy,"* Augustus C. Buell, New York, Charles Scribner's Sons (1906), pp. 335–62.
57. Lovejoy, Bess, op. cit., pp. 171–179.
58. The French ambassador appeared on the banks of the Potomac totally naked but wearing gloves. When the President enquired the reason for the gloves, the ambassador replied: "Mais, M. le President, we may meet ladies!".
59. *Living with Mandela*: and his book, *Going to the Mountain*, Hutchinson (2018).

Appendix

Dates of Exhumations (Not Definitive)

1. Richard III (2012)
2. Thomas Becket (1220, 1538, 1888)
3. President James K. Polk (Moved three times since 1850)
4. President Zachary Taylor (1991)
5. President Abraham Lincoln (1865; 1871; 1874; 1887; 1901)
6. Rudolf Hess (2011)
7. President Zaczynski of Poland (2016)
8. Three members of the Mandela family (2013)
9. Martin Bucer, Paul Phagius, Catherine Danmartin (1557)
10. Pope Formosus (897)
11. Ines de Castro (1361)
12. St. Clement, Pope (868; relic, 2017)
13. John Henry Newman (2008)
14. Emperor Karl of Austria (1922)
15. Mary Tudor, Queen of France (1784)
16. Queen Christina of Sweden (1965/6)
17. Sir Mark Sykes (2007)
18. Oliver Cromwell and Bradshaw (1661) Ireton (1651, 1661)
19. Tut-an-khamoun (1922/3)
20. Anne Boleyn (1876)

M. L. Nash, *The History and Politics of Exhumation*,
https://doi.org/10.1007/978-3-030-24047-9

21. Lionel of Antwerp, Duke of Clarence (1369; 2016)
22. Katherine Parr (1782; 1786)
23. Edward IV (1789)
24. Charles I (1813; 1888)
25. Henry IV (1832)
26. Habsburgs at Konigsfelden (1739;1770;1807)
27. Adelheid, wife of former King Miguel of Portugal (1966)
28. King Miguel of Portugal (1967)
29. Pedro I and Pedro II, Emperors of Brazil (1972)
30. King Carol II of Roumania (2003) Madame Lepescu (2003)
31. Stanislas Poniatowski, King of Poland (1938; 1990; 1995)
32. Peter III, Tsar of Russia (1796)
33. Potemkin, Grigory (1798; 1818; 1859; 1873; 1930; 1984)
34. Grand Duchess Serge (Elizabeth of Hesse) (1918; 1921)
35. The Last Romanovs (2007)
36. Princess Alice, mother of the Duke of Edinburgh (1988)
37. Haile Selassie I, Emperor of Ethiopia (2000)
38. Thomas Paine (1819)
39. John Paul Jones (1905)
40. Matthew Flinders (2019)
41. Roger Casement (1965)
42. Edith Thompson (2018)
43. Fr. Jarzebowski (2011)
44. Witold, Polish boy (1995)
45. Eva Peron (1955; 1971; 1976)
46. Napoleon Bonaparte (1840)
47. King Peter II, Queen Maria of Yugoslavia, Queen Alexandra of Yugoslavia (2013)
48. Salvador Dali (2018)
49. Archbishops of Canterbury (2015; 2018)
50. St. Catherine of Siena (1383)
51. The Princes in the Tower (1674; 1933)
52. Gustav Vasa of Sweden (1945)
53. Erik XIV of Sweden (1958)
54. Lady Anne Mowbray (1502; 1964/5)
55. Richard II and Queen Anne of Bohemia (1871)
56. King John (1797)
57. St. Cuthbert (1827)
58. Katherine of Valois (1509; 1793)

59. Edward the Confessor, King (1089; 1163; 1685)
60. Thomas Beaufort, Duke of Exeter (1772)
61. Edward I. (1774)
62. William the Conqueror (1522)
63. Matilda, Queen (wife of William the Conqueror) (1562)
64. William Rufus (during the English Civil War, c. 1642–9)
65. King Edmund (915; 1095; 1538?)
66. Prince Stanislas Radziwill (2010)

Works Relating to Specific Exhumations

1. **Richard III**: Cheetham, Anthony, *Life & times of Richard III*, (1972); Mancini, Dominic, *The Usurpation of Richard III*, (ed.) C.A.J. Armstrong, (1936); Licence, Amy, *The Road to Leicester*, (2014) Amberley; Langley, Philippa and Jones, Michael, *The King's Grave: the search for Richard III*, (2013) John Murray.
2. **Thomas Becket**: Butler, John, *The Quest for Becket's Bones*, (1995); McCullough, Diarmaid, *Thomas Cranmer*, (1996); Simpson, Helen DeGuerry, *Henry VIII* (1934), Peter Davies; Prescott, Hilda, *Spanish Tudor* (1940); White, Beatrice, *Mary Tudor* (1936).
3. **Presidents Polk, Taylor and Lincoln**: Merry, Robert J., *A Country of Vast Designs: James K. Polk, The Mexican War, and the conquest of the American continent*, (2009) Simon & Schuster; Willard & Marion, *Killing the President*, (2010).
4. **Rudolf Hess**: Conyers Nesbit, *Roy: Rudolf Hess: Myths and Reality*, (1999) Sutton; McBlain, John, Rudolf Hess: the British Conspiracy.
5. **Members of the Mandela clan**: Mandela, Mandla, Living with Mandela (article in the London Times); Going to the Mountain, (2018) Hutchinson.
6. **Pope Formosus**: Wickham, Chris, *Rome & Italy in the late ninth and tenth centuries*; Gregorovius, Ferdinand, *History of the City of Rome in the Middle Ages*, translated from the 4th edition by Anne Hamilton, London, George Bell, (1895); Llewellyn, Peter, *Rome in the Dark Ages*, (1971), Faber & Faber, London; Smith, Julia M.H., (ed.) *Early Mediaeval Rome and the Christian West*, (2000) Brill, Leiden, Boston and Koln.

7. **Ines de Castro**: Hilgarth, J.N., *The Spanish Kingdoms*, (1976) Oxford; Russell, P.E., *The English intervention in Spain and Portugal*, (1955) Oxford.
8. **John Henry Newman**: Cornwell, John, *Newman's Unquiet Grave*, (2013).
9. **Queen Christina of Sweden**: Buckley, Veronica, *Queen Christina*; Hjortso, Carl-Hermann, *Queen Christina of Sweden* (1966); Scott, Franklin, *Sweden* (1977) University of Minnesota.
10. **Oliver Cromwell, Henry Ireton, Bradshaw**: Fraser, Antonia, *Cromwell: Our Chief of Men*; Troutbeck, G.E., *Westminster Abbey*, (1900) Methuen; McMains, *The Death of Oliver Cromwell*, University Press of Kentucky; Worden, A.B., *Introduction to Ludlow, Voyce from the Watchtower, Oliver Cromwell and the Rule of the Puritans in England*, (1901), reprint (1938), London.
11. **Tut-an-Khamoun**: Desroches-Noblecourt, Christiane, *Tut-an-Khamoun*, published by The Connoisseur and Michael Joseph, (1963), Penguin (1965)
12. **Lionel of Antwerp, Duke of Clarence**: Froissart, Sir John: *Chroniques*, translated from the French by Johns, Thomas, (1839).
13. **Edward IV.** Davies, Katherine, *The First Queen Elizabeth*, (1937).
14. **Poniatowski, Stanislas Augustus, King of Poland**: Nisbet Bain, R., *The last king of Poland and his contemporaries*, (1909), G.P. Puttnam' Sons, Methuen & Co.; *Zamoyski, Adam, The last king of Poland*, (1992); Michalski, Jerzy, *Stanislaw Augustus*, (2011) Polski Biographiczy; Butterwick, Richard, *The last king of Poland and English culture*, (1998) Clarendon Press.
15. **Peter III, Tsar of Russia**: Hughes, Lindsey, *The Romanovs: ruling Russia 1613–1917*, (2008) Hambledon Continuum; Hughes, Lindsey, The Funerals of the Russian Emperors and Empresses, in Schaich, M. (ed.) *Monarchy and Religion: the transformation of royal culture in eighteenth century Europe*, (2007) Oxford; Wortman, R, Scenarios of Power: Myth and Ceremony in Russian monarchy, 2 vols., (1995) Princeton; Gendridov, V.B., S.E. Sen'ko, Petropavlovskii sohor, Usypal'mitsa imperatorskogo doma Romanovykh, (1998) St. Petersburg.
16. **Potemkin, Grigory**: Montefiore, Simon Sebag, *The Life of Potemkin*, (2000).
17. **Grand Duchess Serge (Elizabeth of Hesse)**: Smolin, General, Alapayevsk Tragedy; Almedingen, E.M. *An Unbroken Unity, a memoir of the Grand Duchess Serge* (1964) The Bodley Head.

18. **Princess Alice, mother of the Duke of Edinburgh**: Vickers, Hugo, *Princess Alice*, (2000) New York.
19. **Haile Selassie I, Emperor of Ethiopia**: Kapuscinski, Ryszard, *The Fall of an Autocrat*, (1978) translated from the Polish, (2000) Penguin, (2006).
20. **Thomas Paine**: Nelson, Craig, *Thomas Paine*, (2006) Profile Books.
21. **John Paul Jones**: Buell, Augustus C., *Paul Jones, founder of the American Navy*, (1906) Charles Scribner's Sons, New York.
22. **Roger Casement, Sir**: Dudgeon, Jeffrey: *The Black Diaries*, (2018) 3rd edition; Schillinger, Liesel, Traitor, Martyr, Liberator, (article) *New York Times*, 22nd June, 2012.
23. **Edith Thompson**: Rose, Andrew, *The Prince, The Princess and the Perfect Murder*, (2013), Coronet.
24. **Eva Peron**: Ortiz, Alicia Dujovne, *Eva Peron*, (1997).
25. **Napoleon Bonaparte**: Weider, Ben, *Assassination at St. Helena*, (1978) Vancouver, Canada, Mitchell Press.
26. **Salvador Dali**: Ades, Dawn, *Dali*, (1995) Reprint (2002) Thames & Hudson, World of Art.
27. **Catherine of Siena, St.**: Jorgensen, Johannes, *St. Catherine of Siena*, (1938), translated from the Danish by Ingeborg Lund, Longmans, Green & Co.
28. **The Princes in the Tower**: Weir, Alison, *The Princes in the Tower*, (1992); Jenkins, Elizabeth, *The Princes in the Tower*, (2002)
29. **Erik XIV and Gustav Vasa of Sweden**: *Erikson, Lars, Johan III.*

Glossary

Acorn, oak leaves These appear on finials at Westminster Abbey, being the national tree of England, Wales, France, and Germany

Acus A needle, a pin, a bodkin

Fibula Calf bone

Hip-knob An element marking the top or end of some object.

Quatrefoils Decorative element consisting of a symmetrical shape which forms the overall outline of four partially overlapping circles of the same diameter. It is arranged in a cross, with four of them forming a square or rectangle, and a fifth at the centre.

Quincunx Geometric pattern consisting of five points

Sudarium A sweatcloth, see Bible, John 20: 6–7

M. L. Nash, *The History and Politics of Exhumation*,
https://doi.org/10.1007/978-3-030-24047-9

Bibliography

Primary Sources

Conversations with Fr. Gregory Corcoran, Quarr Abbey, Isle of Wight, May 25, 2018; and with Fr. David Middleton, Prior, Clare Priory, Suffolk, January 2019.

The Diaries of Laurence Tanner, F.S.A., Archivist and Keeper of the Muniment Room, Westminster Abbey, 1933–1936.

Drottning Christina: Carl-Hermann Hjortso (1965) Gravoppingen I, Rom 1965 Bokforlarget Corona Lund, 1967.

Hjortson, Carl-Herman, Queen Christina of Sweden: A medical/anthropological investigation of her remains in Rome, Lund (1966) C. W. K. Gleerep, Sweden.

Information received from Ricardo Javier Mateos Sainz de Medrano, on Ines de Castro and on the proposed exhumation of General Franco, 2019.

Scharf, Sir George (First Director of the National Portrait Gallery) Selections and drawings from his 230 notebooks in the Archives of the National Portrait Gallery.

National Archives of Sweden: Vol. 101: Konungahusens urkunder; Vasagraven I Uppsala domykyra: (1956) Gustav Vasa, (1958) Erik XIV.

Ashdown-Hill, John (the late) Updated evidence in respect of the burial of Lionel, Duke of Clarence, and Others, in the choir of Clare Priory, Suffolk (June 26, 2016).

Collignon, Charles, M.D., F.R.S., Professor of Anatomy at Cambridge: Some accounts of a body lately found in uncommon preservation under the ruins of St. Edmundsbury, Suffolk; and some reflections on the subject, 1774.

M. L. Nash, *The History and Politics of Exhumation*,
https://doi.org/10.1007/978-3-030-24047-9

Ayloffe, Sir Joseph, F.S.A., Paper given on the opening of the tomb of Edward I., May 12, 1774.
Herbert, Aubrey: A tribute given to (Sir Mark) Sykes at his Memorial Service, SRO/HP DD/HER/53.

Secondary Sources

General

Bland, Olivia, The Royal Way of Death (1986) Constable.
Brewer, Clifford, The Death of Kings (2000) A medical history of the kings & queens of England, Abson Books.
Conway, Heather, The Law and the Dead, (2016) Routledge.
Farmer, Oxford Dictionary of Saints (1978, 1992).
Green, Mary Everett, Princesses of England (1854).
Haestier, Richard, Dean Men tell Tales (1934).
Hill, Mark, QC, Ecclesiastical Law, 3rd edition (2018).
Kelly, J. D., History of the Popes.
Lovejoy, Bess, Rest in Pieces (2013).
McGrath, Christopher, Mr Darley's Arabian. High life, low life, sporting life: a history of horse-racing in 25 horses. John Murray (2016, 2017).
Nash, Michael L. Royal Wills in Britain from 1509 to 2008 (2017), Palgrave Macmillan.
Nichols, John, Wills of all the Blood Royal (1780); Nicholas, N.H. (ed.) Testamenta Vetusta (1826) London.
Strickland, Agnes and Elizabeth, Lives of the Queens of England (1844 and other editions).
———, Lives of the Bachelor Kings of England (1861).
———, Lives of the Tudor Princesses (1868).
Tytler, Sarah, Tudor Queens and Princesses (1896).
Wheatcroft, Andrew, The Habsburgs: embodying empure (1995) Viking; (1996) Penguin; (2004) The Folio Society.
Yeatman, R.J. and Sellar, W.C., 1066 and All That (1930), Methuen (2005).

Index

M. L. Nash, *The History and Politics of Exhumation*,
https://doi.org/10.1007/978-3-030-24047-9

F

G

I

M

U

The manufacturer's authorised representative in the EU is Springer Nature Customer Service Centre GmbH, Europaplatz 3, 69115 Heidelberg, Germany. If you have any concerns regarding our products, please contact ProductSafety@springernature.com

Printed and bound by CPI Group (UK) Ltd, Croydon, CR0 4YY
30/09/2026
02225656-0016